T0317031

Inventing Edward Lear

INVENTING EDWARD LEAR

SARA LODGE

Harvard University Press

Cambridge, Massachusetts

London, England

2019

Copyright © 2019 by the President and Fellows of Harvard College
All rights reserved
Printed in the United States of America

First printing

Library of Congress Cataloging-in-Publication Data
Names: Lodge, Sara (Sara J.), author.
Title: Inventing Edward Lear / Sara Lodge.
Description: Cambridge, Massachusetts : Harvard University Press, 2019. |
Includes bibliographical references and index.
Identifiers: LCCN 2018015474 | ISBN 9780674971158 (alk. paper)
Subjects: LCSH: Lear, Edward, 1812–1888. | Authors, English—
19th century—Biography. | Artists—Great Britain—Biography. | Natural history
illustrators—Great Britain—Biography. | Arts, Victorian—Great Britain.
Classification: LCC PR4879.L2 Z75 2019 | DDC 700.92—dc23
LC record available at https://lccn.loc.gov/2018015474

*For Charles Lewsen
a scholar and a gentleman*

CONTENTS

A NOTE ON THE MUSIC

Wherever you see a G clef included in the text (as shown below), you will find a link to a piece of music that was composed by Lear or was sung by him. There are twelve specially recorded pieces in this audio trail. Readers are invited to listen along. The music is at edwardlearsmusic.com.

There was an Old Man of the Isles, whose face was pervaded with smiles;
He sung "High dum diddle," and played on the fiddle,
That amiable man of the Isles.

Inventing Edward Lear

INTRODUCTION

E DWARD LEAR wrote some of the best-loved poetry in English. When, in a survey for National Poetry Day in 2014, 'The Owl and the Pussy-cat' was voted Britain's favourite childhood poem, nobody was remotely surprised. Lear's limericks, in which eccentric persons are discovered dancing exuberantly with a raven, eating roast spiders with chutney or playing the harp with their chin, still leap off the page. His longer poems 'The Jumblies', 'The Quangle Wangle's Hat' and 'The Pobble who has no Toes' constitute a playlist of childhood that occupies a familiar place in Britain comparable to that of Dr Seuss's rhyming stories in America. They are performed as children's theatre, reissued with new illustrations and anthologised in collections of nonsense—the genre that Lear reinvented and popularised in the nineteenth century. Many who enjoy his work would also recognise Lear from the self-caricature that he doodled in letters to friends: a genial, tubby, myopic figure with a beard and spectacles—followed by his stump-tailed cat, Foss, who stares wide-eyed, lovably out at us, playing Laurel to Lear's Hardy.

Yet, in another sense, Lear remains unknown. Few casual readers of his most famous poems realise that he made his living chiefly as an artist, first of exquisite ornithological and zoological studies of parrots, yagouaroundis, night monkeys and other exotic creatures, then as a landscape painter, producing over ten thousand beautiful watercolours and some three hundred memorable oil paintings of scenes ranging from France, Italy and Greece to Jordan, Egypt and India. He was also an intrepid and compulsive traveller who published illustrated accounts of his journeys in the wilder and more remote parts of Italy, Greece, Corsica and of Albania, which he was one of the first British tourists to describe. Lear's skill as a painter attracted the attention of Queen Victoria, whom he gave twelve private lessons in 1846; he was, she wrote in her diary, 'very encouraging' and taught 'remarkably well'.[1] Lear affectionately described both the queen and her daughter, the Princess Royal, as 'ducks'.[2] His talent for friendship was perhaps his greatest gift.

Fig. I.1 **Lear and Foss (1876)**

Still fewer people know that Lear was an accomplished musician who regularly sang for private audiences and played on the piano, and in his youth also on the flute, the small guitar and the accordion. He composed and published twelve popular song-settings of Tennyson's poems and improvised many other settings (now sadly lost) of work by poets including Shelley and Swinburne and of his own verses, including 'The Owl and the Pussy-cat'. This book will contend that most of Lear's poems can best be understood as songs. I am fascinated by the musical environment that Lear inhabited, the songs he listened to, sang, wrote and parodied. With the pianist David Owen Norris and singers Mark Wilde and Amanda Pitt, I have recorded these songs—several of them identified for the first time as part of Lear's repertoire, or not previously available to listeners as sound recordings—and made them freely accessible via a dedicated website, edwardlearsmusic.com. I hope that some readers will be inspired to listen along.

Lear was not only attuned to musical culture. He was a dissenter in religion, a vital aspect of his intellectual background that has, until recently, received little attention.[3] It made him peculiarly sensitive to religious and social exclusion and angry about the gap between the teaching embodied in Christ's life and the preaching of 'priests' of any denomination. Lear's writing is full of energetic nonconformity, and of a particular kind of tolerance and beatitude, which expresses itself in the 'hundred and two feet wide' brim of the Quangle Wangle's hat, on which a variety of unlikely creatures make music together. He announced his desire for an "NEW ANTIBEASTLY ANTIBRUTAL ANTIBOSH BIBLE" to counter nonsensical aspects of the original; his own nonsense is a platform for broadmindedness.

Lear, as a scientific illustrator whose work was consulted by Charles Darwin, was also conducting a form of practical research at a time of intense speculation regarding the development of life on earth and the relationships among species. His poems and pictures explore the possibilities of composite identity and interspecies pairings, drawing the science he observed into the world he invented. His delightful verses of 1873 about the Channel-swimming Pobble who has no toes, but 'had once as many as we', gain a new shade of interest when considered in the light of evolutionary theory. They also appear different when viewed as a humorous response to the first attempt to swim the English Channel in 1872, an experiment that failed because the swimmer's feet became so cold he felt they might fall off. In 1870, a reviewer noted that in Lear's 'The Duck and the Kangaroo', the kangaroo has an aristocratic bearing, while the duck, who begs to ride around the world on her tail, is 'plebeian'. This poem of escape is also a fantasy of class mobility. The same reviewer remarked that in 'The Owl and the Pussy-cat', it is the female cat who proposes to the male owl, 'in the true spirit of women's rights'.[4] Interspecies relationships in Lear's work often throw surprising light on gender attributes and sexual relations. When stripped of the layers of varnish created by overfamiliarity, Lear's poems sparkle with unexpected colours.

For Lear, word and image are not discrete entities with separate lives on the page, but organic branches with shared roots. In his children's alphabets, illuminated letters become the creatures they describe—*S* is a snail's shell, *B* a butterfly's wing—communicating a vivid joy in language as something that scintillates, moving and changing naturally within the world we see. Likewise, in sketches for his watercolours, words become part of the landscape, evoking layers of personal and cultural memory. Lear's association in the 1850s and 1860s with the Pre-Raphaelite Brotherhood—a boldly avant-garde movement, whose subjects and stylistics challenged the 'slosh' and 'treacle' of conventional Royal Academy painting—is, like his nonsense, a creative expression both of nonconformity and of the essentially interdisciplinary nature of art.

Critical writing on Lear for many years remained sparse.[5] Most book-length approaches were biographical. This is no accident. Lear's life is an extraordinary story. But in reading Lear's art through biography, there has been a strong temptation to see all his nonsense characters principally in a biographical light. S. A. Nock in 1941 set a trend in asserting that 'Edward Lear seems to have been unique in writing in nonsense his emotional biography'.[6] Ina Rae Hark wrote in 1982 that 'Commentators agree that the Bò is Lear himself, Lady Jingly Jones is Gussie Bethell, and the poem is a fictionalisation of their abortive romance'.[7] If Lear *is* the Yonghy-Bonghy-Bò, his life is all one needs to know. But in fact the relationships between Lear and the characters he invents, including 'Edward Lear', are never straightforward. Both his life and his writing are shaped more by connection than by isolation; he is constantly in conversation with work in a variety of media and with people in a variety of spheres.

Lear was born on a day of political drama, a fact of which he was highly aware.[8] The evening before, on 11 May 1812, the prime minister, Spencer Perceval, had been assassinated by a gunman in the lobby of the House of Commons. There were rumours of an uprising. But these proved false. The only insurgence that followed was the advent of a nonsense poet who would explode limericks on an unsuspecting population. His father was the sugar refiner turned City stockbroker Jeremiah Lear. The Lear family owned property in Whitechapel, in London's East End, where cane sugar was docked, boiled and purified. Lear's mother was a Skerrett, and her family owned property at 'Sunnyside' in County Durham; an early Lear poem, 'The Shady Side of Sunnyside', suggests lingering bitterness about the genteel lifestyle of which the vagaries of inheritance had robbed her. But the Lears were, at least initially, a prosperous middle-class family who by the time of Lear's birth lived in a Georgian villa, Bowman's Lodge, in the leafy London suburb of Holloway. It was a pleasant house with a 'painting room', a 'greenhouse room', a 'play ground' and open views over lime trees and streets down which drovers still herded sheep.

They were friendly with other successful middle-class families, some with county connections to the gentry. The Ayscoughs and the Wilkinsons, whose nieces Lear ogled as a teenager, were 'upholders' (upholsterers) and undertakers who came to own substantial property.[9] The Nevills, whose son William was Lear's first good friend, were manufacturers of hosiery and other woollen and cotton goods.[10] Robert Gale, a fellow illustrator, was grandson of Robert Martin Leake of Thorpe Hall in Essex, who had been Master of the Report Office. This allowed Lear, who frequently visited Gale's home at 10 Queen Square, Holborn, to meet his friend's uncle, William Martin Leake, a diplomat and topographer of Greece and Albania, doubtless inspiring his own later journeys and travelogues.[11] Importantly, even at a young age, Lear felt able to hold his own in company that included 'swells'. He was, as he would later remark testily to a functionary in India who threatened to exclude him from the Brass Pagoda, 'an English gentleman, and that is enough'.[12]

However, all was not well in the Lear home. We can identify at least four separate traumas in Lear's childhood. The first was that his mother gave over his upbringing to his eldest sister, Ann, who was twenty-one when Lear was born. The reasons are not far to seek. Lear liked to claim that he was the twentieth of twenty-one children. The evidence points to at least seventeen named children, and there may well have been others, miscarried or stillborn or not surviving long enough to be baptised, as Mrs Lear seems to have been pregnant almost every year from the time she was twenty-one until she was forty-four. Catherine, the child born before Edward, died in 1811; his mother must still have been carrying this grief within her when she became pregnant with Lear. Loss was part of his inheritance. Whatever her reasons, Lear reciprocated her abandonment. In 1865 he wrote in his diary, '"my mother's" birthday—but that was no great joy for me'.[13] The inverted commas contain a world of pain. Late in life, he read Augustus Hare's *Memorials of a Quiet Life,* in which the author describes being given up by his parents to be adopted by an aunt.[14] It reduced him to helpless tears.

Secondly, Lear's father got into financial difficulties when Lear was four; he became a defaulter on the stock exchange, and the family was forced for a time to rent out Bowman's Lodge and to move into the industrial fog, crowded streets and cramped quarters of inner London. The family's fortunes never fully recovered from this humiliating fall. Lear began adult life with a morbid distaste for debt and a sense (not mathematically but emotionally accurate) of having been thrown upon the world without a farthing. He rarely mentions either parent. A close friend, the artist Daniel Fowler, noted, 'I never heard him speak of any relations'.[15] A cartoon that Lear drew aged seventy-two shows four generations of Lears. Strikingly, the couples appear to be fighting. They confront one another with arms and legs akimbo, as if

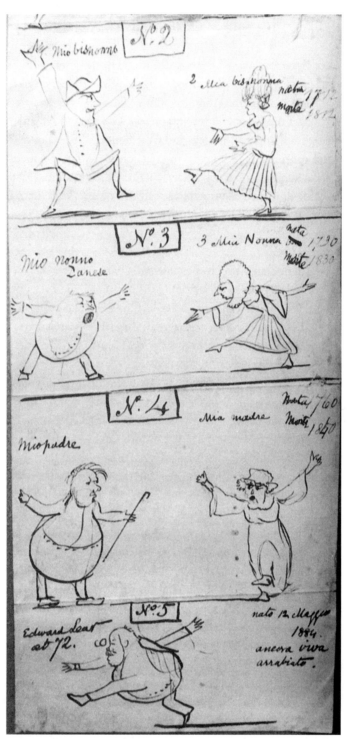

Fig. I.2 Lear and his ancestors (1884)

about to engage in a wild dance or a bout of wrestling. Next to his own figure, captioned 'Edward Lear aged 72', he writes, 'ancora viva arrabiato': still living angrily.[16] One gets a sense of his animated comic figure both escaping from and internalising a history of conflict.

Then there was epilepsy, his 'daemon', 'chain' or 'skeleton', which seems first to have afflicted Lear when he was around five years old and about which he felt such 'horror' and 'disgust' that he concealed it throughout his adult life. Epilepsy in this period was greatly feared and little understood. A sensational *Blackwood's Magazine* story in February 1831 depicted an epileptic patient in a fit of madness, brandishing a razor, threatening all around him and shaving off his eyebrows. This account sounds to a modern reader more like violent psychosis than epilepsy. The article hinted that the 'demoniacal twitchings, & contortions, which are so sudden—so irresistible . . . give the idea of some vague, terrible exciting cause, which cannot be discovered: as though the sufferer lay passive in the grasp of some messenger of darkness'.[17] In the village of Selborne, Lear noted in 1872, the superstitious still asked for nine sixpences from nine different people, which, if made into a ring, would allegedly cure fits.[18]

Lear probably suffered from focal epilepsy of the temporal lobe. He usually had warning of attacks, often in the form of severe indigestion, and his fits seem often to have come on at night and in clusters. Sometimes they lasted only two or three seconds, but the unconsciousness that followed might endure for a couple of hours. Jolting carriages and flickering light could trigger them, but he was also told as a child that masturbation was a cause, which set up a difficult relationship in his young mind between 'will-control', desire and punishment. To the end of his life, Lear pondered the question of his responsibility for his mental state, finally writing in old age that he had 'become aware of late, that inalienable and apparently unalterable physical evils, have been less due to the work of my own will, as I have hitherto imagined, than to overpowering effects of unknown & uncontrollable force, dating from my very birth—or little later'.[19] Lear's brain was a volcano. There were rarely more than ten days between eruptions.

Around a third of epileptics suffer from depression.[20] Lear was one of them. The reasons for this linkage are still not well known. Lear, however, did understand that his physical, mental and emotional life were all one. Excess in any area could cause disturbance in another. This made self-regulation necessary, but also gave to immoderate pleasure a thrill of danger. His curiosity about his own internal processes and how physical symptoms, such as 'disturbance of stomach', could lead to emotional crises, such as 'accesses of passion-rage', helped to turn him into an author and artist who is exceptionally perceptive about the inseparability of thought and feeling. Many of the expressions that Lear uses in his diary, such as 'stunder-thorm' (for thunderstorm) or 'soft-shiny-soppy-shivery day', express the truth that weather can be experienced as both an external phenomenon and an internal one, in which being stunned or shivery results from dwelling within an organic system where everything affects everything else. Lear's 'nonsense' words often convey this porousness. His imaginary places—the Chankly Bore, the Torrible Zone, the Gromboolian plain—are ambigu-ously physical landscapes or inner states.

Lastly, there is evidence that Lear was abused as a child. Easter Monday of 1822 fell on 8 April; aged seventy-three, Lear needed to confirm this pre-cise date, recalling the anniversary of 'the greatest Evil done to me in life, excepting that done by C: & which must last now to the end—spite of all reason & effort'.[21] The culprit was Lear's nineteen-year-old cousin, Fred-erick Harding. But in my view, Frederick did not act alone. Lear refers to the incident as the 'H J & F affair'.[22] H. J. was his brother Henry, who, aged twenty-three, had just been bought out of the army. These young roustabouts hurt the ten-year-old Lear, probably sexually, in a way he never forgot. In 1876, when Henry (then seventy-seven) was threatening to move back to England from America, Lear wrote, 'in any case I must keep clear of a man—who, tho' he happens to be my brother,—is one of whom I have never heard any good—not even from my dear angel sister Ann'. His alarm speaks volumes about the misery Henry represented. Lear was nearsighted (he was obliged to wear extremely strong glasses), sensitive, vulnerable. He attended school briefly, aged eleven, but soon left. Many years later, in 1885, after reading newspaper accounts of boys who had died as a result of aggressive hazing incidents at boarding school, Lear could not sleep for many nights or speak without crying.[23] The incidents must have brought back memories of being bullied that remained viscerally raw.

Sex for Lear would always be fraught with anxiety. He was attracted to women and as a young man had occasional sex, almost certainly with the kind of lower-class women who were available to him as partners.[24] How-ever, Lear was also romantically attracted to men. A poem, 'Regrets', that he wrote out in the 1870s for his closest friend and heir, Franklin Lush-ington, suggests the strength of Lear's feelings for him:

If we had known, if we had but known,
While yet we stood together,
How a thoughtless look, a slighting tone
Would sting and jar forever
Cold lies the turf to the burning kiss,
The cross stands deaf to cries,
Dull, as the wall of silence is,
Are the grey unanswering skies![25]

This is a love poem. Lear, when he transcribed it, was revisiting his diaries of Greece in 1848, when he and Lushington had spent happy days together. This poem seems to be an allusion to a past that both Lear and Lushington knew was long buried, but where, for Lear at least, ardent memories and regrets lay.

Lear had an emotionally difficult start in life. But he also grew up in a culturally rich environment that supported his development into a consummate performer. Lear sometimes lamented his 'small brain', alongside his 'ugly body', and complained that he had been 'badly educated, and by women besides'.[26] This is untrue. He had been home-schooled and had, in certain respects, received a woman's education, in which Greek and Latin were deficient and the decorative and social arts (music, painting, letter-writing, modern languages) were pronounced. But the sisters who taught him, Ann and Sarah Lear, were smart, disciplined and imaginative. They must themselves have received a liberal education. A clue to this may be provided by Sarah's friendship with Anne, Elizabeth and Alice Giles—perhaps the same Giles sisters who ran a girls' boarding school in Stoke Newington in north London, an area that was home to many dissenting academies.[27] We catch glimpses of Lear's education through reminiscences in the diaries he wrote as an adult. When he visits the temples of Abu Simbel in Egypt in 1867, he reflects that they were 'earliest known to me from the tales of my dear sister Ann—48 years ago'.[28] These temples were excavated and described by Europeans only in the 1810s and 1820s; Ann must have been sharing news of them as it emerged. On another occasion he remembers visiting Rupert Ingleby's family with Ann, and seeing the infant Rupert having his fingernails cut and 'nodding like a Chinese mandarin'. Lear, aged seven or eight, was intrigued by the allusion, so Ann took him into London to see two real nodding mandarins—a practical lesson in satisfying intellectual curiosity that stayed with him all his life.[29] Ann referred to Bowman's Lodge, where the Lear family lived, as 'toxophilite' (the Greek word for a lover of archery); this is a piece of classical wordplay, as a bowman is an archer and the villa was indeed built on ground said to have been used for archery in ancient times.[30] These memories suggest the benign climate that nurtured Lear's linguistic skills and his playfulness with language, but also his ever-outward-bound mind, stimulated to both imaginative and practical curiosity about other nations and cultures.

Jeremiah Lear was a life-governor of the Asylum for the Support of the Deaf and Dumb Children of the Poor at Bermondsey.[31] Lear would in later years give money yearly to a children's asylum; he found Constance and Arthur Fairbairn, the deaf children of one of his patrons, Sir Thomas Fairbairn, *'truly beautiful'*.[32] He drew with Arthur, sharing the pleasure of dialogue that was visual rather than spoken. Lear's family connection with work for the deaf has not hitherto been known. It casts a fascinating light on the insistent visuality of his books for children. Lear was brought up to understand that communication takes many forms; the dictionary has no freehold on meaning. He was also taught to value the deep, reciprocal pleasure of giving. The *Times* of 8 August 1860 shows that Lear gave five pounds to the British Syria Relief Fund for the support of 'some 75000 persons (10,000 widows and orphans)' who, as a result of civil war, were reported to be 'scattered in the mountains and seaports, totally destitute, homeless, and helpless'.[33] This was only one of Lear's many charitable donations, but it brings his concern with events in the wider world very close to our own.

By his teenage years Lear spoke French fluently and was an extremely talented painter and musician. He wrote letters that, unlike those of most men of the period, read like animated conversations: funny, performative, self-ironising. His female education was key to what made Lear socially successful. He would be drawn all his life to intelligent women who were linguists (Augusta Bethell), writers (Eleanor Poynter), artists (Marianne North), musicians (Helena Cortazzi) and explorers (Amelia Edwards), and who often combined several of these skills. The men he loved were exceptionally clever, too.

Lear was intellectual, and the word 'intellectual'—which he uses constantly in his writing—is always a term of praise. It is not, in Lear's vocabulary, an alienating word. He praises Lady Aberdare as 'the most sunshiny-intellectual woman one can ever know'.[34] The lawyer Sir Francis Goldsmid, who campaigned for Jewish rights, and his feminist wife, Lady

Louisa Goldsmid, have a beautiful house full of things that are 'intellectual and pretty'.[35] Alfred Tennyson's houses at Farringford and Aldworth are among the happiest places he spends time: 'such is the fascination of this lot of intellectual coves'.[36] He prizes Dr. Lushington's house for its 'intellectual life'.[37] He dislikes 'dilettantism' and disdains the boring, the uninformed and the silly. His friend Evelyn Baring remarked that he was a 'very prejudicial person' ('and truly', confessed Lear).[38] Beneath the warm greatcoat of his friendship, whose generous pockets were stuffed with oranges, there lurked an irritable, razor-sharp intelligence.

He read, widely and voraciously, all his life. He referred to the 'Libery' he built in his villa at San Remo; in this phonetic rendering of 'library', so close to 'liberty', one hears the freedom he found in books.[39] In youth there was moral reading: the Bible, John Bunyan and John Milton, and Samuel Butler's poetic satire on false religion, *Hudibras*. But there were also fantastical stories of adventure and transformation: *Gulliver's Travels*, *The Arabian Nights*, *The Adventures of Baron Munchausen* and Thomas Stothard's illustrated *Robinson Crusoe*. In his sixties, Lear remembered 'the Great Boydell Shakespeare prints—bringing back all the childhood days!!!'.[40] John Boydell's extraordinary Shakespeare Gallery featured work illustrating scenes from Shakespeare's plays by leading artists including Benjamin West, Henry Fuseli and Angelica Kauffman; the folio of prints, issued in 1805, was a landmark publication. One can readily see how the young Edward Lear became fascinated by new techniques in illustration alongside drama. His familiarity with Shakespeare is apparent in his letters and diaries, which quote, among other plays, *Othello*, *Henry VI* and *Troilus and Cressida*. On a couple of occasions, he blends a quotation remembered from Tennyson with one remembered from Shakespeare.[41] Lear's cocktail quotations, like his spoonerisms and portmanteau words, reflect a mixologist's mind. From his transposition of a line from a well-known speech by Lord Mansfield, 'I thought so then and I think so still', into the nonsense of 'The Pelican Chorus' ('we think so then and we thought so still'), we can guess that he also used the ubiquitous school primer, Lindley Murray's *English Reader*. Lear's nonsense is full of literary allusions that have been shaken or stirred.

Lear as a teenager read Sir Walter Scott's novels.[42] He also read a variety of periodicals and a panoply of poets, including James Bird, Thomas Campbell, William Collins, Felicia Hemans, Samuel Rogers and Robert Southey, but most especially Thomas Moore, Percy Bysshe Shelley and Lord

Byron. Byron was Lear's early model of the poet-hero. He recalled, as a
boy, being 'stupified and crying' in the moonlight on hearing of Byron's
death, 'the pale cold moon . . . strangely influencing me'.[43] He visited
Newstead Abbey, which gave him the shivers, and remained fascinated all
his life by biographies and gossip about Byron, seeking out those like Edward Trelawny who had belonged to the Byron/Shelley circle. Lear became friendly with Sir Percy Shelley, the poet's grandson. He embraced
every opportunity to revisit cultural sites connected with these poets.[44] His
artist-hero was Turner, whose 'truly wonderful' work, which he repeatedly
studied in London's National Gallery and in reproduction, filled him with
both delight and despair. 'O!!! Turner!!!' he wrote in 1880.[45] The insistently
personal nature of Lear's admiration for these figures is important. Romanticism shaped his vision of the artist's life as a form and forum of creative expression. His own poetry and visual art would be constantly mediated through personal relationships: given as gifts, inscribed in letters,
performed in company. And, like Byron and Shelley, he was drawn to the
actual and symbolic freedom of the Mediterranean, living as an artist in
Rome, Malta, Corfu, Cannes and San Remo.

From the 1850s Alfred Tennyson—who, being alive, was more receptive
to conversation—jostled Byron for first place in Lear's poetic pantheon.
Lear corresponded regularly with Emily Tennyson and was a frequent visitor, when in England, to the Tennyson home. But his admiration for other
authors always expressed itself in spiky repartee. In 1873, Lear wrote in his
diary, parodying lines Byron had supposedly penned on the eve of his sweetheart's marriage to another man:

> O mummery! torcher me know more!
> The present's all or-cast
> My opes of fewcher bliss is or,
> In Mussy—spare the past[46]

This is Byron as recited by a Cockney housemaid. Literary memory, in Lear's
writing, often involves 'mummery': acting. It can conjure the emotional intensity of regret—'no more!'—which incorporates the loss represented in and by
Romantic poetry as a conduit for more personal losses. But it typically also
performs a critical relationship to existing literature that is funnier and sharper
because it 'knows more'. Lear's post-Romantic art is created in teasing dialogue, both with individual correspondents and with existing work.

Fig. I.3 **Lear's illustrations for 'A Dream'**

This self-conscious dialogue began very early. One of his first cartoon sequences illustrates the words to 'A Dream', a poem published in the *Dublin University Magazine* for February 1833.[47] The poem is written from the perspective of an older man, reliving his happy childhood in sleep, then waking 'with a sigh that memory / should revive what time destroys'. Lear depicts the child skipping with a rope in front of delighted parents and leaping through a field of flowers.

When my heart vos light and my opes vos bright
And my own a appy ome[48]

The child's heart is on its sleeve—quite literally: a miniature heart is depicted on the child's coverlet and clothing. This heart remains as a motif on
the bed of the old man, who is weeping, in company with two cats, to discover that his return to childhood has been only a tantalising dream. Nostalgia for home and happy memories of carefree youth were everywhere in
poems and songs of the 1820s and 1830s; one might compare Thomas Hood's
'I remember, I remember, the house where I was born' (1826) and the ubiquitous song 'Home, Sweet Home' (1823). However, Lear's play with the cliché
of the lost idyll is piquant because he is not an old man but a young one:

When I dreamed I was young and hinnocent—
And my art vos free from care,
And my Parents smiled on their darling child,
And breathed for his [weal] a prayer.

Lear's dreamed-of 'hinnocence' is knowing; the original's 'heart free from
care' becomes 'art free from care', a pun that measures the distance between
being naïve and being artful, as this cartoon sequence is. The point is clear:
the 'heart on sleeve' play of the child in the picture is not the sophisticated
critical play of the young author making the picture. Emotive nostalgia and
ironic distance will henceforward always be partners in Lear's work, which
is poised—like Harold Lloyd on a windowsill twenty stories high—between
comedy and what he refers to as 'dishpear'. When thinking of Lear as a
tearful old man with a cat, we need to remember that this was a tragicomic
role he had caricatured from adolescence.

Later, Lear especially valued poetry by Algernon Swinburne, Arthur
Hugh Clough—with whose railway-mimicking hexameters he experimented—and 'queer Walt Whitman'.[49] He also knew the work of Robert
and Elizabeth Barrett Browning (both of whom he met), of Poe and of
Longfellow. He read reams of novels, from Burney, Edgeworth and Austen
to George Eliot, Charlotte Brontë and Ouida. He admired the fiction of
Elizabeth Gaskell (an acquaintance), Charles Kingsley (with whom he corresponded), Charles Lever (whom he knew well) and Wilkie Collins (a friend
for over thirty years, who sometimes sent Lear fiction for commentary). His

friends likewise included an impressive roster of painters and sculptors, including William Holman Hunt, John Everett Millais, Thomas Woolner and Ford Madox Brown. He became fluent in Italian, functional in modern Greek and read poetry in a variety of European languages. In middle age, he taught himself ancient Greek and read Sophocles, Xenophon and Thucydides, whom he refers to affectionately as 'Thucydiddles'. Travel literature, throughout his life, was amongst his favourite genres. Natural history absorbed him. Political and religious debate interested him. On at least one occasion he stayed up all night reading parliamentary reports. Lear was a committed but moderate Liberal. He met Gladstone and at first was friendly, but came to dislike him as 'fanatical'—although as he noted with bitter humour, 'dirty Landscape painters have no vote in that matter'.[50] He knew many members of parliament personally.[51] Among his closest friends were senior figures in Gladstone's Liberal administration: Chichester Fortescue, Henry Bruce and Thomas Baring, Lord Northbrook. His social, artistic and political connections meant that he was always engaged with the life of his time.

The variety of Lear's intellectual and social interests is suggested by an enjoyable conversation that he described having in 1868 with Julia Philipsohn, a 'really delightful clever merry girl' while walking round a churchyard. They talked of

> Italy—religion—Philosophy—beetles—Via Reggio—toads,— woodpeckers—& the immortality of the soul—David, ladies trains,—Tennyson, mulberries, Calvanism, puns, landscapes, Tunnyfish, Leghorn, laurels & lozenges.[52]

Here, characteristically, long dashes join disparate thoughts like jump leads, sparking connections, suggesting the busy, happy mind that is stimulated by all it encounters. Lear's nonsense also relishes this kind of energetic medley, where foodstuffs and animals, places and ideas rush into unexpected alliances. He once wrote to his friend Chichester Fortescue that 'proper and exact "epithets" always were impossible to me, as my thoughts are ever in advance of my words'.[53] Movement, vivacity and the always-close-to-failing capacity of language and image to keep up with what the eye perceives and the brain conceives are central to the pleasure of his art. His pen catches life on the quick edge of change.

Fig. I.4 **Lear leaping for Leap Year (1872)**

In self-caricatures, he often depicts himself with both feet off the ground: dancing, jumping, flying with birds or being blown away by the wind. In leap years, he liked to take Leap Day off. Indeed one might regard Lear as the patron saint of leapers and Leap Day as his particular festival. Where Lewis Carroll's nonsense likes to dig down, into the rabbit hole of logic, the dominant direction of Lear's nonsense is up and away. There is a powerful, sometimes hypnotic, pull in his lyrical verse towards the condition of infancy: of being carried, by boats, sieves, birds, turtles. But this does not mean that his poetry is simple. In it, the lightness of being and the lightness of verse are shadowed by the possible weight and darkness over which his characters temporarily prevail.

Lear is fascinated by moonlight and by delight, whose magical linkage in his most memorable poems conveys the ephemerality of joy. In a letter to Mrs Stuart Wortley, he describes his trip to the moon:

And these journeys are all done by means of Moonbeams, which, far from being mere portions of light, are in reality living creatures, endowed with considerable sogassity, & a long nose like the trunk of a Nelliphant, though this is quite imperceptible to the naked eye. You have only to whisper to the Moonbeam what you wish to see, & you are there in a moment, & its nose or trunk being placed round your body, you cannot by any possibility fall.[54]

Light is alive. It can transport one magically. Lear's best landscape painting has the same quality of granting us vistas where distance shimmers with light, and with the evanescent promise of elsewhere. Delicate washes conjure the air—what is 'quite imperceptible to the naked eye'—as much as they sketch in the forms and colours of what can be seen. Lear's favourite people were 'luminous'. He liked to send 'nonsense letters' to his adult friends, as well as to their children. In them Lear himself becomes a character within the world of nonsense, chatting with frogs, or slugs, or hanging from the horns of a wild sheep while being carried up the mountains of Crete. Lear's nonsense is as much for adults as it is for children. It opens up a channel of communication between the child-self and the adult-self that, like the living moonbeam, allows safe yet powerful and far-reaching movement.

'Nonsense', to modern readers, means Lewis Carroll and Edward Lear, who are inevitably partnered, like the Walrus and the Carpenter, in all accounts of the genre. In the nineteenth century they were not usually paired. Carroll was twenty years younger, and *Alice's Adventures in Wonderland* (1865) appeared nearly twenty years after Lear's first *Book of Nonsense* (1846). Lear was extolled in 1876 by a reviewer in the *Examiner:* 'we recognise . . . the voice of the first great Nonsense Poet of the age'.[55] There was no mention of Carroll, who was chiefly known for prose. Besides, there were many other 'Christmas Books' that readers were happy to consider under the broad aegis of nonsense. These included poetry, such as D'arcy Thompson's *Nursery Nonsense or Rhymes without Reason* (1864), and collections of graphic images, such as John Parry's *Ridiculous Things* (1854), and tales, such as Charles Leland's *Johnnykin and the Goblins* (1877). There was also musical nonsense, such as the 'nonsense songs' delivered by Tom Barry the clown in Hengler's Circus in 1866, or the 'Great Nonsense Song', which the comedian Harry Paulton accompanied with a 'grotesque dance' in a burlesque of *The Idle Prentice* in 1870. Paulton's nonsense songs were 'thickly studded with crack-jaw words'.[56] (These musical gobstoppers were also show-stoppers: Paulton routinely received four encores.) The diversity of this material suggests that nonsense in the nineteenth century is defined less by its precise constituents than by its function. It is not the meat of communication but the dessert: allowed to be absurd, fanciful, weightless (though far from senseless). Since it is associated not with labour, but with pleasurable idleness, it can perform the surreptitious psychological work of release.

The eminent cultural critic John Ruskin wrote nonsense letters or 'etties' to his cousin Joan Severn, in which he consciously moves from 'professorial' language to 'Pessy-wessorial' and 'Crawleywawlian', allowing his inner infant, 'Donie', to play.[57] This private practice might seem remote from Lear's published nonsense, until one realises that Lear corresponded with both Ruskin and Severn, and that Ruskin was open about the importance that Lear's nonsense had for him: in the *Pall Mall Gazette* he placed *A Book of Nonsense* first in his list of a hundred books that everyone should read.[58] Lear's nonsense was deeply enabling for its nineteenth-century readers, both adults and children. Although Carroll slips in occasionally, I have tried in this book to open up Lear's work to a broader set of comparisons. And I have repeatedly been drawn to the question of intimacy, which seems to me to be at the heart of Lear's achievement.

Lear reaches out to us. His sky-bound self-caricature projects itself into the reader's affections. In a memorable letter of 1865 to Henry Bruce he describes a sudden reversion from gloom to happiness He is in Venice, 'in a fog of disappointment which corroded my soul'. Then he reads in the newspaper that Chichester Fortescue has been appointed permanent secretary for Ireland, which success:

> threw me into a fit of delight—whereby I suddenly tossed the
> paper up to the ceiling, & began to dance on one leg round the
> table, ending by seizing a whiting, & whirling him round my
> head halo-wise till his body flew off & went bang across the
> room, leaving his tail in my fingers.—Conceive my collapse on
> finding at this awful point that I was not alone in the room as
> I thought,—but that a party were in a recess at breakfast, who
> arose evidently perceiving Lunacy looming near!!! All I could
> do was to make an apology directly, saying I had just seen
> some good news of a very dear friend:—& now comes the
> pleasantest part of my story. Had the people I appealed to been
> English, glumness & sneers would have prevailed: but they
> were Italian—& all burst out laughing saying—[in Italian]

'O excellent gentleman! we're delighted too! It's a shame that
we're not having fish for breakfast or we would have had the
pleasure of throwing them around the room in sympathy!'
So we all roared & shouted & the episode ended happily.[59]

In Lear's work, we are all invited to be Italian. Dancing on the table and
whirling fish 'halo-wise' (or hello-wise) suddenly seem like perfect expressions of emotional sympathy. The 'fit' of Lunacy of which epileptic Lear
might potentially have been suspected becomes a 'fit of delight' where being
unbalanced is fun. Indeed, the celebration of sympathetic feeling here that
ripples out from Fortescue's name in the newspaper to Lear, to strangers
and back to Bruce in England draws us in to share it. Semantic accounts of
nonsense have sometimes been inclined to regard emotion as a misstep in
the game it proposes.[60] But one cannot fully appreciate Lear's art without
acknowledging the role of emotion in it, and how that has shaped readers'
often personal and protective feeling about Lear as a character. The close
relationship between feeling and failing, between pathos and absurdity, happiness and loopiness is essential to the delicate equilibrium of his nonsense
and its continuing power to affect us.

  Some may feel that academic discussion of Lear is the equivalent of taking
a sledgehammer to a soufflé. Yet into a great soufflé goes considerable art,
and knowing this doesn't detract from its deliciousness. In the final alphabet
in his final published book of nonsense, *Laughable Lyrics* (1877), Lear imagines the letter *A* injuring his arm and being comforted with various remedies. *K* proposes a picture of a Kangaroo; *S* suggests, 'A Song should now
be sung, in hopes to make him laugh'; *P* counters, 'Some Poetry might be
read aloud, to make him think'. Lear's work offers delightful pictures and
songs to make us laugh, but also poetry to make us think. This book em-
braces that gift.

1

RETURNING TO LEAR
Music and Memory

'I made them laugh by my Pussy and Owl song'.[1]

EDWARD LEAR had an exceptionally quick ear. It was both a gift and a curse. Sounds got to him. He was maddened to the point of misery and fury by unwelcome noise. In adulthood, 'shrieky' parrots and barking dogs, 'shrilly-howly' wind, 'plate-clashing waiters' and crying babies produced agitated anguish. He described in 1859 a woman who was 'practising howling' with a singing master downstairs as 'louse-lunged', 'piddlewobbling' and 'epipopplebottomed'.[2] He liked to pun on 'instruments of torture'; badly tuned pianos fell into this category. But Lear could be kept from sleep even by the 'roaring' of the sea, or sparrows, or silence, or driven wild by someone making tunes with wet fingers on a glass.[3] He once counted a street door banging, presumably so that he could complain about it, ninety-seven times in one day.[4] From an early age he wore strong glasses; acute myopia probably meant that his sense of hearing developed a finer reach. Unwelcome vibration could also trigger his epileptic attacks. This gave sounds enormous power to affect him, physically and emotionally, and he would self-consciously use them to affect others. He often signed himself with an *L* curling into the shell-shape of an ear: L-ear. It is a suggestive motif, the visual and the aural becoming a single ideogram.

He also collected sounds. Foreign languages attracted him. Place-names were play-names, directly inspiring verses: Nárkunda, where the ambient growl of thunder echoed into nonsense that explores the violence of noise; Oripò; Ibreem.[5] A stuttering missionary on the boat to India unwittingly tripped over his words and into Lear's diary:

It is my own idea——idea—r-r-my own idea,——that if the
wind had been –r-r-right—r—favorable for 4 days we should
have arrived—r—r—in Bonn—r Bombay– the coffee is not
hot, in Bombay arrived in sugar my own idea.[6]

Nonsense lurks invitingly in the gaps between what we mean to express and
what comes out of our mouths. In this case, arriving in Bonn and arriving
in sugar are both ideas we visit en route to where the speaker thinks his sentence is going. In a remote region of Montenegro, Lear noted that peasant
women, who carried large, weighty loads, 'have a habit of uttering an extraordinary whistle every now and then—very nearly like that of a railroad
short preliminary puff-whistle. How they do it I could not find out but believe thro' their teeth'.[7] When he travelled, Lear memorised tunes that he
heard: a fishing song in Corsica, a song in praise of Garibaldi in Italy, a
sailors' chorus in Egypt as he drifted down the Nile. 'The sailors are singing
a sort of quadruple chorus song—which is very characteristic and fine. One
set says Tayib, Tayib, & there is a quick answer—Ba boo ban dir—& then
the chorus ai lai—a very pretty song—all minor'.[8] Each region had its
own soundscape, which Lear tried to record—as he recorded the landscape—in words and images. Had he lived in modern times, Lear would
have made, among other things, an excellent radio producer: he is always
attempting to capture the atmosphere of place in sound. He could not read
music from the page. But he played very well by ear, and his lifelong habit
of listening, getting songs by heart and improvising on them would have
far-reaching consequences for his own work as a writer and composer.

This chapter is about Lear's music, particularly the soundscape of his early
life and how his background and practices as a musician shape his nonsense.
But it is also about memory. For Lear, memory and sound are deeply intertwined; as he writes in March 1870, 'Tivoli, Corfu, Sicily Crete,—lonely
& painful echoes alone are their long passed songs of a time long past'.[9] His
memories of people and places are often stimulated by particular musical
cues. The sound of blackbirds singing means Knowsley Hall.[10] Augusta
Bethell, the woman whom he thought for a time he might marry, is represented by 'Les Cloches du Monastère', a nocturne for piano by Lefébure-
Wely that she played beautifully and that imitates a carillon of bells.[11]
Whenever he heard this piece, it brought her to mind. Dying in 1887, Lear
struggled to write down the words of a ballad that Charles Hornby had sung
in the 1830s, 'Land of the Stranger', which recalled Hornby's sweet voice:

> For remembrance is like the compass which guides
> The wandering mariner forth
> Tho' the ship may be toss'd by the wind and the tides
> The needle still points to the north.[12]

Lear's nonsense poems or songs are infused with the emotive power of musical return, both in the sense of internal reprise—repeated words, rhythms and rhymes—and echoes of other literary and musical works.

Lear grew up in a musical environment. From a very young age, he was valued as a singer; he told Edward Strachey that as a boy, 'his voice being a good one, he used to be taken to sing at artists' parties'.[13] He also played on the piano, the accordion, the flute and the small guitar: an instrument with an hour-glass shape and crisp tonality, less sustained than that of a modern guitar.[14] This is important. From the start, Lear was a performer. He was taken into company to entertain and delight people. An early picture of Lear, aged nine, by his sister Ann, shows him holding a flute in an Arcadian landscape with a waterfall and exotic foliage in the background.[15] She was portraying him as a young gentleman, but also as an Arcadian shepherd with a pipe. Playing, for Lear, would always involve role play; private and public performance were enmeshed in his early life. His subsequent development as a nonsense poet can be traced to this early habit of live musical performance. Lear's nonsenses are designed to be sung or recited aloud to an appreciative audience.

Indeed, when picturing Lear it is helpful to conjure him singing. He did so on many hundreds of occasions throughout his life, when visiting friends or entertaining them in his home. Diary after diary entry reads, 'played and sang'. He sang at the lithographer Charley Hullmandel's parties, where he met Turner and forever afterward remembered the great artist singing a tiddly song: 'The World goes around, abound, abound!'[16] He sang comic numbers for Lord Derby's guests at Knowsley Hall in the 1830s; Burns's love songs al fresco in the moonlight in Rome in the 1840s; Tennyson settings in the Gallery at Strawberry Hill and at Farringford in the 1850s, where Emily Tennyson reported that on occasion he performed for two or three hours at a stretch.[17] He sang on the boat to India in the 1870s and at hotel pianos in Italian mountain resorts. Even when 'short of tin', he hired a piano, to which he could flee in the evenings and at times of emotional stress—the 'blessed' piano, he sometimes called it.[18]

Lear enjoyed the element of 'call and response' in songs, the opportunities they offered for acting, the power of sound as a force that precedes other kinds of sense. In 1876, he reported that with Charles Church he 'played old airs & talked of old times till 11pm'.[19] Lear, who loved to conjure floating and flight, is airborne by music. Most unusually, he included scores in his *Illustrated Excursions in Italy* (1846), so that readers could transport themselves musically to the places he described, singing an ancient pilgrims' chant and a traditional Italian air in praise of the swallow. Lear's own poems, which are also songs, have the same quality of enchantment. Their music transports the reader to distant and wondrous places: the Western Sea, the Coast of Coromandel, the land where the Bong-tree grows.

Indeed, music is at the heart of Lear's nonsense, from the Quangle Wangle's hat where the blue baboon plays the flute, to the boat where the Owl plays his guitar and sings to the Pussy-cat, to the Jumblies' songs and the Pelican Chorus. Many of the best of Lear's poems evoke song as the means by which social concert evolves out of loneliness, or characters are carried away on waves that are both musical and literal. The central techniques of Lear's poetry—counterpoint, medley, refrain, leitmotif—are musical techniques.

For Lear, poetry and song are not intrinsically different forms. He referred to his own published nonsense, excluding the limericks, not as nonsense poetry but as 'nonsense songs and stories', which was also the title of his first collection of longer work.[20] His output, he told friends, consisted of 'Learical Lyrics and Puffles of Prose'.[21] We know that Lear sang 'The Owl and the Pussy-cat' to friends including John Addington Symonds, Franklin Lushington and his family, William Bevan and Daisy Terry, though Lear's 'funny little crooning tune'[22] for it has sadly been lost. Lear describes 'The Quangle Wangle's Hat' as 'an absurd poem or song'.[23] In May 1870 his publisher sent proofs of the 'Pussey Cat, Kangaroo, and Floppy Fly songs'. Lear refers in his diary to 'The Yonghy-Bonghy-Bò' as a 'fooly song'; a few days later it and 'Mr and Mrs Discobbolos' are jointly described as 'ballads'.[24] Lear's music survives for only two of his nonsense songs: 'The Pelican Chorus' and 'The Courtship of the Yonghy-Bonghy-Bò'. But Lear sang and played many of his other nonsenses, as did others. His friend Frances Catherine Chattock, a composer of hymns, sang his nonsense songs 'wonderfully well' in Lear's opinion, and she self-published her setting of 'The Two Old Bachelors'.[25] In the 1880s Emily Josephine Troup set to music

'The Owl and the Pussy-cat', 'The Duck and the Kangaroo' and 'The Daddy Long-legs and the Fly'; Lear heard them sung and played 'very nicely' by Mrs Hassall, the wife of his doctor in San Remo, and thought the latter 'by no means a commonplace affair'.[26] These musical settings give an idea of how Lear's circle sang the works—and remind us that they were written with such performance in mind.

Even Lear's limericks have lyrical qualities. John Ruskin admiringly referred to them as 'corollary carols': musical pieces whose end lies in their beginning.[27] A carol is, in origin, a ring dance; it is also a song associated with Christmas cheer and goodwill. Lear's nonsense songs, which were published in December to attract the Christmas gift market, had many of the qualities of carols. In 1876 Mostyn Pryce, a barrister, published *Musical Nonsense Rhymes,* which set twelve of Lear's limericks to music. Price's settings show how the visual and aural symmetries of Lear's limericks were also interpreted musically by Victorian audiences. In Pryce's version of 'There was an Old Man who said, 'Hush! / I perceive a young bird in this bush!', the bird sings, 'tra-la-la' and the man echoes him.[28] Peeping naturally leads to cheeping.

Lear published his settings for twelve of Tennyson's songs and composed music for at least nine other Tennyson poems, including 'The Lady of Shalott', 'The Lotos-Eaters', *Maud* and 'In the Garden at Swainston'.[29] Various commentators testify to the effectiveness of these musical tributes. Chichester Fortescue commented in his diary for July 1855, 'Drove to St Leonards, surprised Lear painting on the lawn, and listened with tears in my eyes to his Tennysonian melodies, "Tears, Idle Tears", "Ellen Adair" etc'. In 1858, he wrote of Lady Waldegrave, 'Sat in the Gallery while Lear sang his Tennyson songs, which *she* enjoyed and felt very much, some of them made her cry'.[30]

Perhaps most intriguingly, Lear sang his own setting of lines from Swinburne's *Atalanta in Calydon* (1865), a provocative attempt at imitating Greek prosody in English.[31] He also delighted in setting Shelley's poems, which in 1863 he sang to Shelley's grandson on his boat, a 'white day' of joy for Lear, who could never resist an opportunity to communicate his own artistic vision to the families of his poet-heroes.[32] Song-settings, for Lear, are tributaries that offer opportunities for swimming back to the source. They are a form of critical response and reconfiguration. Lear's music has received very little critical attention.[33] But we cannot understand Lear's poetry fully without realising that most of it once had a musical accompaniment.

Lear was saturated in the popular musical culture of his age. In particular he knew by heart and parodied the songs of Thomas Moore and Thomas Haynes Bayly, who were the leading poet-songwriters of their era. Moore and Haynes Bayly are far more important to Lear's version of Romanticism than Wordsworth, whom he once met but whose poetry he barely knew until late old age, or Samuel Taylor Coleridge, whom he never mentions at all.[34] The musical work of Robert Burns was formative, and he was drawn to Welsh, Irish and Scottish ballads, such as 'Huntingtower' and 'The Lament for Owen Roe O'Neill'.[35] Importantly, he also sang the comic songs of his era. He enjoyed performing songs that involved comic acting, such as 'The Cork Leg', by Thomas Hudson and Jonathan Blewitt, which has an unstoppable, tongue-twisting refrain, and 'Tea in the Arbour' and 'The Nervous Family', by Jacob Beuler. Lear learned much from this repertoire about comic timing and the possibilities of using sound to comic effect.

Lear also listened to what we now call 'classical' music. Aged twenty, he boasted to George Coombe about going to hear the violin virtuoso Niccolò Paganini. Paganini's London concerts, featuring his own compositions, were oversubscribed and tickets were expensive; Lear must have been extravagantly keen to get in.[36] With George he went to hear Bellini's 'I Puritani'. He knew Mozart's operas,[37] but it was Italian opera that swept Lear off his feet. When he saw an engraved portrait of the great mezzo-soprano Maria Malibran Garcia in 1884, it interested him far more than the portraits of 'Goethe, Volta and Humboldt etc'.[38] Maria Malibran was renowned for her passionate performances and the seductive timbre of her voice in roles from Bellini, Rossini and Donizetti. She came to London in 1834 and died in 1836, taking the town by storm. Lear doubtless heard her and may well have met her. When he heard the aria 'A te, o cara' played by a public band in 1879, 'all the memories' of 'those days—when first I Puritani came out . . . rushed violently over me'.[39] Lear's description of the memory 'violently' overwhelming him is very typical of the physical, emotional chords that music strikes in him.

Lear was always drawn to music in public spaces and loved 'the music gardens' in San Remo, which he often visited on Sundays instead of going to church, 'the music sedoosing me'.[40] In Italy in 1838, he reports listening to an old blind man with a guitar who sang 'o rose! O lily!'[41] In Rome on Christmas Eve, he was moved by the sound of *pifferari* (pipers), one playing a bagpipe and another playing an instrument similar to an oboe, who travelled from southern Italy, playing at wayside shrines as they went, in accordance with ancient custom: '*What* memories these Abruzzi bagpipes recall—masterfully!!'[42] In 1864 he angrily refused to sign William Holman Hunt's paper calling for the suppression of all street music.[43] His own work repeatedly draws on the forms and themes of popular song.

Later, Lear appreciated the works of Beethoven, Chopin and Mendelssohn, which were played in his friends' homes.[44] There are echoes of Beethoven and of Schubert in his Tennyson settings, alongside hymn tunes and effects learned from opera. In the nineteenth century, 'classical' music and popular song enjoyed a particularly close relationship. Beethoven and Mendelssohn both set songs by Thomas Moore. Glee clubs and the minor theatres featured versions of many of the same comic and sentimental ballads that were sung in middle-class parlours equipped with a piano, the newly affordable instrument of mass appeal. A good example of the conversation between what we might regard as 'high' and 'low' musical styles is provided by Lear's friend Edward Rimbault, who transcribed Lear's settings of Tennyson for publication. Rimbault was a classical organist and founding member of the Percy Society, which pursued scholarly research into early music; he also produced popular piano settings that ranged from arias from Verdi's *Macbeth* to blackface minstrel melodies called 'Kiss Me Quick and Go' and 'Hoop de Dooden Do'.[45] On the back of 'Hoop de Dooden Do' appear advertisements for the scores of all thirty-two of Beethoven's piano sonatas, a clear indication that the same audience was expected to enjoy both. Lear would likely have been shocked to know that Jacob Beuler, whose comic songs he sang at Knowsley, had been famous in the wild Regency years for composing and singing libertine songs at the Coal Hole, a tavern in the Strand, including 'Cocky Cock the Cocksmith of Cock-Lane and the Coquetting Cock-Eyed Maid at the Cock Public House'.[46] The combination in this period of music of different eras and styles in the home was exceptionally fertile: it produced the kind of improvised medleys that Lear enjoyed playing on the piano, which led directly to his nonsense songs.

Domestic music-making also brought old and new music together.[47] On successive evenings in October 1869 with the Goldsmids and the Aldersons, Lear heard Miss Alderson sing Mozart, Thomas Moore, Italian songs and a new song by Claribel, published that year, called 'Strangers Yet'. Lear reported that, while she sang the other pieces well, 'Miss Alderson sung—sung?—the last rose of summer—& I had rather have had a tooth taken out'.[48] Lear's loopy comic squiggles in his diary feelingly represent the effect

Fig. 1.1 **Lear draws bad singing (1869)**

of notes that are so drawn out as to be excruciating. The attempt to evoke sentiment could easily spill over into bathos, a descent Lear secretly enjoys.

It is easy for a modern audience to think patronisingly about nineteenth-century domestic music-making as an amateur 'tinkling of the ivories'. But such a view undersells the skill and emotional resonance of these regular performances, which allowed friends and new acquaintances to play together, sharing new compositions, evoking memories and expressing a complex range of feelings. Through his friendship with Lady Waldegrave, Lear knew her four brothers, three of whom were professional singers; their father, John Braham, was the most celebrated English tenor of the early nineteenth century.[49] During one evening with Lear, Ward Braham 'sang a whole French opera'.[50] Another close friend, Marianne North, had been classically trained by an opera singer in Germany and had 'gone through all of Mozart's operas and masses, singing and transposing all the solos and duets . . . and learning many of Beethoven's sonatas by heart'.[51] Lear heard the celebrated Swedish soprano Jenny Lind sing in 1868 at his friends' house; he dined with her after the private concert.[52] The boundary between private and professional music-making could be thin. Lear's performance of nonsense songs to friends preceded their publication and was an important part of their early dissemination amongst adults as well as children. For example in June 1877 he reports that after dinner, 'I sang a lot of nonsense to Lady Baynes—now 84½ years old—but perfectly "young" as to health and intellect'.[53] The emotional work that music, sung and played in the home, accomplishes in this period deserves more consideration than literary scholarship has yet accorded it. Like the private theatrical, it permits heightened communication where lines can be voiced that may be comic or tragic, sincere or affected, hovering between personal intimacy and public masquerade. Lear's nonsense songs explore these liminal dramatic possibilities. He

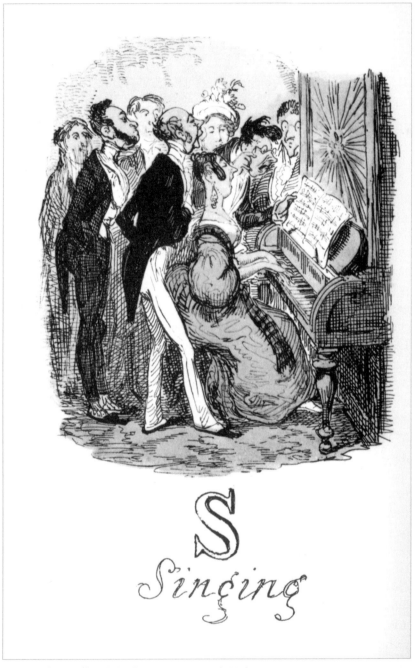

Fig. 1.2 George Cruikshank, *Comic Alphabet* (1836)

absorbed both the comic burlesque and the sentimental musical repertoire of his era, and his work often ingeniously combines aspects of both.

Juvenilia: Sound and Dialogue

When we meet him in his early compositions, Lear is already a performance poet. These early works anticipate Lear's later writing, which is also an exuberantly social performance, directed first at his friends and then at the wider crowd of readers who are imaged, on the title page of the *Book of Nonsense* (1846), as eight children gathering around an entertainer, jumping and jigging and turning handstands. Sound effects are essential to the dialogue they conjure. One of these early poems, written when Lear was thirteen, is addressed to his sister Ann on her birthday, which he celebrates by trying to find one hundred rhymes for the word *relation*.

> Dear, and very dear relation,
> Time, who flies without cessation,—
> Who ne'er allows procrastination,—
> Who never yields to recubation
> Nor ever stops for respiration,
> Has brought again in round rotation
> The once a yearly celebration[54]

'To Miss Lear on Her Birthday' resembles a patter song: voicing it would involve a feat of breath control. It also shows Lear's early interest in recondite vocabulary. *Glomeration, rhabarbaration, trucidation, obtrectation* and *advesperation* are not words one meets with every day. Our response to them is thus primarily visual and aural. They invite us to imagine meaning, or simply to enjoy their sounds and shapes as pleasures distinct from meaning, as Lear's later nonsense vocabulary will do.

As its rhyme-words become more and more obscure, the poem turns into a kind of game, like firing a hundred-gun birthday salute. Some guns don't quite go off—they are repeats, or cheats—but the pleasure that Lear finds in such desperation (an obvious rhyme that he chooses to omit) is apparent. It is as if the poem is literalising the notion of 'many happy returns' by having a rhyme that keeps coming back indefinitely.

In his gift poem 'Journal 1829', we catch a glimpse of the seventeen-year-old Lear dancing. He recalls for his friends the kind of hectic socialising of which energetic teenagers love to boast. First, at a dance in London he jigs 'all the colour out of my face', returning at cock-crow. He then packs til 4.30 am, drinks tea at 6 am and catches the coach down to Arundel, where his married sister Sarah Street lives.

> Chelsea and Fulham and Putney Bridge,—
> And Kingston on Thames with its banks of sedge,—
> Esher and Cobham, how cold they were!—
> Oh! it was enough to make anyone swear!
> —Thumped my feet till I made them ache,—
> Took out provisions, a meal to make,—
> Offered a sandwich,—(I had but three,)—
> To my neighbour, who sat with a shaky knee,
> 'Sir'—said she with a glutinous grin,
> 'I'll thank you for *two,* as they seem but thin,—
> And shall feel quite glad if you'll give one 'arter,
> To this here young lady wot's my darter.'—[55]

The names of places as they flash past form a chant that evokes the rattling wheels of the coach. In other ways, too, Lear makes us listen to his journey, with dramatic exclamation, thumps and reported dialogue. Lear often ventriloquises a stage-Cockney manner, of the kind popularised in the early nineteenth century by comic songs such as 'Dash My Vig!' In 'Journal 1829', he depicts himself in a social whirl of activity, eating, talking, walking, discussing reform and reading Samuel Rogers's *Italy,* illustrated by Turner. The packed itinerary stresses his connectedness—musical, social, artistic and political—and how these forms of cultural engagement are interwoven. The style of his versified teenage diary may be headlong, but it is also rhetorical. It imitates that of Thomas Moore's *The Fudge Family in Paris,* a poem that pretends to be the diary of an impressionable middle-class family who go to post-Revolutionary Paris, where they make many gauche mistakes.[56] Relating his journal in the manner of the Fudges, Lear emphasises his contrasting self-awareness. He is playing back to his friends the record of their shared lives with self-conscious spin.

Another poem in Lear's juvenilia uses sound to explore loss. Aged just thirteen, Lear emulates the framework of William Collins's poem 'Eclogue the Second: Hassan, or the Camel Driver' to present the family's chagrin in a seriocomic light as, after his father's financial failure, they leave Bowman's

Lodge.[57] Collins's Hassan the camel driver proceeds in 'silent horror' through the desert waste, fearing to die of thirst if wolves, tigers, lions and snakes don't eat him first. Lear's family are only moving from a Georgian villa in the leafy suburb of Holloway into rented rooms in the crowded streets of central London. Lear's sedate heroic couplets measure this distance, suggesting the relative absurdity of lamenting their situation (it's not *that* bad) while emphasising that, from the point of view of those affected, it is actually very bad indeed:

> Sad was the hour and luckless was the day
> When first from Bowman's Lodge we bent our way!
> 'What noisome thought could urge our parents so—
> To leave the country and to London go!
> The rural scene to change for houses, brown,
> And barter health for the thick smoke of town!
> What demon tempts him from our home to go
> In horrid New Street to pour forth our woe?—
> Oft—oft we've hoped this hour we ne'er might see,
> Yet London—now at last we come to thee!
> Oh! why was New Street so attractive made,—
> Or why our Dad so easily betrayed?
> Why heed we not as swift we ride along
> The farewell peal of Highgate bells ding dong,—
> . . .
>
> 'At that dread hour the noise of fire shall sweep
> If aught of rest we find, upon our sleep,
> Or some rude thief bounce through the window—smash—
> And wake our dozings with a hideous crash[58]

The familiar church bells abandoned for the 'noise and trouble' of the city, with its potential 'noise of fire' or the 'bounce . . . smash . . . and hideous crash' of an entering thief, replicate in sound the change from an orderly and protected sanctuary to crowded lodgings vulnerable to unpredictable social threats and embarrassments. The Highgate church's 'peal' becomes a personal 'appeal' that should have been heeded. This is parody as a form of voluntary transposition that can help the teenage Lear to bemoan an involuntary transposition. Lear deals with the emotionally fraught move through

making a downsizing move of his own, from romantic orientalism to domestic comedy. Potential reformist agitators in the London streets become
the ironic counterparts of the lions in the desert. The side garden replaces
Zara in 'Hassan' as the romantic sidekick who will be devastated by the
Lears' departure. But Lear's rage at his father's 'betrayal' sings out through
the comedy. He would, ever after, feel a 'strange dread in new places',[59] and
small rooms produced in him an intense claustrophobic reaction. Parody is
an assertive form—the equivalent of buttonholing a celebrity, then giving
them your autograph. Here, the adolescent Lear transmutes the calamitous
fall from Bowman's Lodge to New Street into literary bathos, performing
it back to his family with a brio that is fierce and raw.

All these early pieces involve remembering: the many happy returns of a
birthday, holiday journeys, the revisiting of family losses. They are self-aware
about using modes of literary reprise (recurring rhyme, the journal, parody)
to explore shared memory, counterpointing the form of return against
the theme of return. Lear's family circumstances made him peculiarly alert
to the pull of the past. He was aware, from before a time when most
children have any awareness, that things had been better before. However,
Lear was also born into an era that was culturally preoccupied with the
power of memory. The late 1820s and '30s were the period in which Romanticism reached a mass public, partly through annuals with names such
as the *Keepsake,* the *Forget-Me-Not,* and the *Literary Souvenir* (to whose
editor Lear submitted 'lines about Pisgah'); they printed work, much of it
on the subject of memorial, including pieces by the newly dead Byron and
Shelley. When Lear saw these annuals in the 1870s he remarked, '*What
days do they not bring back*'.[60] Popular song played into this vogue for personal and cultural remembering. As Derek Scott has remarked, 'Nostalgia
emerges as one of the dominant themes of the drawing-room ballad
throughout the entire [nineteenth] century'.[61] Lear grew up at a time when
music and poetry were preoccupied with parting and with the painful pleasure of recollection; his own preoccupation with this subject and that of his
era are impossible to separate. From a very young age he learned to play it
alternately for tears and for laughs.

Contrafactum: New Words to Old Music

He exploited this ability when, in the 1820s, he set comic words to two well-
known melodies, turning their sentimental nostalgia into something more

disruptive. Thomas Haynes Bayly's 'Isle of Beauty, Fare Thee Well!' is a song with stirring music by Charles Shapland Whitmore that could serve as the national anthem of an imaginary state. The singer is departing by sea and, as he sees the shore recede, he expresses his longing for what he leaves behind:

> Shades of Ev'ning close not o'er us,
> Leave our lonely bark awhile!
> Morn alas! will not restore us
> Yonder dim and distant Isle:
>
> . . .
>
> What would I not give to wander
> Where my old companions dwell;
> Absence makes the heart grow fonder;
> Isle of Beauty, 'Fare-thee-well'![62]

The melody, which allows the singer to linger caressingly on 'friends' and the places where they 'dwell', mimics the intense feeling that a departing traveller might undergo. In an era of mass emigration this song touched many people deeply; the line 'Absence makes the heart grow fonder' remains even now a popular cliché. 𝄞

Lear must have played and sung this popular number. In his lyrics to the same music, titled 'Turkey Discipline', he describes nine 'monstrous turkeys' that have got into the kitchen yard and are pouncing on other birds. Instead of being a scene of nostalgic leave-taking, it's a scene of domestic cacophony:

> 'Bless my heart—nine monstrous turkeys!—
> Gracious!—all the garden's full!—
> And one great one with a jerk has
> Pounced upon my favourite gull!'
> —Through the noise of turkeys calling,
> Now was heard, distinct and well,
> From the Southern window squalling
> Many a long and awful yell.[63]

𝄞 Listen to musical link #1 at edwardlearsmusic.com/audiotrail/#isleofbeauty.

𝄞 Listen to musical link #2 at edwardlearsmusic.com/audiotrail/#turkeydiscipline.

Haynes Bayly's song conjures the faint sound of evening church bells, floating through the mist 'like a voice from those who love us./Breathing fondly "Fare-thee-well!"' Lear has characteristically replaced the 'vesper bell' with an 'awful yell'. That yell will recur in various nonsense poems.[64] One of the features of Lear's nonsense is the way in which it counterpoints polite and tuneful noises with wild and discordant ones. Lear loves to substitute, in imagination, yells for melodious bells and to voice squeaks and shrieks, bongs and dongs. It is a very musical joke. Here, he creates pleasurable counterpoint between the high sentiment of the lyric and the violent aggression of the turkeys. It is as if Alfred Hitchcock had set *The Birds* to the tune of 'Danny Boy'.

'Resignation', another early comic piece by Lear about the tiresomeness of baking day, is also actually a song. It has not previously been identified as such, but in fact it is a comic version of another drawing-room ballad by Thomas Haynes Bayly with music by Henry Rowley Bishop, called 'Oh! No, We Never Mention Her'. (It can equally well be sung by a female complainant as 'Oh! No, We Never Mention Him'.) It tells the tale of an abandoned lover who can't get their former sweetheart out of their head:

> OH! no we never mention her, Her name is never heard;
> My lips are now forbid to speak that once familiar word:
> From sport to sport they hurry me, To banish my regret;
> And when they win a smile from me, they think that I forget!
>
> They bid me seek in change of scene, The charms that others see:
> But were I in a foreign land, They'd find no change in me;
> Tis true that I behold no more The valley where we met,
> I do not see the hawthorn tree, But how can I forget![65]

As is often true of pop songs, this romantic lyric turns on the tension between forgetting and regretting: moving away from a loved object and being inevitably drawn back by it. In 'Resignation', Lear spoofs the heartache inspired by insistent and unwanted psychological return. The protagonist can't escape the kitchen: ♭♭

♭ Listen to musical link #3 at edwardlearsmusic.com/audiotrail/#ohnowenever.
♭ Listen to musical link #4 at edwardlearsmusic.com/audiotrail/#resignation.

I wish you would not mention it,
It gives me so much pain!—
Too soon by half I always know
'Tis baking day again!—
From pie to pie they hurry me,—
Loaves—tarts—preserves—and crusts—
And though I've not a moment's peace,
I cry—'What must be, must!'

They bid me seek a change of fruit,
The charms which other see,
But—cherries—currants—plums—or pears—
They're all the same to me!—
'Tis true, I do not pluck the things,
Or clean 'em from the dust,
But though I don't—it's such a bore!—
Although 'What must be, must!'[66]

Lear is ventriloquising a female voice here. One wonders whether he sang this song falsetto. Given the size of the Lear family, the kitchen was likely hot and harassed on baking day, and one can imagine his mother and sisters complaining. The effect of substituting fruit for lover is, however, typically Learish in its absurd humour. The singer doesn't care for pears and doesn't give a fig for plums. A lyric of abandonment becomes a lament about pie.

As with Lear's other comic turns, these songs are geared towards the co-quetry of performance, the exclamation marks pointing the emphasis and the long dashes marking the breaths. Listening to 'Resignation' sung to Rowley Bishop's music, one realises also the quasi-operatic pleasure offered by the ornamental cadenza on the final words, and that certain words have musical values not apparent from the poem on the page: thus *pain, again, see* and *me* are each sung over two beats.

Both these early works by Lear deploy contrafactum: the technique of setting new words to established music. We are assumed to know these songs, and the new lyrics make us laugh because they are at odds with the tone of the original. Contrafactum, here, shares many of the same qualities as parody: it involves responding to the form and style of an earlier work in a manner whose familiarity emphasises critical distance.[67] Yet it also differs from parody in that we hear the familiar music identically through the new lyric; in this sense it is like an aria sung with a pianist in another room who doesn't know that they're now playing for a comedian rather than a tragedian. Lear relishes this juxtaposition—the creative friction between what the music is saying and what he is saying to it. His later nonsense constantly makes use of a similar counterpoint between the musical qualities of the verse and the absurd qualities of the narrative.

A third early example of Lear using contrafactum has only recently come to light. It is a surprising piece because it is highly political. It tells us that as a young teenager, Lear was experimenting with Shelleyan thought, with ideas advocated by William Cobbett and other radicals. These sentiments, if seriously advocated, could have got him into serious trouble in 1826.

> Ye who have hearts—aloud rejoice,
> > For Oligarchy trembles
> Like boxes in a theatre—
> > From shouts at Keans and Kembles.
> Rejoice aloud!—rejoice aloud!—
> > For the Oligarchs must fall
> And the Christianized republic—be
> > One universal all!——
> >   . . .
>
> Coke—Cobbett—Canning—Irving—Hunt,
> > Alike are raising high
> A battering ram to overthrow
> > All Aristocracy!——
> The mighty with a crash shall fall—
> > And Kings, and dukes and princes
> Shall be as insignificant
> > As pips in unripe quinces!——
>
> Delightful thought! equality
> > Alone shall rule mankind,—
> And all the world shall welcome
> > This millennium of the mind;—
> Alike in little gardens—all
> > Shall rear their daily food—
> A universal meal of peace—
> > Its freedom sweet—though rude![68]

This song anticipates the Chartist hymns of the 1840s in its fusion of political with religious millennial imagery.[69] It imagines the advent of a new 'Christianized republic' in which the promises of the Bible have come to pass: the meek have inherited the earth, and the oligarchy of powerful, tyrannical rulers has been swept away. Equality now rules mankind. As the journalist and MP William Cobbett imagined in *Cottage Economy* (1821), ordinary people could grow their own food on their own land, returning Britain to a rural vision of peace and prosperity. There would follow what Shelley, drawing on Godwinian philosophy, referred to as a 'triumph of mind' or 'omnipotence of mind over matter',[70] characterised by a government of reason and justice.

Lear's rag-bag throws some seemingly ill-assorted characters together. George Canning in autumn of 1826 had just taken over the leadership of the Tory party; he was opposed to parliamentary reform. Thomas Coke was a long-serving Whig member of parliament, known for supporting agricultural reform. Edward Irving was a controversial preacher whose oratory attracted large crowds to his London chapel and who believed a religious millennium was at hand. Henry Hunt was a radical orator who pressed for universal suffrage, annual parliaments and other far-reaching democratic reforms; in 1822 he had been released from prison following his part in the Peterloo rally, in which demonstrators were attacked and killed by the cavalry, provoking a firestorm of antigovernment protest. Pairing Canning with Hunt as revolutionists who will batter down the walls of aristocracy now seems odd. But the song is, in any case, not a hand-on-heart paean to revolution. Everything we know of Lear's political views reveals that he was a moderate, though staunch, Liberal. He disliked mobs and the possibility of violence, and his eclogue of 1825 worries about reformist agitators: 'By mischief roused they scour the streets, and fly / While radical reform is all they cry'. In middle age he would copy beneath several of his paintings lines from Tennyson's poem describing Britain as 'A land of settled Government . . . where Freedom slowly broadens down / From precedent to precedent'.[71] This vision of Britain as like a stable tree with a thickening girth, 'broadening down' towards spreading democratic roots, is closer to Lear's real ideal of progress than the almighty crash he imagines in this song.

Still, Lear's enthusiasm for Shelley as a poet, whose work he would continue to set to music, was real and abiding. There are nods in this song to 'Ozymandias' ('tyranny must fade . . . like writing on the sand') and to *The Revolt of Islam* (Lear's concluding phrase 'one universal all' resembles

Shelley's description of the cry of Liberty as 'one universal sound'). We know that Lear attended Edward Irving's chapel for a time.[72] And he carried the ideal of the self-sustaining cottage garden into later life. In the 1870s in San Remo he cultivated 'the pease of my own garding',[73] rather similar to the 'universal meal of peace' he envisioned aged fourteen. A passionate love of liberty is part of Lear's liberal, dissenting inheritance, which flows into his nonsense, where eccentric individuals so often light out for the territory, throwing off the restraints of class and position.

We can, then, I think read this song as a playful exercise, like the other examples of Lear's early contrafactum. The tune was probably borrowed from a dissenting hymn. There are many examples of such hymns, based on the book of Isaiah, that begin in a similar fashion, most famously Isaac Watts's 'Awake my heart, and thou my tongue, / Prepare a tuneful voice'. Lear's imagery of the theatre box shaking with the crowd's voice is telling: this is a piece inspired by the experience of theatrical performance and intended to be performed. The manuscript tells us that it was sung by 'J . . . C . . . G . . .' on 7 October 1826. This may have been a member of the Gale family, who were also dissenters, and in whose Bloomsbury house Lear spent many adolescent evenings. The technique of contrafactum allows for fertile ambiguity, permitting us to entertain seditious thoughts while maintaining a knowing distance from them.

There are tantalising glimpses in Lear's diary of other examples of his early musical habit of burlesque. In December 1874 he recalls 'singing that travesty of one of Edward Francis's poems' at Mrs Arnold's in 1827 or 1828. Certainly, he never abandoned the technique of setting new words to existing music. I have found six instances of Lear deploying contrafactum, and there may well be more. In 1879, aged sixty-six, he wrote the well-known verses '"How Pleasant to Know Mr Lear!"', with assistance from a friend, Miss Bevan. He told her that they could be sung to the tune of 'How Cheerful along the Gay Mead', a song from Thomas Arne's oratorio *The Death of Abel* (1744), which became a popular hymn.[74] In taking the tune of a hymn and making it a song about him, Lear was being mildly sacrilegious, setting autobiographical lines to music that concludes, 'Thee, Lord, who such wonders canst raise. . . . My lips shall incessantly praise'.[75] Arne's music adds to the piquancy of lines that from one viewpoint emphasise Lear's geniality (his 'many friends', his 'hundreds of books') yet also emphasise his oddity ('queer', 'hideous', 'that crazy old Englishman—O'). '"How Pleasant

to Know Mr Lear!'" can be sung in quite a camp manner; the musical colleague whom I invited to record it instinctively performed it this way. Interestingly, the music brings out the poem's theatrical quality of self-conscious
performance. Lear's personality becomes, like the song, something that can
be presented with conscious ambivalence: the conflict between the lyrical
and the ridiculous in the character has a specific analogue in the teasing relationship between the music and the words.

Contrafactum was rife in the early nineteenth century, a standard habit
for composers of comic songs, which were quite often sung back to back
with their 'serious' counterparts and printed in the same collections. Jacob
Beuler produced at least nine series of *Comic Songs to Popular Tunes* in the
1830s. The combination of well-known music with topical words on such
themes as the miseries of carving (a social obligation that made Lear sweat),
steam coaches and infant schools was popular with amateur singers and professional entertainers alike at London's minor theatres, the forerunners of
the music hall. Thomas Haynes Bayly published comic songs such as 'The
Old Bachelor' alongside serious ones like 'Isle of Beauty, Fare Thee Well!'.
Indeed, a glance at any substantial song compilation of the 1820s and
1830s—and there are a great many—reveals that the same air was very frequently treated in a variety of ways. Olivia Clarke in her introduction to
Parodies on Popular Songs (1826) remarks flirtatiously that:

> A pretty air . . . with only *one set of words,* resembles a pretty
> woman with only one admirer; and though the genius of the
> above writers [Thomas Moore, Robert Burns and Lady
> Morgan] has given to national Melody, poetry not unworthy
> of the beautiful strains it embodies, still an adaptation of less
> elevated ideas to the *same* air, may not be unacceptable, nor
> inappropriate, for it is a notorious fact that the same Scotch or
> Irish tune, becomes a jig or a cronon, according as it is rattled
> over the keys of the piano *prestissimo,* or swept over the chords
> of the harp, in the *affetuoso. . . .*[76]

Lear grew up in a musical environment of professional and amateur vocal
performance where genre was a quick-change act. He learned how to play
the same material both *affettuoso* and *prestissimo,* and how to teeter precari-
ously on the edge between the two. Marianne North, his musically gifted

friend, described Lear playing the piano at her house in a manner that captures his keen awareness of the twilight moment at which deep pathos could spill over into high comedy:

> He . . . used to wander into our sitting-room through the
> windows at dusk when his work was over, sit down to the
> piano, and sing Tennyson's songs for hours, composing as
> he went on, and picking out the accompaniments by ear,
> putting the greatest expression and passion into the most
> sentimental words. He often set me laughing; then he would
> say I was not worthy of them, and would continue the intense
> pathos of expression and gravity of face, while he substituted
> Hey Diddle Diddle, the Cat and the Fiddle, or some other
> nonsensical words to the same air. I never was able to appre-
> ciate modern poetry, and still think it is sense worried, and
> often worrit without the sense.[77]

North is commenting here not only on Lear's teasing habits of performance but also on the intellectual question they raise: whether 'serious' poetry is indistinguishable from nonsense when treated as sound effect. I shall come back to this question when discussing the musical qualities of nonsense songs such as 'The Courtship of the Yonghy-Bonghy-Bò' and how these pieces hover deliberately and productively between the conventions of sentimental drawing-room ballad and comic song. For now, however, I would like to examine Lear's early musical repertoire and the ways in which his singing and his visual portrayal of music, from the 1820s to the 1850s, form the foundation on which his nonsense songs of the 1870s are built.

ALBUM CULTURE AND 'THE BRIDE'S FAREWELL'

Around 1829 we find the seventeen-year-old Lear compiling an album for a Miss Fraser, one of the pupils to whom he taught art.[78] Just as published literary annuals of the 1820s offered a decorative mixture of poetry, prose, songs and artwork, so private albums of autographed work became fashionable, particularly for young women, who demonstrated thereby their cultural taste but also, in the days before Facebook, the number of people who 'liked' them sufficiently to add a tribute. Miss Fraser's album and the preparatory album into which Lear copied work by himself and others emphasise the way in which musical, artistic and literary influences intertwined in Lear's formative years.

If one had to guess, one would assume that Lear's albums were not only made *for* a woman but also made *by* one. Butterflies wing their way over the endpapers, and tiny, fancy sketches of birds, including a woodpecker, a goldfinch and collared doves, are so delicate in their detail that one needs a magnifying glass to appreciate them fully. The most striking poem in both albums is 'Ruins of the Temple of Jupiter Aegina, Greece', which Lear accompanies with a sketch of the temple, no bigger than a postage stamp. This is Romanticism miniaturised, as it is in the Brontës' tiny Angrian notebooks:

> The moss is on thy walls—
>   Silence and deep despair;—
> And the ruin as it falls
>   Gives the only echo there!—
> Thy music is not heard,—
>   Thy high-raised roof is gone,—
> And the solitary bird
>   Sits on the topmost stone:—
> There are sunbeams lingering still,
>   Through thy far white pillars sun,
> But they only seem to tell
>   Of what thou once hast been!—
> And oft in silence o'er thee,
>   The dark cloud passes on—
> And it sheds a deeper glory—
>   O'er thy wild oblivion!
> Aegina!—with the dead
> Thy fame hath perished!—[79]

Lear's adolescent ejaculations are overstrained: the dramatic apostrophe at the end of each verse is almost comically heavy-handed. Nonetheless the poem is striking for its use of musical echo to make a political point. The ruined temple on the island of Aegina had only recently been excavated. Turner painted it in two major oils, *The Temple of Jupiter Panellenius* and *The Temple of Jupiter Panellenius Restored,* displayed together at the Royal Academy in 1816. In Lear's poem the temple becomes the 'type' for Greece, which has fallen into political subjugation to Turkish rule. Lear quotes Shelley's *Revolt of Islam* in the phrase 'wild oblivion', while the shadow of Byron, who notoriously died of fever while fighting for Greek independence, falls over the setting and the sentiments.

Lear's direct dialogue with Turner in this poem has not previously been considered. There is no evidence that Lear saw these pictures in the original, but he must have seen engravings. As Gerald Finley notes, Turner's paintings themselves made a direct political comment:

> The first picture shows the Greek dance taking place against
> the background of a temple in ruin, a sky with a late afternoon
> sun (which for Turner often symbolises cultural decline) and
> the presence of Greece's Turkish oppressors; these elements
> together seem to suggest that Greek culture merely survives.[80]

Turner's second picture, *The Temple of Jupiter Panellius Restored*, which depicts an ancient Greek wedding procession in morning light, symbolically alludes to the possibility of Greek independence and a restoration of Greece to its former freedom. Both paintings had lines of poetry attached to them, the latter a verse by Robert Southey. Lear in choosing this subject was thus asserting his own place within an interdisciplinary dialogue that already existed between the leading painter and the poet laureate of the day. Lear had clearly studied Turner's first painting with some care. He, too, uses music and ritual—the shouts of revelry and the cymbaled votary, ceding to ghostly echo—to represent the silencing of Greek culture.

Into his own album Lear also copied out an extract from *Dunwich: A Tale of the Splendid City* (1828), a poem by the working-class Suffolk poet James Bird:

> Thou trackless, dark, and fathomless and wide
> Eternal world of waters!—ceaseless tide
> Of power magnificent! Unmeasured space,
> Where storms and tempest claim their dwelling place
> Thy depths are limitless—thy billow's sound
> Is nature's giant voice—thy gulph profound
> Her shrine of mystery . . .[81]

It was clearly the sound that drew Lear to this passage: the onomatopoeic pleasure of rolling it around one's mouth. Four of Lear's most famous poems are set at or by the sea. He learned from poems like Bird's how one can use rhythm and assonance to evoke its sound, and the tidal reversion of the line to re-create its movement. Bird's poetry is a hitherto-unrecognised influence on Lear's later nonsense songs.

Another work in Lear's 1829 album, 'The Bride's Farewell', has been included in Lear's *Complete Verse*, but, as I believe I am the first to realise, Lear is not the author. He was copying out a popular song. Lear doubtless had it in his repertoire; perhaps one of his sisters sang it and he accompanied her. The lyrics are by Miss M. L. Beevor (a regular contributor to the *Forget Me Not*) and the music by Thomas J. Williams. It was published in *The Sylph or Annual Pocket Melodist* in 1830, in precisely the form that Lear has copied, but the fact that Lear's album is dated 1829 suggests that he may have encountered it slightly earlier. Its presence in the album provides an important clue that Lear as a young man was up to date, playing new songs as they came out. 'The Bride's Farewell' derives in turn from a poem by Felicia Hemans, published in 1828.[82] The speed of the adaptation shows how closely poetry and parlour song were related at this time.

'The Bride's Farewell' is, like 'Isle of Beauty, Fare Thee Well!', a sentimental drawing-room ballad. It is also a song about the pains of leaving home. The bride trembles and hesitates, bidding goodbye to her mother, father, sister and brother in turn. She is weeping. It is open to the audience to interpret her crying as the natural hesitation of a modest maiden on the threshold of childhood or as something more sinister—she hints that she is marrying someone who may 'deceive' and 'wound' her. Drama prevails:

> Farewell Mother! tears are streaming,
> Down thy pale and tender cheek!
> I in gems and roses gleaming
> Scarce this sad farewell may speak,
> Farewell Mother! now I leave thee,
> (Hopes and fears my bosom swell)—
> One to trust who may deceive me
> Farewell Mother! Fare thee well.[83] 𝄞

𝄞 Listen to musical link #5 at edwardlearsmusic.com/audiotrail/#bridesfarewell.

Fig. 1.3 Music for 'The Bride's Farewell' (1830)

When we look at the music for 'The Bride's Farewell', we can glean more information than is in Miss Fraser's album and gain a sense of how Lear and his friends likely played and sung it. The expressive marks on the score offer notes for performance: *andantino espressivo* (a little bit slower than walking speed, as if the bride is hesitating to leave). Certain words (such as 'tender') are represented by more notes than syllables. These trills suggest a quaver of emotion in the phrasing. The song rises up the octave in the penultimate line of each verse, where the speaker addresses each relative for the last time, suggesting a rising emotional intensity, a swell that the singer will instinctively phrase with a crescendo.

Most significantly, once we know this is a song, we know that each verse is sung to the same tune. The song as a form has its own intrinsic relationship to memory: the song enacts the process of remembering as the same musical notes recur, matched to new words, in each succeeding verse. 'The Bride's Farewell' talks about leaving home, but its song-form talks about returning, over and over again. That tension is emotionally expressive. A similar tension imbues many of Lear's nonsense songs, in which never coming back is a recurrent trope. This dynamic counterpoint between what the song says and what it does gives 'Calico Pie', for example, an emotional weight that far exceeds its feather-light lyrics of birds, mice and syllabub:

> Calico Pie,
>   The little birds fly
> Down to the calico tree,
>   Their wings were blue,
>   And they sang 'Tilly-loo!'
>   Till away they flew,—
> And they never came back to me!
>   They never came back!
>   They never came back!
> They never came back to me![84]

This poem or song talks of not coming back, but its lyric form is one of insistent return. The contradiction between its outward images (of flight) and its inward music (of return) sets up an aching, conflicted dynamic that we feel in our bones to be unresolved. The fact that we can hear a nursery song in the background of 'Calico Pie' (1869), whose opening lines recall the rhythm of 'Hey Diddle Diddle', adds to the sense that we are being lulled and unsettled at the same time. Birds 'fly' as a matter of course, but here their flying seems to contain the secondary meaning of departing from the subject in a manner that means abandonment. Their song, 'Tilly-loo', thus has the symbolic quality of a farewell.

Similar tensions haunt 'The Pelican Chorus'—another Lear song about flight, this one involving a pelican princess who has left to be married. As in 'The Bride's Farewell', marriage should mark a joyful progression, but the musical refrain keeps returning us to the 'multitude-echoes from Bird and Bird' that emphasise her parents' loss. Repetition is Lear's secret weapon, his simplest yet most effective technique. His lyrics keep coming back to us—and they are meant to do so. As a singer and a pianist, he knew the power of musical sobbing, and of the counterpoint between figured departure and musical reprise. It is instructive that Lear's deeply sensitive editor, Vivien Noakes, imagined 'The Bride's Farewell' to be Lear's. So many of Lear's own poems are songs that its qualities of song argued for his authorship.

The Knowsley Period: 'Standards' High and Low

In Lear's twenties, the Earl of Derby invited him to stay at Knowsley Hall, the earl's country house near Liverpool, to paint the animals and birds housed in the extensive menagerie. This was Lear's lucky break. The Derby family became his patrons and friends, introducing him to a wide circle of fellow aristocrats who would become clients for his artwork and subscribers to his books. Lear performed a complex role in the Knowsley household as both resident artist and entertainer: somebody who could play and sing, who wrote and illustrated limericks and who could show sketches to enliven the long evening after dinner, creating as it were an oasis after dessert. Music was an important part of the way that Lear harmonised, literally and figuratively, with people whose educational and social ambits were different from his own. In 1835, he recorded proudly in letters to his Arundel friends George and Fanny Coombe that he was a valued contributor to musical evenings at Tabley Hall, where he and Lady de Tabley accompanied one another:

> Every evening at this lovely house—we had lots of music;
> Lady de T[abley] & I duet wonderfully—& I only marvel at
> my not being hired as nurse to the baby—who was always
> quieted by my playing Accordion.[85]

On a tour in 1836 to the north and west of Liverpool, Lord Derby's letters of introduction gave Lear access to some of the finest houses in England and Wales. Music cut across class barriers: it was an immediate shared language that allowed him to perform with distinguished company. In the Lake District he crowed:

> —The landscape however was my least pleasure; for the 3 Miss Bradylls are 20 degrees beyond perfection—& what with all sorts of singing & music with them, their father, & Brother, & Admiral Sothern,—a band of 2 Accordions—flute—harp—guitar & piano—we minded not the rain a tittle.[86]

Lear's repertoire at Knowsley was varied, but it certainly included comic songs such as Jacob Beuler's 'The Nervous Family', of which Lear produced two versions in 1834 and 1836, which he was still distributing among friends (and therefore probably also singing) in the 1860s and 1870s. This song, which was sung to the traditional tune 'Nid, Nid, Noddin', incorporates in its lyrics the shakes of the overanxious protagonist and his relations. Beuler's score helpfully indicates the diction: 𝄞

> We all are ner . . . vous, shake shake trem. . . . .bling
> We all are nervous at our house in town.
> My self and my Wife and my Sis . . . ter and my Mo. . . . ther,
> If left in the dark are all frightend at each o. . . . .ther;
> Our dog runs a. . . . .way if a stran . . . ger's in the house,
> An our great tab . . . by Cat, too, is frightend at a mouse.
> And we all are ner . . . . vous shake shake trembling
> We all are nervous at our house in town.[87]

Songs like this offer wonderful opportunities for acting: the singer works a semi-stutter into his rendition, making the absurd *tremolando* of the nervous family into a musical joke worthy of comic opera. We can imagine Lear hamming it up. He also, typically, adds some absurd sound effects that are not in the original:

𝄞 Listen to musical link #6 at edwardlearsmusic.com/audiotrail/#nervousfamily.

Our nerves in stormy weather are particularly *bad,*
And a single peal of thunder is enough to drive us *mad.*
So, when a storm comes on, we in a fright begin
To lock ourselves in closets where the lightning can't come in.
And for fear a little thunder to our nervous ears should come,
We each turn a barrel organ, and my Mother beats a drum.[88]

Like the squawking and yelling in 'Turkey Discipline', these lyrics turn domestic discord into something literally loud and wild. The four beats in the
bar become, in this climactic verse, a marching rhythm to which we can
imagine Mother thumping her drum while other closeted family members
try to drown her out.

Lear was clearly drawn to songs that created a crescendo of comic effects. While visiting Blithfield House in the 1840s, he sang 'Tea in the
Arbour' so well that Alfred Bagot recalled the performance forty years
later.[89] This song features an urban protagonist, invited to visit Mr, Mrs
and Miss Barber, who live in a villa 'out of town', and to take tea in their
garden. It captures the class comedy of conflict between the awkward cit
and the Cockney cottagers who have moved out of the Big Smoke to
cultivate 'turnips and flowers'. A marvellous series of mishaps befalls
him:

Of little green flies on my dress came a host,
And a bee put me all in a flutter;
A great daddy-long-legs stuck fast on my toast,
And left one of his limbs in the butter.
On the sugar, six blue-bottles sat hob-a-nob,
And while I discours'd with *Old Barber,*
From above a black spider swung bibbity bob
In my chops as I sat in the Arbour.[90]

It gets worse. Like Dickens's Pickwick, our hero falls victim to all the haz-
ards that a rural idyll can afford. A frog makes him jump, much to Miss
Barber's amusement. A caterpillar falls in his tea. The gravel is damp, and
he fears catching cold (this line must have been especially funny, as Lear
did indeed fear damp). He is peppered by boys who are shooting at crows,
gets tar on his breeches from a newly painted fence and finally gets caught

in a man trap. Perhaps, however, the literal man trap is better than the romantic one presented by Miss Barber, which our hero narrowly avoids. This series of misadventures is worthy of a silent film starring Harold Lloyd, and we can imagine Lear convulsing the company by performing the comic antics. The chorus runs:

> Where there are Sweet-Billies and Daffy-down-dillies
> Perfumes like the shop of a barber;
> And roses and posies to scent up your noses
> Then *Come* and take *Tea* in the *Arbour.*

The lyric nicely addresses the theme of the song, which is the relationship between nature and artifice. The Barbers may have replaced the artificial perfumes of the barber's shop with those of rustic bowers, but they aren't perfectly at home, and their visitor's misery reflects his own displacement. When Lear sang this song at an aristocratic country house he was, perhaps, dealing with the precariousness of his own status by miming discomfiture. Lear would repurpose a line from 'Tea in the Arbour' in his limerick about the 'Old Person of Wilts, Who constantly walked upon stilts', wreathing them with 'lilies and daffy-down-dillies'.

Another Jacob Beuler song that Lear almost certainly knew, 'Wery Pekooliar or the Lisping Lover' (1826), features a vocal tease similar to that in 'The Nervous Family': the lisp-afflicted lover woos his sweetheart with his tongue between his front teeth:

> To the mighty god, KOOPID, I've been a great thlave,
> He thot in my buthom a quiver of harrows,
> Like naughty boys thoot at cock robins & thparrows
> . . .
> Then ye Gods only know how I lov'd one Mith JULIA,
> There was thomething about her tho wery pekooliar![91]

This song likely inspired Lear's own comic poem 'O Thuthan Thmith! Thweet Thuthan Thmith!', in which, as in Beuler's original, both the lover and his beloved lisp. The speaker's imagined vocal impediment gives his high-flown romantic sentiments an absurd twist. Lear writes:

The thlender Thrimp itth gabolth playth,
The thiny thprightly fitheth thwim,—
The thandy thore, the dithtant hillth,—
All these I watth;—but nothing stillth
The thindy that my bothom fillth
In gathing on thy thape tho thlim![92]

The vocal tics explored in this comic song can easily segue into nonsense. Imaginary 'nonsense' words may be visual phonetic renderings of words that we hear, contorted by bodily quirks. The imaginary gap between the singer's teeth here comes to signify the possible gap between the subjective and objective view of the romantic protagonist: Lear exploits its theatrical possibilities. Performance is written into the dynamics of these pieces, as is the pleasure of sound. We know that in middle age Lear sang Thomas Hudson's 'The Cork Leg', a comic-grotesque ballad about a rich Dutchman whose false leg, punishing him for killing a poor relation, carries him on an unstoppable, fatal dance.[93] The joke is that, even after the merchant dies, the leg keeps on going; we wonder if the song will ever end. Its mimetic, dancing refrain—'Ri too ral too ral too ral too ral too ra lal too ral ri tol tu ral lay'—demands that the singer has very deep reserves of energy. There are no fewer than thirteen verses.[94] Again, we can imagine Lear performing this song for his child-friends the Congreve brothers, exploring the delight that children take in repetition and in violence. Lear often uses choruses in his nonsense: 'flippetty chip—Chippetty flip'; 'Jikky wikky bikky see,/Chicky bikky wikky bee'. It is traditional in folk music for the chorus to feature sounds that may be largely improvised. However, in Lear's nonsense these choruses also frequently explore the debatable land between human and animal language. Music offers particular opportunities for expressing the physical nature of utterance and the way that the body's peculiarities can be reflected in it. The physically compromised underdogs of Lear's nonsense songs—the Dong, the Yonghy-Bonghy-Bò, the Duck, the Daddy Long-legs—bring to their narratives an awkward charm similar to that of Beuler's lisping and trembling protagonists.

Sentimental Journeys: Moore, Mee and Excess

George Cruikshank's illustration on the cover of Beuler's 'Tea in the Arbour' demonstrates the close relationship between cartoon and comic

Fig. 1.4 Title page, 'Tea in the Arbour' (1830)

song in this period. *The Universal Songster or Museum of Mirth* was similarly illustrated by George and Robert Cruikshank. It was probably from this kind of cartoon that Lear got the idea for his comic storyboards, drawn in the 1830s and 1840s, which respond humorously to the narratives of well-known romantic songs. They utilise yet another way of exploring the fertile gap between the sentimental drawing-room ballad and the ways in which its lyrics might be interpreted by a wayward comic hand.

Several of Lear's comic storyboards subject Thomas Moore's *Irish Melodies* to humorous treatment, but songs by Thomas Haynes Bayley, Robert Burns, Lady Anne Lindsay and William Mee—as well as the gypsy glee from the opera *Guy Mannering,* with words by Joanna Baillie and music by Henry Rowley Bishop—are also included, giving us a helpful guide to Lear's Knowsley repertoire.[95] One can imagine the pleasure Lear gave his audience not only by singing after dinner but also by improvising these visual spoofs of the same songs.

In Lear's musical cartoons, the ladies are typically large, ugly and over-dressed as pantomime dames. His men are weak: buck-toothed, silly suitors, pathetic drunks or prissy hermits. This comedy anticipates his nonsense, in which females are so often stronger than males. In his cartoon version of Thomas Moore's 'By That Lake, Whose Gloomy Shore', Lear depicts St Kiven running away to avoid his amorous pursuer, the 'Gentle' Kathleen. Lear's Kathleen is a hefty dame in a checked gown, lolloping after the thin, anxious ascetic, his loincloth trembling in the Irish breeze.[96] When Lear visited Ireland in 1835 with Arthur Stanley and Edward Penrhyn, he enjoyed the full tourist experience, which involved, among other things, ascending a narrow ledge shoeless and being 'popped into a hole' called 'St Kiven's bed' by an 'old woman surnamed Kathleen . . . saying all the time, "Don't be fretful my dear"'.[97] Doubtless a memory of this unmanning experience and of the other tourist guide, who shouted Moore's 'Glendalough' at the top of his voice, contributed to Lear's comic version of Moore's 'By That Lake'. Moore's skylark 'warbles on high'; Lear's skylark 'wobbles on high', like an ode by Shelley recited in a shaky voice. This symbol of Romantic lyricism can't quite get it up. There is the beginning of a joke here about the relationship between lyric transcendence and male ascendancy that recurs in Lear's nonsense.

In Lear's cartoon version of 'Bonny Doon', the line 'when ilka bird sang o' his love and fondly sae did I o' mine' is illustrated with a grotesque old

Fig. 1.5 **One of Lear's illustrations for 'The Banks O' Doon'**

woman dancing while the birds sing from sheet music on a stand.[98] If music is supposed to be the signifier in Burns of what is natural and heartfelt, Lear will depict it as something cultural and performed. This is Romantic ballad seen through the proscenium arch of Victorian theatre. In 'Miss Maniac', a similarly coy but hideous protagonist acts out the familiar narrative of the woman deserted by her lover who is cast out with her illegitimate child by her tyrannical father and, descending into madness, meets a tragic end. The original on which this storyboard is based has not been discovered, but a sign reading 'beware of the bog' hints that it is Irish.[99] It follows the pattern of the folk song 'Mary of the Moor', which was reworked by many authors, including Wordsworth and Southey. Hundreds of poems and songs about maniacs were published between 1800 and 1840. Operas, including *I Puritani,* had an obligatory mad scene. Henry Rowley Bishop's popular 1810 opera, *The Maniac,* featured Mad Margery and the refrain 'Then thunders rage and roar thou batt'ling wind, / For what your storms to tempests of the mind'.[100] Significantly, Bishop's *The Maniac* was billed as a 'Serio-Comic Opera'; Lear's contemporaries also saw the comic potential in the cliché of melodramatic madness.

In Lear's illustrations to 'Auld Robin Gray', the mother makes her daughter cry so much that a fish and a duck are depicted swimming below the bed.[101] The line in the song is 'My mother did not speak / *But* she looked

My mother did not speak
'But—she looked in my face, till my heart was like to break!'

Fig. 1.6 One of Lear's illustrations for 'Auld Robin Gray'

in my face, till my heart was like to break!' The silent look is a figure for the emotional work of music in this ballad. Lear replaces it with another kind of silent communication: the cartoon. One suspects that the bulbous-nosed, grotesquely huge mother in this picture reflects some of Lear's anger towards his own mother and her perceived neglect. The literal flood of tears, however, wells up in various Victorian works for children: in *Funny Books for Boys and Girls* (1856), 'Crying Kate' blubbers so much that she floats off and has to be fished out by her mother with a net.[102] More famously, Lewis Carroll's Alice in Wonderland (1865) regrets having cried so much when she nearly drowns in a pool of her own tears. This recurring literalised image of 'drowning in woe' performs a shared comic reaction to the drama of Romantic melancholy. For Lear, reaction to Romantic emotionalism—with its high and low notes of extreme feeling—is always mediated through a musical sense of the possibility of performing the material ironically, or at least in a histrionic manner that threatens to go so far over the top that, like one famous prima donna playing Tosca, it topples over the battlements only to bounce up again on an artfully placed trampoline. For Lear, the song of lost love always has a comic alter ego lurking in the wings.

Thomas Moore is the most consistently spoofed of authors in Lear's songbook. Lear met him around 1846,[103] and Moore's work is probably the single greatest influence on Lear's musical habits. He knew Moore's work so well that it amounts, in his diary, to a kind of code. When Lear is considering the subject of marriage, he writes, 'as a beam o'er the face of the waters may glow———So I fear most matrimonies be'.[104] The rest of Moore's verse runs:

> While the tide runs in darkness and coldness below,
> So the cheek may be tinged with a warm sunny smile,
> Though the cold heart to ruin runs darkly the while.[105]

When he has missed a ferry, Lear writes that he is 'left on the bleak shore alone'. This is from Moore's 'I Saw from the Beach', which was sung to the air 'Miss Molly':

> Ah! such is the fate of our life's early promise
>   So passing the spring-tide of joy we have known;
> Each wave that we danced on at morning ebbs from us,
>   And leaves us, at eve, on the bleak shore alone![106]

Another striking diary entry uses the shorthand of Moore's songs to reference thoughts that Lear could not address explicitly even in the private space of a diary. Lear in March 1877 was caught up in intense feelings for Hubert Congreve, the teenage son of his neighbour at San Remo, whom he had hoped to train as a professional artist and, perhaps, to live with. They went to Rome together. On their return, Hubert rejected Lear's proposition and elected to go to Cambridge to train as an architect, causing the 'downfall of dreams'. Lear was shattered. He writes, 'I cannot weave as once I wove'. This is a line from Moore's *Evenings in Greece*, specifically the song of 'Sappho, the love-sick lesbian Maid', who sings at her loom:

> "Oh, my sweet Mother—'tis in vain—
> "I cannot weave as once I wove—
> "So 'wildered is my heart and brain
> "With thinking of that youth I love!"[107]

This is perhaps the closest that Lear ever came in writing to a direct expression of homosexual desire. Sappho was (as Lear would have known from his reading both of Greek and of Swinburne) a classical symbol for homosexuality. In giving himself Sappho's line, Lear covertly alludes to a feminine aspect of his attraction to a 'youth' whom he could not with propriety offer anything more than avuncular affection. *Evenings in Greece,* which offered a mixture of passages to be read aloud and passages to be sung, was Moore's attempt to programme evening entertainments that could be performed at home by the musical and nonmusical members of a nineteenth-century household. In late middle age, Lear recalls these lines to voice thoughts that lie below the surface of acceptable speech.

Like Robert Burns and Sir Walter Scott, Moore was not only a song-writer but also a song collector. He recorded Neapolitan and Sicilian and Maltese and Catalonian airs, saving this traditional music in the oral tradition from potential disappearance. During his travels in the Abruzzi, a then-remote region of Italy, Lear committed to memory several songs and airs that he encountered; he follows in the tradition of Scott, Burns and Moore in seeking to preserve folk song. However, his teasing response to Moore reflects a widely shared reaction to Moore's sentimentalism (what Lear in a nonsense version of a line from Tennyson calls '*Tom-Moory* Pathos')[108] and to the Irish nationalism implicit in his lyrics.

Lear's cartoon storyboards demonstrate how similar his comic vision was, in the 1830s, to that of other comic writers of his era. For example, Lear drew comic illustrations to Moore's well-known song 'Rich and Rare Were the Gems She Wore'.

> Rich and rare were the gems she wore,
> And a bright gold ring on her wand she bore;
> But oh! her beauty was far beyond
> Her sparkling gems, or snow-white wand.[109]

The heroine of Moore's song is an ideal embodiment of Irish nationhood; the fact that nobody tries to rob or violate her as she walks through the land testifies to the purity of national honour. The piece offered a rich and rare temptation to nineteenth-century humorists. Thomas Hood, the comic poet and cartoonist, illustrated it in his *Whims and Oddities* (1826) with a picture of a cannibal wearing a huge ring through her nose.[110] A musical parody current in 1834, by the female vocalist Miss Bryant, runs:

> Ragged and Rough were the clothes she wore!
> And a bottle and glass in her hand she bore;
> But, oh! her red nose shone far beyond
> The sparkling rum in her dark brown hand.[111]

Bryant's indigent alcoholic protagonist collapses and dies. Since the female figure in Moore's song represents Irish national pride, the fact that in Hood's version she is an 'uncivilised' tribeswoman and in Bryant's version a tipsy tinker casts aspersions on the idealistic mode in which Moore celebrates Irish identity. Lear's protagonist in his comic illustrations to 'Rich and Rare', rather like Hood's (which he may have seen), has an enormous nose ring and earrings, but she is white and wears a crucifix around her neck, suggesting her function as a symbol of Catholic Ireland.[112] The fact that she is ugly and carries a big stick constitutes, in this context, not only a reversal of stereotypes of female loveliness but also a refusal to view Ireland romantically. Lear visited Ireland in 1835 and was well aware of the political battles that had followed the 1800 Act of Union. His cartoons of 'Rich and Rare' and 'gentle Kathleen' figure Ireland as a tougher, older, more knowing political partner than Moore wished to present.

In Lear's cartoon version of William Mee's song 'Alice Gray', he similarly transforms Mee's heroine, with her 'brow of spotless white', into a black woman with a ruff. The song begins, 'she's all my fancy painted her—she's lovely—she's divine'. Perhaps it was hyperbole that made this song such a ripe target for humour. Lewis Carroll also spoofed it, in the *Comic Times* of 1855, a parody that finds its way into *Alice in Wonderland*, where the white rabbit confuses the jurors by describing an affair conducted between shifty pronouns.[113] As with his other song spoofs, Lear allows his illustrations of

Fig. 1.7 **One of Lear's illustrations for 'Rich and Rare Were the Gems She Wore'**

'Alice Gray' to form their own commentary—one that, to a modern eye, is racially troubling. The heroine is black and she is minuscule. The lover's inordinate passion for her, as he chain-weeps and exclaims, 'O! my heart, my heart is breaking', is thus revealed as melodramatic excess that has teetered into comedy, as he threatens to teeter off his chair. The 'O!' is a great inky circle, underlined, and almost as big as Alice's face.[114]

Excess is, crucially, the running theme of Lear's cartoons of the 1830s and early 1840s, as he moved from his teens to his late twenties. Overindulgence of woe, or appetite, or romantic passion leads to comic results that are equally outrageous in their physical absurdity; the ardent lover cries tears that fall as numerously and vertically as raindrops, his arms flung wide. The melan*choly* lady is impaled on a *holly* bush, as if her inner pain has become a literal pain in the butt. The man of the South with his 'immoderate mouth' is killed by swallowing a dish the same size and shape as his enormous 'O' of a palate, while the suicidal man of New York impales himself ecstatically on a fork the size of Neptune's trident, 'but nobody cried, though he very soon died, for that silly old man of New York'. Lear's unsentimental approach to tragic self-impalement is reminiscent of Thackeray's 1851 verse on the suicide of Goethe's Werther:

> So he sigh'd and pin'd and ogled,
>   And his passion boil'd and bubbled,
> Till he blew his silly brains out,
>   And no more by it was troubled.[115]

Lear during the Knowsley years was experimenting with different possible approaches to the egotistical sublime and to the lyrical performance of melancholy. He recalled with pleasure that on one boat trip with the Hornbys in 1837:

> When one's merry one's soon set off in a giggle—very shortly
> Colonel Hornby who is the oddest creature in the world—
> came to us & said he had discovered a mermaid or a devil in
> the shape of a most queer woman on board:—I shall never
> forget her certainly—but you will one day see my sketches of
> the creature—we called her 'the dejected'—& the day passed
> in fits of laughter—duets—& fun. . . .[116]

One suspects that cross-dressing was involved in this comic scene, and that the 'dejected' siren was in fact a giggling member of the party.

But the tidal music of sea-seduction and lunar attraction could also be sincere in its expressive sympathy with the elements. Lear recalled with a yearning delight happy evenings in 1837 at Bovisand, near Plymouth, where, like the owl in 'The Owl and the Pussy-cat', 'We all adjourned to the rocks with guitars . . . & there we sate singing to the sea & the moon'.[117]

These musical beach parties sometimes lasted until two in the morning. Nothing could be more self-consciously romantic than singing and playing in such a setting. In 1836, the year before Lear's moonlight concert at Bovisand, a German critic had dubbed Beethoven's most famous piano piece the 'moonlight' sonata; Chopin was in the midst of composing his set of twelve 'nocturnes'. The fact that social music usually happened at night, after the formalities of the meal and conversation, is significant. This was the time of day for play, a time when games, such as acrostics, charades, riddles or 'epitaphs', were sometimes introduced. After dark, our visual sense is narrowed and our aural sense heightened. The possibilities of magic, melancholy, erotic love, humour and the variety of otherwise suppressed thoughts that immediately precede sleep: all these infuse the late-night concert with particular power to divert and to move us. It is helpful to conjure Lear singing his songs by candlelight and moonlight, to engage imaginatively with their potential emotional affect as something that is built into their composition as songs designed for performance in such conditions.

This was an era of increased expression in vocal and piano music; the habits and tropes of the stage were filtering into domestic music-making. Muzio Clementi's influential *Introduction to the Art of Playing the Pianoforte* (1801) explained terms such as *affettuoso* ('in an affecting and tender manner') and *agitato* ('agitated, with passion and fire'); he glossed *con espressione* as 'with expression; that is, with passionate feeling; where every note has its peculiar force and energy; and where even the severity of time may be relaxed for extraordinary effects'.[118] Lear's settings of Tennyson utilise many of these terms. Everything we know of Lear's music from his Tennyson settings emphasises drama. He was highly aware of the possibilities of acting offered by both voice and instrument: through phrasing, dramatic contrasts in volume and tempo, unexpected discords and key changes and mimicry of sounds produced by objects within the landscape of the narrative.

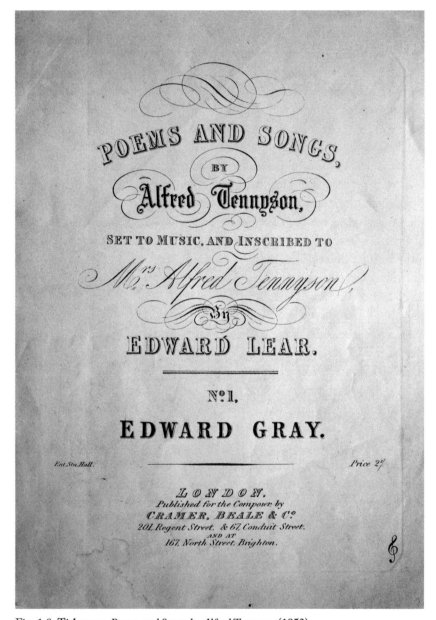

Fig. 1.8 Title page, *Poems and Songs by Alfred Tennyson* (1853)

Playing (with) Tennyson

Lear's twelve published song-settings of Tennyson's poetry deserve to be better known, both for their inherent quality and for what they tell us about Lear's musical methods, particularly his use of medley and counterpoint and his mastery of dramatic effects, techniques that also energise his nonsense songs.

Lear got to know Alfred Tennyson socially in 1850 through their mutual friendship with the Lushington family.[119] Lear sent Tennyson and his new wife, Emily, some landscape drawings as a wedding present—a typical gesture and one way in which Lear found himself a permanent place in others' homes. Lear's relationship with Tennyson was from the first that of an acolyte who celebrated Tennyson's poetry as 'real and exquisite' in high and deep matters, his 'genius in perception and the beautiful in Landscape' and his painterly power 'of calling up images as distinct & correct as if they were written from . . . images, instead of giving rise to them'. Lear hints, in fact, that Tennyson's gift is truly vatic—that he sees and describes places poetically that he has not seen in reality, with uncanny accuracy 'as true as if positively drawn in the places themselves'.[120] The fact that Lear *has* seen these places gives him the subservient yet also quasi-mystical role of acting as Tennyson's artistic medium, not only illustrating Tennyson's lines but authoritatively reuniting them with the landscapes that their visionary stanzas were unconsciously channelling all along.

Lear's relationship with Tennyson, then, although sincere and ardent in its enthusiasm and admiration for the verse, contains from the start an element of competition. Like Lear's response to Thomas Moore's lyrical verse, it is characterised by assertive and often comic repartee. In his early letter asking for permission to illustrate the poems, he quotes a line from 'The Poet', which imagines the 'viewless arrows' of the poet's thought being carried by the winds, which they fill 'with light / And vagrant melodies' until 'like the arrow-seeds of the field-flower' they fall to earth and germinate into multiple new forms:

> . . . springing forth anew
>> Where'er they fell, behold,
> Like to the mother-plant in semblance, grew
>> A flower all gold.

Lear hopes that his illustrations will be these artistic progeny; the deferentially quoted metaphor images Tennyson's work as seminal and his own as secondary. Yet he also alters the line he quotes, suggesting that if his illustrations are badly executed they will

> *Un*like the mother plant in semblance grow
> a flower all mud——or all cold——or all anything
>   else totally disagreeable[121]

He then dares to hope that, if successful, the project might be financially lucrative: 'to parody the lines above once more—"might grow "a flower all *tin*'''. Lear walks a fine line between homage and parody that will characterise all his dealings with Tennyson, whom he found often rather grumpy and selfish in person (Lear's sympathies lay with Emily), though his work was inspirational and swiftly became the verse that Lear read and quoted with the greatest regularity. Lear thought from time to time of buying some land in the neighbourhood of the poet's house and going to live there, as if he were literally a flower seed that wanted to take root near its parent plant. But of course he didn't do this. Instead, he built his own houses at San Remo, the first of which he named the Villa Emily and the second the Villa Tennyson. Lear chose to inhabit Tennysonian stanzas, but in his own place and on his own terms.

Lear began setting Tennyson's poetry to music in the early 1850s. This proved a more successful mode of asexual reproduction than the illustration project, which lasted over thirty years but bore disappointing fruit. In particular, Lear's beautiful rendering of 'Tears, Idle Tears'—a song from *The Princess*—compares favourably in performance to settings of the same poem by Arthur Sullivan and by Ralph Vaughan Williams. Lear's music provides an emotional exposition of the poem that maps its inner drama onto the musical phrasing and, through the relationship of the voice to the piano accompaniment, suggests the welling up of suppressed emotion. Indeed, Lear's settings of Tennyson deploy the full gamut of dramatic techniques for voice and piano to explore the ways in which music can echo feeling: the way that it can ascend and descend the scale, swell and diminish in volume and intensity, break off and return with unexpected force and mimic contradictory impulses in uttered and unuttered thought through contrasting the vocal line with the piano's subterranean murmuring.

The musical markings on Lear's 'Tears, Idle Tears' tell us from the first that it is to be played and sung emotively. It opens with a series of chords that echo those in Beethoven's 'Farewell' Sonata. The instruction is *larghetto* (slowly, but with musical associations of expressive flexibility), and the player is directed to mark the emotionally resonant discord on 'idle' with further deceleration and emphasis. Interestingly, Lear chooses to treat the four stanzas as two pairs; the first is sung to one musical theme and the second to another, creating a dynamic relationship like that between verse and refrain. This means that the first stanza has the quality of a reflection, *thinking* on 'the days that are no more', while the second—with faster, lilting arpeggios that create movement—brings the memories rushing back. The arrangement creates dramatic opportunities for the singer to voice shifts in emotional mood. Another resonant discord on '*all* we love', with a sudden high note for which the singer has to reach, is like a musical cry; this and the ornament on 'verge', where the voice lingers and caresses the margin between death and life, shows how much Lear learned from the opera he listened to as a young man. ♪

Lear chooses to repeat the final line of each of Tennyson's stanzas, so each verse ends with a doublet. But the line is repeated with different phrasing. The first iteration of 'so sad, so fresh, the days that are no more' separates 'so sad' and 'so fresh' with small musical gasps—as if the singer is weeping. The second iteration places its emphasis differently, lingering on 'fresh' and 'the days that are no more', as if the singer chooses to concentrate, finally, on the beauty of memory rather than its regrets. In another dramatic manoeuvre, the piano part withdraws in the last line of the final verse, leaving the voice to stand alone, abandoned but brave. The song starts in D major, but concludes in G major, in the subdued subdominant. Lear takes us on an emotional journey that ends in a different place from where it began.

'Tears, Idle Tears' was one of Lear's own favourites of his Tennyson settings, and it stands out for its effectiveness. But they all display similar characteristics. Many of the lines and phrases are reminiscent of ones in other drawing-room ballads, light operas and even hymns of the era. Lear was a master of musical bricolage, building his own nest with strands from diverse sources. In 'Edward Gray', for instance, one can hear a distinct echo

---

♪ Listen to musical link #7 at edwardlearsmusic.com/audiotrail/#tearsidletears.

of a hymn tune known in Lear's era as 'Rockingham' (now played to 'When I Survey the Wondrous Cross'), which is perhaps apt in a ballad that deals with the repentance of a man who haunts the grave of the woman whose love he failed to requite in life.

There is a great deal of cleverness, originality and subtlety in the way that Lear writes for performance, exploring the words as an actor explores a play script, finding musical means of drawing out inner conflict and resolution. For example, in Tennyson's 'As Through the Land at Eve We Went', a song that deals with a couple who 'fall out' but who 'kiss again with tears' over the grave of their dead child, Lear begins with a stepped series of two notes sounding on their own, as if to represent the two figures going through the fields, whose reconciliation will be imaged in an embrace of chords. In 'The Song of Love and Death', he gives each of Tennyson's four verses a different musical treatment, shadowing an emotional progression towards a fatal, dramatic decision. Lear uses interrupted cadences to mark punctuation expressively. He creates musical tension between the pull of love and that of death; the final line, 'Call and I follow, I follow! let me die', introduces a rush of unexpected dramatic arpeggios, supplying the adrenalin to carry us towards a bravura operatic climax. Lear as a pianist was fond of arpeggios, or 'spread chords', and we might consider these to be the musical equivalent of the long dashes he favoured in prose: a means of communicating ideas in breathless rushes, sequences that travel and invite us to follow.[122] As with 'Tears, Idle Tears', Lear chooses to repeat the final line of each three-line stanza so that the song mimics the internal echo of memory.

More obviously, in many of the other settings, onomatopoeic effects represent thematic motifs within the song: in 'A Farewell' we hear the flowing river; in 'Home They Brought Her Warrior Dead' we hear a drum solemnly beating the fallen soldier's return; in 'Sweet and Low, Sweet and Low', we hear the rocking cradle; in 'Turn, Fortune, Turn Thy Wheel', Lear gives us the sound of the spinning wheel. Lear had likely heard Schubert's song 'Gretchen at the Spinning Wheel' (1814), which uses the same musical idée fixe to evoke the singer's obsessive, restless psychological state as she constantly revolves thoughts about Faust. Lear's musical spinning wheel of Fate makes a more cheerful, lively sound as its treadle turns, the singer reflecting that 'man is man, and master of his fate' and 'thy wheel and thee, we neither love nor hate'. Lear scores the words such that an initial emphatic push is followed by a flurry of faster notes; the music hastens us forward, rolling one line emphatically towards the next. These musical effects bear comparison with those in Lear's later nonsense poems, where characters like the Dong ('The Dong! The Dong!') have their own particular leitmotif. ♪

Perhaps the most effective of Lear's uses of musical mimicry is his setting of 'The Time Draws Near the Birth of Christ' from *In Memoriam*, in which he gives us an extraordinarily realistic and resonant peal of bells. The right hand descends the scale in eighths, while the left hand, unusually, descends in sixths. With the rather blurry pedal marked in the score, the effect is uncannily like that of church bells. This is not an easy piece to play, and it testifies to Lear's skill at the piano; the singer, too, has to work hard to keep the diction crisp above the falling peals, with their rising crescendo. Emily Tennyson, who also wrote song-settings of Tennyson's poems, spoke of this composition as 'beloved' by her and told Lear:

> If I can yet [be] strong once more & be able to sing them to
> Alfred my pleasure in them will be complete. . . . Hallam
> delights in the bells 'Mr. Lear's Bells' as he calls them &
> learns to play his scale in sixths in humble imitation.[123]

When Emily sang and Hallam played these songs for Tennyson they closed a loop, carrying Lear's musical responses back to the laureate and asserting Lear's own right to be heard interpretively alongside him. (Several of the published settings misspell *Tennyson* as *Tennison;* that's not Lear's fault, presumably, but a mistake that emphasises Lear's primary billing and the fact that Tennyson's name wasn't universally known.) Their respective song-settings also highlight the role that Lear and Emily shared as musical interpreters, and occasional moderators, of Tennyson's genius.

Lear sometimes offered unsolicited advice to Tennyson: in July 1877 he begged Tennyson to write a 'Moslem hymn' to 'counteract the Russian sympathies evoked by his Montenegran Sonnet', published in May alongside an opinion piece by Gladstone in the *Nineteenth Century*.[124] This bold suggestion was a form of political as much as of literary criticism: Lear disliked Gladstone's Eastern policy and had sympathy with the Ottomans, particularly when Russia declared war and marched to the gates of Constantinople. It is intriguing that Lear's attempt at poetic diplomacy involves requesting a Moslem 'hymn'; musicality and tolerance go hand in hand.

♪ Listen to musical link #8 at edwardlearsmusic.com/audiotrail/#turnfortuneturn.

Much earlier, in 1858, Lear commented on some of Tennyson's martial verses on the Indian Mutiny: 'I did not like them. They were forced & pedantic & unmelodious'.[125] Musicality is again here a sign of sympathetic emotional resonance; its absence produces unnatural, unpleasing verse. Lear's opinion of Tennyson and of Tennyson's poetry was always framed by a critical eye and ear. Often, what he saw in Tennyson's character were traits he deplored in himself: Tennyson could be irritable, egotistical, petulant, petty about money and high-handed in the home. As Lear exclaimed after one annoying encounter, 'How queer is the smallness and Egotism of such a man! . . . To hear AT talk—one would fancy him a mere child & a foolish one too'.[126] When Lear comically reset Tennyson's lines, as he did in his diary ('Trouble on trouble—pain on pain / The drain smell is beginning again'), he was poking fun both at his own hyperbolic tendencies and at the laureate's exaggerated habit of complaint.[127]

Tennyson's lyrical poetry resonated with Lear partly because he understood the underlying themes that Tennyson and he shared in life: a sense of childhood abandonment, powerless longing and overwhelming bouts of depression. Lear and Tennyson must have talked freely about the 'morbids'. Certainly Lear knew the history of depression in the Tennyson family, and that Tennyson's younger brother Horatio, when he heard street criers singing 'water-cresses' in a 'slow minor key', heard 'water-increases' and was inundated with terrible thoughts about the Deluge that made him 'cry in the street', sobbingly.[128] The power of language to produce psychological affect was something that Lear and Tennyson both understood from intense personal experience.

Tennyson approved of Lear's musical treatment of his poetry, reputedly saying that compared with settings by other composers, they only 'cast a diaphanous veil' over his words.[129] One can see why he found them pleasingly transparent: they are more respectful of Tennyson's phrasing than many by other composers. Yet they are also powerfully histrionic. All the indicators of performance, from the verbal notation ('aggitato', 'accelerando', 'callando') to the musical marks—such as the double hairpin in 'Sweet and Low' that tells the singer to expressively swell then fade the second iteration of 'Blow him again to *me*'—emphasise the emotive possibilities of the songs. We can't determine how much Edward Rimbault contributed to the notation, but everything we know about Lear's singing style suggests that most of the expressive effects are his own. In March 1861 he complained in his diary that Frank Massingberd sang with a fine voice but 'no feeling or emphasis'.[130] His own singing was, in his own word, 'unscientific' but characterised by feeling. He liked to 'take the attention of people' and was caustic about inattentive listeners who dozed or rustled newspapers; notes had to be 'distinct' and words 'well-pronounced'. A memory of Lear singing in the Gallery at Strawberry Hill lit by a single candle suggests the kind of dramatic effect he cultivated.[131] Notably, almost all the Tennyson poems that Lear chose to set to music involve weeping. Anecdotes about Lear singing often allude to him bringing tears to the eyes of the audience and himself.[132] This is a vital aspect of the work that song does in Lear's oeuvre: it is designed to move us, and his settings of Tennyson's songs remind us what a formidable battery of musical techniques he possessed to achieve that end.

Writing for performance, however, Lear is highly conscious of the varied possibilities that exist for playing and receiving the material in different emotional lights. Several friends describe the same thing: Lear at the piano, moving from sentimental to comic numbers or treatments. Evelyn Baring noted that Lear made himself cry when singing his setting of 'Vivien's Song', from *Idylls of the King* ('In Love, if Love be Love, if Love be ours'), but the following morning presented a nonsense version of it: 'Nluv, fluv bluv, ffluv biours'.[133] Lear treats Tennyson like a record played at too high a speed, exposing love poetry as fluff poetry. Occasionally, the transition happened inadvertently. In May 1877, the Drakes 'made me sing & play, but as Edith Drake screamed with laughter at "O that t'were possible", I stopped'.[134] Evidently Lear's rendition of lines from Tennyson's *Maud* was hysterical, at least to some listeners some of the time.

We need to imagine the way in which one set of musical notes can be rendered plangent or preposterous to appreciate Lear, whose art so often plies this borderline. Lear's best nonsense poetry often makes use of a musical tension between the lyrical colour and movement of language and rhythm, which evoke strong and deep emotion, and the self-consciously absurd nature of the actors and situation. The seeming froth of 'nonsense' deliberately belies the powerful emotional undertow of the musical currents in play. His nonsense songs utilise everything that he learned in his career of singing, playing and composing drawing-room ballads. They also deploy his long-standing experience of comic song, with its emphasis on absurd characters, vulgar dialogue and the use of sound as itself a vehicle of comedy.

Fig. 1.9 **Self-caricature of Lear at the piano**

NONSENSE SONGS: PATHOS AND ABSURDITY

One of the first things to notice about Lear's nonsense songs is how often they incorporate music-making within the frame of their own narrative. Thus, 'The Broom, the Shovel, the Poker, and the Tongs', from Lear's first collection, *Nonsense Songs, Stories, Botany and Alphabets* (1871), takes the form of a singing competition of the kind practised by shepherds in Renaissance poetry. In Lear's urban version, however, the rustics are fire irons, taking a break from serving the grate. Each of the 'male' implements sings of his ardour, but in such a way that he enrages the object of his affections. The poker addresses 'Shovely so lovely':

> When you scrape up the coals with a delicate sound,
>   You enrapture my life with delight!
> Your nose is so shiny! your head is so round!
>   And your shape is so slender and bright!
>   Ding-a-dong! Ding-a-dong!
>   Ain't you pleased with my song?[135]

Then the tongs serenades the broom:

> Ah! fairest of creatures, when sweeping the room,
>   Ah! why don't you heed my complaint!

> Must you needs be so cruel, you beautiful Broom,
>> Because you are covered with paint?
>>> Ding-a-dong! Ding-a-dong!
>>> You are certainly wrong!

Lear has fun with the physical likenesses between people and domestic tools—it is quite apt for a Victorian heroine to be 'slender and bright' and her full skirts might well 'sweep the room'. But a 'shiny nose' and 'paint' (the Victorian word for makeup) are certainly not attributes that any romantic suitor should mention, while the scraping of coals is scarcely a 'delicate sound'. The fire irons think they are singing romantic lyric, when in fact they are making a ding-dong row. Indeed the women threaten their menfolk with violence that is both noisy and funny:

> Said the Shovel, 'I'll certainly hit you a bang!'
> Said the Broom, 'And I'll sweep you away!'

The fact that the women are in charge is very typical of Lear's nonsense. Far from being romantically transported, they are the ones offering to sweep— or brush—men off. Only when they are back at the hearthside, waiting for the kettle to boil, is musical harmony restored. This four-verse song offers itself as a piece potentially shared by four voices. Each of the men sings and the two women reply; one imagines that in the end all join in a quasi-Mozartian aria of reconciliation.

Domestic utensils revolting against their class position and having a day of holiday is a very old theme in nursery rhyme. In *Mother Goose's Melody* (1791), 'the dish jump'd a top of the table, / To see the pot wash the ladle; / The spit that stood behind the door / Called the dishclout dirty whore'.[136] The gridiron has to be called in as constable to break up the resulting brawl. Lear's politer nonsense, in which the nutcrackers and sugar tongs ride off on horses and the table and chair escape to 'take the air', is indebted to this tradition of domestic Saturnalia. But he explores this idea within the lyrical dynamics of comic opera.

Hugh Haughton rightly remarks on the frequency with which Lear uses pairings and symmetries in his poems, a habit that is offset by his sometimes intricate and unusual metrical forms, where the lines in a stanza may be odd in number.[137] These pairings and symmetries are typically musical— they create opportunities for recitative and reply, counterpoint, duet, reprise.

Thinking about musical performance can sometimes explain seeming anomalies. When Lear sang 'The Broom, the Shovel, the Poker, and the Tongs', for example, it is quite likely that he repeated the last two lines of each stanza as he does in so many of his Tennyson settings, to give a regular twelve-bar musical structure. With all his metrical variations, Lear's nonsense lyrics are written so that they can be sung, with a regular number of beats in the bar. The fact that his rhythms echo those of popular song is one reason why his work has remained so popular to this day: it is quite literally catchy. His songs also frequently contain a musical element of 'call and response' that seeks to resolve itself in the union of harmony, though this harmony may prove elusive or temporary.

Mr Daddy Long-legs and Mr Floppy Fly sing to each other about the reasons they have lost their confidence (long legs and short legs respectively) and won't go to court any more. The fly begs his friend:

'I wish you'd sing one little song!
  One mumbian melody!
You used to sing so awful well
  In former days gone by,[138]

The Daddy Long-legs responds by singing that he can't sing because he has lost his voice—a classic *opera buffa* line. Lear plays on the strange truth that, for insects, their voice lies *in* their legs. One could thus perform this song with one 'high' and one 'low' voice and a good deal of musical buzzing, of the kind that Offenbach employs in *Orpheus in the Underworld* (1858) when Jupiter sings in the guise of a fly. Lear may have been aware of the recent discovery that each insect did perform in its own distinct key; thus 'the gnat hums in the note A on the second space; the death-watch calls (as the owl hoots) in B flat, and is answered in G; the three notes of the cricket are in B . . . the buzz . . . of the house-fly F in the first space'.[139] The insects exit in concert, to sail away and play eternally at 'shuttlecock and battledore' on the great Gromboolian plain, a fate that seems to imitate their back-and-forth musical dialogue.

Most famously, the Owl and the Pussy-cat embark on their romantic voyage in a song that contains its own song, like the money wrapped up in a five-pound note that they also carry with them:

The Owl and the Pussy-cat went to sea
  In a beautiful pea-green boat,

They took some honey, and plenty of money,
    Wrapped up in a five-pound note.
The Owl looked up to the stars above,
    And sang to a small guitar,
'O lovely Pussy! O Pussy, my love,
    What a beautiful Pussy you are,
        You are,
        You are,
What a beautiful Pussy you are!'[140]

Here the chorus has fused with the verse, creating a rippling series of phrases repeated four times with a lulling, dreamlike effect. The apostrophe, 'O lovely Pussy! O Pussy, my love'—so typical of Lear, who loves to write 'O!'— passes to the repeated image of the ring in the second verse, and the moon in the third verse. That visual series of enchanted circles is a mirror of the form of the song itself, of the way that it keeps coming back to its beginning, mesmerising us with the fragile possibility of perfect accord that, like a ripple, exists only briefly before it breaks.

Impossible animal pairings are a feature of several traditional songs. In 'The Frog He Would A-Wooing Go', which dates from the sixteenth century, the frog is courting a mouse. Another common nursery lyric, which dates at least from the seventeenth century, announces 'Fiddle de dee, fiddle de dee / The Fly has married the Humble Bee'.[141] But Lear's odd couples negotiate more complex relationships than those in rhymes from ancient times. There is a strong element of modern sexual comedy in his uneven

Fig. 1.10 The Owl and the Pussy-cat

unions, where the females are often larger or bolder than their male counterparts, and the male is often tu-whit-tu-wooing dreamily without a realistic
hope of consummating his desires. Indeed the pairings hint at the possibility of incompatible sexualities within marriage, as well as the uncertain-
ties of masculine social and sexual potency. Physical harmony is elusive,
but musical harmony can offer a dream of duetting across corporeal lines.

'The Jumblies' is the most formally complex and haunting of the lyrics in
Lear's first collection of nonsense songs. It tells of another impossible
voyage—the Jumblies set sail in a sieve to the Western Sea. The Jumblies
have green heads and blue hands, associating them with the colours of nature, of sea and sky, that Lear loved best to paint. Their rash journey is con-
demned by public opinion, but to the naysayers' surprise it is a spectacular
success that everyone afterwards wants to imitate. The Jumblies arrive at 'a
land all covered with trees' where they buy 'a hive of silvery Bees', 'a Pig,
and some green Jack-daws' and 'a lovely Monkey with lollipop paws'. They
also sing as they sail:

> And all night long they sailed away;
>   And when the sun went down,
> They whistled and warbled a moony song
> To the echoing sound of a coppery gong,
>   In the shade of the mountains brown.
> 'O Timballo! How happy we are,
> When we live in a sieve and a crockery-jar,
> And all night long in the moonlight pale,
> We sail away with a pea-green sail,
>   In the shade of the mountains brown!'
>   Far and few, Far and few,
>   Are the lands where the Jumblies live;
>   Their heads are green, and their hands are blue,
>   And they went to sea in a Sieve.[142]

Lear's genius in this composition lies in its internal counterpoint. Each
fourteen-line stanza is divided, as a sonnet might be, into a ten-line narrative passage with an intricate rhyme scheme that involves three couplets,
but not where you would expect them in sonnet form (here the pattern is
ABCCBDDEEB), followed by a four-line chorus that is repeated throughout,
recurring six times in all. The rhythm and rhyme of the narrative passages

whirl us onwards, 'while round in our Sieve we spin!' The chorus, contrarily, has a lulling, rocking, hypnotic rhythm. Its crooning chant directly recalls that in Tennyson's cradle song 'Sweet and Low', which was one of the most admired of Lear's musical settings. When thinking about metre in Lear's poems it is useful to bring a musical awareness to bear on them. The binary, Morse-code logic of classical metre, which reads poetry in terms of stressed and unstressed beats, doesn't fully capture the fact that Lear is thinking in musical terms, where individual notes may be held for up to four beats or for fractions of a beat. For example, in Lear's song-setting of Tennyson's 'Sweet and Low, Sweet and Low', the first iteration of 'Sweet and low, sweet and low,/Wind of the western sea' gives the first note as a crotchet (quarter note), the second as a quaver (eighth note), and the third as a dotted crotchet. 'Low' is thus held for three times as long as 'and'. If one then sings the first line of Lear's 'The Jumblies'—'Far and few, Far and few'—to the same music, 'few' becomes an extended note that echoes three times longer than its neighbour. 𝄞

Indeed it is an interesting experiment to sing the chorus of 'The Jumblies'—'Far and few, Far and few'—to Lear's tune for 'Sweet and Low'. It emphasises the extent to which 'The Jumblies' is a kind of lullaby: a song of reassurance that sails us back to childhood and its dreamland of desires that can be reached by night, in spite of all adult opposition. Tennyson's lullaby calls on the 'Wind of the western sea' to bring the imagined child's father back, with his 'silver sail' under a 'silver moon'. Lear's Jumblies, in their moonlight voyage to the Western Sea, are sailing straight into Tennyson's musical territory.

But Lear's song does something that Tennyson's does not. In counterpointing the strange choric lullaby, 'Far and few', with the passages that chart the Jumblies' progress, Lear creates a dynamic musical tension—a swell and slap of water against vessel—that remains unresolved. And this musical counterpoint echoes an emotional counterpoint between joy and sadness, looking forward and looking back. As a child, I was hypnotised by 'The Jumblies', but even then I heard the unrequited wistfulness in its music as well as the joyful wish-fulfilment in its text. It is a song that is somehow both a lullaby for children and a lullaby for childhood. For when the Jumblies return, everyone says, 'How tall they've grown!'—a remark that

---

𝄞 Listen to musical link #9 at edwardlearsmusic.com/audiotrail/#sweetandlow.

suggests that they are children, whose magical invulnerability has permitted them to go to fantastical places of which adults can only dream. But if this is so, then there is no way back. Childhood is that Xanadu (which sounds rather like 'Far and few') from which there is only a one-way ticket. Lear described himself as 'moony' when he was apathetic with depression. The word suggests moaning (which is Lear's specialist subject), as well as 'mooning about', perhaps influenced, as he felt his emotions to be, by the phases of the moon itself. When the Jumblies warble their 'moony song', they internalise the way in which the buoyancy of delight is always shadowed by the waning and sinking that singing only temporarily staves off. Like the sieve, we can bear things we shouldn't be able to—but only for a time. This melancholy awareness makes the power of the Jumblies' successful refusal of the laws of physics as poignant as it is pleasurable.

The insistent returns of poetry and of music can be, in Lear's self-aware culture of totemised memory, both deeply emotional and highly calculated. He inhabits a post-Romantic moment in which themes of loss and nostalgia are both enshrined and demystified, largely because of their increasing popular and commercial ubiquity. The breaking heart and its excesses of sorrow; the solitary seeking solace in nature; the remorseful adult wishing himself back to childhood; the deserted or bereaved lover wandering an inhospitable landscape. All these themes can be handled alternately *con espressione* or *scherzando*, and indeed music that suggests one mood may be set off against words that suggest another.

Recognising this counterpoint is valuable when approaching Lear's later works. In his 'nonsense', he creates characters—from the wistful Dong to the rejected Yonghy-Bonghy-Bò—who are unaware that they are acting out the well-worn roles of plaintive relict and spurned hero. They stay true to the genre in which they find themselves. Hearing their lyrics of loss with knowing ears, however, we can respond both to the art with which Lear remembers and reprises earlier work in the genre, casting sidelong light on its conventions, and to the feeling with which the characters inhabit their impossible longing, resonant and real longing that is embodied in the music of their refrains.

'The Dong with a Luminous Nose', published in *Laughable Lyrics* (1877), involves a medley of remembered chords out of which it creates a fantasy of strange and original brilliance. Most prominently, the opening couplet is a version of the opening couplet in James Bird's poem *The Emigrant's Tale* (1833):

O'er the wide empire of CANADIAN plains,
O'er their vast solitudes deep silence reigns,
Tired echo sleeps by silent dale and hill,
The boundless woods, the mighty lakes are still[143]

Lear's transformation of these lines shows the continuing influence of his early reading on his later compositions. Bird's narrative involves a man who, in a fit of mistaken jealousy, attacks his sweetheart's brother and thinks he has murdered him; he has to flee to the New World, where he struggles with remorse and a love that, he fears, cannot now be consummated. In Lear's now-famous opening, 'Canadian' has been replaced with 'Gromboolian', but the imagery of loneliness and lost love is the same.

When awful darkness and silence reign
    Over the great Gromboolian plain,
        Through the long, long wintry nights;—
When the angry breakers roar
As they beat on the rocky shore;—
    When Storm-clouds brood on the towering heights
Of the hills of the Chankly Bore:—

Then, through the vast and gloomy dark,
There moves what seems a fiery spark,
    A lonely spark with silvery rays
        Piercing the coal-black night,—
    A Meteor strange and bright:—
Hither and thither the vision strays,
    A single lurid light.[144]

Lear's imagery also recalls that of Thomas Moore's ballad 'The Lake of the Dismal Swamp'(1806), in which a man dies while pursuing his vanished Indian lover, following her 'firefly lamp' and 'meteor bright' across the dark surface of the lake. Lear may well have sung this ballad alongside the many others by Moore that we know were in his repertoire.[145] Moore steers away from direct invocation of slavery by making the *ignis fatuus* a Native American girl; the vast Dismal Swamp between North Carolina and Virginia was in fact famously the haunt of Maroons, refugee slaves who had escaped from their masters. Interestingly, a memory of doomed interracial romance lingers around Lear's poem, where the Dong wanders vainly in pursuit of a 'Jumbly' girl who has departed across the sea.

'The Dong with a Luminous Nose' is a poem about musical echoes. Its protagonist plays 'the plaintive pipe', an ancient Greek instrument *(querula tibia)* mentioned by Pindar, Horace and Lucretius. In *De Rerum Natura,* Lucretius explains the relationship between the plaintive pipe and echoes in 'lonely places . . . among sombre mountains', which 'return as many as six or seven cries':

> Such places are fancied by local people to be the haunts of
> nymphs and goat-footed satyrs, and to be the homes of fauns,
> by whose night-pervading clamor . . . the still silence is, they
> say, often broken; sounds of strings are heard, and sweet notes
> ripple from the plaintive pipe. . . .[146]

The plaintive pipe, then, is associated with night, lonely landscapes and with a mythology of echo that attributes it to semi-human creatures. When the Dong dances 'in circlets all night long' with the Jumblies to the sound of his pipe, he is following in distinguished classical footsteps.

Intriguingly, his 'luminous nose' also looks like an instrument: it has stops like a pipe, through which light or sound might equally be transmitted. He resembles both the 'Old Man in a barge', whose large nose supports a light, and the 'Old Man of West Dumpet/Who possessed a large nose like a trumpet'; that nose, when blown aloud, astonishes the crowd. We do, of course, 'blow' our noses, but in Lear's fertile imagination this act produces a musical fanfare.

The Dong is an echoing sound; his name, his nose and his noise are one. But he is also a beacon, a 'fiery spark' moving through the darkness. Both his light and his sound are described as 'silvery'. The poem, then, plays on the relationship between the visual and the aural senses and how both light and sound can reach us over distance and through darkness. It explores what Coleridge in 'The Eolian Harp' calls 'a light in sound, a sound-like power in light'. The magic of its internal music, its chant, is one of regular resonance contrasted with flickering light—like an arpeggio in the right hand overlaying a constantly repeated note in the left. Lear as a pianist loved to play arpeggios. He brings his musical gift for restless movement together with the counterpoint of vocal chime (Dong! Dong!) to create a scene that is operatic in its mixture of visual and aural drama:

Fig. 1.11 **The Dong with a Luminous Nose**

Slowly it wanders,—pauses,—creeps,—
Anon it sparkles,—flashes and leaps;
And ever as onward it gleaming goes
A light on the Bong-tree stems it throws.
And those who watch at that midnight hour
From Hall or Terrace, or lofty Tower,
Cry, as the wild light passes along,—
    'The Dong!—the Dong!
  The wandering Dong through the forest goes!
    The Dong! the Dong!
  The Dong with a luminous Nose!'

Here are Lear's characteristic long dashes, dramatising and lengthening the pauses between words, and his exclamation marks, indicating ringing emphasis. These marks take us some of the way towards musical scoring, in that they suggest where long notes will fall. There is also musical counterpoint. The bell-like refrain 'The Dong!—The Dong!' is answered by the wistful repeated chorus from Lear's earlier poem, 'The Jumblies' ('Far and few, far and few / Are the lands where the Jumblies live'), which has the rise-and-fall rhythm of waves. Both the Dong and his Jumbly girl possess a musical leitmotif that dramatises their predicament within the structure of the verse: they cannot meet, but their respective melodies recur in sequence. One might compare Wagner's *Tristan and Isolde* (1865) or, more obviously, Lear's song-settings of Tennyson, in which he makes use of motto-themes to dramatise within the music persons and objects that feature in the text.

The Dong has many of the characteristics of a Romantic protagonist. He is 'lonely and wild'. His plaintive note of abandonment sounds a little like 'Gone! Gone!' Like 'Miss Maniac', he wanders 'by lake and forest, marsh and hill' and he seems to have lost his mind: 'What little sense I once possessed / Has quite gone out of my head!' Yet Lear's expression is deliberately equivocal. Has the Dong been maddened by lost love, or was he always just silly to begin with? The poem allows us to entertain both thoughts simultaneously: to read the Dong as a comic character and as a symbol of the night-side of human existence, which relies on signal and symbol to convey its unspeakable woes. Previous commentators have tended to resort to comparing Lear himself with the Dong. Self-evidently one can do this: Lear in his diary once depicted himself with a swollen nose like a blister on the point of bursting.[147] However, the poem, like Lear's cartoon version of 'Bonny Doon' and other Romantic lyrics, is also a commentary on the naturalness of song, on the way in which it might be a lyrical extension of ourselves—a cry from the heart, or at least the inner organs—and simultaneously an absurd form of self-projection, an insupportable mask that theatrically draws attention to itself.

'The Courtship of the Yonghy-Bonghy-Bò' is another nonsense song in *Laughable Lyrics* that repays close reading in the light of Lear's mixed musical heritage. It is a song about a rejected lover, like 'Alice Gray' and 'Oh! No, We Never Mention Her!', which we have seen Lear spoof with youthful comic brio. Humorous ballads about men who lost their loves to tradesmen were common in the period.[148] 'Dash My Vig!', for example, which was sung to the tune 'Derry Down', featured a Cockney who lamented that the woman he was courting dismissed his proposal, preferring a 'journeyman-grocer . . . Mr Figg'.[149]

Lear's song shares some of the features of these comic turns. Our hero, who lives in the middle of the woods, is a 'Hoddy Doddy' whose head is many times larger than his body. This term was commonly used to describe babies and cuckolds: significantly, it suggests a presexual or emasculated form, a figure who is bound to be rejected as a mate.[150] Many of Lear's courting males fall into this category of *castrati innamorati*. Lear in his diary sometimes refers to his bottom as his Bòhind: the Bò might be considered a sort of ambulant arse.[151] He tells Lady Jingly, whom he encounters one day in his lonely wanderings, that he is 'tired of living singly,—/ On this coast so wild and shingly'. (One is reminded of Jacob Beuler's lisping lover.) We shouldn't be surprised that the object of his affections is already taken.

> 'On this Coast of Coromandel,
>   Shrimps and watercresses grow,
>   Prawns are plentiful and cheap,'
>   Said the Yonghy-Bonghy-Bò.
> 'You shall have my chairs and candle,
> And my jug without a handle!—
>   Gaze upon the rolling deep
>   (Fish is plentiful and cheap;)
>   As the sea, my love is deep!'
> Said the Yonghy-Bonghy-Bò,
> Said the Yonghy-Bonghy-Bò.[152]

The Yonghy-Bonghy-Bò's assurance to Lady Jingly that 'As the sea, my love is deep' is a version of Juliet's promise to Romeo: 'my bounty is as boundless as the sea,/My love as deep'. When, however, he assures her in the same breath that 'Fish is plentiful and cheap', we sense there may be more comic flounder than tragic soul in the relationship. Indeed the poem smacks of a comic inversion of Tennyson's *Enoch Arden,* his long, sometimes awkward poem about a fisherman marooned on an island whose wife remarries, thinking him dead. There is also a dash of comic Cockneyism in the deliberately bad rhyme between 'talking' and 'Dorking'. When the Yonghy-Bonghy-Bò exclaims, 'You're the Cove for me' to the 'large and lively Turtle' that is to bear him away from his lost love, the cheerful slang is at odds with his sentimental predicament; in this coastal romance, 'cove' should really be an inlet, and 'turtle' should really be a dove. The name of Lady Jingly's absent husband is Handel, of 'Handel, Jones Esquire and Co'; a handle is a name, and (in German) 'Handel' is a generic word for business. 'Jingly' (a word coined in 1806, meaning 'characterised by affected recurrence of words or sounds') also suggests money. It is as if the language of commerce and the language of romance had tried to embrace and the result was farce.

And yet. As ever with Lear, the music of the lines forms an affecting counterpoint to the 'nonsense' of the topic. 'On the Coast of Coromandel/ Where the early pumpkins blow' is, in its own way, as lyrical a phrase as the famous opening of Mignon's Song in Goethe's *Wilhelm Meister:* 'Kennst du das land, wo die Zitronen blühn?' Her dreamy landscape of laurels and myrtles and Lear's 'slippery slopes of myrtle' are both associated with *sehnsucht*, impossible longing that is the essence of the Romantic imaginative quest. Lear's 'silent-roaring ocean' has never been bettered as a metaphor for the incommunicable inner life of grief:

> Through the silent-roaring ocean
>   Did the Turtle swiftly go;
>   Holding fast upon his shell
>   Rode the Yonghy-Bonghy-Bò.
> With a sad primaeval motion
> Towards the sunset isles of Boshen
>   Still the Turtle bore him well.
>   Holding fast upon his shell,
>   'Lady Jingly Jones, farewell!'
> Said the Yonghy-Bonghy-Bò,
> Said the Yonghy-Bonghy-Bò.

'The Courtship of the Yonghy-Bonghy-Bò' is a song preoccupied with weeping and with being 'too late', as are Lear's serious settings of Shelley and Tennyson ('Too late, too late! Ye cannot enter now'). The Yonghy-Bonghy-Bò possesses only a jug without a handle, two chairs and half a candle. This makes him ridiculous as a potential suitor, but also aligns him with the figure of the poet-exile. Lear in his diary for 1863 recorded a particular jug without a handle on a Greek island: it belonged to Byron, the poet-hero of Lear's younger self.[153]

There are many subtle allusions in Lear's poem, both literary and musical.[154] The setting recalls Byron's *Childe Harold's Pilgrimage:*

> There is a pleasure in the pathless woods,
> There is a rapture on the lonely shore,
> There is society, where none intrudes,
> By the deep Sea, and music in its roar[155]

However, the 'sunset isles of Boshen' are an inverted, 'boshy' version of Goshen, that Biblical 'place of plenty or light', the fertile land allotted to the Israelites during the plague of darkness. In the Houghton manuscript of Lear's poem, Lady Jingly 'weeps and warbles airs from Handel', a clue that Lear is thinking of opera and its arias and duets of unrequited love, which this nonsense song burlesques. When she 'twirls her fingers madly', Lady Jingly behaves like the prima donnas of Donizetti and Bellini, whose love triangles inevitably produce a 'mad scene' that is the showstopper for the female voice. It is interesting that when Lear mentions this poem in his diary he usually calls it 'Lady Jingly'. It is the story of a frustrated female as well as the story of a disappointed male. When he sang or recited it in India in 1874, it was evidently funny: 'A very pleasant day . . . Punning bad puns & telling stories & laughing (Lady Jingly Jones)'.[156] Philip Hofer has argued of Lear that 'he could clown in his verses: in his music he was in earnest'.[157] But this distinction is a false one. 'The Courtship of the Yonghy-Bonghy-Bò' is funny *and* sad, a musical burlesque and a lyric of plaintive power. 𝄞

Critics persist in casting Augusta Bethell as Lady Jingly—but in 1871, it had been four years since Lear had decided against proposing to her, and she would not marry another man until 1872. In San Remo he sang the song accompanied on the piano by the novelist Eleanor Poynter, whose books and whose society he enjoyed. 'Too late, too late!', he recorded in his diary.[158] He was sixty-three. She was thirty-five and never married; she might well have been available had Lear chosen to court her. But he didn't. It was more enjoyable to act the role of comic suitor and respondent at the piano. This is, like all of Lear's music, a performance piece whose truest love is its audience.

Hearing 'The Courtship of the Yonghy-Bonghy-Bò' as a song is a subtly different experience from reading it on the page. The rhythm is sprightly and reminiscent of light opera. But the third and eighth line of each verse has rising musical emphasis, with longer beats and in the latter case six identical notes. This means that we hear certain phrases (among them 'will you come and be my wife?'; 'your proposal comes too late'; 'will you please to go away?'; and 'on that little heap of stones') more vividly than they appear in the written text. Indeed the music points up the rhetorical potential of the dialogue and invites the possibility that the piece might be performed as a duet, with a female voice singing the verses in which Mrs Jingly Jones responds to her suitor. Lear's music here is reminiscent of that of W. S. Gilbert and Arthur Sullivan, whose first joint burlesque was performed in 1871. It exhibits the same alertness to operatic convention and the possibilities

---

𝄞 Listen to musical link #10 at edwardlearsmusic.com/audiotrail/#yonghybonghy.

of musical parody. In particular, the sharp staccato scoring at the end of the first line of each verse creates a comic judder, which pulls the sentiment up short. However, it is noteworthy that this song, like 'The Pelican Chorus', is in the key of E major, the same key that Lear uses for Shelley's 'O World, O Life, O Time!' and for the vast majority of his Tennyson songs. It is—as nobody seems to have noticed before—quite literally Lear's signature key: the key of E for Edward. The songs' shared key points up the musical continuity between Lear's expressive drawing-room ballads, as settings of Romantic poetry, and his nonsense songs.

A critic in the *Examiner* for 1876 noted the 'Byronic melancholy' of some of Lear's verse and its 'totally new sensation of humour, *welt-schmerz*, mystery, and farce combined'; he thought 'The Courtship of the Yonghy-Bonghy-Bò' the finest of the *Laughable Lyrics*, 'deeply tinged with the Nonsense Poet's pervading melancholy'. Crucially, this critic responds to Nonsense Poetry as a distinct new form characterised by its unique, sweet-sour genre fusion.[159]

Another contemporary critic, in the *Times*, compared *Laughable Lyrics* with W. S. Gilbert's *Bab Ballads* and commented, 'there are some lines . . . descriptive of the Turtle's swiftly going through the "silent roaring ocean" . . . which for the melody of their nonsense are as good, almost, as "Laura Matilda's Dirge" in Rejected Addresses'.[160] This is an intriguing remark that deserves further consideration. *Rejected Addresses* (1812), by James and Horace Smith, was a highly popular comic text in the early nineteenth century. It pretended to contain submissions for a poetry competition to celebrate the rebuilding of the Drury Lane theatre after a fire. These supposedly rejected entries were 'by' Wordsworth, Byron, Southey, Coleridge and others. They set a high standard for spoof of Romantic stylistics. Among the more obvious parodies was an oddity: a 'dirge' by 'Laura Matilda' that made all the right noises for a piece of lyrical poetry, but was, in fact, nonsense:

> Where is Cupid's crimson motion?
>   Billowy ecstacy of woe,
> Bear me strait meandering ocean,
>   Where the stagnant torrents flow.[161]

One can see why the rhyme ('motion'/'ocean') and the command to carry the protagonist across the waves made the *Times* reviewer connect this piece with Lear's 'Yonghy-Bonghy-Bò'. The critical thrust of 'Laura Matilda's Dirge' was that this was the kind of vacuous poetry young ladies produced:

woeful. But the stanza form became unexpectedly influential. A. E. Housman at the very end of the nineteenth century admired it. And it sparked serious debate about the relationship between poetry and music. Citing the Laura Matilda stanzas, one early sematologist in 1831 argued:

> . . . no one will pretend that a piece of music expresses, or can express, independently of words, a series of rational proposi-tions; yet it awakens some sentiments or feelings of a suffi-ciently definite character to occupy the mind agreeably. Now perhaps it is not an unwarrantable libel on one half of the reading world, if we affirm, that they read poetry and other amusing composition for no further end, and with no further effect, than the pleasure of such vague sentiments or feelings as spring from music: and to such readers it is of little moment whether the words make sense or not.[162]

By comparing Lear's 'Yonghy-Bonghy-Bò' and 'Laura Matilda's Dirge', the *Times* reviewer was reading Lear within a debate, which began surprisingly early, about whether *all* poetry produced emotion chiefly because of its sound. William Dobson, writing on nonsense verse in 1882, reflected on 'how thin the partition line is between true nonsense verse and many of those pieces which were wont to be known by the name of Album Verses'.[163] The 'true' nonsense verse is, presumably, a self-conscious form. But the possibility that a parody of album verse (verse intended to be included in a keepsake album) can be identical to a nonsense poem in 'the melody of their nonsense' raises the question whether the lyrical voice of nonsense is critically assumed or personal, or can somehow be both. Is nonsense in essence a parodic mode, or does its nearness to pure sound in fact bespeak a relationship with unmediated feeling that offers a direct route to emotional expression and psychological truth? These contemporary reviews alert the modern reader to the range of echoes that nineteenth-century readers heard in Lear's work, and their competing identifications of him as a master of genre fusion, whose 'pervading melancholy' was Byronic, and as a comic showman, whose work was poised between that of the Smith brothers (who also wrote songs) and W. S. Gilbert.

Early twentieth-century commentators, such as Maurice Bowra, were apt to see in Lear a *'reductio ad absurdum* of Romantic methods' that exposed the tendency of Romantic poetics towards lyrical 'vagueness' that could become ridiculous.[164] Émile Cammaerts argued, 'Nonsense stands, with regard to Romanticism, very much in the same position as Satire and Epigram, with regard to Classicism'.[165] More recently, Michael O'Neill has persuasively argued for 'Romantic delight in particularity as well as suggestiveness' as a 'point of origin' for Lear's departures.[166] But these accounts do not attend to the nuanced relationship between Romanticism and song that infuses Lear's work. Unlike Carroll, whose parodies of Romantic poetry in the Alice books are pointedly designed to be read as critical takedown, Lear's echoes of Moore, Bayly, Bird, Byron, Tennyson and others are part of a practice best understood in musical terms: of medley, contrafactum and internal counterpoint. A sparkling response to Romantic excess and cliché is part of Lear's comic inheritance, which comprises also a keen awareness of how easily lyric can descend into bosh. A delight in the expressive and affective possibilities of lyric and its identically rooted capacity to transcend meaning, to express the infinite and the unsayable, is, however, also essential to Lear's nonsense, which uses its song-lines to bind us to it, over and over, with fine emotional threads. The fact that often these processes are working simultaneously, making us laugh and cry at once, is Lear's real genius.

In Lear's work, pathos and absurdity typically form a feedback loop. To be subject to one is to invite the other and vice versa. This self-conscious loop is one of the most important things to understand about his writing; it is why it is insufficient to say that Lear's work expresses his 'emotional biography', or to feel sorry for the writer's losses, which he 'veils' under the mantle of absurdity. Lear's writing is not only about his own deprivations and failures and longings. It explores the hyperbolic and hopeless nature of emotion itself, via a consciousness of genre that teeters between sincere echo and parody, exposing the nature of reprise as always potentially melancholy and funny at the same time. In his songs the bricolage of seemingly familiar notes and sequences can add to our sense of return as ironic; yet the musical inevitability of return, the sense in which the song imitates memory by re-calling melody, is also essential to the way the lyrics stay with us, producing their own plangent emotional echoes.

Once we have begun to hear it, music is everywhere in Lear's writing. It is in his diaries: travelling in Egypt in his fifties, he is moved to laughter by the sound of *sakkias* (waterwheels used for irrigation), which make a sound like 'flourishes and scales on the violin, with chords—& violincello accompaniments in a wonderful style. 10 or 20 fiddles are all of them shaking at once—then come long drawn notes & scrapings,—and every kind of orchestral tuning. One thinks a stray opera band has been left on shore & are practising'.[167] An object, as so often in his nonsense verse, has a voice of its own. Lear tries to capture this strange and captivating sound by drawing a rough stave with notes on the page. Music animates Lear's letters: while in Italy, he sends George and Fanny Coombe a couple of new verses for a song he was singing before he left, 'My Old Home Is No Longer Mine'.[168] Music also plays a part in the vivid soundscapes of Lear's published travelogues, perhaps most memorably where he alludes to fleas and bedbugs as 'F sharps and B flats'.[169] We can imagine these tiny creatures, the plague of the Victorian traveller, as small black notes on the white bedsheet that in turn produce a song and dance of misery.

The nonsense word itself could be thought of as a kind of 'blue note'—a deliberate musical slur that enables us to hear and see notes played together that we recognise separately but are not used to hearing fused to produce a distinctively new sound. Certainly, nonsense has qualities of musical improvisation. Its shrieks and squeaks, bongs and dongs invoke the primacy of sound to language in human development from childhood and the thin veneer of control that conceals indecorous noises that are always threatening to explode. In a letter of 1860 to Emily Tennyson, Lear describes the commotion created by a bursting boiler at the Oatlands Hotel, where he was staying:

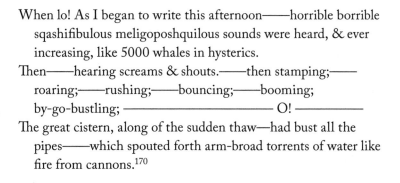

> When lo! As I began to write this afternoon——horrible borrible sqashifibulous meligoposhquilous sounds were heard, & ever increasing, like 5000 whales in hysterics.
> Then——hearing screams & shouts.——then stamping;——roaring;——rushing;——bouncing;——booming; by-go-bustling; ——————————— O! ———————
> The great cistern, along of the sudden thaw—had bust all the pipes——which spouted forth arm-broad torrents of water like fire from cannons.[170]

Together, Lear's long dashes as he conveys the onomatopoeic crescendo and the 'O!' of release approach the quality of musical scoring. At some point the human noises and those of the plumbing merge. It is as if the pipes have given voice to something huge and unseen (the five thousand hysterical wails we all suppress) that is simultaneously alarming and very funny. Lear's nonsense offers many such dramatic outlets. It demands to be voiced.

Lear published his first collection of limericks, *A Book of Nonsense,* under the pseudonym 'Derry down Derry'. Derry down Derry was one of the fools of the traditional mummers' plays, and thus a name linked to comic entertainment. But 'Derry Down' is also a tune, best known as the air to the English folk song 'The World Turned Upside Down', a title that suggests the inversions and impossibilities in which nonsense delights. 'Derry down derry' is, moreover, a popular refrain in many folk songs, both tragic ('The Twa' Sisters', 'The Three Ravens') and comic ('Past Twelve O'Clock', 'How to Tell a Story'). This is apt, for Lear's nonsense keeps returning us to song and explores song as a vehicle of return: through its repetitions, whether comic or sad, and its capacity to evoke the emotional beats of personal and shared memory. Its sociable lyrics with their strong rhythms and rhymes draw on musical forms and themes; the narratives also frequently contain characters who sing. Often the inner music made by the characters is counterpointed with the music made by the poem as a whole, creating a dynamic tension between the harmony and circular resolution towards which the song formally reaches, and a different cadence, of traumatic repetition and unresolved desire.

Looking at Lear's early work is useful as it reminds us not to read his nonsense songs merely as a rueful, self-parodying reflection of his later personal life, but as pieces that emerge from a long immersion in a fluid musical culture, where comic and sentimental airs were frequently played to the same tune. Lear's early experiments also alert us to the wide range of cultural influences—from Byron to Bird and Bayly to Beuler, from Turner to Thomas Hudson and Tennyson—that play into his oeuvre, and how visual art, literature and music constantly combine in his life and work to produce pieces defined by their interdisciplinarity. Lear's work is intensely social. It is rhetorical and affective at the same time: deeply aware of the conditions of performance and the emphatic techniques of producing drama, yet also alive to the capacity of art, particularly music, to transcend the limits of its own apparent subject and become the key that opens the door to emotions that precede conscious thought.[171]

Music comes to us in waves. The internal music of Lear's songs, which often drifts across water or is performed in the open air, catches the magic of this movement and the ripples of memory it invokes. In 'Eight Cousins'

(1875), a story by Louisa Alcott, a crew of little boys sail boats on a lake. Alcott concludes, 'Then the boats parted company, and across the water from the "Petrel's" crew came a verse from one of the Nonsense Songs in which the boys delighted.

> Oh, Timballoo! how happy we are,
> We live in a sieve and a crockery jar!
> And all night long, in the star-light pale,
> We sail away, with a pea-green sail,
> And whistle and warble a moony song
> To the echoing sound of a coppery gong.
>   Far and few, far and few
> Are the lands where the Jumblies live
> Their heads are green, and their hands are blue
>   And they went to sea in a sieve.'[172]

It is a lovely parting image: the children's voices echoing across the water as they enact the Jumblies' impossible voyage, sailing away into the space beyond the page's end. The interesting thing is that they aren't singing the song Lear wrote. They lyrics have shifted and changed position like sand on a beach. Moonlight has become 'star-light'; 'Timballo' has become 'Timballoo' (coming closer to Timbuctoo); and 'they' has become 'we'. The singers own the song. This is as it should be. For Lear's is a magpie art and an inclusive art. When he plays, we are all invited to join in.

Fig. 1.12 One of Lear's illustrations for 'Sing a Song of Sixpence'

2

NONSENSE AND NONCONFORMITY

'Verily priesthood of the orthodox! You walk blindfold!'[1]

EDWARD LEAR is usually remembered as a genial figure: 'he is so good and kind and gentle', Emily Tennyson reflected in her journal, choosing words that were often used to describe herself.[2] But Lear, although a funny, generous and deeply affectionate human being who drew others to him by his capacity for sympathy, also had a tendency to sudden outbursts of anger. As he frequently puts it in his diary, 'I became enraged'. The topic most likely to produce this reaction was religion.[3] 'Alas! Alas! Going to church is my *bête noir*', he fulminates in a letter of October 1875 to Chichester Fortescue, in which he also threatens to 'snort' and 'dance' and 'fling my hat' at the 'abomination of sermonpreaching'.[4] Gussie Bethell teased Lear that churchmen were his *bêtes noires*.[5] He refuted the charge, mentioning several men of the cloth, such as Charles Church and the controversial cleric Arthur Penrhyn Stanley, whose society he valued highly. It is true that Lear had friends 'both laymen and clerical', as his poem '"How Pleasant to Know Mr Lear!"' avers, but Gussie's arrow was well-aimed. Over and over in Lear's diaries and letters we find evidence of his irritation and contempt for 'priests', by which he denotes clergymen of any stripe whose views he finds offensive. Of Mr Rogers, a parson, he writes, 'a high example of the base-priest. . . . Heavens! what a foul canker are these men!'[6] In one diary-sketch of a seating plan at dinner, he places 'The Reverend Fooly Philpott'[7] at the head of the table; in another he notes that the chair of the bishop of Bath and Wells, whose religious views he opposed, collapsed, and 'I was almost sorry to pick him up'.[8] Lear's diary is peppered with snorting

reactions to 'absurd' sermons, such as a 'disgusting foolsermon'[9] of forty minutes at Cannes, or one in which 'a sad idiot bored me by preaching folly and
lies'.[10] He delights in an imaginary invention at the Great Exhibition of an
extinguisher, like a candle snuffer, to snuff out any clergyman who preaches
for too long.[11] A threat of comic violence often hovers above the pulpit when
Lear is in the congregation. This angry Lear is a figure whose voice we need
to hear, whose dissent is as important to his art as his benevolence.

   A consideration of religion is key to a full understanding of Lear, of his
nonconformist heritage, his politics, his value system, his intellectual independence and his approach to reading. Lear referred to parts of the Bible as
'boshy' (for example the 'Book of Boshua'),[12] and to exclusive forms of worship, particularly the Athanasian Creed, as 'nonsense and blasphemy';[13]
his own nonsense owes much to his resistance to doctrinal authority. The
Bible in Lear's view was a historical artefact and subject to the errors and
prejudices of its time; Christianity that didn't reflect a broad, tolerant
and progressive view of morality and which insisted that those whose beliefs lay outside Anglicanism were 'damned' was, in his inventive coinage,
'Christinanity'.[14] The steam-force of Lear's anger about aspects of preaching,
'puritanism' and piety energises his writing, producing virtuosic bursts of
vehemence. As he explained to Emily Tennyson when describing an 'odious'
church service at Stoke Newington, 'I became gradually crosser & crosser
& crosser & crosser & crosser & crosser. . . .'[15] I am especially interested in
the metaphorical 'flinging'—of hats, of dances, of words—in which Lear's
religious views involve him and in the creative consequences of his nonconformity. In particular, a better understanding of Lear's dissent can help us
to see his nonsense not merely as whimsical but as oppositional; he is writing
work for children and for adults that rejects the proselytising of compliance
as the standard of morality.

A Dissenting Education

Lear's parents were dissenters. We know this from the fact that their
children's births were registered in Dr Williams's Library, the repository established by dissenters for recording births and deaths outside the Anglican
parish-record system. Their birth certificates, moreover, show that the Lear
children were all baptised by a single preacher, the Reverend Joseph Brooksbank, who signed himself 'Protestant Dissenting Minister'. Brooksbank
(1762–1825) was for forty years pastor of the Independent church that

assembled at Haberdashers' Hall, Staining-Lane, Wood Street, London; this is likely where Jeremiah Lear got to know him, when working in the heart of the commercial City. Of Joseph Brooksbank, a colleague noted that 'though he retained much of his Yorkshire accent, and was by no means remarkable for the easy or elegant flow of his diction, he drew to himself for years a large measure of the public regard. This, perhaps was mainly owing to the decidedly evangelical tone of his pulpit addresses, delivered as they were with earnestness and becoming zeal for the salvation of souls. . . . He did not understand the art to soften down sturdy principles'.[16] If Lear listened as a child to Brooksbank's sermons (as seems probable), one wonders how he reacted to their blunt evangelism. Brooksbank was a founder member of the London Missionary Society; this personal connection may have inspired Lear's brother, Charles, to pursue missionary work. By contrast, Lear's pronouncements on missionaries are generally scathing; he alludes to one as 'a browny Clerical—Missionary—dummy & queery'.[17]

Haberdashers' Hall was one of the oldest dissenting societies in London, having been formed in 1650, a little before Cromwell assumed power. Independent congregations, as the name suggests, believed that each chapel was sovereign and should determine the nature of its own worship. The earliest ones, such as the congregation that worshipped in Haberdashers' Hall, were founded by rebel Puritan groups, and as such had a particular, historical opposition to the Catholic church. After 1830, many of these Independent congregations banded loosely together as 'Congregationalists'. This is the form of faith shared by two other liberal-minded poets whom Lear knew socially: Robert and Elizabeth Barrett Browning. It is estimated that by 1851 there were around half a million Independent worshippers in Britain; they were widely spread, but northeast London, where Edward Lear grew up, was an area of concentrated strength.[18]

It matters, for several reasons, that Lear was brought up in a family of nonconformists of an independent Protestant cast. First, it helps to explain why socially and politically he always felt himself to be 'an outsider and by nature and habit a Liberal'.[19] Dissent from Anglicanism was popular and growing in Victorian England, especially among the mercantile classes where Methodist, Unitarian and various other kinds of chapel were on the rise. Still, those who chose to stand outside the bourn of the Anglican church faced exclusions and disabilities with serious social consequences. Until 1829 they could not technically hold public office;[20] they could not attend the great universities of Oxford and Cambridge; baptism, marriage and burial were not legally recognised unless they were performed within an Anglican church; and until 1868 dissenters were obliged to pay church taxes for the upkeep of buildings and clergymen whose views they did not uphold. The fight for equal recognition of dissenters within nineteenth-century Britain mirrored the wider movement for legal and political reform. There was thus a very strong regional and social correlation between dissent and liberalism.[21]

Lear was a lifelong Liberal. His views were moderate—he had 'a set feeling that gross and violent Radicals ought never to govern or help in governing more than virulent Tories'[22]—but it is notable that *Tory* is always a pejorative term in his vocabulary, and that he often uses the word *narrow* in connection both with Toryism and Anglicanism. In describing the Countess Lonsdale, for example, Lear notes, 'she had a kind of social amiability—but was so narrow & vulgar a Tory, that she could conceive no person to be human or Christian who was not a Tory'.[23] In November 1861, he writes of a Mr Graham, 'Wonderful asinine Tory!—spoke of the downfall of Austria—& their reward and consolation being the fact of never having admitted Jews in their society'.[24] For Lear, the Establishment was inevitably both a political and a religious entity, and dissent was a form of democratic freedom that threatened its control. In a fit of rage about Cardinal Manning's declaration that Protestantism was dead in England, Lear fumed to Emily Tennyson in 1865:

> for every advance of the Upper Caste to a form of religion allied to repression retrogression & Toryism—the Masses will protest more & more against such a creed by a nearer approach to Democracy. The Dogmas they care little for;—but that all human thought is to be controlled by some set of priests (any one—R. C.—calvinists or what not,) headed by one man,—— this the English will protest against & screamingly one of these days.[25]

As his repeated use of the word here attests, the 'protest' in Protestantism remained very much alive for Lear. To him, Catholicism was not the main threat (though he regretted it when friends converted); it was repression and control. He hated the idea that 'Popes and Parsons' would 'sit on our brains' and that the broadening stream of religious belief would flow backwards to one 'head', whether that head was Catholic or Anglican. Such exclusive power was inimical to individual freedom of conscience. Screaming—like the Old Man of Ibreem in Lear's limericks—is one possible response to the kind of intellectual-cum-physical suffocation that Lear imagines when the plurality of human thought is menaced by any such claim to supreme doctrinal authority. Later he would denounce with similar fervour the Pope's opposition to Italian unification, which threatened similar oppression by religious authority in the political sphere.

Lear is often remembered as personally eccentric—which he undoubtedly was—but it bears remembering that, from a religious viewpoint, he was born outside the mainstream and, amongst the big fish of Victorian society whose custom he courted, he would have to learn to swim carefully in order to avoid being caught out. Dissenters' views about the status of the Bible as a text, the role of preachers and worship in religious life and the conduct of services were different from Anglicans'. The raison d'etre of an Independent Protestant chapel was lay responsibility: the idea that each individual member should interpret the Bible for themselves. In Independent congregations Bibles were open during services as members considered sermons that might involve ambitious theological wrangling. Prayer was always extemporary, and sermons usually were. These practices were important to the active, independent model of reading, critical engagement and theological debate that Lear must have absorbed, and which he favoured throughout his life. The individual in this religious model is not dependent for salvation on the intercession of a priest or on receiving communion. Indeed, like many dissenters, Lear did not believe in transubstantiation, the Virgin birth and other 'supernatural' aspects of the Bible; for him Christ was a human figure, and the Christian's duty, as he reminded himself in his diary on the first day of the year in 1860, was to 'endeavour to praise God rather by solid acts, & self-improvement, than by forms of loud prayer—the trade of priests'. Lear often uses the word *priestcraft*, a term dating from the 1680s that has the sense of 'scheming, guile, or deceit'; this echoes a very old tradition of Protestant invective against dogma, ritual and church corruption. As he told Chichester Fortescue in 1862:

> I still maintain that Blasphemy and lying are the Prerogatives
> of Priestcraft or they would not say that the Almighty damns
> the greater part of his creatures. So far I agree with you—that
> which they *should* preach (them there practical truths you
> elude to) is worthy of all love and veneration,—but since as a

body they have ever given the lie to such preaching by their dogmas and lives—cui bono the preaching? Whereby— though I sincerely like and respect many individually, I object to the whole biling.[26]

Lear favoured 'simple word reading'[27] over religious ceremony, and his distaste for aspects of ritual response extended to the rhythms as well as the words that were used. Visiting the home of the Blencowes family, he recorded with horror 'O! those prayers! The little disjointed sentences— uprisings & c!'[28] At a visceral level, his teeth were set on edge by certain forms of religious observance as well as certain topics, such as Lot's wife, whose recurrence in sermons he totted up, like a disgruntled diner noting the wearying reappearance of a hated dish.[29] It is intriguing to think of how Lear's mental and physical reactions to rhythm in language may have been shaped by his resistance to certain kinds of ritual responses. In a diary entry he talks not only of a 'hideously long sermon' but also of visits to church as 'those disgusting functions', remarking, 'such compulsion is enough to make a man turn Mahametan; which I gladly would do, were it not for being circumcised'.[30] Lear's thoughts drift towards his private parts as, with sharp humour, he considers the relative misery of enduring church versus the pain of losing one's foreskin. It is an extraordinary comparison: Lear's hatred of 'compulsion' has a deep physical and emotional basis. 'Those disgusting functions' would, in somebody else's sentence, refer to urination and defecation; it is telling that, for Lear, church rituals (functions) evoke a similarly strong physical repugnance. Lear's 'disgust' with aspects of church doctrine and practice was influenced by the heated context of nineteenth-century theological debate—with which, as we shall see, he was fiercely engaged. But it was also a matter of early training and habits that made 'kneeling, responses etc' abhorrent.[31] As he put it to Emily Tennyson, Protestantism to him meant 'daring to think'.[32] He took this obligation seriously.

Dissenters typically chose to educate their children using texts reflective of their distinct views. A comment that Lear made in 1859 about a Quaker autobiography, *The Life of Mary Anne Schimmelpenninck,* is important for what it hints about his dissenting upbringing. He notes that the book 'has many curious anecdotes of the people of the end of the last century, & to me is peculiarly amusing, as bringing back much of my early life'.[33] Schimmelpenninck's memoir gives a very detailed account of her childhood that combines nostalgia with anger. Like Lear she suffered from asthma and had 'a deep melancholic tinge' in her character, and like Lear she suffered from her mother's withdrawal, in her case due to her mother's illness.

Like many dissenters, Schimmelpenninck learned natural history as the touchstone of her engagement with God's creation. Her father, who was a member of the Lunar Society, a group of experimental scientists and thinkers, liked to instruct her in 'the rudiments of science', and 'it was my delight to hear my father explain the Linnean Orders; and to have him show me the teeth and claws of my various pets, classifying them'.[34] She studied anatomy, conchology and botany. Her father had a scientific room for experiments; family tradition asserts that this was also true of Lear's father, who had a 'work shop with a forge' at the top of the house and spent Sundays in there from four a.m.[35] Such Sunday experiments would have been a significant departure from the habits of most nineteenth-century families. Schimmelpenninck's reading, which is typical of that in dissenting households, included Thomas Day's *Sandford and Merton*, Arnaud Berquin's *L'Ami des Enfants* and Anna Letitia Barbauld's popular *Hymns in Prose for Children;* Barbauld particularly encourages the child to appreciate God's grace through close observation of the wonders of nature: flowers, birds and animals.[36] There is strong evidence that Lear also read Berquin and Barbauld as a child. In a letter to Ann, he refers to Stoke Newington (then a village north of London) as 'respectable' and 'Barbauldy'; Barbauld lived at Stoke Newington and was buried there, a fact Lear evidently knew.[37] He also read Bunyan and Milton—'types of ancient goodness'—which gave him a strong background in seventeenth-century Protestant dissent.

If this was his upbringing, it is little wonder that Lear's education began with meticulous study of birds, animals and plants and accurate depiction of their beauty. Later in the nineteenth century Beatrix Potter, whose family were Unitarians, would similarly study natural history in scientific detail, a habit that laid the foundation for her illustrated tales of Peter Rabbit, Tom Kitten and the Two Bad Mice. Both Lear and Potter use animal characters to explore the naturally rebellious inclinations of children, with a sympathetic eye. Dissenting education tended to foster interest in science and the child's independent questioning and discovery of answers to life's mysteries through observation, controlled experiment and dialogue. Schimmelpenninck writes that her Sundays were spent in going over a text from the

Sermon on the Mount, one of the commandments or one of Joseph Priestley's questions from the scripture catechism. Similarly, we know that Lear's sister Ann trained him to learn a biblical text each Sunday, a practice he was still alluding to aged nineteen. Like many dissenters, Lear was not 'sabbatical': he felt free to write letters, sketch, work on book projects or go for walks on a Sunday, and often skipped church attendance when he felt under no social obligation to go. In a telling diary entry of September 1861, he bursts out:

> Pouring rain . . . Sleep and deadly AngloSunday Godhating
> idolatrous puritan Pharisee silence and sermonreading . . .
> I weary of English Sundays, & must break off from lying
> conventionality.[38]

Anglo-Saxon is a loaded term in Lear's writing: it distances him from aspects of English culture and climate that he dislikes.[39] Here, the nonsense word 'AngloSunday' combines the idea of Anglicanism with something more tribal. In the blast of words that follows, puritanism is associated with the Pharisees, idolatry and Godhating, implying that those whose worship involves socially policed self-denial are setting up a false god and rejecting the true and loving one.

Lear's conception of faith is essentially private in its relationship with God and public in its good works. Lear regarded Schimmelpenninck's Quakerism as 'splombonglified religion', but he observes that she is 'as broad a Xtian' as such a narrow sect could produce.[40] Still, his description of her account as 'bringing back much of my early life' suggests that the educational methods employed in her family bore similarities to his own childhood experience. His upbringing, in turn, would help to explain why Lear's approach to writing for children was so interactive, and so invested in 'entering into the child's mind', fostering individual agency and thought rather than praising obedience and passive learning. Lear's work is very different from that of William Blake or Anna Letitia Barbauld, but they have in common a refusal to believe in original sin, and a commitment to the child's pleasure as good in itself; childhood is a state to be relished and cherished rather than reformed.

While they clearly shared a dissenting education, Lear differs wholly from his siblings in his use of biblical allusion and religious language. The extant letters of his sisters Ann, Ellen, Sarah and Mary are steeped in religious discourse. Ann, who was in the habit of distributing tracts, writes to her sister-in-law Fanny:

> I often think of you dear—and go back to days *long past now* when you first began to seek Him who is the "Way, the Truth, & the Life"—and I've rejoiced often to hear that you have been *pressing on in your pilgrimage*. . . . I hope dear Rosa, is also in the narrow path . . . the younger branches, I hope will think of this sweet promise. . . . 'I love them that love me, and they that *seek me early,* shall find me'.[41]

Mary, writing to her brother Fred, exclaims, 'O dear Fred . . . my heart *longs* to hear that *you* have secured the everlasting Inheritance. Your outward condition may be trying—but the *precious Soul*—Oh . . . Do not let care engross your every faculty—Give yourself up to Christ. . . .'[42] Lear, by contrast, is allergic to evangelical discourse. He almost never quotes the Bible directly. When he does mention it, the words are often transported into a nonsensical form. For example, in August 1877 he revises a phrase from Psalm 102, 'like a pelican in the wilderness', to announce that he is 'like a sparry in the pilderpips and a pemmican on the Housetops'. Pemmican is canned meat—an early form of Spam. Biblical phrases, in Lear's vocabulary, are not preserved from absurdity; rather they threaten to become absurd preserves. In a letter of July 1879, bugs infest the Sermon on the Mount: 'sufficient unto the day is the weevil thereof'.[43] When Lear announces that he has a 'horror of great darkness', he is alluding to the British climate. Lear's occasional and very free use of biblical language is a marker of his determination to self-edit a text that, in his view, contains much error and superstition as well as truth. It is striking how often Lear uses the words *nonsense, absurd* and *bosh* pejoratively to describe religious pronouncements and practices with which he disagrees. If some of the authorised Bible is nonsensical—beastly, brutal, burlesque Bosh, as Lear asserted to Chichester Fortescue in 1864—then Lear's nonsense can form a benevolent, inclusive alternative to its cruelty and exclusions.[44]

He loved his sisters, but he did not share their religious outlook. He refers to Eleanor as having 'narrow Calvinistic theories'.[45] Lear believed that religious observance was relatively unimportant, that leading a good life was all, a position Eleanor strongly rejected. A rare, brief and testy letter to his brother Frederick reveals the surprising fact that even with his beloved Ann, Lear avoided discussing religion in order to avoid mutual offence:

> It has long been a rule with me not to discuss subjects con-
> nected with religion, either by writing or speaking: and this
> rule, during the many years I lived with my dear sister Ann,
> we both of us adhered to, nor ever broke through it.[46]

Lear is fibbing shamelessly here; he routinely discussed religion with like-minded friends. But the dramatic turn of phrase 'nor ever broke through it' suggests that when he lived with Ann this house rule served as a supporting wall that kept the roof from falling in. Ann was Lear's moral fulcrum. She taught him to 'Put yourself in other people's places',[47] and Lear describes her as 'the harbour of my salvation',[48] using a phrase applied to God himself in the *Philokalia*, a religious text supposedly compiled by St Nikodemus and St Makarios: 'I take refuge in Thee, the harbour of my salvation. For I know by Thy grace that "Thou art my God"'.[49] (This compliment is typical of the way that personal fidelity and textual infidelity often consort in Lear's writing.) Yet intellectually he differed from his sister. When Lear was re-reading the Comte de Volney—who argued that in a tolerant world society, all religions would eventually be subsumed into one—he kept the book from Ann, knowing she would disapprove.[50]

It is important to recognise that Lear was not only born into a dissenting family but actively developed his own individual mode of nonconformity: one that rebelled from his evangelical upbringing. He was not a chapel-goer. Yet, when he did attend Anglican services, he refused communion, would not repeat the creed and often denounced sermons as 'blasphemous', 'hideous' and 'absurd'. In 1863, he confided to Chichester Fortescue that he had been reading Ernest Renan's recently published *La vie de Jésus*, a heterodox account of Christ's life as purely human that rejected accounts of his miracles. Lear reported that 'the people of the lodgings have nevertheless conceived a favourable idea of my piety by seeing [Renan's book] on my table . . . little conceiving the opposition of that volume to their views & their topics of faith'.[51] Lear delights in appearing to conform while quietly rejecting orthodoxy. His self-invention in this respect, as in many others, involves refusal to worship 'the greatest of all English gods, conventionality'.[52]

Nonsense and Religious Language

From the first, Lear's antipathy to clerical authority affects his nonsense. For example, at some point before 1835 he wrote a new verse to Jacob Beuler's comic song 'The Nervous Family' on the topic of churchgoing, a subject never broached in the seven-verse original.

> We're too nervous to get ready in time to go to church,
> So we never go at all, since we once went late one day;
> For the Clergyman looked *at* us, with a dreadful sort of frown,
> And my poor shaky Mother caught his eye and tumbled down;—
> And my Aunt and Sister fainted,—and tho' with care and pain
> We dragged them slowly out,—yet we've never been again . . . [53]

This comic scenario imagines the power of the clergyman as akin to that of the Old Testament God: his wrathful judgement brings the three female sinners low. But the matter of timekeeping is too trivial to make such drama reasonable. Overkill is implied that touches not only the clergy but, perhaps, Old Testament judgement itself. And the reaction that Lear imagines, of *never* going to church again, turns anxiety into something that looks suspiciously like resistance. He did, indeed, often avoid going to church, 'for church is simply intolerable, if there is no absolute duty to oblige one to do so'.[54]

Lear's unconventional view of the Bible also affects his visual imagery. Around 1828, Lear designed a frontispiece for the book *Sketches of Animals in the London Zoological Gardens*. He drew 'The Peaceable Kingdom', with carnivores and herbivores lying down amicably together. The tableau echoes Isaiah 11:6–8, a passage that had inspired the American artist Edward Hicks, who was a Quaker, to produce a series of Peaceable Kingdom paintings that Lear may have known. Biblically faithful renderings of the subject depict the lion and the lamb; some also include the ox, the wolf, the leopard and the bear. Lear changes this formula. In his picture, the lion is lying down with the *llama*. A couple of smiling spotted hyaenas hint at laughter, while an owl and a couple of ostriches hover in the background. The pun on *lamb/llama* is typical of how Lear enjoys unorthodox pairings, riffing on religious language in a way that refuses to grant it immunity from fresh interpretation. We might think of many of the pairings in Lear's later nonsense, such as the Owl and the Pussy-cat, as comic versions of the

Fig. 2.1 **Illustration for** *Sketches of Animals in the Zoological Gardens* (c. 1829)

peaceable kingdom in which unlike creatures can put aside their differences and love one another. In one of his early nonsense poems, 'Mitres & beams, / Thimbles & Creams' and 'Tea Urns & Pews, / Muscles & Jews'[55] form free-associating partnerships. The 'Muscles' in the picture are shellfish, which appear in a V-shaped composition with the urns, pews and Jews, menaced by a large cat. This picture poem, with its 'two by two' couplets and corresponding images (two mitres, two beams, two thimbles and two creams) explores multiple ways in which things can be unlike and yet similar: visual symmetry, rhyme, pun. One might logically associate a mitre (a wooden joint) with a beam, but the mitres Lear illustrates are bishops' mitres. Similarly, one might associate burial urns with pews, but tea urns and pews, Jews and mussels (which observant Jews are obliged not to eat) don't go together, except in the dreamlike dating-service of nonsense, which delights in the 'impertinent', daring us to perceive relationships between categories and sects seemingly defined by their differences.

As Ina Rae Hark has observed, the illustration of the Jews in this poem is crude and reflects the ubiquity of anti-Semitic caricature in the early nineteenth century. It depicts men with hooked noses wearing several hats atop one another; Jews were associated with 'old clo' dealing' in London.[56] However, Lear's understanding of Jewish faith and his appreciation of Jewish culture grew enormously over his lifetime, as he became extremely close to families like that of the pioneering politician Sir Francis Goldsmid and his wife, the vocal feminist Lady Louisa Goldsmid, whose intellectuality he appreciated and whose kindness he extolled. Lear read the *Jewish Chronicle,* of which the Goldsmids were active sponsors;[57] he admired Agnes Zimmermann, Julia Phillipsohn, the Warburg family (who translated Tennyson into German) and other talented intellectuals and artists in this circle.[58] Lear often expressed the opinion that Jews behave less divisively towards their fellows and more morally towards others, thus imitating more closely the spirit of Christ's life and teaching, than Anglicans do. In Lear's view it is following Christ's example rather than the Christian faith that makes one a Christian; he relished the paradox that non-Christians were frequently more Christian than Christians. He was appalled by acquaintances who argued that the Jews should convert to Christianity. He told Chichester Fortescue in 1858 that Jerusalem was a 'mass of squabblepoison' and that the idea of a society to convert Jews there was 'fully as absurd' as one to 'convert all the cabbages & strawberries in Covent garden into pigeon-pies & Turkey carpets'.[59] The colourfully genus-bending metamorphoses in this nonsense are a fitting rebuke to the preposterous conversions proposed by bigots.

In Lear's writing, nonsense is always lurking, like a smile or a snort, at the corners of the mouth of religious language. He told Amelia Edwards, 'a friend of mine in India, gave a Hindoo—studying English—the 100 Penitentiary Psalms to copy as a punishment, which the youth did, but headed his paper thus . . . "The 10penny Ten Sherry Sarms"'.[60] In this joke, repetition that is intended as morally improving is reformed into riposte. Caveat Redemptor. Lear's awareness of how the word of the Bible is constantly susceptible to falling into nonsense reveals his liberal approach to textual authority and form in general. He delights in the way that the unstable and disruptive qualities of language foreground the necessity of reading and interpreting for oneself. He frequently notes in his diary examples of children responding to religious questions posed by authority figures with answers that are delightfully incorrect. The Inspector of Schools asks, 'What is the pestilence that walketh in darkness?' and a boy answers, 'a flea'.[61] Lear's humour sides with the child who won't be catechised, whose answer is simultaneously reasonable and insubordinate.

Lear loves to record and to relate occasions when religious language has slipped into secularity. In 1859 he shared a joke with the organist Edward

Rimbault about 'instances of bad singing', when spiritual airs had been truncated such that they seemed to refer to physical desires:

O my poor Poll————————(uted soul)
Jesus & Sal————————(vation)
I want a man————————(sion in the skies)[62]

On an earlier occasion, he related gleefully to Fortescue how the poor articulation of a tipsy church clerk had turned the reading of Psalms into nonsense. Instead of 'white as snow in Salmon', the clerk had enounced, 'white as an old salmon'; 'alien to my mother's children' had become 'a lion to my mother's children'; 'they are not guiltless' had turned into 'they are not guinea pigs'.[63] It is noticeable here that animals unexpectedly pop up in church, undermining the dignity of scripture. The metamorphoses of words becomes a vehicle for another kind of metamorphosis, in which the animal body—subordinated or repudiated in the original text—asserts its lively presence. Animals tend to remind humans, in Lear's imaginative universe, of their active physicality and their shared appetite for pleasure. Words and animals have much in common: they resist confinement, breaking into frolics that defy all attempts at constraint. They constantly speak (or squeak or shriek) of repressed energies. When the lion and guinea pigs burst out of the Bible, they give voice to a playfulness temporarily silenced but ready to roar in a congregation obliged to listen dutifully to sermons and prayers. Guinea pigs will reappear in Lear's nonsense, in his story 'The History of the Seven Families of the Lake Pipple-Popple' (1865), where they become hypnotised by a gigantic lettuce. Its permissive attractions ('Let us, O Lettuce!') prove immediately and comically fatal. Their fall combines elements of the biblical story of Eve and of Homer's lotus eaters within a sequence of filial disobedience leading to untimely death (sixty-three fatalities in twenty pages) that must have made young readers squeal with laughter.

When writing 'The Seven Families', Lear may well have been thinking of works like Darton's *Moral and Entertaining Fables* (1806), in which a fly disobeys its mother and hovers above a boiling cauldron before dying horribly (in an unintentionally comic fashion), admitting as it expires, 'How wretched is the child who disregards the admonition of its parent, and prefers its own wisdom to maternal experience'.[64] Lear's animal children perish with a perverse persistence that turns repetition into farce.

Mindless reiteration is one means by which language deliquesces into nonsense, discovering absurdity within itself. For Lear, this kind of repetition is inherent in 'parrotprayers'[65] and prescribed responses. Having grown up with a model of worship in which sermons and prayers were brief and improvised, he appreciated jokes like the following, which he heard from Mr Hayward and recorded in his diary:

> What is Liturgy? A sleepy disease
> What is Lethargy————————a religious observance[66]

Wordplay can be a wake-up call—the transposing mindset that exposes the lethargy of mouthing formulae without questioning them. For Lear, who was naturally restless and required constant activity to keep both physical and mental illness at bay, morality lies not in the repeated forms of conventional worship but in active self-improvement and practical aid to those in need.

Lear's attitude to language was vitally shaped by his belief in the openness to interpretation of all texts, of which the Bible is the prime example. A telling argument he had in July 1859 with Richard Bethell, the lord chancellor, began with Lear defending Tennyson's poem 'The Two Voices'. Lear disputed Bethell's assertion that 'all fine poetry could never be understood or interpreted but in one way':

> On my [mentioning] the Psalms—he and lady B grew very
> angry—& declared the Gospels were the finest etc etc on Lord
> B going he became vastly angry and blew me up—'Lear if you
> grow so testy—no one will converse with you Lear! . . . You
> are quite a breed' on which he was perfectly right—only in the
> argument he was perfectly wrong.[67]

This dispute relates religious doubt to textual ambiguity. Tennyson's poem 'The Two Voices' is about religious doubt: one inner voice advocates despair and suicide, the other counsels endurance and hope. Lear defends the expression of such doubt, and extrapolates ideas of interpretability from Tennyson to the Psalms. Bethell finds this approach to the New Testament unacceptably irreverent. Lear accepts criticism of his behaviour but stands his argumentative ground. Given the formidable intellectual powers of the lord chancellor, who seeks to isolate Lear with an insult that glances at

Lear's humbler birth and existential oddity ('You are quite a breed'), this exchange imparts a sense of Lear's chutzpah. His determination to defend the intertwined nature of literary and religious doubt, rooted in textual ambiguity, is very striking. The lord chancellor, as befits his role, defends authoritative judgement. Lear seems to insist that the Bible is not exempt from ambiguity, that acknowledging poetic language as debatable territory does not undermine its 'fineness' but may indeed pay tribute to it. Lear's investment in the multiple ambiguities of nonsense is a product of this mindset. The nonsense word is, from this perspective, not a special case but a type—an emblem of the joyfully polysemous nature of signification and of the power thereby devolved to each individual reader. We glimpse here the resistance to authority involved in Lear's dissenting position as a reader as well as a writer.

Lear's resistance to authority is visible everywhere in his writing. In particular, it is evident in 'The Two Old Bachelors', a nonsense poem or song that Lear privately called 'Sage and Onions'. In it, two old men with an empty larder go to seek nourishment from an 'earnest' and 'ancient' Sage, who lives amongst 'purpledicular crags'. They want, in fact, to turn the Sage directly into stuffing, making of him a very practical form of content. But the Sage proves to be large, bearded and indigestible—certainly unwilling to transmute his word into flesh. He gives them nothing. Instead he 'takes certain aim' at their heads with his 'awful book', and the bachelors roll down the hill, browbeaten and hungry, emigrating forever from the text.[68] The poem gently guys the philosophical and poetic quest for higher wisdom that animates much ponderous verse of the early nineteenth century and the identification of the poet as mystic.[69] But there is also something about the outsize authority figure on top of a mountain, deploying an awful book with a 'perplexing page' as a weapon, that speaks of Lear's distaste for a punitive Old Testament vision of God.

REFUSING TO PREACH: THE BOOK OF NONSENSE

Lear's *A Book of Nonsense* (1846) is delightful and groundbreaking for many reasons, but the most obvious to a Victorian child must have been the fact that it eschews didacticism. It is difficult to convey how unusual this made it in a period when literature for children was almost inevitably associated with learning, and usually with moral sentiment. James Orchard Halliwell complained in 1849 that children's books were dominated by 'the present

cold, unimaginative,—I had almost said, unnatural,—prosaic good-boy stories'.[70] Lady Eastlake, in an 1844 survey of 'Children's Books', which she
considered to be already an 'overstocked' department of literature, remarked
that 'the one broad and general impression left with us is that of the excessive ardour for *teaching* which prevails throughout'.[71] William Lisle Bowles's
*The Little Villager's Verse Book; Consisting of Short Verses for Children to Learn
by Heart* (1837) was typical of early nineteenth-century poetry books for
children in using insects to inculcate the lessons of industry and contentment: the busy bee scorns the idle butterfly. In 'The Path of Life' the child
is encouraged to learn and repeat the lines:

> Oh, Lord,—in sickness and in health,
> To every lot resigned—
> Grant me before all worldly wealth,
> A meek and thankful mind.[72]

To a modern reader, it is striking how often in these books such lessons are
extended not only to children but also to the labouring class. Another poem
in the same collection, 'Old Labourer', inculcates the virtues of gratitude,
humility and 'murmuring not' at one's honest toil. Books of grammar, punctuation and elocution also associated reading with the learning of moderation
and self-control: *Punctuation Personified* was, suggestively, taught by a
character called Mr Stops. Sara Coleridge's *Pretty Lessons in Verse, for Good
Children* (1845) tells the story of 'The Boy That Would Rather Be Naughty
than Good', who prefers to walk in a wood rather than say his lesson. He
reforms, abandoning 'ridiculous raving and rant,/ I will and I won't and I
shall and I shan't'.[73] It is as if the forbidden 'wood' represents the child's
indulgence of self-will (what he 'would'). He must learn to retrain and re-
strain his will, to absorb the lesson of social duty and compliance.

Against this background, Lear's headstrong and wayward characters who
will and won't and shall and shan't, leap off the page like genies escaping
from a bottle. Everywhere, it seems, from Quebec to Tartary, Melrose to
Moldavia, the world is full of people whose feelings and behaviour are so
strange and excessive that they can't be contained. The fact that some are
'young persons' who ought to submit to discipline but the majority are 'old
persons' who ought to set an example makes their perversity all the more
delightful. The man of Bangor has a face distorted with anger; the lady of
Russia's screams are so extreme that no one can hush her. Whether they

are standing on one leg reading Homer, dancing jigs while eating figs or committing suicide by jumping into the river, these persons are the largest figures in their own dramas, the most spectacular ids on the block. Embodying the unruliness and compulsiveness of desire, they take the very notion of the exemplary (the figure who represents a place) and turn it into a blackly comic celebration of oddity, where normality has no place at all.

Most books for children in the early years of the nineteenth century were small, and many were tiny; illustrations, being expensive, were usually rationed and often rudimentary. The freedom and largesse of Lear's *Book of Nonsense* lie therefore not only in the rhymes but in the layout. The original book was not a miniature duodecimo but an oblong octavo (215mm long by 145mm tall) in two volumes. Since Lear, like Blake, designed, drew and 'arranged' both drawings and text, he was able to control the relationship between them. Each limerick has a double-page spread to itself, and the large, active pictures with their bold and free use of line dominate the text rather than remaining subservient to it: bodies throw their limbs out left and right, jumping stiles, swallowing rabbits, walking on tiptoe and even splitting in two. Bodies, indeed, are front and centre of each story: a celebration of physical energy in characters immune to corporeal shame. Lear's first limericks had been created as comic performances in real time. The *Book of Nonsense* retains that sense of surprise. The form of the limerick is like a box. It may be arranged over three lines (as in the first edition of *A Book of Nonsense*) or four lines (as in *More Nonsense*) or five lines, but the repeated pattern has symmetry.[74] Out of that box jumps a theatrical succession of new and outrageous acts. There is pleasure in the contrast between the predictability of the form and the capriciousness of the contents.

Early twentieth-century critics, such as Aldous Huxley and George Orwell, were inclined to read Lear's limericks as an allegory of conflict between the individual and society.[75] 'They' (the crowd) in the interwar years took on the sinister guise of willing executioners, 'sober citizens in bowler hats'[76] of the kind who smashed the noncompliant. This is a powerful reading, darkened by its historical moment. It is, however, perhaps equally important to note that Lear's limericks refuse spiritual ends or moral consequences. The *Book of Nonsense*, unlike, say, the book of Job, makes no claim to admonition. On the contrary, it suggests that more often than not people do what they want and that those desires constitute a litany of perversity. These are nonconformist narratives that revel in difference, eccentricity and disregard for prevailing hierarchies. The 'provoking' Young Lady of Parma, whose conduct grew calmer and calmer, responds with 'Hum' when people ask if she's dumb. The lady of Peru bakes her husband in the oven, in a 'mistake' that the smiling illustration reveals as outrageously intentional.

Lear's religious mores were founded on ideas of tolerance towards all his 'fellow humanbeans' (*beans* suggests the fundamental similarity of all people, like peas in a pod). He could, however, as he recognised, also be 'intolerant'; ironically, the forms of strict Anglican worship were among those things most likely to make him aggressive and intemperate. Lear's limericks allow the reader to experience both tolerance and intolerance. We take the side of the willful and the weird, discovering in them a wild individualism that animates us all; but we can also laugh and gasp at their absurd antics, relishing the physical discomforts that often attend their actions.[77] In this respect the limerick is rather like the pun, which Victorians (including Lear) enjoyed precisely because it acted out a dialogue between pleasure and 'badness', the 'letting' of a double meaning (like a fart) that could be acknowledged as both socially inappropriate and riotously funny. In one limerick a censorious beadle or church officer puts the 'bad old man' of Cheadle in the stocks; in another, a beadle/beetle has run up the neck of the old man of Quebec, who declares that he will slay him with a needle. If the beadle is the social conscience who polices our behaviour, then he is sometimes on the front foot but mostly on the back foot. See him run.

Lear did not invent the limerick. He copied the form from a couple of small books for children that were popular in the 1820s, *The History of Sixteen Wonderful Old Women* (1820), and *Anecdotes and Adventures of Fifteen Gentlemen* (1821). Some other limerick books published in the 1820s maintain a didactic element; *A Peep at the Geography of Europe* (circa 1824) highlights the capital cities mentioned in each limerick so that children can learn them. Lear's limericks do not. The *Spectator* wryly drew attention to this feature by imagining a 'mock-examination' on Lear's limericks in which candidates were asked, among other questions, 'What do you gather from a study of Mr. Lear's works to have been the prevalent characteristics of the inhabitants of Gretna, Prague, Thermopylae, Wick, and Hong Kong?'[78] Its playful eight-question anticatechism suggests how much adults, as well as children, enjoyed the limericks' resistance to the idea of forcing the reader to learn facts.

It is interesting to compare Lear's limericks with other contemporary examples of the form: his exhibit a freedom, both in their illustrations and in their outlook, that is nimbler and more buoyant. Lear drew his 'nonsenses' remarkably fast. Although he returned to them and perfected his books with a critical eye for detail, the confident speed of his line is part of the animated impulsiveness that makes his cartoons so successful. Among the collections that Lear learned from, several limericks do make a moral or social judgement on their eccentric protagonists. In *The History of Sixteen Wonderful Old Women,* the women are implicitly criticised for being stingy, cross-tempered and vain. The Old Woman of Croydon 'to look young . . . affected the Hoyden / And would jump and would skip, / Till she put out her hip; / Alas poor Old Woman of Croydon'.[79] Another limerick in the same volume sneers at an 'Old Woman at Lynn, / Whose Nose very near touch'd her chin', cattily suggesting 'You may easy suppose, / She had plenty of Beaux; / This charming Old Woman of Lynn'. In a third limerick, a loquacious 'Woman at Glos'ter' pays two guineas for a parrot, 'but his tongue never ceasing, / Was vastly displeasing, / To the talkative Woman of Glos'ter'. The garrulous parrot—imitating her as parrots do—serves her right.[80] The volume closes with the improving moral example of an 'Old Woman at Leeds / Who spent all her time in good deeds, / She work'd for the Poor / Till her fingers were sore; / This pious Old Woman of Leeds'.[81]

By contrast, Lear's limericks, promiscuously mixing young and old persons of both sexes, present characters neither as commendable nor as cautionary. His young lady 'whose nose was so long that it reached to her toes' simply hires an old lady to carry it for her. The resourceful young lady 'whose chin resembled the point of a pin' has it sharpened, purchases a harp, and plays tunes with it. These wacky characters allow us to imagine what it might be like to live if one were, even momentarily, oblivious to social judgement; it is no accident that many of them consort with animals and birds, whom they come to resemble. Lear borrows from *The History of Sixteen Wonderful Old Women* the theme of 'an old lady of Leeds, / Who was always a' doing good deeds', but Lear's old lady 'sate on some rocks with her feet in a box, / And her neck was surrounded by beads'.[82] This comes close to parody. The do-gooder, perhaps wearing her rosary as a necklace, turns out to be just as odd, confined and antisocial in her private life as everyone else. In a later version, Lear has the lady of Leeds sit on a stool and eat gooseberry fool. Such antics must have been even more amusing and surprising to the original readers of his nonsense books—like the three young men Lear encountered at the offices of Bush, his publisher-bookseller, who were reading the limericks and falling about with laughter.[83] Among the energetic nonconformists Lear added to the 1861

16

OLD WOMAN OF LEEDS.

There was an Old Woman at Leeds,
Who spent all her time in good deeds,
She work'd for the Poor,
Till her fingers were sore;
This pious Old Woman of Leeds.

Fig. 2.2a **(left) Old
Woman of Leeds,** *The
History of Sixteen Wonderful
Old Women*

Fig. 2.2b **(below) Lear's
Old Person of Leeds**

There was an Old Person of Leeds, whose head was infested with beads;
She sat on a stool and ate gooseberry-fool,
Which agreed with that Person of Leeds.

edition of his *Book of Nonsense* is the 'Old Man in a pew',[84] who tears his waistcoat in pieces to give to his nieces. Whether the pew is in a church or not, the Old Man's free-spirited behaviour rides a nice line between the kind of generosity that echoes Christian values (for example, St Martin giving his cloak to a beggar) and a tendency to violence and public undress that might be regarded as profane. Here is the benevolence that characterises so much of Lear's poetry, yet here also is a tendency to acts of sudden destruction that is equally characteristic. An impulsive and potentially antisocial vehemence is the flip side of tolerance, and it often strikes Lear amongst the crowds and compulsions of church. It gives his work edge. Such undress will recur, in a more radical form, in his poem 'The New Vestments'.

EDWARD LEAR AND THEOLOGICAL DEBATE: RATIONALIST AND REFUSENIK

The time and energy Lear applied to considering theological and moral discussion throughout his life, but particularly from middle age onwards, belies what he sometimes modestly referred to as 'my small brain'. He was a shrewd, active and broad reader, attracted by ideas; by intellectual range, 'cleverness' and 'information' in those he met; and by religious debate. Lear launched into the latter whenever the social water was safe, as it was with his close friend Chichester Fortescue, whose mind was, in Fortescue's own words, 'highly or deeply unorthodox'.[85] In a letter to Fortescue from 1857, Lear reported that he had arrived safely in Dublin but had passed an uncomfortable ride in the railway compartment thither with a very fat woman: 'just exactly like a picture of Jonah's whale I used to see when a child in a picture bible. I was horribly afraid she would eat me up & sat expecting an attack constantly till the arrival of the train relieved me from apprehension'.[86]

Such naughtiness is typical of Lear on two counts. It allows him to enjoy the comedy of the large female swallowing the smaller male (in a way that might remind us of sex in the animal world), and it transposes biblical myth to a modern context that highlights its absurdity. Lear often jokes about the 'big fish as swallowed Jonah', among other Old Testament 'legends' that he considered foolish subjects for modern representation. In January 1865, he wrote to his friend the Pre-Raphaelite artist William Holman Hunt that he had heard a rumour that Hunt was going to paint 'Dannel in the lion's den'.

Lear jeers that 'popular delight' would be assured if one could create a painting featuring 'Balaam's ass seen thro' a window——Jonah's whale on a distant shore—Elijahs ravens—& the Gadarene piggywiggies . . .'[87] His imaginary cavalcade of biblical animals hints, not very tactfully, that these topics are calculated to please a public whose taste for the full menagerie of Old Testament myth is childish. Hunt should instead aim for a 'truer and broader caste of poetry'. Lear's use of the word *caste* in this context is telling.[88] For Lear, the notion of 'broad' views relates not only to religious sect, but to a form of ideological inclusiveness that is also artistic.

Lear could, like Holman Hunt, have catered profitably as a visual artist to the Victorian public's sweet tooth for religious subjects. His journeys of 1858 and 1867 to Palestine furnished him with ample scenery for landscape paintings on biblical themes, and he did sell views of Jerusalem, the Mount of Olives and Bethlehem. But Lear actively chose to veer away from bib-lical quotation in titling his artwork. He joked (typically) to Emily Tennyson in May 1865 that the public couldn't tell the difference anyway. He over-heard two gallery visitors discussing a Palestine drawing to which he'd given as a title a line from Tennyson: 'I will see before I die / The Palms and temples of the south'. The visitors disputed about the 'Motto . . . as to whether it was in *Jonah*, or Jeremiah!'[89] When Louisa, Lady Ashburton bought Lear's major oil painting *The Cedars of Lebanon*, she had the sentence 'The Lord Brea-keth the Cedars of Lebanon' inscribed on the frame. Lear requested that it be removed.[90] His stated reason was that the inscription was 'so injudiciously divided as to be a mistake'. But we can, I think, infer from Lear's habits in naming his pictures that he found the application of this single biblical line invoking the power of divine anger injudiciously divisive in other ways, lim-iting the painting's allusive field and (perhaps) suggesting its own vulnera-bility to attack: it had not been critically acclaimed as Lear had hoped.

Lear's deep-rooted nonconformity affected his artistic choices in ways that are not always obvious to a modern viewer. For example when drawing picture alphabets, which Lear did regularly to give as gifts to friends' children, he chose subjects that were commonly also represented in scrip-ture alphabets of the period: the ass, the whale, King Xerxes. But Lear's alphabets, like his nonsense books, refuse to point a moral. One popular book, *The Child's Alphabet Emblematically Described and Embellished by Twenty-Four Pictures*, illustrates *W* with the text 'In the Whale's belly Jonah lay / Three whole nights and days. / Whales in the sea / God's voice obey'. For *X* it has 'Xerxes the Great did die / And so must you and I. / Death and his

Dart/Strikes the youngest heart'.[91] The smiling, roly-poly whale in Lear's alphabet, by contrast, obeys nothing but his own whim: 'W was a whale/With a dreadful long tail/Who rushed all so frantic/Across the Atlantic . . . Roll about Whale!' *X* for Xerxes is also, rather than an emblem of mortality, a loud and lively figure of incontinent human desire: 'X was King Xerxes/Who more than all Turks is/renowned for his fashion/Of screaming with passion . . . Shocking old Xerxes!'[92] The message is not one of submission to God's word and its power to define and control, but of enjoying language as something in motion, emphatically present and active, validating the child's own willful exuberance.

Lear found many Old Testament subjects ridiculous and distasteful. In March 1862 he noted, 'Clark preached from those dreadful old bores Jacob and Esau'.[93] The previous Sunday, he sighed, 'Craven preached on Lot's wife. Lord! How one remembers the Arabs' comments on that Lady—at the wery spot of her extinction! It is really wonderful—the inert absurdity of these poor priests. Yet they "know no better"'.[94] Absurd priests are 'inert': their mindset does not move to embrace a modern understanding of the Old Testament as myth rather than literal truth. Lear reacted derisively to allusions to patriarchs living for multiple centuries, to 'the hill of 4skins' and to 'an ass like sermon of Herodias & Salome, & fornication generally'.[95] The latter comment implies that he objected not only to the topic but to violent rebuke for sexual sin. Lear rejected spiritual chastisement. In 1860, he seethed that a 'tiresome Mr Burgon' had preached for forty-two minutes 'all about the Debble': 'this enthusiast warping always on positive spiritualities—Eve & what not, & the serpent—and much artistic phrase—sketch, draw, paint, picture—outline—& "that accursed Artist, Satan!"'[96] Byron or Burns might have embraced the comparison between the artist and Satan. Lear, however, is disgusted by warped language that links art to artfulness and hence to sin. His preference is always for the clemency of the New Testament, which as an adult he made time to study in the original Greek. When Lear praises a sermon, it is typically brief (twenty minutes or less) and almost always on a New Testament text, such as Romans 12, which exhorts us to 'be kindly affectioned to one another with brotherly love . . . Bless them which persecute you: bless, and curse not'.[97] It is notable that when, late in life, Lear decided to undertake the education of his servant Giorgio's youngest son, Dimitri, he gave him the Lord's Prayer, parables including that of the prodigal son and the good Samaritan, passages from the Sermon on the Mount and Psalm 103. The Beatitudes recur. Probably these texts had also been central to his own education. There is a clear pattern here: Lear favours texts that are about forgiveness, compassion and blessing.

He rejoiced heartily when there was no sermon whatever and at San Remo often quietly left church before the sermon was delivered. He always timed sermons to the minute and almost always commented on them (usually negatively) in his diary; these habits mark both his active intellectual engagement with religious discourse and his impatience with it. He did not like to be preached to: 'sermons bore me horribly'. Nor did he take communion. For a brief period the Reverend Fenton's San Remo church experimented with a choral service, replacing the sermon and liturgy. Lear enjoyed this interlude and was upset when it was abolished: 'we are to be wholly Calvinisticaldummytediousbothery again'.[98] 'Calvinistical' is a general term of abuse in Lear's vocabulary: he detested the idea of an elect who were predestined for salvation. Boredom, stupidity and irritation churn together, so wildly impatient that their adjectives have run in the wash, when he reacts against such exclusive thinking.

Often, as here, Lear's dissent is visible not only in his narratives, but in his language. It is a motor driving his deeply felt affection, his determination that 'one's fellowbeans of any nation class or age'[99] deserve sympathy. But it also propels his disaffection, which produces exuberant linguistic rushes and rants—such as his condemnation of the 'muttering, miserable, muttonhating, manavoiding, misogynic, morose, & merriment-marring . . . Monx' of Mount Athos.[100] Repetition here conveys both the repressed obsessiveness of the monks and the anger that their senseless, sexless self-denial inspires in the writer. The two become linked. Lear's irascibility is like magma beneath the surface of his affable persona: when he erupts, inventive verbal compounds fly. The connection between his disaffection and his creativity is energetic.

One might ask why Lear, with his dissenting heritage, attended Anglican services at all. One reason is that in the French and Italian towns where he spent much of his adult life, there was usually only one 'English' church where the expatriate community gathered. This was certainly true at San Remo, where Lear settled between 1870 and his death in 1888. Another reason was that, as he explained to Fortescue, he did not want to appear 'wholly unconventional . . . bitter as the hideous talk is'.[101] He found it convenient to attend family worship at the various English country houses he visited during the summer, reconnecting with friends and securing artistic commissions. One gains a sense of how poisonously dissenters were treated by some of the gentry in a conversation Lear records after dinner at the Woodwards' in 1859:

Presbyterians and Dissenters coming to church was spoken of, &
I vindicated their doing so on the grounds of their being but one
Church in Rome.—All 4 flew at me . . . Mrs W said then things
about Quakers and Presbyterians—'they may be called Xtians' etc
etc of so shocking a nature that I was really perfectly disgusted &
distressed . . . I scarcely spoke again all the evening . . . & I
believe I shall never go to see them again—since the company of
bigots & fools is not good for anyone who can avoid it.[102]

Clearly Lear is incensed by this topic because it touches his own behaviour. He
has been 'passing' as Anglican in these circles, but refuses communion[103] and is
secretly at odds with aspects of Anglican worship. They damn *him* without
knowing it. Lear's religious life here seems to mirror other aspects of his life—
particularly his epilepsy, a demon he painstakingly concealed from all but a few
close friends, but perhaps also his sexual ambivalence. We might thus link his
dissent and a more general 'queerness' that affects Lear's self-perception as
someone who is isolated, always an outsider by birth and circumstance. Lear
invested a great deal of energy in 'passing', and the result was a short fuse: a
propensity for rage at exclusion, of which damnation is the ultimate form.

A focus of Lear's hatred and abhorrence was the Athanasian Creed, with
its condemnation of those who do not 'hold the Catholic Faith . . . whole
and undefiled' to 'perish everlastingly'.[104] This judgement struck Lear as a
'curse', one that was morally repugnant in its consignment of dissenters and
those of all other faiths to burn forever. He saw it as a projection into eter-
nity of the 'bonfire days' when so many had suffered 'torrents of blood and
cries of torture' because of '*disputable* "idols" of belief'.[105] He referred to Sundays when the creed was read in his local Anglican church as 'cursed Athanasian blasphemy days'.[106] The question of eternal punishment was during
the mid-nineteenth century a smouldering fire within the Church of
England that for a time seemed to threaten the entire fabric of the building.
It is important to recognise this in order to realise how germane Lear's liberal theological stance is to the central religious debates of the era.

There were three areas in which, by the mid-nineteenth century, church
doctrine and liberal intellectual debate were increasingly at odds. Natural science, particularly discoveries in geology, biology and paleontology, cast doubt
on miracles and on the literal truth of Genesis. Historical scholarship cast
doubt on the authorship and authenticity of certain texts within the Bible.
Lastly, moral feeling tended increasingly to reject hellfire—particularly the

idea that it would consume unbaptised infants or non-Christians who had led a moral life. Lear was convinced by all three heads of the argument for a rationalist approach to the Bible.[107] His extensive reading included the works of William Hartpole Lecky: *A History of the Rise and Influence of Rationalism in Europe* (1865), which Lear found 'a delightful book', and *A History of European Morals from Augustus to Charlemagne* (1869). Lecky defined rationalism not as 'any class of definite doctrines or criticisms, but rather a certain cast of thought, or bias of reasoning, which . . . leads men on all occasions to subordinate dogmatic theology to the dictates of reason and of conscience, and, as a necessary consequence greatly to restrict its influence upon life'.[108] Lecky was revolted by the 'absurdity' of the idea of transubstantiation, the Calvinist doctrine of reprobation and the idea of damnation of the unbaptised infant; he wrote that 'such teaching is in fact simply daemonism, and daemonism in its most extreme form'.[109] Lear often echoes Lecky in referring to the 'devil-inspired', 'filthy' and abhorrent nature of the 'dark creed' that rejects the possibility of universal salvation. Lear also read Darwin's *On the Origin of Species* (on his trip to Egypt in 1866–1867). He was interested by the revisionist work of liberal Protestant theologians such as David Strauss and of Jewish scholars such as Emanuel Deutsch. In 1870, Lear complained to Thomas Woolner about William Holman Hunt, who did not share his 'advanced' theological views:

> I had spoken about the increase of rationalistic & antimiraculous thought & hoped his future pictures would point or express such progress. Whereas I find I never made a greater mistake, & that on the contrary, he is becoming a literalist about all biblical lore, & has a holy horror of Darwin, Deutsch, & I suppose of Jowett & A Stanley, tho' he don't name them.[110]

He was 'consoled'[111] by the work of liberal Protestant historian John Lothrop Motley, whose *The Rise of the Dutch Republic* (1855) told a story of the power of the commons struggling and eventually triumphing against arbitrary rule and religious persecution: 'liberty, often crushed, rises again and again'. Lear believed strongly in the progress of human thought towards greater tolerance and religious freedom. Works like Motley's helped Lear place the 'persecution' in the 1860s of men such as Frederick Temple within a long history of religious oppression that would one day cede to more enlightened views.

The era was one of trials in which the Church of England closed ranks against those who departed from faith in the literal letter of the Bible and the Thirty-Nine Articles, sacking some and prosecuting others. The most famous of these controversies surrounded the publication of *Essays and Reviews* (1860), a book of essays by liberal churchmen that triggered what one historian has called 'the greatest religious crisis of the Victorian age'.[112] It produced a hurricane of criticism in the press, in which the authors were accused of seeking to bring down the Anglican church.[113] In his contribution to *Essays and Reviews*, 'The Education of the World', Frederick Temple argued that the Bible should be treated as an historical document rather than a record of literal truth, and that it was limited by the time in which it was written and interpretable anew in the light of modern science. Conscience should be the 'supreme authority', and modern religion should 'modify the early dogmatism by substituting the spirit for the letter, and practical religion for precise definitions of Truth'.[114] Lear clearly agreed with this position and was 'rabid' about the threat to deprive Temple of the bishopric of Exeter. He warned Holman Hunt, who must have grown somewhat tired of Lear's frequent injunctions not to paint 'supernatural' religious subjects:

> I am nursing the hope that you may not have selected any subject connected with miraculous, or mythical, or even traditional interest. There seem to me such a host of moral-historic truths to illustrate, that fables may nowadays be well left aside. Some parts of Jewish History (I don't mean traditions, speaking asses & Lions dens) are most touching & grand: & so also are some of the undoubtedly historic parts of the New Testament. All that tends to strengthen the hands of priests—of whatever Creed—the race who have preyed for ages on the foolish & helpless—should, to my fancy—be avoided. (We are all in a rabid state here about Temple: Shaftesbury & Pusey uniting—for Theologians alas! have ever one point of union,—that of hatred.)[115]

Lord Shaftesbury and Dr Pusey were leaders of the High Church Party. Lear's pun is biting: priests, rather than praying for their congregations, are in fact *preying on* them. They represent exploitation, not intercession. Lear replicates a pun deployed by another Victorian comic poet, Thomas Hood, who was part of the middle-class resistance to Sabbatarianism and whose work Lear enjoyed. In 'An Open Question' (1840), Hood had argued for the zoo being kept open on Sundays, noting that the puma 'preys extempore' as well as certain preachers.[116]

Lear was close to two families, the Lushingtons and the Bethells, that had members involved in the judgement handed down to the authors of *Essays and Reviews*. Two of the essayists, Rowland Williams and W. B. Wilson, were prosecuted in an ecclesiastical court, the Court of Arches. Franklin Lushington's uncle, Dr Stephen Lushington, was the judge of this court and convicted the two men of heresy. They appealed (successfully) to the Privy Council, where Sir Richard Bethell (father of Gussie Bethell and Emma Parkyns) delivered the judicial committee's opinion. In January 1862, Lear reported:

> I am on thorns for Dr. Lushington's decision about Williams.
> Should Williams be condemned, I think you will not be
> surprised by my openly becoming a Unitarian some day—: for
> if Popes and Parsons are to sit on our brains, it behoves them
> as has any to stir, & show they have not succumbed to the
> chains of Priesthood altogether.[117]

Lear aligns himself with the Unitarian position—which rejected the Trinity, the deity of Christ, the unquestionable authority of the Bible and eternal punishment—though he does not yet choose 'openly' to join that faith. Despite the relative moderation of his political views in this period, we can hear echoes here of Lear's interest in Shelleyan radicalism: he rattles the chains of oppression that threaten the 'millennium of the mind'.

Lear erupted again in 1864 when John William Colenso was deposed as bishop of Natal for heterodoxy. Colenso, an admirer of F. D. Maurice—a leading figure in the 'Broad Church' movement—had published *The Pentateuch and Book of Joshua Critically Examined*, which frankly expressed his view that the first five books of the Bible were not written by Moses and could not be regarded as 'historically true'. Colenso, who had studied a variety of German rationalist theologians, pointed to the 'absolute, palpable, self-contradictions of the narrative'[118] and regretted that the Anglican church's insistence on literalist interpretation was preventing the progress of education and of scientific research. Lear read Colenso's work and was a fervent supporter, calling his persecutors 'ravening fanatics . . . devil-inspired'.[119] He confided to Lady Waldegrave:

> The battle about Colenso interests me immensely. . . . In the
> nature of things it was not to be supposed that the Bps were to
> forward Colenso's views, but they might have done another

thing—to wit, let him alone. A broader creed,—a better form of worship—the cessation of nonsense and curses—and the recognition of a new state of matters brought about by centuries, science, destiny or what not—will assuredly be demanded and come to pass whether Bishops and priests welcome the changes or resist them. Not those who believe that God the Creator is greater than a Book, and that millions unborn are to look up to higher thoughts than those stereotyped by ancient legends, gross ignorance, and hideous bigotry—not those are the Infidels,—but these same screamy ganders of the church, who put darkness forward and insist that it is light.[120]

His wordplay is significant. 'Screamy ganders' depicts the conservative churchmen who refuse to brook modern interpretation of the Bible as silly geese, hissing loudly at what they do not comprehend. But the odd combination of adjective and noun also phonetically suggests 'screaming anger'. There is a buried level of aggression here, which is Lear's. His impassioned denunciation of 'hideous bigotry' reveals deeply personal affront. As a dissenter who rejects the doctrine of eternal damnation, Lear is aligned with Colenso. In threatening to defrock the bishop, these churchmen impugn Lear's own claim to lead a Christian life. Their 'nonsense and curses' stand in opposition to his own 'nonsense' of the period, which is a form of gift and benediction. Lear, in the same letter, humorously urges Lady Waldegrave to ask Lord Shaftesbury and the bishop of Oxford, leaders of the High Church movement, to buy his revised *Book of Nonsense*. The joke positions *The Book of Nonsense* as a direct riposte to the 'stereotyped thoughts' of the bigots.

In further response to Colenso's deposition, Lear proposed to Chichester Fortescue that Fortescue should produce a 'NEW ANTIBEASTLY ANTIBRUTAL ANTIBOSH BIBLE' with all the 'filthy, savage, or burlesque-upon-the Deity' passages left out.[121] Rather than a cornerstone of morality and the sacred work that proves Man's dominion over the animals, in this radical re-reading the authorized version of the Bible is, in certain respects, boshy and beastly: it enshrines aspects of man's inhumanity—brutality—and lack of moral superiority to other creatures. Such a nonsense text requires a countertext. In Lear's three later books for children, *Nonsense Songs, Stories, Botany and Alphabets* (1871), *More Nonsense* (1872) and *Laughable Lyrics* (1877), the brute is on the other foot: beasts and humans are often indistinguishable in their behaviour, and even their bodies are ambiguous or contiguous.

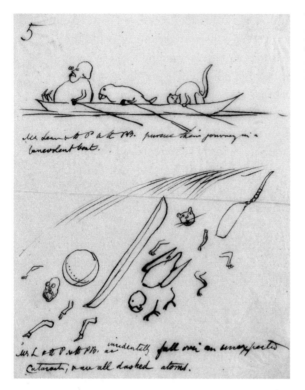

Fig. 2.3a & b **Some of Lear's illustrations for 'The Adventures of Mr Lear & the Polly & the Pusseybite' (1866)**

Fig. 2.3b

The Pusseybite and the New Vestments: Stripping Authority and Resolving Difference

'The Adventures of Mr Lear & the Polly & the Pusseybite on Their Way to the Ritertitle Mountains' is a cartoon storyboard that Lear produced for Gussie Bethell's sister, Emma Parkyns, and her children in 1866. It doubtless contains personal jokes, but Lear intended to publish it in one of his nonsense volumes during the 1870s, which suggests that he considered it meet for a wider public who would enjoy its absurd narrative. In the cartoons, Mr Lear goes out walking with the Polly (a parrot) and the Pusseybite (a cat). They buy umbrellas to shelter from the rain, they arrive at a broken bridge, they tumble into the river, they row in a 'benevolent boat'. Then, falling over an 'unexpected cataract', they are 'dashed to atoms'. Two 'venerable Jebusites' fasten the remains of the three creatures together 'but fail to reconstruct them perfectly as 3 individuals', and the story concludes with them all tumbling with some 'Jerusalem artichokes' into a deep hole.[122]

This is nonsense, so trying to decode it may seem perverse. But 'Pusseybite' is surely a play on 'Puseyite'—a High Churchman. We have seen how angrily Lear responded to Pusey's hostile intervention in the *Essays and Reviews* crisis. It would not be surprising if he depicted the High Church as being willing to bite. Perhaps there is also a pun on 'polytheism' in the 'Polly', or a buried allusion to the kind of 'parrotprayers' that Lear accuses the monks on Mount Athos of muttering from habit rather than with discernment.[123] Lear depicts himself in the middle, between the Polly and the Pusseybite. This seems to be a story about a journey towards 'right to title'—authority or ownership—that is being undertaken by believers of different religious complexions. The Jebusites were members of a tribe that once inhabited Jerusalem and whom God in the Old Testament promises to drive out of the Promised Land.[124] God asks the Israelites to destroy them and not to intermarry with them.[125] The fact that in Lear's story it is they who rescue the travellers and reconstruct them seems significant. It pits the benevolence of the excluded against the forces of division. Lear's own journeys to Jerusalem had made him keenly aware of the disputed territories in that region and the mudslinging—which he deplored—between rival Christian, Jewish and Muslim organisations. Since Jebusites are identified with the original inhabitants of the city of Jebus, which became Jerusalem, Lear may be hinting here that it is the inhabitants of Palestine who have to 'pick up the pieces' of the confusion that has resulted from religious divisions.

The turn this nonsense story takes, whereby heads and tails of different creatures recombine to produce cross-breed creatures, has elements of grotesque that are traditional in folk art.[126] But there is also a strong flavour of contemporary commentary: different parties set out as independent factions but find that they have got muddled up. The result is that they end up in a hole.[127] Is this an indication that the divided church has got itself into a hole-y mess? There is a shade of a Darwinian joke here, too: the combination of a parrot and a cat would give you a 'pollypuss', which echoes the Victorian word for an amoeba, 'polypus'. Thomas Hood makes similar play with 'Polly-Puss' in an illustration published in his *Memorials* (1860), which Lear read more than once. Lear plays with hybridity in ways that are nonsensical yet topical. The fact that this piece was never published in Lear's lifetime, despite his intention to include it in his nonsense books, suggests that he or his publisher may have been wary of its possible interpretation as religious satire.

Fig. 2.4 Thomas Hood, 'A Polly-puss' (1860)

Another work of Lear's that we might specifically reread through the lens of his dissenting background is 'The New Vestments', published in *Laughable Lyrics* (1877). In this poem, an 'old man in the Kingdom of Tess' invents 'a purely original dress'. It consists of items that can be consumed as food: a shirt of dead mice, a waistcoat and 'trowsers' made of pork chops. 'His Coat was all Pancakes with Jam for a border, And a girdle of Biscuits to keep it in order'. The man walks into town, but he is rushed upon by 'all Sorts of Beasticles, Birdlings and Boys'. Pigs eat his drawers, dogs eat his trowsers, and cats descend screeching from the rooftops to devour his shirt:

Two Cows and a Calf ate his Cabbage-leaf Cloak;—
Four Apes seized his Girdle, which vanished like smoke;—

Three Kids ate up half of his Pancaky Coat,—
And the tails were devour'd by an ancient He Goat;—

. . .

They swallowed the last of his Shirt with a squall,—
Whereon he ran home with no clothes on at all.[128]

The story is reminiscent of Hans Christian Andersen's 'The Emperor's New Clothes': there is the same pleasure in seeing the exposure of an adult who ought to know better. He has to run home, like a baby, in his birthday suit. (Lear was an admirer of Andersen's stories, praising him as 'a real poet—but "too" melancholy'.)[129] However, 'The New Vestments' is also a poem involving a mob, with some of the same violent comic energies as Robert Browning's 'Pied Piper of Hamelin' or Thomas Hood's 'Miss Kilmansegg and her Precious Leg'—poems Lear would have known. In all these fantasies, consumption becomes an out-of-control engine that is both pleasurable and threatening.

Hood and Browning criticise the reifications of unfettered capitalism, whose failure to distinguish between person and thing bites back to destroy humane values. In Lear's 'The New Vestments', the point is, rather, a stripping of authority that explores the debatable territory between physical shame and desire. The array of delightful and disgusting foods surrounding the body mimics our mingled delight and disgust surrounding the body both as a consuming subject and an object for others' oral and sexual pleasure. The 'scoffing' in this poem combines childish glee in feasting and laying bare with adult sexual horror at public exposure, to produce a frisson of uneasy pleasure—rather like Lear's anecdote about the whale-woman threatening to swallow him, Jonah fashion, on the train.

The title of this poem seems significant: not 'The New Clothes', but 'The New Vestments'. *Vestment* is a word strongly associated with the church; one definition is 'a garment worn by a priest or ecclesiastic on the occasion of some service or ceremony'. The phrase 'The New Vestments' must inevitably also have reminded Victorian readers of 'The New Testament'. There is something in this nonsense that flirts with the sacrilegious. An old man is divested of his cabbage-leaf cloak of respectability. In this poem Lear has created a kind of Nude Testament. It is the opposite of Genesis, in which Adam and Eve perceive their sin and their nakedness in God's sight and, out of shame, clothe themselves as a sign of their Fall, their original sin. In Lear's narrative, an old man begins with an 'original dress'. But animals—particularly apes—and children (Beasticles, Birdlings and Boys) eat through this concealment, and the old man, stripped of the culinary trappings of civilisation, is revealed in his full creatureliness. The 'kids' who eat the pancakes may be goats or humans; the consumption of the man's 'tails' and 'skins' reminds us of the similarity between human and animal bodies. While not as vehement as Blake's work, Lear's vision refutes the doctrine of original sin: in his poems, people and animals naturally share essential appetites. 'The New Vestments' is, whether you read it in religious or in Darwinian terms, a leveling poem.

THE SCROOBIOUS PIP AND THE QUANGLE WANGLE: ODD ONES IN

Many of Lear's poems involve perversity that is also a kind of integrity. The Jumblies and the 'Pobble who has no Toes' refuse to do as they are told. According to the moral logic of most Victorian verse for children, these disobedient creatures ought to come to grief, but instead—wonderfully, against all expectation—they come to happiness. Lear passes a judgement on them that, rather than punitive, is redemptive. Universal salvation in the land of nonsense is not only possible but true.

The Quangle Wangle is another delightful creature who, having seemed to be excluded from society by oddity (his face concealed by his ginormous hat), turns out to provide a platform for an array of marvellous creatures to build on.

> On the top of the Crumpetty Tree
>   The Quangle Wangle sat,
> But his face you could not see,
>   On account of his Beaver Hat.
> For his hat was a hundred and two feet wide,
> With ribbons and bibbons on every side
> And bells, and buttons, and loops, and lace,
> So that nobody ever could see the face
>   Of the Quangle Wangle Quee.
>
> The Quangle Wangle said
>   To himself on the Crumpetty Tree,—

'Jam; and jelly; and bread;
    Are the best of food for me!
But the longer I live on this Crumpetty Tree
The plainer that ever it seems to me
That very few people come this way
And that life on the whole is far from gay!'
        Said the Quangle Wangle Quee.

But there came to the Crumpetty Tree,
    Mr and Mrs Canary;
And they said,—'Did you ever see
    Any spot so charmingly airy?
May we build a nest on your lovely Hat?
Mr Quangle Wangle, grant us that!
O please let us come and build a nest
Of whatever material suits you best,
        Mr Quangle Wangle Quee!'
. . .

And the Golden Grouse came there,
    And the Pobble who has no toes,—
And the small Olympian bear,—
    And the Dong with a luminous nose.
And the Blue Baboon, who played the flute,—
And the Orient Calf from the Land of Tute,—
And the Attery Squash, and the Bisky Bat,—
All came and built on the lovely Hat
        Of the Quangle Wangle Quee.

And the Quangle Wangle said
    To himself on the Crumpetty Tree,—
'When all these creatures move
    What a wonderful noise there'll be!'
And at night by the light of the Mulberry moon
They danced to the Flute of the Blue Baboon,
On the broad green leaves of the Crumpetty Tree,
And all were as happy as happy could be,
        With the Quangle Wangle Quee.[130]

This is, to use an expression Lear used to describe a letter that pleased him, a 'soothy-beautiful' poem or song.[131] Its lyrical movement from plaintive one-note melody to social harmony is intrinsic to its power. From being shut out and isolated by his vast brim, the Quangle Wangle becomes the quiet centre of a joyful concert of diverse forms of life. His hat has transformed itself into a habitat. 'When all these creatures move / What a wonderful noise there'll be!' is a line of particular brilliance. It is not only the Blue Baboon playing the flute or the singing of Mr and Mrs Canary that produces the lovely sound in this poem. It is the subtler music of creatures moving together, swaying, perhaps, as the branches of a vast tree do in the wind. The wonderful noise of their moving moves the reader likewise. They dance on the 'broad green leaves of the Crumpetty Tree', and 'all were as happy as happy could be / With the Quangle Wangle Quee'. They seem to be pleased *by* him and happy *alongside* him; these two senses of 'happy with' coexist. One can, the song seems to say, share one's life with others in more than one way. It is possible to be apart and simultaneously to be integrated.

Lear's poems are often about happiness: its elusiveness, its magical power to transform. When we read or sing 'The Quangle Wangle's Hat' we are beckoned into its chorus. Its happiness has the power to transfer itself to us, like a hat. This poem can be read as a description of emergence from depression: the gradual quickening of the mind from concentration on the self and its miseries ('very few people come this way / And . . . life on the whole is far from gay!') to an awareness of the ability to attract and satisfy others that produces emotional plenitude, where one's head is not a prison but a dance floor. Lear certainly knew this pattern of withdrawal and emergence well. But the narrative is also reminiscent of the parable in Matthew 13:32 where the kingdom of heaven is said to be like a tiny mustard seed that grows into a tree so large that 'the birds of the air come and lodge in the branches thereof'. The broad leaves of the tree and the astonishing breadth of the Quangle Wangle's hat offer ample room to join its throng of strange creatures from all manner of countries who live together in amity. Lear, for whom *broad* is always a term of commendation—in religious, intellectual and social terms—has created a piece of nonsense that sings of inclusion, a peaceable kingdom where all dance by the light of the Mulberry moon.

Nowhere is the relationship between perversity and integrity in Lear's characters more evident than in his poem 'The Scroobious Pip', a work from 1870 that was not published in Lear's lifetime. It features a creature who refuses to be parsed by species or genus. When others ask, it metaphorically flips them the bird:

> The Scroobious Pip from the top of a tree
> Saw the distant Jellybolēē,—
> And all the birds in the world came there
> Flying in crowds all through the air.
> The Vulture and Eagle—the Cock and the Hen,
> The Ostrich, the Turkey, the Snipe and Wren,
> The Parrot chattered, the Blackbird sung,
> And the Owl looked wise but held his tongue,
> And when the Peacock began to scream,
> The hullaballoo was quite extreme.
> And every bird he fluttered the tip
> Of his wing as he stared at the Scroobious Pip.
>
> At last they said to the Owl,—'By far
> You're wisest Bird—you know you are!
> Fly close to the Scroobious Pip and say,
> "Explain all about yourself we pray!—
> For as yet we have neither seen nor heard
> If you're Fish or Insect, Beast or Bird!"'
>
> The Scroobious Pip looked gaily round
> And sang these words with a chirpy sound—
>   flippetty chip—Chippetty flip—
>   My only name is the Scroobious Pip.'[132]

This is another musical poem of pleasure both in waywardness and in the variety of modes of being. Different groups (birds, animals, fishes, insects) pose their question in turn, and the Pip responds with noises appropriate to the creatures it is addressing. Indeed the poem operates rather like Benjamin Britten's musical work for children *The Young Person's Guide to the Orchestra*, in which the strings, brass, woodwind and timpani all have their moment, demonstrating the beauty of their distinctive sound before joining together in harmony. Lear's poem ends with the birds and fishes and animals and insects dancing and swimming round the eponymous refusenik in a circle, joyfully confirming that 'its only name is the Scroobious Pip'.

Lear's illustrations for the poem depict a Pip who, like the polymorphous animals in 'The Adventures of Mr Lear & the Polly & the Pusseybite', has parts belonging to different classes of creature. In one drawing its torso resembles that of an echidna (an animal Lear especially loved), its wings resemble a fly's, its tail a snake's, it has the spurred legs of a man, but a bird's beak with a parasol and decorative feathers that suggest the feminine. The fact that the Pip has both male and female characteristics is interesting. It may reflect Lear's own bisexual ambivalence. But it also reflects the poem's wider, teasing refusal of commonly accepted principles of difference. This creature is both and all and none. Women are biblically associated with serpents; here, no such principle is entertained. Neither are humans privileged over animals; they have, in a comic composition typical of Lear's visual experiments, feet and hands that can be fused with wings and tails. One can see in this poem reflections of Darwin's theories concerning evolutionary adaptation, which suggested that reptiles had become birds and that humans' predecessors had once had tails. No distinction of genus is absolute in perpetuity. The palindromic Pip is an apt word for a creature whose rank or identity is opaque: it could develop any which way.

However, the poem also seems to contain memories of Lear's favourite passages from the New Testament. The Scroobious Pip gathers all the 'birds of the air', the animals, the insects and the fishes of the sea around him 'by the beautiful shore of the Jellybolee'. The 'birds of the air' (an expression that also occurs in Lear's limericks) is a direct quotation from the gospel of Matthew. In 'shore of the Jellybolee' the name of the body of water sounds like 'jellybowl', but the complete phrase also echoes 'shore of the Sea of Galilee', where Jesus gathered his disciples and delivered his parables. Like the 'sunset isles of Boshen' this is a biblical landscape transposed into nonsense. The universal gathering itself also has the qualities of a peaceable kingdom. It would, in a religious context, be God or Jesus who attracted all the creatures of the world to surround him and to listen to his words. The Scroobious Pip's rebuff to attempts to define him also savours of a religious antecedent: in Exodus 3:14, God tells Moses, who has asked his name, 'I AM THAT I AM'. This scrupulously inscrutable reply is the basis of faith, and it accompanies the promise of the Israelites' liberation from oppression in Egypt.

Lear's 'The Scroobious Pip' is typical of his later nonsense in that it weaves together strands from multiple sources, creating a bricolage of ideas and moods similar to the fusion of body parts in the illustration. What interests

Fig. 2.5 Lear's 'The Scroobious Pip'

me particularly, however, is the relationship between benevolence and defi-
ance. Lear has created an animal character who refuses to self-identify as
part of an established group, yet who can unite disparate creatures; who is
a fully paid-up member of the awkward squad, but who might also be
considered to be Christlike or Godlike in its benign inscrutability. This
combination of characteristics reflects Lear's particular mode of nonconformity, at once so prickly and so warm.

Even that most familiar of Lear's poems, 'The Owl and the Pussy-cat',
looks slightly different when we read it in the light of Lear's dissent. It is a
story of strange liberties. Since this is a poem we all know almost too well,
it is easy to miss the fact that the central characters are eloping. Contrary
to the proper moral sequence, they have their honeymoon (their honey and
money) before their wedding. They call no banns; they sail for a year and a
day, then marry immediately. They marry using pig metal. (There is a hint
of sacrilege in the pun.) And the parson is a turkey, another playful pun. In
the nineteenth century, any black-and-white bird or animal could be called
a 'parson'. There may even be a joke within the joke: the 'parson's nose' is
the piece of fat on a turkey's rump.

Victorian readers recognised that this was an unconventional poem. In
1870 a critic in the *Spectator* noticed that the female cat, 'in the true spirit

of women's rights',[133] asks the male owl to marry her. Indeed, early readers may have wondered momentarily about whether the cat was male and the owl female: the cat in some illustrations seems larger than her mate; she is steering the boat, and her rudder-like tail has a phallic assertiveness. Daniel Karlin rightly notes that the final lines of 'The Owl and the Pussy-cat' resemble those of Milton's *Paradise Lost* (in which Adam and Eve leave Eden) but reverse the punitive scenario imagined in Genesis, as the couple leave 'hand in hand' to enter a state of bliss.[134]

'The Owl and the Pussy-cat' has become a popular reading at modern weddings, and this reflects, I think, a deep appreciation of the way in which it performs its own ceremony and confers its own blessing. The most powerful line is the last: the happy couple, 'hand in hand, on the edge of the sand', become a mirror reflection of perfect harmony.

> They danced by the light of the moon,
>> The moon,
>> The moon,
> They danced by the light of the moon.[135]

Like the characters in 'The Quangle Wangle's Hat', these two creatures of darkness don't dance 'in the moonlight' but 'by the light of the moon': we hear 'delight' in 'the light', and a quiet joyfulness shimmers off the page.

Poems are rituals. This is particularly true for children, who absorb the rhythm and tone of a phrase and revel in its insistent repetition, prior to knowing what words mean, or that some words have no agreed meaning. Lear's poems offer a particular kind of ritual pleasure, and the ritual they enact is one that, rather than reinforcing the claims of a higher authority, consistently endorses the child's point of view: waywardness is normal; pleasure is liberating; and words are what we make of them. Lear loved the fact that several children he met had chosen to learn his nonsense 'by heart'.[136] The expression dates back to the fourteenth century.[137] It suggests knowing something from its core, completely, but also conveys the truth that words we learn 'by heart' are somehow transfused into our internal circulatory system, becoming part of us; they have passed beyond the field of reading and comprehension into the domain of ownership and emotional expression that is inseparable from our inmost selves. As indigenous societies sometimes eat the hearts of other animals in order to incorporate their desirable qualities, so we absorb words we wish to carry within us. Lear's poems commend themselves to this process to a high degree. One reason for this is that their musical qualities and their vivid, dreamlike images pass readily into the subconscious; their flow circulates to rhythms that even in childhood are readily internalised. Another reason is that they are, explicitly or implicitly, gift poems,[138] whose kindness and sympathy—often conveyed in narratives that move the characters towards happiness—offer a benediction that retains its magical power to comfort and enchant.

Various critics have described the mystical qualities of Lear's poetry. G. K. Chesterton in 1901 argued that:

> nonsense will, in a very unexpected way, come to the aid of the spiritual view of things. Religion has for centuries been trying to make men exult in the 'wonders' of creation, but it has forgotten that a thing cannot be completely wonderful so long as it remains sensible. So long as we regard a tree as an obvious thing, naturally and reasonably created for a giraffe to eat, we cannot properly wonder at it.[139]

For Chesterton, Lewis Carroll's nonsense is essentially intellectual. Lear's is of greater value because it opens our hearts to the inexplicable joy of creation. It has a purity that wit and logic lack, because unreason is closer to the state necessary to 'draw out the soul of things'.[140]

Holbrook Jackson would in 1912 describe Lear as a 'prophet' whose work countered the materialism of an age of 'factories and ironclads, locomotives and guns, and banking accounts'—an age that equated 'good sense' with shrewdness and acquisition and was oblivious to values outside this ideology. In this context, Lear's nonsense is not the 'obverse of sense' but a negation of the materialist definition of its terms. He 'has given us the keys of the heaven of nonsense, and as we turn them in the doors and enter therein we breathe lightly and without care of the morrow, as though we were one with a rout of children dancing and shouting'.[141] The miraculous effect of nonsense that Jackson describes sounds rather like that of a sunbeam striking through a church window and turning a Bible into a bird: 'It is as though a dignified ritual, long become exanimate by repetition, had suddenly been reversed by an unseen but jocular power, and creating, instead of shallow laughter, fathomless joy'.[142] Both Chesterton and Jackson suggest that Lear's nonsense awakens the reader to joy beyond reason. Thomas Byrom's seminal

1975 study, *Nonsense and Wonder*, follows in this critical tradition. These critics convey something important about the capacity of Lear's art to transport, to entrance and to console.

However, it is important also to register the questing intellectual curiosity and angry resistance to doctrinal authority and dogma that are part of Lear's dissenting inheritance and that also inform his writing, producing wit that, as we have seen, can be both barbed and defiant. Nonsense can be a form of invective as well as blessing. As Mr Discobbolos says before he kills his family, 'O! W !X !Y !Z! / We shall all presently be dead'. And as Lear remarks in his diary, 'Went to Church. Scissars! What a bore—& the Sermon the 150th I have heard for that text'.[143] Contrariness and independence, the preservation of ambiguity and the refutation of mindless repetition, are as important to Lear's nonsense as benevolence and faith.

LATER LEAR: INVENTING A CREED

In his diary for 7 December 1879, Lear devised his own creed, noting that it was 'one all can unite in—or most':

> I believe in God the Father Almighty
> Maker of Heaven & Earth. And in Jesus
> Christ our Lord, who was crucified
> Under Pontius Pilate.
> I believe in the Forgiveness of Sins
> And in the Life Everlasting, Amen.[144]

Inventing a creed is quite a remarkable thing for a sixty-seven year old to do; it is typical of Lear's restless intelligence, which refused to repeat words without fully weighing their meaning. Lear's creed resembles the Apostles' Creed, but its omissions are significant: he doesn't believe in the immaculate conception, in Christ as God's 'only begotten Son', in the resurrection or in the day of judgement. He also, seemingly, prefers to believe in a 'Life Everlasting' that does not involve the resurrection of the body.

Lear wanted to believe in an afterlife and mostly did. As he expressed it to Chichester Fortescue, he was 'willing to hope dimly',[145] a formulation quite similar to Thomas Hardy's later poetic expression of uncertainty: 'hoping it might be so'.[146] Lear's reasoning was largely based on his sense of how unbearably sad and unfair temporal life would be if there were no second act. As he wrote to Gussie Parker (nee Bethell) in 1880:

> Why should we have to suffer so intensely here, if not for some good end to be made known hereafter? Of all the theoretical botherations published, surely materialism is the most odious: since it takes away all that renders life tolerable to millions, & gives them blank blackness instead.[147]

His ideas about what might possibly come after this life, however, varied. Sometimes he felt that it would be terrible if we did not retain our identities in a putative Paradise; in that case, he would be unable to be reunited with Ann. At other moments, he gladly accepted the possibility that the next world might be so completely different from this one that all trace of our former identities would disappear:

> As I grow older I think more—& it does not now seem to me horrible nor an injustice that we may never have consciousness of this life—if we live in another. To be quite changed—to have no memory of this life would not be pain . . . [148]

There is a strong strain of rationalism in Lear, which coexists with a desire to embrace unknowing. In 1860, he was reading Plato's *Republic*. In 1870 he ordered further volumes of Plato to read. In a whimsical mood, Lear considered his own chances of metempsychosis; he might return after death as 'a tree—a cloud—a cabbage—or silence in the next world: but most possibly an ass'.[149] Lear's humour, which can't quite allow this reverie to float into the aether without a pop at his own pretensions, coexists with wistfulness, a feeling that life is a dreamlike veil and its mystery involves the numinous qualities of the natural world. Being quite changed is something with which his nonsense experiments. A man topples into the Thames and seems to become a fish; a man and a bird stare at one another, in a mirror pose of identical astonishment. Such transformation is a joke yet echoes the underlying truth that bodies do transmigrate, through evolutionary adaptation, but also through the food chain, and perhaps through processes of reincarnation beyond human understanding. A scientific and a mystical perspective on the elemental relationship between humans and other forms of life can produce quite similar ass-imilations.

Lear was highly conscious of the positivist theories of Comtism; he lived close to and was for a time on friendly social terms with Walter Congreve and John Congreve, brothers of Richard Congreve, the prominent Comtist philosopher. The idea that scientific philosophy might one day supplant the rituals of formal religion was, as we shall see, not wholly inimical to Lear. He was sufficiently interested to buy the *Nineteenth Century* of June 1877 and read Frederic Harrison's essay on the soul.[150] However, the quasi-Catholic hierarchy of Comtism enraged him in a manner typical of his inherently democratic nonconformity. He referred to John Congreve as a Comtist 'high priest' and, latterly, wrote of Comtism that 'more impudently violent fanatical priestcraft, I fancy does not exist'.[151] The irritable terms of his rejection reveal his awareness of the tension between admitting intellectual possibility and requiting emotional need:

> Bother your materialists & Comptists,—I had rather *hope* to meet good women or men again—than *know* I cannot do so. Such *knowledge* is pain—not pleasure.[152]

Because he was uncertain about the supernatural and what might follow death, Lear disliked ghost stories. His remarks about Wilkie Collins's *The Haunted Hotel,* which Collins (a friend for over thirty years) had sent him for comment, are interesting: he didn't approve of it.

> I think ghosts & future states may be & probably are quiet realities,—yet I don't like them used as mere talk. One of my old friends . . . wrote to me lately 'so & so has accused me of being materialist & unbeliever in a future state because I won't talk on the subject. The very contrary is the fact;—yet I feel sure it is not intended for us to know what is beyond this life. If I dislike talk of my dead friends, it is not because I doubt of their existence, but because I feel that all definite notions about them are absurd & outrageous. Are they to be all like Adam & Eve in Paradise?—Or are they to wear dress preserves & high heeled shoes?'[153]

It sounds as if Lear is defending himself against the suspicion of materialism. He was uncertain about how to represent a future state. In his occasional cartoons of Paradise, he and his friends are birds with human heads sitting in the trees or, alternatively, are surrounded by the birds and beasts of Paradise while 'eating ice creams and pelican pie'.[154]

Many Victorians dabbled in spiritualism; the possibility that invisible powers might allow communication beyond the material sphere was compelling. Lear, however, abhorred 'table-turning' and spiritualist practices. Dining with the Batemans in 1868 he found to his horror that 'the man is a spiritualist who believes in tableturning & willow wands finding water & says Faraday's fallacies have been exploded. I wish I were of a nature to make the best of these silly eccentric fungi:————not being so, they make me sulk & grieve'.[155] Lear's scientific background comes to the fore here. The Batemans' spiritualism is of a piece with their insistence that Michael Faraday's practical work in the field of electricity and magnetism is a hoax that has, ironically, been 'exploded'. They become, in his account, themselves odd specimens, primitive 'fungi', of the kind that a scientist might collect and dissect. It is interesting to observe how Lear turns the tables on the tableturners, marshalling the language of science to consign the views of such 'silly eccentric fungi' to the intellectual backwoods. A diary entry of 1870 similarly compares the swelling growth of churchiness to that of mushrooms: 'I weary of ecclesiasticism,—the fungus growth of which outweighs reason in these days'.[156]

Lear's disparaging attitude to spiritualism led him in May 1875 to consider producing a series of caricature 'spiritual objects', including a Spiritual Snail, whose composite figure has a tortoise head with an elephant's trunk attached to a snail shell and what is perhaps a hyaena's bottom.[157] He was parodying 'spirit drawings' of the kind that were on sale at the Spiritualist Bazaar in London, which had been organised to raise funds to promote the study of pneumatology and psychology and to obtain permanent premises for spiritualist use. A journalist for the *Thames Star* reported:

> Well a bazaar is a very mundane, not to say trifling and
> frivolous thing; no way serious or spiritual in its arrangements
> and doings, albeit often undertaken for what other people
> beside professed spiritualists call 'spiritual' or 'serious' objects;
> but then you see, at this particular bazaar a great number of
> the articles exhibited were of spirit manufacture. These were
> only for exhibition; the articles for sale, described as 'useful

and ornamental', were, we are told, marked at reasonable
prices; for the spirit productions, it is to be presumed, no
reasonable price would suffice, and yet to an unspiritual critic
the pictures looked 'mere dashes of colour laid on with a paste
brush'.[158]

The fact that the phrase *spiritual object,* which usually meant 'noble aim', was
applied at this bazaar to concrete items supposed to have been manufactured
by spirits, was irresistible. Lear's imagination was fired by the implicit oxymoron. As we have seen, Lear often produced composite creatures that combined aspects of animal, bird, insect and fish. Here the tension between the
material and the ethereal implicit in the verbal pun on *spiritual object* inspires a visual grotesque. It may reflect the possible melding of identities in
a future state; it may be the sort of muddle a charlatan would pass off as
spirit work. This particular cartoon shows how firmly Lear's nonsense could
be rooted in contemporary events.

   Another example of Lear's nonsense verse inspired by contemporary debate
occurs in June 1880. While staying with Gussie Parker (formerly Bethell) and
her husband, Lear wrote and illustrated 'O Brother Chicken! Sister Chick!', a
short poem that considers the mystery of First Causes. The newborn chick
looks around confusedly, wondering: 'However did I get inside? Or how did I
get out?/And must my life be evermore, an atmosphere of doubt?' Asking
'Can no one solve, this mystery of Eggs?', the chick concludes:

>   May it not seem to me,
> That we were merely born by chance,
>   Egg-nostics for to be?[159]

This quickly improvised poem again suggests how interested Lear was in
argument about religion and its relationship to science. *Agnostic* was a term
coined by the scientist and philosopher Thomas Huxley in 1869 for a state
of 'not knowing'; in Huxley's view agnosticism was not a creed but a state of
mind with which one could approach the mysteries of science and philosophy, content that all knowledge was relative and incomplete. Lear was
aware of Huxley's views. He wrote in his diary in 1867 that 'Darwinism
and Huxleyism may be true but are uncomfortable'—a remark addressed
further in the following chapter.[160] It is worth noting here how Lear's comic

verse literalises the question 'which came first, the chicken or the egg?' Eggs may not, to humans, be mysterious objects, but the ultimate origins of life *are* unknowable. If it is absurd for a chick to worry about how it got here, and to conclude gloomily that life in 'an atmosphere of doubt' is the natural inheritance of birdkind, then is it not doubly absurd for men to assume that they are the outcome of chance events, doomed to agnosticism? The poem doesn't tell us that Huxley's position is nonsensical, but it hints that the comic undecidability of the pun is preferable to the troubled undecidability of the agnostic mindset.

Lear's diverse intellectual reading in this period included Matthew Arnold's *Literature and Dogma* (1873), T H Green's *A Prolegomena to Ethics* (1883), Monier Monier-Williams's *Brahmanism and Hinduism* (1883) and Eliza Lynn Linton's *Under Which Lord?* (1879), an anti-Tractarian novel that expressed her fundamental dislike of institutionalised religion. 'But why— granting that there is need of endless reform in Christianity', Lear asked in his diary after reading Lynn Linton's work, 'why this hatred of the system and of its Organisation? Is there no medium way? May we not dislike all extremes, without trying to uproot good along with evil?'[161]

In 1882, aged seventy, he was reading *Christian Theology and Modern Scepticism,* by the Duke of Somerset, 'with the very sage and moderate con- clusions of which I cannot but mainly agree'.[162] Lear tells Fortescue that he does not feel that, for the present, humanity 'can dispense with religion of some kind'.[163] But the future may bring a more perfect state of scientific and philosophical understanding in which religion is transcended. In his letter, Lear partially quotes the following passage:

> In the present imperfect state of human knowledge the
> endeavor to construct a positive philosophy is obviously
> premature. A genuine philosophy of the mind may eventually
> disclose a system as sublime and ennobling, as the discoveries
> revealed by science in the visible universe. For these results
> however we must wait, remembering that truth is the daughter
> of time, and not of authority. . . . Since religion may be judged
> by its fruits, that form of Christianity which develops the
> highest qualities of human nature and furthers the continued
> improvement of society may be safely accounted as the nearest
> approach to religious truth.[164]

This approaches a utilitarian view of religion: the belief that makes people behave best must be the best belief. The phrase that Lear repeats with emphasis is 'truth is the daughter of *time*, and not of *authority*'. Lear, as we have seen, is suspicious of claims to religious authority. He regards religion, like science, as an evolving body of knowledge that may eventually lead to a more perfect comprehension of the world and our place in it. Early in life, Lear had been fascinated by Shelley's radicalism, imagining a 'millennium of mind'; in old age, he retains a sense that truth belongs to the future, which may develop a new 'philosophy of the mind'.

In Lear's personal philosophy we are constantly led away from authority, back to individual responsibility, intellectual liberty and freedom of conscience, to self-reflection and social philanthropy. The onus is on us. He used his diary, which he kept every day throughout his adult life, as an aid to reflection, noting in retrospect when he had been hasty or wrong and hoping to mark signs of moral improvement. I find myself deeply touched by the strength of his commitment to doing better by others. In Addison's essays from the *Spectator*, which Lear was reading in 1886, he marked passages that resonated with him. He emphasised, 'It is an endless & a frivolous pursuit to act by any other rule than the care of satisfying our own minds in what we do'.[165] Frivolity is often associated with pleasing oneself, but here the opposite is true; it is frivolous *not* to 'satisfy our own minds'. Giving and receiving pleasure may be one way in which we legitimately account for our moral existence.

In April 1881, in a pipe dream of plenipotential prosperity, Lear pictured himself in a chocolate-coloured carriage, 'wherein, sitting on a lofty cushion composed of muffins and volumes of the Apocrypha', he would 'disport himself all about the London parks, to the general satisfaction of all pious people'.[166] In this delightful vision, Lear is borne aloft, satisfying the 'pious', but secretly turning his backside to the Bible's most questionable texts. The mixture of muffins, chocolate carriage and biblical texts is mildly subversive, muddling as it does edibility and inedibility with credibility and incredibility. One wonders whether the 'pious' people he will 'satisfy' are religious or just people who love pie—like the inhabitants of the moon in one of his nonsense letters,[167] whose devotions consist in the consumption of Ambleboff pies (a nonsense compound that evokes both apple pie and humble pie). Lear's vision of 'disporting himself' while being carried is typical of the way his play often combines pointed irreverence with childlike innocence.

In April 1885 he pictured himself for Chichester Fortescue as a nonsense Archbishop of Canterbury.[168] Again here he is being frivolous, yet there is also a buried truth in Lear's depiction of himself as a comic alternative head for the Anglican church. James T. Fields in a biographical sketch of 1877 referred to Lear's 'ministry of good-nature about the world'.[169] Lear's work reflects both his nonconformist belief in the necessity of reading and thinking for oneself and his delight in the way that words resist simple reading, constantly inviting plural ideas and entertaining unexpected meanings, making a Broad Church of their own infinity. Nonsense can give voice to irreverence and irritation, while also expressing tolerance and compassion.

In the final years of his life, Lear experimented with various drafts of a nonsense poem, which became 'Some Incidents in the Life of My Uncle Arly'. As many have noted, it has an autobiographical resonance. The name 'Lear' peeps out between the final two words. Yet Uncle Arly is also a version of the word *unclearly;* the poem makes play of its own resistance to interpretation. In the endpapers of the books where he was scribbling, Lear tried out a different version of the poem from the one he eventually settled on: a revealing road not taken. In it, the bald Uncle Arly has sat on and de-

Fig. 2.6 **Lear as Archbishop (1885)**

stroyed his hat. He is thus exposed to the elements. In this calamity, he is rescued by the ducks he has faithfully fed over the years:

> Many thousand chicks had followed
> All his footsteps as he
> Day by day and year by year
> . . .
> And when now of hat bereft . . .
> All the ducks remembered that . . .
> They had breakfasted & dined (while other birds in hunger pined)
> On those Nicodemus pills
> So by scores they fluttered round him
>   Like a vast umbrella . . .
>
> Quacks vobiscum Uncle Arly
> Silly on your heap of barley
> Quacks vobiscum—every Duck
>
> Quacks vobiscum—as they flew
> Quacks vobiscum—two by two
> Through the morning sky so blue . . .
> Quacks vobiscum—what a lark![170]

This may be an allegory of Lear's final years at San Remo, where old friends clubbed together to lend or give money for a new house, a roof over his head. The first villa that Lear had built in San Remo, the Villa Emily, had been rendered miserable to him by the construction of a hotel in front of it that blocked the light from his studio and obscured the sea view from his terrace. Aged sixty-eight, he thus embarked on building the Villa Tennyson, in a different location—a financial undertaking that was costly and risky for an artist nearing the end of his working life. The ducks who flock round Uncle Arly by scores, protecting him from downpours and, perhaps, transporting him to a new location, are like the friends who enabled Lear to flee from the Villa Emily and spend the last eight years of his life in peace.

The poem is, however, also reminiscent of the story of St Francis, who squandered his early inheritance and became a poor itinerant, feeding birds and preaching to them. Lear liked to feed 'unfortunate' birds in winter and depicted himself doing so in a letter to Emily Tennyson during the very harsh British January of 1861, when Lear also pitied the human poor and gave money to various charities to support them. In this cartoon, Lear is so bundled up in furry clothing that he resembles a giant egg, a natural brother to the birds who eat out of his hand. The ducks who follow Uncle Arly invoke the possibility that he is a sort of saint. His 'silliness'—a word that derives from the word *seely*, whose meanings include 'holy, 'innocent' and 'blessed'—as he sits on his heap of barley, is in this reading less dependent and more assertive. As an avatar for Lear, this Uncle Arly may embark on a journey heavenward that has the qualities of religious ascension—an ascension that is inescapably comic, both larky and lark-like. It is the ducks who act as priests to Uncle Arly, performing a nonsense version of the Latin mass (*pax vobiscum*—peace be with you).[171] Gabbled religious responses are for the birds; quacks may suggest quackery. Yet the 'mercy and affection' that '*no body* doubts . . . being good'[172] are very near the surface of this abandoned allegory of salvation.

Lear sent out twelve copies of 'Some Incidents in the Life of My Uncle Arly' (the duck-free version that most readers know today) to close friends, dubbing it 'the last Nonsense poem I shall ever write'.[173] One cannot escape the thought that Lear was distributing his literary body to his twelve friends before he died, just as Christ distributed bread to the twelve disciples. Like so much else in Lear, this literary act hovers between impiety and fidelity.

Even in this final poem one can glimpse Lear's ambivalence towards religious language and the trade of priestcraft, and his tendency to transpose ideas of heaven and its ministers from religious to secular contexts. Lear wrote to Norah Bruce in 1870 that nonsense was 'the breath of my nostrils',

Fig. 2.7 **Lear feeding unfortunate birds (1861)**

a lovely and odd description of how nonsense was to him as natural and inevitable as breathing.[174] This sounds very like Job's biblical affirmation of integrity: 'All the while my breath is in me, and the spirit of God is in my nostrils. My lips certainly will not speak unjustly, nor will my tongue utter deceit'.[175] As is so often the case, Lear's play here succeeds in making a substitution (nonsense for God) that might be considered scandalous, yet is also touching. Nonsense is its own kind of truth. It emanates from the body; in offering innocent pleasure to thousands of children it offers a mode of communion that is wholly in keeping with Christ's mission. Yet Lear's work also reflects exasperation with the traditional forms and divisions of religion and the repressive uses to which they are turned. His poems prefer to confer their own blessing and to offer their own model of salvation through kindness and reciprocal affection, imaging a flight 'two by two' that is not into the ark but into the blue.

3

QUEER BEASTS

'Hanimal—? he ain't a hanimal . . . if you sees beasts &
birds alongside of each other at the same time, you may call
them Hanimals: but when they's alone they be beastesses &
birdesses'.[1]

EDWARD LEAR began his working career as an artist whose spe-
cialism was depicting birds and animals with such precision and vivacity that the brilliant flash of a parrot's plumage, the shiny, hard texture
of a tortoise's shell or the strange, hairy body of the whiskered yarke sprang
out of the illustration as if the purchaser of the lithograph possessed a specimen of the creature itself, each page a cage in an infinite aviary or zoological garden. Lear developed a flair for observing and recording other life
forms that no other poet has surpassed.

His work was not merely aesthetic. As someone engaged in close study
of rare species, he was part of the ongoing scientific project of the era: to
catalogue and classify the extraordinary wealth of life existing on the planet,
and to try to understand its behaviour and its place within a larger system.
In 1862, when he was almost fifty, Lear was contacted by the Linnean
Society, to which he had been elected an associate aged eighteen; they
asked if he was still engaged in 'communicating science'.[2] We may not
think of Lear 'communicating science' at all, but that was his first role as an
artist. By 1862 Lear had made his living principally as a landscape painter
for two decades. But he had not given up his interest in zoology. The previous month, in Corfu, he had sent '3 green frogs and 2 trap spiders' to Mrs
Naylor.[3] In October 1861, while in London, he had made his usual, regular
pilgrimages to the zoo, where he 'admired bears'; in May he went there to
observe the 'Bore Constructor' (boa constrictor) eat rabbits and ducks.[4] In

February 1861 he attended a dinner of scientific enthusiasts who talked about insects and spiders. Afterwards they repaired to Burlington House, home of the Linnean Society, in a way that reminded Lear of 'the old routine'.[5] From there, they walked to the Royal Society to hear the experimental physicist John Tyndall give a lecture on thermodynamics in gases. (Lear spotted Alfred Tennyson in the audience.) Tyndall, who discovered infrared radiation, gave a dense lecture that included reflections on the influence of carbon on the atmosphere.[6] Lear found the lecture difficult to understand and left before the end, but his presence at the Royal Society is instructive. Lear throughout his life participated in the exploration and discussion of phenomena observable in the natural world.

He corresponded with Joseph Hooker, the leading botanist of his day and head of the Royal Botanical Gardens at Kew, trying to identify the botanical names for species of tree that he had seen and painted in India. A keen plantsman, he smuggled seeds and roots though customs to grow in his garden in San Remo, where he specialised in varieties of *Ipomoea:* columbines with trumpet-shaped flowers in shades of white, pink and indigo. One of these species still bears Lear's name. Three birds were also named for him: Lear's cockatoo *(Lapochroa leari),* a colourful parakeet *(Platycercus leari)* and the now-endangered Lear's macaw *(Anodorhyncus leari).* The latter was identified in 1856 by Charles Lucien Bonaparte, Napoleon's ornithologist nephew, after detailed study of a lithograph by Lear revealed it to be a species distinct from the hyacinthine macaw. The attentive, prolonged looking and accurate depiction embodied in natural-history illustration enabled many of the discoveries of early nineteenth-century science. John Gould, the entrepreneurial former taxidermist who employed Lear to illustrate works including *The Birds of Europe,* was responsible for ornithological insights that shaped Darwin's vision. As Jonathan Smith has noted, 'It was Gould who had correctly identified Darwin's Galapagos finches and mockingbirds as separate but closely related species, and who provided the crucial observation that specific differences seemed to obtain among specimens from different islands in the archipelago'.[7] Lear supplied illustrations for volumes that helped naturalists to distinguish and characterise species that were in many cases new to Western study. His contribution to this field was real and salient.

Letters from Lear's travels are peppered with observations of trees, flowers, birds and animals. Writing to his sister Ellen from India in June 1874, he noted:

At [Mahoolee] there are immense banyan trees, & on some
there were great quantities of what appeared a sort of black
fruit, but in reality they were thousands of bats—(as large as
good-sized cats,) . . . [that] flew about the trees. There were
some most respectable apes also, with wonderfully long tails,
& all the Mrs apes carried their little apes below them when
they made extraordinary leaps—yet the Master and Miss apes
never fell off. Some of these monkeys stand nearly five feet
high when upright.[8]

In Lear's nature notes, a desire to study the animal accurately ('nearly five
feet high'), a compulsion to rhyme (bats with cats) and an anthropomor-
phic flair for creating story (respectable Mrs apes) combine in prose that is
naturally exuberant and enjoys conveying through its own irrepressible leaps
and exclamations the abundance and vitality of flora and fauna.

Lear's ornithological and zoological drawings are wonders. They rank
alongside the best work of John James Audubon, whose son Victor was a
friend of Lear's, ensuring that Lear had early access to volumes of *Birds of
America*.[9] Lear's early work in natural history was formative in shaping his
tree of acquaintance and friendship among the 'scientific gentry', which provided shelter and sustenance for the rest of his life. He was, for example,
introduced in his teens to the Drewitt family of Peppering, Sussex; his first
visit to their house was to examine a cabinet, probably of butterflies and
moths. John Drewitt was also famous as a collector of ornithological specimens; his granddaughter recalled that he could 'whistle the call of any English bird'.[10] John Drewitt's daughter, Fanny, married George Coombe, and
Lear's early letters show that he acquired fossils for George, who was an
enthusiast for the emerging science of palaeontology, and read at least one
'Fossil Book' that George lent him.[11] Lear's early writing reveals a fascinating interplay between his work in natural history and his humorous
correspondence. He refers to one of his missives to George as a 'Megatherium' of a letter.[12] A megatherium was an extinct giant sloth; Lear was slyly
deprecating his letter as humongous and slow. The first instance given in
the *Oxford English Dictionary* of *megatherium* being used in this extended
sense is dated 1850; Lear uses it in 1835. He was a pioneer of a new vocabulary that was bringing scientific discovery into ordinary speech.

Lear had been sketching birds and plants since he was very young, but
most of his early work is decorative and miniature; birds such as the 'Javanese

peacock' are figured against imaginary exotic landscapes of the kind that appeared on fans or screens. Once he was studying and painting live specimens, however, Lear progressed in proficiency with astonishing speed. He brought the careful minuteness of his early fancy work to bear on his sketches, taking detailed notes and colour samples for future reference. But the parrots, and indeed Lear's other studies of birds and beasts, are remarkable for the way that they combine fastidious attention with a rapid quality of encounter that catches the surprise and delight of seeing something for the first time. Lear's visual art is at its best when, like his writing, it harnesses his innate sense of drama. His birds and animals are presented as personalities whose unique costume and physical posture arrest us: we instinctively react to their apparent introversion and extroversion. The sensitive hedgehog has its eye turned away; its gentle yet prickly body, rendered in soft dun and grey wash, occupies the middle distance, as if shuffling towards the wings. By contrast, the brilliantly coloured toucan, who seems to be bowing forward to get a better look at us, leans curiously over the edge of a branch like an actor breaking the fourth wall.

Lear's work in natural history is innovative and experimental; it explores looking. While working on plates for *The Naturalist's Library,* Lear wrote to his employer, Sir William Jardine:

> Naturalists—it appears to me—don't pay sufficient attention to the colour of the eyes in their figures of birds . . . the colouring of the eye is frequently a very strong point which marks genera—or natural groupes—call them what you wish:—*all* the Platycerce have dark hazel eyes—& I think nearly all the Palaornis irides are white—most of the lories a double iris—particularly the Trichoglossi:—& when have Cockatoos the iris of a light colour?—the same might be traced much farther.[13]

The detail of this observation, and the independent hypothesis about the distinguishing marks of genus that it has led him to frame, mark Lear as himself a gifted naturalist: one who looks birds directly in the eye and notices what others miss. In another letter to Jardine, Lear hinted, 'I have been talking & wishing very much lately for a work on the *Genera* of birds only: there is no good arrangement of them,—& one with figures would be very desirable'. Jardine's *Naturalist's Library* aimed to illustrate as completely as possible each separate genus of birds, but Lear suggested going further: 'could you not in this new series, set about them—so as to be able to bind up the genera in families—or Classes—eventually?'[14] One way of proceeding to 'form a connected & systematic illustration of ornithology', Lear proposed, would be to begin with the struthious (flightless) birds.

This exchange shows how invested the young Lear was in the ongoing scientific project of classification. However, the 'struthious' birds might also remind us of Lear's comical picture of 'The Scroobious Bird' and his later nonsense poem 'The Scroobious Pip': a creature that refuses every question about whether it is bird, beast, insect or fish, responding with delightful obtuseness, 'my only name is the Scroobious Pip'. Here, as in Lear's 'Nonsense Botany', we can see a complex relationship between Lear's work in scientific illustration and his nonsense. At first glance, one might conceive his nonsense to be the fairground mirror of his natural history: twisting and resisting its impulse to order and categorise. Where science appears to favour the line of reason, nonsense favours the curve of imagination. There is an element of truth in this. Yet the relationship is not as binary as such a division would suppose. Often, Lear's work in both fields serves to highlight the shared inventiveness of science and literature: the sense that in producing new nomenclature, in imagining new hybrid forms, they are engaged in similar projects, which in turn respond to the wild creativity of Nature herself.

As an artist involved in 'communicating science', Lear was proof of the fluidity of boundaries that were, in the 1830s, just beginning to be established between art and science. The British Association for the Advancement of Science, founded in 1831 'to give a stronger impulse and a more systematic direction to scientific enquiry', in 1833 proposed the term 'scientist' (in contradistinction to 'artist') to denote those who practised science professionally. Daniel Brown has posited that Lear, for all his innovative techniques in lithography, belonged to an 'old world' approach to science that was fast becoming outmoded: his 'hand-coloured lithographic plates, "a form of visual natural theology", found their subscribers and other patrons amongst the wealthy, often aristocratic, Anglican scientific amateurs and connoisseurs that the emerging professional science of the BAAS was defining itself against'.[15] However, Lear was himself a member of the BAAS, as were several of his aristocratic patrons. Lear attended the 1835 conference of the BAAS in Dublin. Darwin was on his *Beagle* voyage, so Lear didn't meet him at the conference, and there is no concrete evidence that he did so at a later date. We do know, however, that Darwin was sufficiently aware of Lear to borrow his *Gleanings from the Menagerie at Knowsley Hall,* from the Royal Society's library in 1856.[16] In Dublin, Lear would have had the opportunity to meet fellow BAAS members including Charles Babbage, future inventor of the computer, and Darwin's teacher Adam Sedgwick, Woodwardian Professor of Geology at Cambridge.

Looking at the programme for the conference, one is struck by how much of it was concerned with inventing terms. Sedgwick during the meeting proposed the now-standard adjectives *Silurian* and *Cambrian* to refer to rocks of certain geological eras. His reasoning was imaginative rather than analytical: these were the names of ancient British and Welsh peoples who had lived in the areas where certain rock types predominated. Meanwhile the chemist John Dalton was proposing atomic symbols. Naming was provisional. Many creatures in this period occupied a position that was both linguistically and generically vague. In his *Voyage of the Beagle,* Darwin testily admitted that one bird was known as *Milvago leucurus, Falco leucurus, Falco australis, Circaëtus antarcticus,* and *Falco Novae Zelandiae,* despite the fact that it had never actually been found in New Zealand.[17] Thomas Bell's *History of British Quadrupeds,* which Lear also illustrated, documented the 'Reddish-grey Bat'. John Gould, in a letter to Sir William Jardine, mentioned that he would send a specimen of 'a green Bird', collected in a remote part of South America, which he thought 'will form a new genus', but which he would leave Jardine to 'describe and characterize'.[18] Lear's later pictures for children of 'The dark green bird', 'the pink bird' and 'the spotty bird' seem less purely whimsical in a world where many species had yet to be identified and where scientific taxonomy was labile. His nonsense creatures, like the Quangle Wangle, are no more inherently strange than many of the real species he was depicting, such as the whiskered yarke, the banded mungous and the eyebrowed rollulus.

At the BAAS conference, Lear attended the Zoology and Botany subsection. At its meetings, he would likely have heard lectures on 'the Formation of a Natural Arrangement of Plants', on fossil fish and on the 'principles of animal classification in general, and particularly on that of the mammalia, and on the connection which exists between the natural orders of the different classes in the animal kingdom and the order of fossil succession in the different beds of the crust of the earth'. Professor Louis Agassiz argued, 'Comparative anatomy has furnished facts most important in the classification of animals; yet it is undeniable that diversities of organisation exclusively considered, would lead to very artificial divisions, because there are as yet no established principles by which the importance of these divisions can be accurately estimated'.[19] If, Professor Agassiz continued, man was the 'type of creation', then it made sense to think of other creatures as classed according to the number of their internal organs and their resemblance to man's organic systems. But Agassiz's lecture opened the door to the possibility of other principles, admitting the lack of a sound and agreed basis for classifying animals. Lear was involved in scientific enquiry at a moment when its ontological basis, and man's place within its narrative of development, were in doubt. This discussion predated by over twenty years the publication of Darwin's controversial theory of natural selection as the mechanism of evolutionary development.

Lear greatly admired Darwin. He was so impressed when he discovered in January 1869 that his acquaintance Edmund Langton was Darwin's nephew that he wrote in his diary, 'nephew of DARWIN!!!!!!!!!!!!!!'[20] Lear also knew Erasmus Darwin, Charles Darwin's brother, as one of the patrons who visited his artist's studio.[21] Interestingly, however, it seemingly took seven years after the publication of *On the Origin of Species* for Lear to get around to reading it, which (diary notes suggest) he did during his Egyptian excursion of 1866–1867.[22] One can see Darwin's vocabulary filtering experimentally into Lear's. In February, he talks of the buildings he sees on the Nile: 'natural selection of heaps and houses which may all be sand hills one day by reason of want of strength to hold their own'.[23] It seems as if Darwin's views on evolution have met with Lear's natural preoccupation with loss to reinforce the idea of transience, in human habitation as in animal life, where some survive and others do not. After a long talk with Langton in April 1870 on 'Huxleyism and Darwinism', Lear concludes that they 'may be true—but are uncomfortable'.[24] Lear is trying on evolutionary theory like a horsehair shirt that fits but also itches.

When thinking about the impact of natural history on Lear's nonsense, then, it is important not to see Darwin in isolation. From the age of around eight, Lear had carefully copied apes from the Comte de Buffon's *Histoire Naturelle*, in which the author considers the possibility of man's descent, with other species, from a common vertebrate ancestor.[25] His varied and considerable reading in natural history ranged from the ornithological works of Charles Waterton (whom he met in Rome) to Henry Walter Bates's *The Naturalist on the River Amazons* (1863). Lear's lifelong friendship with Thomas Bell, with whom he worked on *A History of British Quadrupeds* (1837) and

A Monograph of the Testudinata (1836–1842), connects him to the ecological tradition of Gilbert White, the eighteenth-century curate whose letters so beautifully observe the flight of birds and the emergence of the small animals that populate the countryside around his rural parsonage. Bell, from 1862, occupied White's Selborne home, and Lear often stayed there. In *British Quadrupeds*, Bell introduces the ten species of British bats, which, he observes, have traditionally 'not only furnished objects of superstitious dread to the ignorant, but have proved to the poet and the painter a fertile source of gloom and terror'.[26] Bell counters this superstitious dread by demonstrating the beauty and interest of bats, and showing their similarity to humans. He notes that their wings contain the same bones as those in the human hand. They have a 'sixth sense' that enables them to avoid objects in the dark. Also:

> The female bat brings forth one or two young at a birth, which
> she nurses with great tenderness and care, carrying it about
> with her and holding it enshrouded in her ample cloak, which
> preserves it from all intrusion.[27]

The 'ample cloak' of the bat's wings invites the reader to identify with her 'tenderness' as she maternally clasps her young. Lear's sympathetic knowledge of live bats, which he had kept in his room (along with two hedgehogs, mice and weasels) when he was illustrating Bell's *Quadrupeds*, directly influences his children's alphabet in which *B* is for 'Beautiful Bat' (an unusual sentiment for its time), and 'The Quangle Wangle's Hat', on whose brim the Bisky Bat companionably roosts.[28]

Lear's artistic understanding of creatures and his scientific understanding are not separable. Unusually for his period, Lear insisted on working from live specimens whenever possible, noting the mistaken scientific assumptions that arose when artists sketched from skins. He huffs that 'a very erroneous figure' of *Pezoporus formosus* (a ground parrot) lately published depicts the bird *perched*, whereas 'these birds seldom or never perch—any more than a partridge'.[29] In terms of artistic method, Lear was also making it new. He learned the recently invented art of lithography from Charles Hullmandel, who became a close friend. Whereas engraving requires making cuts in steel—a process that Lear sometimes described as 'woundy, hard'[30]—lithographs are created with the use of a soft crayon on stone. Lear is particularly adept at communicating the texture of other living

Fig. 3.1 'B was a Bat' (1857)

creatures: the convex, shiny carapace of a tortoise contrasted with its vulnerable underbelly, birds' soft feathers, mammals' fur. Lithograph gives him the means to communicate feeling, in which the sense of touch and that of being touched mirror one another aesthetically and emotionally. *Lagothrix humboldtii*, Lear tells Jardine, has a grey coat 'very like wool shorn' and is 'more gentle than any monkey I ever met with,—he is in the habit of putting his lips forward as I have sketched him'.[31] Note that this monkey is 'he' rather than 'it'. The woolly monkey's pout comes towards us, like a kiss, in a way that we cannot respond to neutrally.

Lear is always interested in finding new artistic means of conveying life. He uses egg white to create sheen, bringing eyes alive.[32] He also experiments with posture. Even in a very early work, *The Gardens of the Zoological Society Delineated* (1831), Lear's illustration of two blue and yellow macaws—where one bird is pointing upward and the other downward, like jokers on a playing card—reminds us of the mirroring involved in engraving while suggesting the way in which parrots also mimic humans, their habit of topsy-turvy looking commenting on our self-conscious ability to change perspective. 'Come-parrot-ifly' is one of Lear's creative spellings; it allows us to see the animal mimicry in analogy.

Lear had admired Albrecht Dürer's watercolours on a visit to Vienna. He was highly aware of modern work in the field of zoological painting by Audubon, by Thomas Landseer and by William Harvey.[33] At Knowsley Hall, he had access to an unrivalled library of works in natural history, including Lady Impey's collection of Indian watercolours. Exquisitely painted in the Mughal miniaturist tradition, these studies feature birds, plants and insects in diagonal arabesque compositions that counterpoint their shapes and colours. Lear was constantly learning. It is evident that he admired the Knowsley volume containing Pierre Joseph Redouté's paintings of the Liliaceae family: he copied a pink amaryllis from it with extreme delicacy. Lear made active stylistic choices that reflect his awareness of competing styles in painting subjects from the natural world.

It is helpful to contrast Lear's work with Audubon's; they succeed in such different ways. Audubon's birds have a grandeur and splendour echoed in the sweep of the sublime landscapes they occupy. Audubon is the Gainsborough of ornithological art, painting birds who inherit a New World of wonders, of palm-fringed creeks and infinite bays. There is a Miltonic abundance in these vistas empty of Man, suggesting the perfection of Nature before the Fall. The Louisiana heron's aquamarine plumage mirrors the

Fig. 3.2 **Blue and yellow macaw,** *The Gardens and Menagerie of the Zoological Society Delineated* (1831)

colour of the creek. It has something of the quality of sculpture within a landscape garden: the bird is part of a harmony of line and tone of whose effect it cannot be aware. This unconsciousness is essential to its charm.

By contrast, Lear does not set his birds in detailed landscapes. In his early work, often the background is merely a deliberately sketchy branch and some leaves in outline, rendered in pen and Indian ink.[34] This has the effect of making the brilliantly rainbow-hued parrots, in particular, seem to leap off the page like a vivid butterfly trapped in a newspaper, which is taking flight from the drab two-dimensional field of print into the three-dimensional reality of space. Lear conveys life by making it stand out and stare out towards the viewer from the not-life behind it. This is an aesthetic theatre that echoes consciousness, a vivid articulation of difference between the subjecthood of the self and the object nature of the scenery in which that consciousness takes place. Although Lear sometimes obeys the convention of portraying the male and female of the species together to illustrate differences in coloration, his most successful works usually portray an individual bird or animal; it is the singularity of character rather than the identification of type that really fires his imagination. The position and expression of the eyes is always important in Lear's bird and animal portraits. He often raises the position of the subject in the visual field so that the viewer's and the creature's eye meet. Lear's splendid eagle owl for *The Birds of Europe* looks so proud of his superbly feathered chest and mortarboard eyebrows that he resembles a bumptious professor, while the red and yellow macaw for Lear's *Illustrations of the Family of Psittacidae* glances coquettishly over one shoulder, flaunting the gorgeous scarlet, yellow, green and aquamarine of his waistcoat wings. A preliminary study of the 'night monkey', now in Harvard's Houghton Library, reveals how much time Lear spent understanding the structure of the creature's huge eyes, which are adapted to its nocturnal habits, compared with his sketchier treatment of its hands and feet. Splashes of colour (references for the finished portrait) both aid Lear's precise recall and lend such sketches a joyous, flamboyant air of improvisation: here a surprising wash of blue brings out the lustre of the night monkey's black tail.[35] Sometimes the energy of the portrayal is comic; the variable chachalaca—aptly enough, given the onomatopoeia of its name—appears to be laughing. The spectacled owl's eyes have an amber glare that conveys ruthlessness. In every case, however, it is the dynamic of mutual vision that interests Lear—not a world from which man is absent, but one in which behaviour, on both sides, is adjusted to incorporate consciousness of being seen.

Lear was working with animals and birds who were, in many cases, pets as well as specimens. Some had colourful histories; Lear drew a specimen of *Brotogeris pyrrhopterus* that had previously been the pet of the queen of the Sandwich Islands. Lear commented in a letter to Jardine, 'Lord Stanley has a Parrot—or rather a monster, from which I believe I could obtain a drawing: it is like nothing but itself & will puzzle all makers of genera'.[36] Lear's humorous insistence that this parrot is a 'monster' suggests that he may have experienced its difficult behaviour. The parrot is, however, also unique in a biological sense, as its genus is uncertain. Lear's description, which hovers between these two understandings of 'like nothing but itself', highlights the tension between responding to the bird scientifically, as an unclassified specimen, and responding to it socially, as an idiosyncratic personality. This tension is evident, too, in *The Naturalist's Library;* the volume on parrots that Lear illustrated claims that one specimen of the 'Ash-Coloured or Grey Parrot' lived domestically for ninety-three years, eating biscuits dipped in Madeira. It was 'distinguished for its colloquial powers' and would 'fetch its master's slippers when required' or call the servants.[37] A reviewer in a new journal, the *Naturalist* (1837), was so charmed by this particular picture that he noted, 'Mr. Lear has given a resemblance so faithful and accurate that we can almost swear to the sly old rascal'.[38] Whether the writer is imagining swearing to the picture's likeness or cussing with the parrot is creatively uncertain.

In a delicate watercolour for Lord Derby from the mid-1830s, Lear has drawn a chimpanzee in a blue-spotted shirt with a child's hoop in its hand. This was Thomas, a Gambian chimp bought by the Zoological Society in 1835, whose short, sad life Isobel Charman has recently chronicled.[39] He survived only until the winter of 1836 but became a celebrity at the zoo, where he lived with the keeper Devereux Fuller and his wife in their cottage. Many visitors reflected on the human-like behaviour of the 'monkey-child'. George Cruikshank's *Comic Alphabet* of 1836, featuring *C* for *chimpanzee,* shows an ape-like dandy, startled, looking through the bars as the chimp, in its spotted shirt, swings from a branch, holding out its hand as if to shake his.

In Lear's depiction, the chimp's grip on the hoop suggests the similarity between the habits of human children and those of primates. The portrait is disturbing to a modern eye: it recalls the long history of treating apes as humans manqué, yet it also displays a sensitivity, so characteristic of Lear's work, to the interior life of the creature's mind, preoccupied as it is with objects outside the realm of our picture. Lear has subscribed the study *Anthropithecus troglodytes,* using the Latin he employs in his specimen drawings of creatures in the menagerie. But a list of the pictures hung at Knowsley in the 1830s reveals that the chimp was known as 'Master Thomas Chimpanzee'; his portrait by Benjamin Waterhouse Hawkins hung in Lord Derby's bedroom, suggesting Derby's intimate bond with a much-loved favourite.[40] In a setting where creatures were studied, bred and anatomised, yet also sometimes clothed, the potential conflict between placing them according to their 'scientific' denomination and using their 'family' name must have been very apparent.

The implied self-awareness of Lear's creatures has struck several commentators. Daniel Brown remarks:

> His animals are endowed with an autonomous subjectivity, a
> quality that appears anthropomorphic only through the
> assumption, entrenched in modern philosophy since Des-
> cartes, that human beings have the monopoly of such being,
> that it distinguishes us from the rest of nature.[41]

The selfhood that Lear's bird and animal portraits seem to convey is necessarily a form of projection, an interpretation of character that relies on human perspective to imagine the inner life of those whose experience is ineluctably different from our own. But, from the human perspective, it succeeds in dramatising visually the wordless communication of posture and behaviour, just as cartoons do—drawing our imaginative attention to the predicament that humans and animals share, of being able to convey only part of what they mean or feel or are. There is a dynamic connection between these early natural-history studies and Lear's nonsense—not just in the brio and sense of movement that Lear imports to his nonsense drawings but in the gift for mime—the potential comedy and pathos involved in communicating without words. Lear's pictures convey the myriad ways in which the body speaks for itself. It can express exuberance, pleasure, anger, vulnerability. It isn't accidental that creatures in his work are often partners in acting out unaccountable desires. Animals and birds, in Lear, can stand in for what we are saying when we are not saying anything, or when we think we are saying something else. Lear in a letter reported that Lord Derby, who was rather deaf, misheard Lear's kind enquiry after his health as an enquiry about his aviary. The results were both nonsensical and telling:

> 'I hope your head is better'—for he had had a bad headache
> the day before. 'Oh!'—replied he—'I have found a remedy for
> that. I have taken out all the little birds—& put in one
> cockatoo & three large red Maccaws'.[42]

Often, animals and birds are what issue accidentally from an unwary speaker's mind. The nonhuman suggests the restless subconscious life that we try to domesticate, but which nonetheless escapes our conscious control. Animals are notionally our 'others', but they also allow us to visualise repressed aspects of ourselves.

Lear notes in his diary for 26 November 1865:

> Some Spanish friend of the Marks—puzzled them by
> declining to dine or go out in the evening—because of his *cow,*
> which annoyed him constantly, & he could not get rid of.—
> meaning *cough*—(*bough* spell *bow,* why not cough *cow?*) . . .
> Among other, queer things, Dr. Barry the old Inspector
> General of Hospitals—has lately died, & has been discovered
> to be a woman! Queer old critter.[43]

We imagine the persistent cow that troubles the Spanish gentleman and can't oust the image once it has entered our heads, although it proves to be a misapprehension. Similarly, the discovery about James Miranda Barry, whom Lear would have met in Corfu, being anatomically a woman revises our comprehension but doesn't alter the male character that s / he successfully inhabited for fifty-six years. We are all queer creatures in one way or another, subject to social misreading; animals and birds in Lear's comic illustrations convey this unruly truth.

Harvard University possesses fascinating sketches that Lear made in the parrot house at the London Zoo when he was drawing studies for the Psittacidae volume. In them, the parrots appear large, looking out thoughtfully on their visitors; Lear has also sketched in a variety of human zoogoers who are little by comparison. One is a stout man with spectacles; one is a crippled woman hobbling with a stick; one is an absurdly thin man striding along. Spending time drawing in the parrot cage made Lear think of how parrots might see humans: as odd types, or as a crowd of jeering faces, indistinct and threatening. In another early pen-and-ink cartoon, produced for the children of his close friends George and Fanny Coombe, Lear drew 'Ye Hippopotamouse or gigantick Rabbitte'. The text beneath explains:

> This large beaste doth belonge to ye familie of Geo Coombe
> Esq of Preston. It dwelleth in a large boxe, and feedeth on
> lettuce leaves or other salads. Alle day longe he moveth his
> nose up & down, but in other respectes he is a harmless beaste.

Fig. 3.3 **View from the parrot cage (c. 1830–1832)**

On one side ye picture doth represent one who offereth a bit of
domestick spinach for ye Hippopotamouse Rabbit, his supper.[44]

The human keepers of the gigantick Rabbitte are tiny. The comedy of reversal again invites the viewer to reconsider the traditional subject/object
position of human and animal. Lear parodies the antiquated language of

Fig. 3.4 'Ye Hippopotamouse or gigantick Rabbitte'

bestiaries to define his Hippopotamouse: a creature whose absurd hybridity, resembling simultaneously a mouse and a hippopotamus, is evoked through the nonsense of the portmanteau word. This cartoon anticipates ideas that will be important to Lear's nonsense world. Strange crosses and pairings attract him, linguistically and visually. By making humans comically small compared with animals and birds, Lear also creates a remarkably level playing field of sympathy.

For George and Fanny's children he also produced around 1838 the visual cartoon 'Portraites of the inditchenous beestes of New Olland'.[45] Intriguingly, this evoked real Australian animals such as the duck-billed platypus, a semiaquatic egg-laying mammal which, when a skin was brought back to Europe in 1798, was at first thought to be a taxidermic hoax: a beaver with a duck's beak. James Bischoff in his *Sketch of the History of Van Diemen's Land* (1832) noted that the platypus appeared 'to blend several of the characters of the quadruped and the bird, and in one of the species even of the fish'. He compared the creature to a duck united with a seal's body.[46] Lear, who regularly attended meetings of the Royal Society, may have been aware of discussion there in 1832 of the platypus, also known as *Ornithorhynchus paradoxus*, which would have signal importance for naturalists trying to understand the developmental narrative of evolutionary biology.

The ornithological trip of Lear's employer, John Gould, to Australia in 1838 would also have flagged the variety of real Australian mammals that Lear draws in his cartoons for the Coombe children, including the wombat and the possum.

Lear's fantastical antipodean creatures also include the fictional 'Owly-Pussey-catte a new beaste found in ye Island of New-South Wales'.[47] This cartoon, also drawn for the Coombe children, is probably a companion piece to the 'inditchenous beestes'. The strange, pipe-smoking creature Lear depicts sitting on a tree branch in the moonlight is owl above the line and (mostly) striped cat below it, the feline tail dangling like a candy cane. As an inhabitant of New South Wales, it aptly wears a Welsh hat, but with a couple of peacock feathers protruding from the brim. Perhaps Lear was inspired by the idea of a catbird, a species of bowerbird that inhabits Australia. Or perhaps he had read William Bingley's *Animal Biography; or Anecdotes of the Lives, Manners and Economy of the Animal Creation* (1803), which noted how similar cats and owls were in the physiognomy of their heads and their habits of ridding fields of mice: 'In their general modes of life, the Owls may be looked on as the Cats of the feathered species'.[48]

However he came up with the notion, it is fascinating that Lear's first thoughts about the possible union of an owl and a pussy-cat are rooted in hybridity. Like the Hippopotamouse and the 'Froglodytes', which appear in a letter of 1847 to Chichester Fortescue, this invented 'new species' explores the possibility of being more than one thing at once in a way that is traditionally comical, as mismatched heads and tails are comical. Yet it also reflects a new awareness in scientific circles of real animals that combined unlikely biological characteristics. If a duck and a kangaroo had sex, might the result be a duck-billed platypus? If an owl and a pussy-cat had sex, might the result be an owley-pussey-catte? These combination-creatures make Lear's later poems of improbable love seem less wholly abstract in their romance.

There is just a hint that the Owley-Pussey-catte is both male and female. Welsh hats are usually worn by women as part of their traditional costume. But this smoking owl seems more of a gent.[49] Lear would return to the idea of the offspring of owl and cat in the sequel to his most famous poem. In this subsequent history of the Owl and the Pussy-cat, the Pussy-cat has committed suicide, leaving the owl to bring up their children alone. These children are 'partly little beasts and partly little fowls'. It appears that the male children are owls, while the female children are cats. At a time when

Fig. 3.5 'Umbrellifera Kendal' (1836)

the X and Y chromosomes had yet to be discovered, Lear uses species difference as a way of thinking about sexual difference, and also about the possibility that one might not belong exclusively to one sex. I will come back
to this idea when looking more closely at Lear's poems of jumbly relationship, where conventional sex is so frequently frustrated by physical incompatibility. But it is interesting to see how early it is seeded. Lear's composite
creatures are creatively enabling, breaking down category boundaries between species, which can stand as a proxy for boundaries pertaining to
gender and sexuality that may seem fixed but turn out to be fluid.

Viewing Lear's nonsense against this background, we can see how his
many composite creatures reflect not only a habitual joy in doodling, but
also his awareness of current discussion in zoological science: how creatures
may sprawl across the boundaries once held to separate plant, animal, insect and fish; how they may develop new characteristics to adapt to varying
environments; and the difficulties of classification in the face of such organic
fluidity. In a letter of 1836 from the Lake District, Lear joked that the 'dear
little babies' of Kendal were born with 'fins' and 'webbed feet' because of
the perpetual rain.[50] He produced a sketch of 'Umbrellifera': a group of
people carrying umbrellas who, since their faces are obscured, are like plants
of the carrot family Umbelliferae, which have inflorescences of many flowers

from a single stalk. This drawing anticipates Lear's later nonsense botany, where people and plants are fused, and the Umbrageous Umbrella-Maker in one of his nonsense alphabets, whose face is wholly obscured by his umbrella. A similar riff in a letter of 1847 from Italy explains that he has encountered a friendly family of 'Froglodytes':

> At the caves of Ispica we became acquaint with a family of original Froglodytes: they are very good creatures, mostly sitting on their hams, & feeding on lettuces & honey. I proposed bringing away an infant Frog but Proby objected. . . . [51]

Here, his invented portmanteau word 'Froglodyte' (frog-troglodyte) is a linguistic crossbreed that mimics the imaginary fusing of bloodlines that such an amphibious 'original' cave-dwelling race would entail. One recalls *Anthropithecus troglodytes,* otherwise known as Master Thomas, the monkey-child he painted in 1836. One kind of human/animal ambiguity seems to have inspired another. In a cartoon of Caius Marius hiding in the swamps of Rome that Lear drew in 1841, he decorated the marsh with 'bullfrogs', which sport the heads of bulls and the legs of frogs. Again, the linguistic frisson of the pun becomes a cue for imaginative visual hybridisation.

The Clangle-Wangle, Clangel-Wangel or Quangle Wangle, which appears in three of Lear's nonsense works, is another 'amphibious' creature, 'dangerous and delusive', whose contested name is analogous to its uncertain biology. Language furnishes a model for exploring hybridity and amphibology: for effecting new organic crosses, such as the 'plumpudding

Fig. 3.6 'All among the bullfrogs' from *The tragical life and death of Caius Marius Esqre* (1841)

flea', and splits, such as the Seeze Pyder. In *Glaucus* (1855), Charles King-sley introduced children to the sea-spider, a creature who 'has this pecu-liarity, that possessing no body at all to speak of, he carries his needful stomach in long branches, packed inside his legs'.[52] In Lear's alternative etymology, which is also an alternative biology, the Seeze Pyder is a sea monster with fangs that *seizes* the boat of the little children who go round the world.

Darwin himself, in *On the Origin of Species* (1859), commented on the likeness between language and biology in preserving vestigial relics of former evolutionary phases: 'Rudimentary organs may be compared with the let-ters in a word, still retained in the spelling, but become useless in the pro-nunciation, but which serve as a clue in seeking for its derivation'.[53]

Lear was, in the 1830s and 1840s, already playing with the way in which linguistic forms can image morphological between-states and putative an-cestry. Nonsense words—words that have no prescribed meaning but whose shape and sound are suggestive of meaning—are able to convey the essen-tially fluid experience of being, its priority to the social identity conferred by naming. They also call attention to the uncertainty of the process by which organic forms develop, merge and change their usage. Nineteenth-century anatomists attempted to trace species development by looking at homologous and analogous structures. Homologous structures, like the human hand and the bat's wing, share characteristics because they derive from a common ancestor. Analogous structures are similar because they have evolved separately to meet similar evolutionary needs. When Lear, in 'The Story of the Little Children Who Went Round the World', plays with the idea that Blue-Bottle-Flies live in bottles, he tests the proposi-tion that the name of the creature is the equivalent of a homologous structure—that it derives from the word *bottle*, meaning a vessel, which is the creature's home. In fact, however, the word *bluebottle* first meant a cornflower and was then humorously applied to beadles, policemen and other officers in blue clothing.[54] It is through this analogous reasoning that the fly acquired its name. The body of language, like the animal body, con-tains visual and aural similarities that may or may not denote common ancestry. Nonsense relishes these decoy ducks in the family tree of etymology. It enjoys mimicking Nature, creating composites (Froglodytes, the hippo-potamouse) that do not yet exist but might as well do so.

The Zoo: A Two-Way Mirror

While scientific meetings that considered newly discovered species, producing new taxonomy and new theories of relationship were one source of inspiration for Lear's art, another was more direct. Lear's close working relationship with the Zoological Society of London whose Gardens (now Regent's Park Zoo) opened to the public in 1828 meant that he spent much of his early life as a painter there. In later life the zoo became a place of pilgrimage whenever Lear returned to England; he often ate his dinner there, never failing to spot something of interest, from the hyaena to the orang-outang, whom Lear initially remarked was 'a great brute' then, when a subsequent visit elicited greater sympathy, 'a sight to see . . . eating bread and butter, & "propping" herself up in a shawl'.[55] Such 'props' as shawls and bread and butter aided the process of seeing such animals as like humans. The zoo was a social theatre of mutual spectatorship. In July 1872, aged sixty, Lear wrote to Lady Wyatt:

> I have been again to the Zoological Gardens. . . . And while looking at
> that queer beast the g[ian]t Anteater, I heard the following comments.
> (Placid & obese Man.) "Thems the Hanteeters."
> (Irascible female.) "Thems?—They ain't thems—there be only one."
> (Placid man.) "Well—leastways he's a coorus hanimal"
> (Irascible F.) "Hanimal—? he ain't a hanimal: he's a beast."
> (Placid M.) "A beast's a Hanimal"
> (I.F.) "He ain't no such thing: if you sees beasts & birds alongside of
> each other at the same time, you may call them Hanimals: but
> when they's alone they be beastesses & birdesses."[56]

In this letter, looking at animals becomes a way of looking at people. The 'placid and obese man' and the 'irascible female' are types of curious animal, 'curious' as spectators but equally as specimens, whose misplaced *h*'s and irregular pronouns mark them as working class. Their viewing defines them; in turn, Lear's verbal portrait of the couple marks the degrees of social difference he perceives between them and him. The 'female' insists that when creatures are seen together in the plural they are 'Hanimals'. But a creature on its own is a 'beastess' or 'birdess': rather grand words which imply that, although she calls the anteater 'he', she is identifying such solitary creatures as female like herself. The 'irascible female' is a figure of fun, yet her assertion that identification is not absolute—but depends on relationship—is acute.

As she perversely but rightly observes, an animal on its own is not an animal. In Lear's travel writing, human characters are described as like 'a caged armadillo' or an 'encaged macaw', a locution that sounds very like 'enraged'.[57] Lear's art often inspires reflection on how we erect psychological barriers to keep from being animals as strong as any we erect to keep animals from us.

Many books have been written about Darwin's influence on Victorian literature, but the impact of the zoo preceded this influence and was in its own way equally profound, changing forever the public's capacity to identify and to identify *with* once-exotic animals. After all, Darwin's *On the Origin of Species* sold 104,000 copies before the copyright expired in 1901; by the 1850s, the zoo was admitting 350,000 visitors a year.[58] Previously, Londoners had taken their children to see the animals at the Tower of London and in menageries such as that of Edward Cross at Exeter 'Change. But the zoo was different. An institution designed to promote scientific study, but also to bolster Britain's domestic industry (by considering animals that might be worth breeding commercially) and international reputation, it sought to house over three hundred kinds of creature within a landscape garden where they were continuously open to view. It produced a rush of works in various media that responded to the psychological dynamics of human-animal scrutiny.

A tiny illustrated guide to the zoo from 1835 commented that there was some debate as to whether the secretary bird was a 'vain bird'. A 'great naturalist' had noted that when a painter was drawing it, 'it approached him, looked attentively at his paper, stretched out its neck, and erected the feathers of its head, as if admiring its own figure'.[59] Had the bird seen itself in the drawing? Or did this behaviour arise from 'nothing more than the love which almost all domesticated birds show of having their heads scratched'? Ordinary zoo-going members of the public were invited to look and to ponder the deep scientific question of animal subjectivity.

Thomas Haynes Bayly's comic song 'The Monkey Jacket' (1835) noted:

At Gardens Zoological,
    If monkey tricks attract them,
The girls see monkies large and small,
    Then why should dandies act them?
The hairy phiz that suits an ape,
    I own you do not lack it—
But why assume the monkey shape
    Why wear a monkey jacket?[60]

Such lyrics hinted, long before Darwin's *The Descent of Man* (1872), at the similarity between human and anthropoid courtship tactics. If animals were so like us in their habits, it followed that their feelings might also be similar, and that captivity made them anxious and unhappy. An 1831 article in the *Atlas*, describing a visit to the zoo, noted that 'there seem to be among these creatures the elements of humanity, separated and dispersed as the rays of light are separated by a prism'.[61] Earlier in the same article the author had compared the zoo to a debtors' prison, reflecting that if the

A STRANGE BIRD.

Fig. 3.7a Thomas Hood, 'A Strange Bird', *Comic Annual* (1831)

brute creation was *indebted* to man, he was making them pay by depriving them of their liberty. The author describes female zoo-goers who view the ostrich and are led to wonder about where the plumes come from that they wear with evening dress. The zoo emphasised the need to display, shared by humans and animals, but also the alienation that both human and animals might experience when subject to enforced scrutiny.

Thomas Hood, the comic poet and artist, was a regular zoo-goer, which influenced his designs for woodcuts in his *Whims and Oddities* and the

UNCONSCIOUS IMITATION.

Fig. 3.7b Thomas Hood, 'Unconscious Imitation', *Whims and Oddities* (1827)

immensely popular *Comic Annual*. His cartoon 'Unconscious Imitation' (1827) shows a man on crutches and a giraffe staring at one another in mirror pose; 'A Strange Bird' (1831) uses the resemblance between a man's coattails and a bird's tail feathers to create a visual pun. Hood also explores the possibility of plants developing animal characteristics, and vice versa. In 'From the Zoological Gardens' (1831), a bunch of flowers stares challengingly at us with a crowd of eyes. His accompanying ode to the zoo's secretary, Nicholas Vigors, imagines him gardening his menagerie, 'earthing up' beavers and setting 'early Kangaroos in pots'. These images are part of a common currency of imaginative hybrids and doubles that emerges in the early nineteenth century, largely stimulated by the zoo.

George Cruikshank, in his cartoon 'Zoological Sketches' (1834), also has men in coattails resembling bird's tails. He depicts 'A Species of Macaw' (a man with a hooked nose in splendid coloured regalia), a human male 'Tom tit', 'Black bird', 'Booby' and 'Gigantic Crane'. At first, entrance to the zoo was limited to fellows of the Zoological Society and their guests, a scheme (ineffectually) designed to exclude the lower social orders.[62] Cruikshank's clever cartoon 'Fellows of the Zoological Society' in the *Comic Almanack* (1851), explores a different kind of fellowship: between visitor and animal. The lion and the social lion, hippo and man-hippo, man and monkey stand next to one another, highlighting their physical resemblances and hinting that they may be cousins beneath the skin. The same magazine considers how orang-outangs might react if a man strolled into their midst; the apes wonder if the 'monster' might eventually gain sufficient intelligence to speak their language. John Parry's 'Zoological Oddities', in *Ridiculous Things* (1854), shows a fish in a cockade and a parrot in boots; 'a lion' is a man with whiskers, while 'a deer' is a doe-eyed lady.[63] His vignettes of absurd hairstyles, 'a la peacock', 'a la crow', 'a la black swan' and 'a la Piggywiggy', anticipate by some years the flurry of *Punch* cartoons on the theme of women preening like birds, using feathers and elaborate coiffures to give themselves an advantage in the competition to find a mate. Significantly, a reviewer in the *Illustrated Times* of 1862 thought that Lear had based his limericks and visual humour on Parry's.[64]

It is important to recognise that Lear produces his drawings of people, animals and birds mimicking or becoming one another in a rich context of early nineteenth-century play on this theme. Lear certainly knew Hood's and Cruikshank's work and was likely influenced by it. However, Lear's drawings also differ from those of his contemporaries. Cruikshank's young

Fig. 3.8 George Cruikshank, 'Fellows of the Zoological Society', *Comic Almanack* (1851)

bucks and boobies are presented satirically. By contrast, Lear's birdmen and fishwomen do not satirise any particular social group. Rather, Lear is fascinated by the way in which pairings between human and nonhuman can image both a release from social inhibition and its opposite: the way that such escapes often prove temporary or unsatisfactory.

> There was an Old Man of Whitehaven,
> Who danced a quadrille with a Raven;
> But they said, 'It's absurd to encourage this bird!'
> So they smashed that Old Man of Whitehaven.[65]

In the illustration accompanying Lear's limerick, the man, uninhibitedly dancing with a raven, has a silhouette nearly identical to the bird's; his dance partner, who ought to be a woman, is in fact his avian double. This strange homology is visually delightful but proves socially problematic, a refusal of the customary differences involved in dancing. The quadrille was a formal square dance performed symmetrically by two couples; it had five different 'figures', the third being 'Le Poule', 'the hen'. Perhaps this is where the man and the bird make a faux pas. For whatever reason, their capers are ill-omened. Whether the 'bird' that shouldn't be encouraged is really the man or the raven is ambiguous. The limerick concludes by coolly informing us

There was an Old Man of Whitehaven, who danced a quadrille with a raven;
But they said, "It's absurd to encourage this bird!"
So they smashed that Old Man of Whitehaven.

Fig. 3.9a–d **Limericks from the** *Book of Nonsense* **and** *More Nonsense*

There was an old person of Bree,
Who frequented the depths of the sea;
She nurs'd the small fishes, and washed all the dishes,
And swam back again into Bree.

Fig. 3.9b

There was an Old Person of Ems, who casually fell in the Thames;
And when he was found they said he was drowned,
That unlucky Old Person of Ems.

Fig. 3.9c

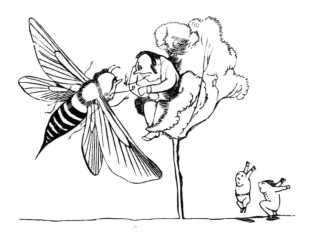

There was an Old Man in a tree, who was horribly bored by a bee;
When they said, "Does it buzz?" he replied, "Yes, it does!
It's a regular brute of a bee!"

Fig. 3.9d

that 'they smashed' the man. There is just a hint here of species difference standing in for sexual difference. If the Man of Whitehaven prefers the wrong kind of partner, he pays a heavy price.

The old person of Bree who is nursing the fishes also seems perfectly contented, but her behaviour is rather disturbing if we pause (which we may not do) to think about it.[66] If she is nursing the fishes in the sense of breast-feeding them, it implies that she has misunderstood how fish reproduce; she can't give them what they need, and they can't be anything more than surrogates for her maternal impulse. She may become a mermaid—the illustration shows her dress becoming a tail—but can she really be a mer-mother? The man of Ems who falls into the Thames looks like a flounder. The 'casual' (i.e. accidental) fall seems a euphemism for suicide, a habit that Goethe's Werther had forever associated with Germany in the British imagination. If his impulse is to swim with the fishes, it is an attraction with fatal results. These are comic illustrations, but there is an undertow of desperation to the attempted escapes into a different body that the humans engineer. If we are looking for the source of the pathos that haunts Lear's comedy, it is often here—in the gap between being animal and being human, the powerlessness of the one and the self-consciousness of the other. There is impossible desire on both sides. In this gap we can also see figured the separation between childhood and adulthood and the inevitable frustrations that attend both states, where child and adult look at one another, resemble one another yet can never fully share each other's inner world.

In Lear's work, sympathy constantly stretches in two directions. We look at animals, such as the frogs Lear claims in a letter pay him a visit with their two eldest tadpoles, and are led to consider, albeit humorously, their inner lives—their domestic cares and aspirations. But looking at animals, in Lear, is always also a way of looking at ourselves—at our unfreedom, which is the fruit of our self-consciousness, and at the social anxieties that cause us, like the scroobious snake, to wear a hat that obscures our face, for fear of biting someone. That tragicomic fear is an inverted one, a preloaded anxiety about ourselves and what we might do, which is the very essence of the internalised guilt that Freud would identify in *Civilisation and Its Discontents* (1929) as the force that renders us socially amenable but psychically inhibited. Freud asks how civilisation controls the aggressiveness of the individual that might threaten its communal structures. The answer is: 'His aggressiveness is introjected, internalized; it is, in point of fact, sent back to where it came from—that is, it is directed towards his own ego'.[67] By presenting animals, the very life forms that should represent the alternative to man's introjected aggression, as subject to similar inhibition, Lear opens a window to viewing humans as estranged from themselves.

> There was an Old Person of Dundalk,
> Who tried to teach fishes to walk;
> When they tumbled down dead, he grew weary, and said,
> 'I had better go back to Dundalk!'[68]

Lear's animals are not fully anthropomorphised in the way that Beatrix Potter's animals are; they do not have Christian names and homes with furniture in them. Rather, they appear with minimal props, as if caught in transition to awareness of the bizarre habits and norms of human society. In 'There was an old man of Dumbree', a production line of eighteen be-mused owls stares at a man with owl-like spectacles who is teaching them to drink tea rather than eat mice, which isn't 'proper or nice'. The man re-sembles a missionary from the human to the animal world.[69] His cultural assumptions about what is 'proper' (polite) for humans threaten to deprive the owls of their proper (correct) diet. Decorum breeds starvation. In an-other limerick, ducklings are taught to dance by a feather-headed old lady of France, whose terpsichorean whimsy seems to reflect more on her need for nature than the ducks' need for nurture. (Her wild profile in some ways recalls that of a maenad of the French Revolution, which would give a po-litical twist to her French dancing.) Lear has adapted this limerick from one in the *History of Sixteen Wonderful Old Women:* 'There came an Old Woman from France,/Who taught grown up Children to dance,/But they were so stiff,/She sent them home in a miff,/This sprightly Old Woman from France'.[70] In Lear's version, the ducklings answer back; they cannot or will not be taught ('When she said, 'Tick-a-tack!'—They only said, 'Quack!'/Which grieved that old lady of France'). One sees clearly how animals in Lear can occupy the position of 'grown-up' and 'child' at the same time, and also how Lear's limericks engage a kind of resistance in animals to human choreog-raphy that is deeply suggestive of humans' own struggle with cultural constraints. The Old Person of Dundalk tries to teach fishes to walk, with predictably fatal results. He can go back to Dundalk, but the fishes can't go back to being fishes. Becoming human, in Lear, is a dangerous path to tread.

Other Old Persons in Lear's limericks are attempting to fly from terres-trial life, nesting with the birds or consorting with insects. Perhaps they have been reading Wordsworth's 'The Tables Turned' and are trying to adopt its wisdom: 'come forth into the light of things / Let Nature be your teacher'. If so, however, the results are not overwhelmingly positive. The 'Old Person of Hove / Who frequented the depths of a grove / Where he studied his books with the wrens and the rooks' is 'tranquil'. But the 'old person of Crowle, / Who lived in the nest of an owl', is 'depressing', screaming out with his fellow birds as if seeking maternal care that never arrives. Another owl-featured man sitting on a fence with an owl is troubled by its continuing to 'bother and howl'. Yet another nonsensical nature-lover is hiding out in a humanoid tree, where he is menaced by a huge bee with a human face. Lear liked to use the self-invented past participle 'bebothered', meaning irritated or upset; this man is bee-bothered, but the bee's face, which resembles his own, suggests that the source of the man's buzzing anxiety comes as much from within as it does from without. The bee not only mirrors the man's profile and expression; its proboscis has become a pipe, so that it seems to be smoking, as he is. Lear's flies and bees always have human faces. It as if the 'bee' confronts us with our existential state: our selves are confirmed but also unsettled by our awareness of other creatures and their alternative, but ultimately unknowable, modes of bee-ing. Culture finds no permanent escape from itself in nature; humans discover in nature, rather, a reflection of themselves that is also a reflection on their own behaviour and the animal needs it expresses or represses.

Where George Cruikshank's *Comic Alphabet* of 1836 illustrates *P* for 'Pretty-Poll' with a boy whose fingers are bitten by a parrot, Lear's quizzical limerick about the man of Dunrose depicts a man with a parrot who is 'pulling him by the nose', evoking a figurative Victorian sense of the phrase: 'to ridicule'. The parrot's attack on the man's embarrassingly similar beaky proboscis is not only sharp; it is pointed. The bird is a painful mirror for his self-consciousness.

In Lear's animal alphabet of 1870 for Daisy and Arthur Terry, creatures are discovered compensating for their animality in all sorts of peculiar ways.[71] The Fitzgiggious Fish always walks about upon stilts because he has no legs. The picture might well make us think about the awkward evolution of aquatic animals onto land. The Obsequious Ornamental Ostrich wears boots to keep his feet 'quite dry'. Ostrich feathers were routinely used as ornaments by ladies in Victorian society, but the idea of the male ostrich as intrinsically 'ornamental', and troubled about getting wet, is humorously discomfiting. Animals should not see themselves thus. Indeed, they should not be self-conscious at all. As so often in Lear, feet here suggest other sensitive body parts whose wetness can cause anxiety. The Queer Querulous Quail smokes tobacco on a teakettle—perhaps his grouchiness comes from his humanoid addiction to stimulants—while the Worrying Whizzing Wasp plays sweetly on the flute with a Morning Cap. Normally one would expect a wasp to 'worry' in the sense of harassing humans. But here the sense is that the wasp is harassed by an obscurely felt pressure to *be* human. Her fussy dress, like that of the Kicking Kangaroo, makes us aware of the tension between her aggressive capacities and her demure performance of a social role. The pale-pink muslin cannot quite cover the kangaroo's powerful tail, which sticks out like a metaphor for the phallic self, escaping from the cover of social decorum. The fact that the kangaroo is female complicates the politics of dress as a screen for sexual identity that Lear is hinting at. The snake who wears a hat *for fear he should bite someone* and the umbrageous umbrella maker (one of three human creatures in this animal parade), 'whose face nobody ever saw because it was covered by his Umbrella', are similarly suggestive of the way in which social role play can amount to self-effacement

There was an old man of Dunrose ;
A parrot seized hold of his nose.
When he grew melancholy, They said, " His name's Polly,"
Which soothed that old man of Dunrose.

Fig. 3.10 The old man of Dunrose, *More Nonsense* (1872)

Fig. 3.11 George Cruikshank, *Comic Alphabet* (1836)

The Scroobious Snake,
who always wore a Hat on his Head, for
fear he should bite anybody.

Fig. 3.12a The Scroobious Snake, *More Nonsense* (1872)

The Kicking Kangaroo,
who wore a Pale Pink Muslin dress
with Blue spots.

Fig. 3.12b The Kicking Kangaroo, *More Nonsense* (1872)

or even self-castration. The symbolically or actually castrated male figure will appear in various of Lear's longer works.

Some of the same animals appear in other contemporary alphabets for children.[72] In *The Alphabet of Animals Intended to Impress Children with Affection for the Brute Creation,* 'A—is the Ass, / Meek and patient, though slow / Oh! Do not ill-treat him, / Nor give him a blow. For the poor he works hard / while on thistles he'll feed: / Contentment learn from him / And help those in need'.[73] Lear's ass, by contrast, is an 'Abstemious Ass, who resided in a Barrel, and only lived on Soda Water and Pickled Cucumbers'. It is hard to resist the hint that such abstemiousness is ass-like. In his diaries and letters, Lear routinely uses *ass* to describe idiocy. In Greek philosophy it was Diogenes the Cynic who lived in a barrel, claiming that true happiness was not to be found in material luxury or power; he lived like a dog, claiming brotherhood with animals. Lear's ass is thus a nonsense figure that, to the adult eye, is far from straightforward. Is he a human whose cynicism and self-denial has turned him into an ass? Or is he a Diogenes-in-reverse, an animal so bent on human fellowship that he has become self-limiting? The latter possibility is more persuasive, because the ass is the lead figure in a procession of animals and birds who are all behaving like humans, in ways that are mildly neurotic. The tom-tommy tortoise beating a drum in the wilderness is a case in point. Tortoise shells were often, in indigenous Mesoamerican and Pacific societies, used as percussion instruments. One suspects that Lear's tom-tommy tortoise with his drum is metaphorically beating himself up. These creatures are delightful—and faintly troubling—because they are so intent on performing activities that are foreign to their nature. They paint a picture of the contrivance, the self-suppression, involved in being human.

The power dynamic involved in the animal-human continuum, where humans dominate and control the movement of animals while also petting and educating them, is a useful parallel for thinking about child-adult relations. At the beginning of our lives, we are all comparably clumsy in grasping small objects, etiquette is mysterious and effortful and most children wonder, at some stage, why they have to wear clothes at all. Adult social life may well seem as bizarre and needlessly fussy to a child as the lobster mending his clothes with a needle and thread. In this alphabet, the child is invited to ponder the motives of the animals who are trying to behave like humans. Amidst the pleasurable silliness of these characters playing human roles, there is a submerged acknowledgement of real social and existential anxieties, of a form of role play that is required of us if we are to participate in the long and forbiddingly complex game of social life.

NATURE, CLASS AND NEUROSIS

Natural history in children's literature had long been used as a means of exploring social class and hierarchy. Lear must have grown up with Catherine Dorset's *The Peacock 'At Home'* (1809), which he echoes more than once in his own verse.[74] In this appealing revel, the peacock throws a party and invites all the other birds, asking rhetorically:

> And shall we like domestic, inelegant fowls,
> Unpolish'd as Geese, and more stupid than Owls,
> Sit tamely at home tête-à-tête with our spouses,
> While the offspring of grub-worms throw open their houses?[75]

The guests include Dowager Lady Toucan, Baron Stork, Doctor Buzzard, Admiral Penguin and members of the avian hoi polloi: 'A London-bred *Sparrow*—a pert forward Cit!/Danced a reel with Miss *Wagtail*, and little *Tom Tit*'. The poem imagines a class system amongst birds akin to that in human society. In doing so, however, it raises the question of how natural any such hierarchy really is; toucans are, after all, no more ladies than sparrows are Cockneys. Sarah Trimmer's famous fable 'The Robin Family' (1786) also uses birds to illustrate the similarities between human social structures and those of other creatures, asserting the natural order that held every creature in its appointed place. Lear's work draws on memories of these earlier children's stories but takes the fantasy of flight in an unexpected direction, using it to consider the obsessive anxiety that social viewing can produce.

In his poem 'Mr and Mrs Spikky Sparrow' (from *Nonsense Songs, Stories, Botany and Alphabets*, 1871), as in the 1870 alphabet for Daisy Terry that includes the Scroobious Snake, neurotic creatures shine a reflected light on human behaviour. Here, the loving husband and wife with five chicks in the nest begin to develop concerns about each other's health. Their hypochondria has a mildly hysterical quality. They conceive the need for clothes. The sparrows fly to 'Moses' wholesale shop' and return with a gown, a sash, slippers and hats. Their children are full of admiration, exclaiming, 'O Ma and Pa!/How truly beautiful you are!' The adult birds also appear quite satisfied with their transformation:

Said they, 'We trust that cold or pain
We shall never feel again!
While, perched on tree, or house, or steeple,
We now shall look like other people . . . [76]

However, the amused spectator may question whether the sparrows have really bought the protection they need. The clothes offer warmth. But they are no guarantee against pain. As the ambiguous final lines convey, it appears that the Spikky Sparrows are suffering from a displaced social anxiety—these sparrows want to keep up with humans.

Matthew Bevis rightly remarks that the sparrows '"look like" other people not only because they resemble them, but also because they have started to see with other people's eyes'.[77] They are more worried about being out in the cold of social ostracism than about the winter chill. They have fallen into a common error in attempting to better themselves. By endeavouring to keep up with their human neighbours, they look neither like 'other people' nor like sparrows. Here, classification within the animal kingdom and the status of social class mirror one another, suggesting the possibility that aping another species/class will lead to trouble in a future beyond the last verse. The poem's chirpy ending hangs in the air like a balloon in a pin factory.

To understand 'Mr and Mrs Spikky Sparrow', it is helpful to compare it with a children's story that likely inspired it: 'The Discontented Sparrow', written by Augusta Bethell and published in 1865. This story, never before identified as a source for Lear, illuminates his poem's background and subtext.

Augusta Bethell was the woman Lear came closest to marrying. As we tend to see her through Lear's diary entries as 'dear little Gussie', a quiet and considerate potential helpmeet, it is useful to step back and recognise her as a successful and spirited children's author in her own right. Between 1863 and 1883 she published seven works for children as well as translations of novels for adults by the female Spanish author Fernan Cabellero and the Norwegian author Björnstjerne Björnson. (Those inclined to regret that she did not marry Lear might consider how much she would have published had she done so.) Her story collection for children *Echoes of an Old Bell and Other Tales of Fairy Lore* (1865) contains 'The Discontented Sparrow'; Emma Parkyns sent this book to Lear in February 1865 and he enjoyed it.[78] The central narrative concerns Bobby and Jenny Robin, who have been fighting. Bobby wants Jenny to stay on the nest all day and tend the eggs. Jenny is bored and wants to seek food and entertainment. Bobby asks the bell to tell his flighty wife stories to amuse her while she broods the nest. This domestic argument is in itself interesting, suggesting that maternal devotion may not be wholly instinctual, and that the female of the species might require persuasion and even bribery to bear the tedium of remaining always at home.

Bird life in Bethell's stories, indeed, draws attention to social pressures exerted on women and on men. In 'The White Owl', a woman who is in fact a human princess in owl form, has to fight off a variety of bird suitors so that she can escape a marriage that would be a grotesque misalliance. In 'The Discontented Sparrow', Mr Cocky Sparrow is a disaffected youth who wants to fly to Africa with the aristocratic swallows. His home life is annoying: his father is dead (killed by sitting on an electric wire); his mother scolds him; and he has a disabled younger brother, Hoppy, who needs to be fed by others. Bethell borrowed aspects of Trimmer's 'The Robin Family', in which the father of the family is also dead, and a young cock bird also shows an impatience with restraint and a determination to see the world, a desire that will lead him to permanent injury. Bethell's story, however, is funnier, and is set in a Victorian world of colonial emigration. The 'Cockney sparrow', long an informal expression for a pert city dweller, is here literalised. Ambitious Cocky is dazzled by his invitation to join the fast set: swallows who wear tailcoats, eat on the wing and travel to distant climes. His friend introduces him:

> 'You will doubtless be surprised that a swallow should call an insignificant sparrow friend, but Cocky is somewhat above his station in life, and I have therefore condescended to notice him'. All this time Cocky was bowing and scraping in a great state of delight at finding himself in such grand society, and feeling very much flattered at his friend's words. 'Haw, haw!' said the other swallow, examining Cocky from head to foot in a supercilious manner. 'Did you say a *sparrow*? Dear me, this is the first time I have ever seen one of those birds so close'.[79]

Cocky attempts to emigrate with his new 'friends' but cannot manage the long flight. Faint and hungry, he alights on a ship; once he arrives in Africa he is perpetually thirsty, and he narrowly escapes the cannibalistic butcher bird. Chastened, he finds a passage back on a British-bound ship and is overjoyed to return to the family nest, where he sings 'Home Sweet Home' for the rest of his days.

'The Discontented Sparrow' has many flashes of humour. Bethell includes, as she admits, 'a very bad pun' when she notes that African sparrows gather glowworms in their nests, creating a 'light repast'.[80] Such jokes
mark common ground on which she and Lear probably played in conversation together. Nonetheless her story is more moralistic than anything Lear
would ever write. Comparing her tale 'The Discontented Sparrow' with
Lear's 'Mr and Mrs Spikky Sparrow' is instructive. It draws attention to
the ambiguity in which Lear delights and the way in which 'nonsense' lib-
erates his piece from other genre expectations, allowing it a lightness akin
to that of the birds themselves. In Lear's poem, the idea of changing
species-behaviour as a metaphor for class aspiration and the lure of emigration are both also present, but they are much more subtly indicated. Lear's
sparrows buy their new clothes at a real Jewish clothing merchant: Elias
Moses Ready-Made Clothing Emporium at Aldgate, near the Monument,
was reputedly the largest shop in London in the 1860s, and several branches
opened throughout the world. Moses had been a purveyor of secondhand
clothes, but as prices for fabric fell in the first decades of the nineteenth
century, he began to deal in ready-made clothes, an expanding market
amongst those of the aspiring working class and the lower middle class who
couldn't afford a dressmaker. From the 1840s onwards there was a boom in
emigration, particularly to America and Australia; Moses's store was especially popular with prospective emigrants. These real-world clues would have
helped an adult Victorian reader to recognise the Spikky Sparrows as members of an avian working class or lower middle class who were trying to behave like human members of their social group, getting nearly new clothes,
perhaps in preparation for a new life abroad. 'Span-new' means 'brand new'
and was an expression most often used of clothes. The Spikky Sparrows
sound as if they are 'spick and span-new', trim and fashionable.

Unlike Bethell, Lear doesn't overtly judge this behaviour. Instead he fo-
cuses on the odd and arresting nature of the suddenly conceived need for
clothing itself, an anxiety that—like the Ornamental Ostrich's anxiety to
wear boots to keep its feet quite dry, or the Scroobious Snake's anxiety
to wear a hat—speaks of a fretfulness that is not confined to any one class
but attends the psychic work of human self-consciousness. We cannot dismiss Lear's sparrows as upstarts. They are an affectionate couple whose
mutual concern leads them unwarily to consumer culture and its emphasis
on acquisition and appearance as the keys to safety and comfort. They have
learned to wonder what they look like, and how they might like to look.

Lear does not scoff at this attitude or lament it or punish it. Instead he in-volves us in the act of spectatorship, implicating us in the viewing that has stimulated the sparrows' wish to be 'quite galloobious and genteel'. If the Spikky Sparrows are awkwardly performing human domesticity and gen-tility, then we are both the mirror and the lash.

Again, in 'Mr and Mrs Discobbolos', Lear uses the betweenness of his protagonists, who do not clearly belong to the realm of either human or an-imal, to examine the precariousness of domestic life under the social pres-sure of being viewed. *Discobolus* is the name of a sculpture of a discus thrower by the Athenian sculptor Myron from the fifth century B.C.E. It formed an aesthetic standard of physical beauty much copied by later artists. The sculpture survived only in imitation. Lear worked from such models during his brief period of studying at the Royal Academy schools. In San Remo in 1872, when he was teaching his neighbour's sons, Hubert and Arnold Con-greve, the principles of drawing, he set up a kind of ball and a "Discobolos" for them to paint, to demonstrate the effects of light and shade on colour in a multifaceted solid form.[81] Sculptures are by their nature vulnerable to breakage; this may have inspired Lear to imagine the Discobbolos couple, who conduct their lives on top of a wall in a state of anxiety about falling, yet proud to stand above 'household cares'. Lear was, at the time he wrote the poem, acutely angry with his neighbour in San Remo, Miss Kay-Shuttleworth, who had reneged on a verbal agreement not to sell the land at the bottom of his garden. She had sold it to Germans (a fact that, to Lear, compounded the fault) who were building the West End Hotel, which blocked his light and spoiled his view. The builders noisily blew up rock, destroying the wall at the bottom of the Villa Emily's garden. Lear was in retreat. He was also furious. These mixed feelings of withdrawal and a desire for violent revenge find their way into this poem and its darker sequel.

Miss Kay-Shuttleworth was above Lear in the social scale of San Remo. When he refused to 'see' her or her friends—to blank them socially—he damaged himself in the English-speaking community of this relatively small town. He was threatened with a libel action. This biographical background is important, but it is also vital to realise how Lear channelled the energies it generated into characters who reflect both certain aspects of the woman who had wronged him (snobbery, the erection and destruction of walls) and his response to such aggression (social withdrawal, angry blasting, the erec-tion of new walls of his own). The mirror work of his early limericks is in this late poem translated into a fable about mutual spectatorship; reading the poem, we can experience both the absurdity of the Discobboloses' position and the validity of their feelings.

As in 'Mr and Mrs Spikky Sparrow', there is an awkward and interesting conflation between physical vulnerability and social ignominy. The sparrows worry—apparently about illness but actually about appearance. The Discobboloses' worry about falling is both laughably concrete and socially nebulous. The extra *b* in their name hints that these beings may be 'cobbled' together; perhaps there was always a metaphorical crack in their plasterwork. This is a 'model' couple who are absurdly sensitive to position. Their anxiety, like the sparrows', has a neurotic edge; their basiphobia culminates in complete social withdrawal:

> 'Suppose we should fall down flumpetty
>   Just like pieces of stone!
>   Onto the thorns,—or into the moat!
>   What would become of your new green coat?
>   And might you not break a bone?
> It never occurred to me before—
> That perhaps we shall never go down any more!'
>   And Mrs. Discobbolos said—
>   'Oh! W! X! Y! Z!
>   What put it into your head
> To climb up this wall?—my own
>   Darling Mr. Discobbolos?'

> Mr. Discobbolos answered,—
>   'At first it gave me pain,—
>   And I felt my ears turn perfectly pink
>   When your exclamation made me think
>   We might never get down again!
> But now I believe it is wiser far
> To remain for ever just where we are.'—
>   And Mr. Discobbolos said,
>   'Oh! W! X! Y! Z!
>   It has just come into my head—
> —We shall never go down again—
>   Dearest Mrs. Discobbolos!'[82]

The metrics are interesting here. The poem is written as a musical dialogue, where each partner has passages of call and response before they join in a seemingly harmonious duet at the end. However, the stanzas are awkward, consisting of a seven-line rhyming structure with a five-line reply that, toppling into rhyming triplets, begins to sound increasingly panicked, until the 'Darling' and 'Dearest' echo like desperate pleas for marital accord.

Like the Spikky Sparrows' poem, 'Mr and Mrs Discobbolos' ends in apparent happiness, with the accomplishment of their desire for splendid isolation on a height. But it has an outrageous sequel, prefigured in the shaky dynamics of part one. In 'Mr and Mrs Discobbolos Part Two', written some eight years later, the mother of the family worries that they 'have no more room at all' on the wall, and is 'driven wild' by the thought that her six daughters and six sons will be unable to move in society, prevented from attending garden parties and other functions that lead to finding partners. Her offspring are 'admired by all' (as sculptures would be), but they have never been to a bazaar or a ball. The paterfamilias is so irritated by her outburst, which seems to imply that they should stoop to mingle, that he calls her a 'runcible goose' and an 'octopod'—a word Lear tellingly used to describe vulgar crowds at hotels, whose multiple legs presumably stood for their prolific families and their pestiferous spider-like manner of occupying space. Mr Discobbolos is, it seems, already imagining his wife's descent in the order of species, a threat that mirrors the family's fear of falling off the social scale. Lear's own family, of course, had suffered such a fall, before his birth and after it. Financially they had 'gone to the wall'. This poem moves on very sensitive territory. When Lear was angry with people he would 'blow them up' in the sense of yelling at them. Mr Discobbolos, however, blows his family up in a shockingly literal fashion. He dynamites the wall, precipitating the fatal fall whose anticipation caused so much anxiety in the first poem. The atomised family 'flies up to the sky so blue' in little pieces, having been destroyed by its head. As a blackly comic allegory of what anxious heads can do to us, the poem has no equal in literature.

Through these nonsense creatures who are neither quite human nor quite animal, Lear is able to explore class and self-consciousness by different lights in a multifaceted form. The family Discobbolos can be seen as social climbers who are, in the end, destroyed not by an angry proletarian revolutionist but from within, by their own extreme snobbery. But their internalised anxiety and its self-contained final solution also has a more existential quality. It is of a piece with the animals in 'The Seven Families of the Lake Pipple-

Popple', who jump into pickling jars to simultaneously extinguish and preserve themselves. Anxiety in Lear's work often breeds this kind of crisis, where creatures are drawn to embrace the end rather than face the endless worry of averting it. Nature in this post-Romantic world cannot offer a permanent release from the anxiety of being human. Rather, the animal-human continuum offers an alternative mode of viewing ourselves and our anxieties in which we can view with humour and compassion our own desire for the escape that being animal seems to confer and its simultaneous impossibility.

Odd Pairs: Interspecies Love and the Complexities of Sex

In Lear's poems of love and courtship, species can stand ambiguously for other kinds of difference that couples frequently have to work around. The author of 'The Science of Nonsense', an article in the *Spectator* of December 1870, saw the relationship between the two protagonists in 'The Duck and the Kangaroo' as a story of social climbing:

> First, there is the Kangaroo towering up in lofty-prim reserve above the suppliant Duck in its nasty pond, which looks the very picture of urgent humility,——of passionate plebeian yearning; while the Kangaroo's small elegant head reared at a vast height above the Duck, and her dropped paws, indicate respectively aristocratic breeding and a certain indifference to the Duck and her humble sphere. In the second picture, where the Duck's wheedling is evidently taking effect, the condescension with which the Kangaroo stoops from her immense height to listen to the Duck's pleadings, and the lackadaisical expression with which she takes pity on the poor waddling thing,—who is drawn in an attitude inexpressibly vulgar, cook-maidy, and self-humiliated, as she approaches the Kangaroo,—are quite irresistible.[83]

The *Spectator* reviewer's reading of this poem is dominated by class. Species here is seen to echo social hierarchy; the larger, exotic kangaroo is a higher form than the duck, which, in its 'nasty pond', is a lower-class citizen, but manages to form an advantageous union that will transport it into high society, travelling the world.

Fig. 3.13 **The Duck and the Kangaroo**

The reviewer's focus on class diverts attention from a reading of gender that is equally intriguing. He or she evidently regards both kangaroo and duck as female characters. If this is a love affair, 'all in the moonlight pale', then it is a same-sex romance. Interspecies relationship has inspired the writer to think about another kind of relationship where union between the parties does not result in procreation. The text offers no concrete information either way; its ambiguity allows readers to make their own gender assumptions about this delightfully odd couple:

> 'Please give me a ride on your back!'
>   Said the Duck to the Kangaroo.
> 'I would sit quite still, and say nothing but "Quack,"
>   The whole of the long day through!
> And we'd go to the Dee, and the Jelly Bo Lee,
> Over the land, and over the sea;—
>   Please take me a ride! O do!'
>   Said the Duck to the Kangaroo.
>
> Said the Kangaroo to the Duck,
>   'This requires some little reflection;
> Perhaps on the whole it might bring me luck,
>   And there seems but one objection,
> Which is, if you'll let me speak so bold,
> Your feet are unpleasantly wet and cold,
>   And would probably give me the roo-
>   matiz!' said the Kangaroo.

Said the Duck, 'As I sate on the rocks,
    I have thought over that completely,
And I bought four pairs of worsted socks
    Which fit my web-feet neatly.
And to keep out the cold I've bought a cloak,
And every day a cigar I'll smoke,
      All to follow my own dear true
      Love of a Kangaroo!'[84]

As is often the case in Lear, the peculiarities of species difference invite us to think again about gender difference. The 1835 illustrated guide to the Surrey Zoological Gardens (a competitor to the Regent's Park zoo) notes that the kangaroo is one of the 'most curious animals discovered in modern times'. 'Its fore feet or hands are very feeble, and its mouth is useless as a weapon of defence', but the tail is said to be 'of such strength as to break a man's leg at a single blow'.[85] The kangaroo's delicate physiognomy and posture, particularly its hands, suggested femininity—what D H Lawrence would later describe as 'her little loose hands, and drooping Victorian shoulders'.[86] But the kangaroo's kick and the swipe of its phallic tail conveyed a violence and power that could injure, even kill, an adult human. New animals with these unexpected combinations of physical traits invited new ways of considering the natural attributes and propensities of male and female. Leigh Hunt thought giraffes looked 'like young ladies of animals . . . naturally not ungraceful, but with bad habits';[87] if all giraffes seemed like gawky female teenagers, what did this suggest about masculinity in the animal kingdom? Might it in some species be passive, awkward, even invisible?

In the avian world, amongst birds of prey for example, females are quite commonly larger than males. In some species, the male and the female both brood the nest. Lear would have been very familiar with these facts, both from close observation and from books such as *The Gardens and Menagerie of the Zoological Society Delineated* (1831), which he helped to illustrate. This volume asserts that ostriches 'might almost be said to belong to the Class of Beasts' rather than birds, having organs similar to those of ruminating quadrupeds, and that the male ostrich sometimes sits on the nest, 'taking his share of the duty' of hatching the eggs.[88] It notes, moreover, that the male ostrich in the London zoo was so henpecked by the female that he had been evacuated to a cage of his own. Doubtless zoogoers framed their own private comparisons. Lear's 'The Duck and the Kangaroo' makes delightful capital out of the oddities of a relationship in which one party can bear the other only if it stays behind, out of sight.

Personally, I have always read the duck as male and the kangaroo as female. Absurdly small males wooing larger females, as in 'The Courtship of the Yonghy-Bonghy-Bò', is the pattern of Lear's nonsense.[89] If the suitor is a small male duck who is wooing a large female kangaroo, Lear is experimenting with an imaginative leap in sexual relations. The female is all-powerful. The male is the one with cold feet. But socks will keep his extremities and her fur from ever meeting directly; their happy union is premised on him riding around on her tail with his wet feet wrapped in socks to prevent them making her cold. There is a broad hint to the knowing adult that this happy relationship is founded on not having sex, or at least not any kind of sex that a naturalist would recognise. Sometimes, as Freud famously remarked, a cigar is just a cigar. But in this poem, the contentedly carried, cigar-smoking duck seems to have put his masculine organ in a place where it can comfort him without bothering her. Like the boot-wearing ostrich who fears to get his feet wet, or the scroobious snake who hides under his hat for fear of biting anyone, this duck is typical of Lear's male characters who cover or remove their extremities to avoid annoyance.

This kind of virtual castration is a signal feature of Lear's comedy: females are usually driving and males are usually riding shotgun. A previously unpublished dialogue that Lear wrote for Chichester Fortescue, now in the Pierpont Morgan Library, is revelatory in its explicit sexual comedy. The scene is 'One of the Planets', where a dialogue takes place between 'two disembodied Mammals or Quadrupeds'. These beasts are in fact the imagined full-grown spirits of two calves that Lear saw regularly when visiting Fortescue at his aunt's Irish property, Red House, in Ardee, in 1857. The bovines hail each other delightedly:

1st Quadruped: Is it possible! Do I see the companion of my earliest youth?
2nd Quadruped: Yes; it is I.—I recollect you well; that is, I recognize the sound of your voice, otherwise I could hardly have known you, since in a quarter of a century you are so much changed that only the extreme end of [your] nose remains the same.

1st Quadruped: You had a habit of rapidly twinkling your ears & of
suddenly elevating your tail,—(for you had a tail then,)—and
these shadows as it were of past life recalled you to me at once.
You were always sweet looking, & of a playful disposition.[90]

A flirtatious conversation follows in which the two creatures allude to
Fortescue's transformation into a seal (i.e. the Lord Privy Seal). They con-
fide that when a 'blasted Butcher' cut their throats, they became winged
creatures, thinking themselves at first the Beast in Ezekiel and then the
Beast in Revelations. Their mutual affection and desire never to separate,
however, has survived their translation into the planetary sphere. The cow,
like the Pussy-cat in 'The Owl and the Pussy-cat', proposes with striking
assertiveness, 'We are both old enough to marry now, so let us be married
at once'. But there is a problem, and it is sexual. Her male companion is not
a bull, but an ox. He lacks the wedding tackle necessary to satisfy his bo-
vine bride.

1st Quadruped: It is impossible, I tell you! I *cannot* marry! I am an Ox!
2nd Quadruped: Heavens! what difference can a name make in so
solemn a subject?
1st Quadruped: The difference is not in *name*, but in *fact*. If I had got,——
2nd Quadruped: Explain what? Or how?
1st Quadruped: I cannot, to a Lady. It would be a gross impropriety!
2nd Quadruped: You drive me mad!—Explain yourself!

The ox whispers in her ear, after which, 'A peal of lightning & a flash
of thunder are heard. The female Mammal or Quadruped flies off into space:
the male ditto lies down on his back and Frix [i.e. masturbates] for 8 years'.
    Future biographers will doubtless plumb this dialogue for evidence of
Lear's own sexual life. It certainly communicates feelings of frustration and
impotence, which may relate to his early encounters with sexually transmitted infections; his conviction that masturbation could trigger his epileptic fits; or a more general anxiety reflective of his mixed feelings about
his sexuality and the direction his desires might take. What interests me
most here, however, is the relationship between the ox and the cow and how
similar it is to other relationships in Lear's nonsense: between the duck and
the kangaroo, Lady Jingly and the Yonghy-Bonghy-Bò, even Mr Daddy
Long-legs and Mr Floppy Fly. After reading in 1883 Walter Savage Landor's

Imaginary Conversations, Lear considered further dialogues between creatures: an industrious and a common flea; a blue bottle and a common fly; a cat and a dog; a sparrow and a swallow; a frog and a toad.[91] All these imaginary pairs are different in 'class'—where class may relate to species, social grade or sexual viability. The conversation between two unlike yet related creatures clearly attracts Lear as a topic. The ox and the cow are not different species; and, goodness knows, if they are 'disembodied' and eating 'Paradise pickles', they ought to be able to get it together. But Lear is fascinated by comic—in this case cosmic—incompatibility. His couples can love at a distance but they can't effectively mate. Lear creates a nonsensical comic drama whose sense of timing is worthy of the stage. In a realm where even the thunder and lightning have swapped the customary verbs to which they are attached, sexual consummation becomes a physical release of energy that just isn't going to happen à deux.

It is interesting that the ox and the cow allude to Fortescue's transformation into a seal. From one perspective this is merely a weak pun—one that Lear frequently revisited. Yet it also relates Fortescue and Lear (described by the ox as 'a queer friend') to the animal characters in the drama. Animal selves are sexual selves, yet they cannot overcome the inhibitions that human society has imposed upon them—a situation ripe for comedy and simultaneously sad beyond measure. This piece of epistolary nonsense reaches outward to incorporate the real; it contains allusions to real places and events and expresses a sincere affection. Fortescue was one of Lear's closest friends, and one with whom he could speak sexual truths.[92] This epistolary flight of fancy is an oddity in Lear's output because of its dramatic form and its sexual explicitness, yet it is also characteristic. Lear's interspecies couples allow him to explore the difficulties that can attend romantic love when both parties are not similarly sexually aligned.

Lear's most famous picture poem or song, 'The Owl and the Pussy-cat', is a case in point. It was written notionally for Janet, the daughter of John Addington and Catherine Symonds, Lear's friends and neighbours at Cannes. But in fact it was designed equally to cheer Janet's depressive father, to whom Lear sang it. Lear knew from the first that the physical and mental health of this couple was not strong. In private life, Symonds was open (from his children's account, embarrassingly open) about his homosexual desires and his difficulties containing them within a heterosexual marriage. In 1869 John and Catherine agreed to a platonic marriage, with Symonds given liberty to decamp to Venice with a male lover. In Lear's 'Growling Eclogue', written for John and Catherine around a week before 'The Owl and the Pussy-cat', Lear comically depicted himself and John as competitive moaners, between whose choruses of complaint Catherine has to adjudicate. In that poem Symonds is given the line 'if I suffer, am I then an owl?' It is not far-fetched, then, to conceive the owl and the pussy-cat, in Lear's follow-on poem, as embodying in idealised form the relationship between Symonds and his wife Catherine (Cat). The two creatures who are incompatible in their biological forms and avocations, but who manage nonetheless to marry and to dance hand in hand on the edge of the sand, would have had particular resonance for this sexually incompatible couple, who struggled to be happy in their seaside retreat. 'The Owl and the Pussy-cat' offered Janet, but also her parents, a narrative of comfort. There was at this time no acceptable public language in which to describe bisexuality or homosexuality. The romance between unlike creatures provides an open equation in sexual algebra, an imaginative space for figuring the ways in which seemingly impossible unions can sometimes be possible, despite the challenges they face.

Still, interspecies love remains fraught with complications. As with 'Mr and Mrs Discobbolos Part Two', the sequel to 'The Owl and the Pussy-cat' is a darker poem. It revisits the domestic harmony set up in the first poem and discovers that events have taken a tragic turn. The Pussy-cat has committed suicide, leaving the owl to raise their children in the trees alone. These children are 'partly little beasts and partly little fowls'—the female offspring have taken after their mother and are cats, while the male offspring are owls. The children prefigure—imagined in terms of species—what later scientists would call the expression of the X and Y chromosomes. It is a powerful way of imagining the profundity of sexual difference: the female and male are so far apart biologically as to have not only different shapes but, to all appearances, wholly different identities. This strange conclusion harks back to Lear's drawing of the Owly-Pussey-catte from around 1834, the crossbreed creature smoking a pipe while his (or her) pussycat tail hangs down below the branch that conveniently divides top from bottom, like the crease in a folded piece of paper. Sexual difference and species difference are clearly connected in Lear's mind; his composite creatures often have the traits of more than one sex, as well as more than one species. His reading in natural history would have made him aware that some creatures did indeed possess traits that were both 'male' and 'female'. Although we cannot know for sure that Lear was himself bisexual, there is convincing evidence to suggest that his desires moved in both directions. He often describes himself as 'queer', a word he also uses to describe Walt Whitman and the transgender doctor James Miranda Barry, with whom he was acquainted in Corfu. Lear's 'queer beasts'—his composite creatures and interspecies unions—often seem to reach towards forms of being that lie outside conventional paradigms of sexual identity.

Forty years after Lear's death, the bisexual Cole Porter wrote his innuendo-laden song 'Let's Fall in Love': 'birds do it, bees do it. / Even educated fleas do it'. But even if sexual desire is the one thing we all have in common, Lear quietly insinuates that what seems most natural may actually be fraught with complication. If gender difference is as profound as species difference, then maybe it makes more sense to pair with someone of our own gender. If, despite all difficulties, we are drawn to mate with a different 'species', then the crossbreeds that result may well have problems in finding mates of their own. Evolution here seems to sound a warning about the loss of selfhood in procreation generally. Lear feared the 'annual infants' that, coming from a family of twenty-one offspring, he knew could be the corollary of marriage. In 1865 he wrote to Emily Tennyson that humans ought not to reproduce at all, in which case 'we should be gradually extinguified, & the world would be left to triumphant chimpanzees, gorillas, cockroaches & crocodiles'.[93] The best response to the Darwinian possibility of man's future redundancy might be to embrace it, as the parents of the 'Seven Families of the Lake Pipple-Popple' do when they jump into pickling jars. As Lear reflected morosely in his diary in April 1862, 'That we do not all kill ourselves seems the wonder,—of those at least who think'.[94] Perhaps, on the whole, sex is better avoided.

Lear wrote to Emily Tennyson from Rome in 1859:

> I don't think at all much nowadays. When I die I shall become an oyster or a Zoophyte of some sort, & live for several hundred years in the Red sea very placidly—at least quite as pleasantly as I do in this vulgar foolish place, which I grieve ever to have come to. . . . Besides I hate a crowd—& am by no means of a gregarious nature—though not unsocial. . . .[95]

Lear imagines himself living for centuries at the bottom of the ocean. The image is one of social and sexual isolation. It is reinforced by a later passage in the letter in which Lear imagines himself as a hermit taking 'a single cell' on Mount Athos, whence, if he was bothered by the other four thousand monks, he tells Emily he would 'suddenly return to Cheapside or Piccadilly', places emblematic of frenetic social encounter. Lear's poems such as 'Mr and Mrs Discobbolos' and 'The Quangle Wangle's Hat' often explore the conundrum of satisfying the social urge while preserving one's integrity or protective boundaries—of not being 'gregarious' but maintaining social connectivity. Taking a single cell or becoming something closer to a single-celled organism are equivalent possible escapes.

It is striking that Lear, in this figured metempsychosis, identifies himself as an oyster or zoophyte—a class of marine invertebrates including sponges, corals and barnacles—because the sexual habits of such creatures had become a topic of intense public interest in the 1850s.[96] A group of scientists including Darwin had performed experiments in which they observed the floating ova of zoophytes, which were released like seeds into the water and then fertilised by sperm from males of the species, who were little more than sperm sacs attached to phallic organs. The zoophyte hovered between plant and animal; as Charles Kingsley remarked:

> no branch of science has more utterly confounded the wisdom
> of the wise, shattered to pieces systems and theories, and the
> idolatry of arbitrary names . . . than . . . zoophytology,
> in which our old distinctions of 'animal', 'vegetable', and 'mineral'
> are trembling in the balance, seemingly ready to vanish. . . .[97]

The zoophyte's reproductive cycle entailed, rather like the activity of Lear's masturbating ox, sexual effusion without tactile copulation. Lear may not have known the detailed facts of zoophyte reproduction, but he clearly expected Emily Tennyson to understand the *noli me tangere* joke he was making.

Again, natural history here allows for the expression of sexual ambivalence that would be difficult to voice in another way. Zoophytes are primitive organisms. Yet, as Lear's allusion points out, they can live for many centuries. Lear's projection of himself into the form of an oyster or zoophyte is a mode of infinite going forward that is also an infinite going back. He becomes, in one sense, an ur-ancestor who achieves a kind of immortality, remaining alive when the scions of other, less tenacious races are long dead; but, in another sense, Lear imagines himself as a primitive vegetable-animal, with no active desire. Becoming such a creature entails a kind of resignation of the complexities that being an adult human involves, a return to a simpler, 'placid' form of presocial, presexual life that is analogous to returning to the womb. Several of Lear's nonsense works explore the relief of return that such involution would entail.

The Pobble who has no Toes and the Pleasures of Involution

The finest of these is 'The Pobble who has no Toes', a poem begun in 1873 that itself went through several evolutionary phases before arriving at the form that usually appears in anthologies. This is a poem that wears its interest in species adaptation on its sleeve.

> The Pobble who has no toes
>   Had once as many as we;
> When they said, 'Some day you may lose them all;'—
>   He replied,—'Fish fiddle de-dee!'
> And his Aunt Jobiska made him drink,
> Lavender water tinged with pink,
> For she said, 'The World in general knows
> There's nothing so good for a Pobble's toes!'[98]

This could be a just-so story: 'how the Pobble lost his toes'. It predates by almost thirty years Rudyard Kipling's *Just-So Stories* (1902), which tell 'how the elephant got his trunk' and 'how the camel got his hump', but it shares their combination of playfulness and self-awareness about contemporary scientific debate on how species arrived at their present anatomical state. In *Feathers and Fairies* (1874), Gussie Bethell retells legends about how the hoopoe got his crest and how the bullfinch got his red breast; the air of children's literature at this time was full of origin myths that hovered between fairy tale and natural history. 'The Pobble who has no Toes' in the poem is an individual, but the title could equally demarcate a species, like the 'short-toed eagle' that Lear depicted in an early lithograph. 'Had once as many as we' could invoke the long timescale of species change, implying transition over millennia from a five-toed creature, something like a human, to a creature with fins or a tail. Othniel Charles Marsh, a palaeontologist in America, established in the 1870s a sequence of fossils of extinct animals believed to have evolved into the modern horse. The sequence entailed transition from a four-toed animal like a tapir to the modern, single-hoofed equine. This sequence of creatures losing toes in successive generations was frequently cited by Thomas Huxley as the primary example of evolutionary progression established from fossil evidence.

Lear would certainly have been aware of contemporary debate surrounding homologous and analogous structures in the hands and feet of man and other animals. His interest in the comparative structure of the foot is evident in 'The Pelican Chorus' where he imagines the King of the Cranes wearing pea-green trowsers with 'a delicate frill' to conceal the fact that his feet are not webbed like those of the Pelican Princess he is wooing: '(For though no one speaks of it, every one knows, / He has got no webs between his toes!)'. As ever in Lear, this distinction in natural history becomes analogous to a matter of social class or form. To the crane seeking to mollify his royal in-laws, the webbed foot figures as a 'higher' adaptation; his unwebbed feet require to be concealed with a 'delicate frill', rather like the human female's ankles. Lear invites us to smile at the way in which anatomical difference between species produces its own snobbery. But the joke might also make us glance at our own feet and consider what practical use we get from our five toes, which are neither prehensile, with opposable big toes for gripping, like those of apes, nor webbed for swimming, like those of beavers and otters. One is reminded of the web-footed and finned babies Lear imagined living in Kendal, adapting to the constant rain, and the cave-dwelling Froglodytes. These transitional creatures suggest the advantages of combining mammalian with amphibious characteristics. Lear, who was sometimes irritated by his footwear, suggested in 1859 to Chichester Fortescue that 'it is a mistake to have toes at all: hoofs would have been simpler & less expensive, as precluding boots'.[99] But would losing one's toes be a developmental step forward or backward?

'The Pobble who was no Toes' allows us to have it both ways. The Pobble will lose his appendages: a loss that at first, from the warnings and careful prophylactics of Aunt Jobiska, seems as if it might be a disaster, a failure to progress. However, it turns out—at least if we believe his aunt's reassurances once they are gone—to be a relief. Like the castrated ox in Lear's tragicomic dialogue, the Pobble loses a part of his nether regions that seems essential and yet proves inessential. Such losses may prevent full maturation and procreation, but they also free us to reject the unwelcome advances that growing up and pairing up entail. Involution or loss of this kind can be paradoxically liberating.

Fig. 3.14 **The Pobble**

Perhaps, as Lear's illustration to the poem half suggests, the human-like Pobble, with his underside merging with the water, actually wants to be more fish, fiddle de-dee. Like the old person of Bree who nurses the fishes, or the man of Ems who casually jumps in the Thames, he is becoming the thing he was covertly angling for. *Pobble* is a word that connotes infancy: babies toddle and wobble, and they are sometimes wrapped in flannel, as the Pobble is. Lear even in adulthood wore flannel shirts to protect his weak chest from the cold. In an earlier draft of the poem the Pobble's nose is 'swaddled' with flannel. Babies are also commonly fed gripe water or rosehip syrup (analogous to 'lavender water tinged with pink') by caring females who in the nineteenth century feminised infant experience prior to the breeching that marked gender differentiation outside the nursery. Yet the Pobble in Lear's illustration looks like an adult male. He has side whiskers. At one level, then, this looks like a nonsense poem that expresses a very deep desire: to go back indefinitely to the womb, a place that precedes the complications of sexual differentiation, or at least a place where one is reliably fed and carried and soothed.

> The Pobble who has no toes
>   Was placed in a friendly Bark,
> And they rowed him back, and carried him up,
>   To his Aunt Jobiska's Park.
> And she made him a feast at his earnest wish
> Of eggs and buttercups fried with fish;—
> And she said,—'it's a fact the whole world knows,
> That Pobbles are happier without their toes.'

Vivien Noakes reads this as a poem that alludes to masturbation and the threats often identified with it in the Victorian nursery.[100] She is right, I am sure, in her instinct that the Pobble's toes, whose sudden loss follows the prohibited removal of a cover from his nose, are members that cover for that member which must always remain covered in polite society: the male organ. Conks and cocks have long been imagistically and medically linked, not least by Hogarth, who depicts several syphilitic characters with missing noses. Lear's illustration of the Pobble with the flannel wrapped around his nose contains just a ghost of an allusion to the syphilitic's bandaged proboscis.

However, in my view the Pobble's loss is less a nursery threat than a nursery promise—a promise to continue nursing. The presexual state of infancy can continue as long as we need it to. The unusual name Aunt 'Jobiska' recalls Jocasta, Oedipus's wife, who is also his mother in *Oedipus Rex,* which Lear read ('to my great delight') in 1859.[101] In Sophocles that incestuous combination is terrifying; here, the solicitous woman who is neither mother nor wife offers a safe haven between oedipal anxiety and sexual desire. Buttered eggs is just the sort of feast with which one would comfort a frightened child. 'Eggs and buttercups fried with fish' produces a synaesthetic sensation of warmth and yellowness that is a feast for the mind's eye. The potential compound nouns floating in the sound of this line include 'eggcups' and 'butterflies'. Words can lose their attachments, metamorphose and yet magically recombine and be as good as new. Their flexibility offers a vital exposition of emotional regrouping in this conso-latory fable. The friendly Bark (not the aggressive kind of bark), like the 'benevolent Boat' in 'The Polly and the Pusseybite', rescues the traveller. He is offered a way back, a mode of reconstruing his narrative of loss as gain. This is as powerful as it is strange. One can read it both in personal terms and as a fiction about species. Going back to simpler aquatic forms may be a kind of involution that frees us from the anxiety of constant self-monitoring, the kind of burden that swimming while keeping your nose dry and your head above water imposes.

Surprisingly, 'The Pobble who has no Toes' was originally conceived by Lear as a different narrative poem: 'The Story of the Pobble, who has no toes, and the Princess Bink'. This is a courtship poem. In it, the Pobble swims across the Bristol Channel and encounters the lively Princess, who agrees to be his wife if he will give up his scarlet flannel and his toes, which—remarkably—can be screwed on and off, like piano keys. He assents to her

demands and they elope, though one notices that the Pobble's reason for marrying is social recommendation rather than overwhelming personal desire.

> The Pobble went gaily on,
>   To a rock on the edge of the water,
> And there,—a-eating of crumbs and cream,
>   Sat King Jampoodle's daughter.
> Her cap was a root of Beetroot red,
> With a hole cut out to insert her head;
> Her gloves were yellow; her shoes were pink,
> Her frock was green; and her name was Bink.
>
> Said the Pobble,—'Oh Princess Bink,
>   A-eating of crumbs and cream!
> Your beautiful face has filled my heart
>   With the most profound esteem!
> And my Aunt Jobiska says, Man's life
> Ain't worth a penny without a wife,
> Whereby it will give me the greatest pleasure
> If you'll marry me now, or when you've leisure!'
>
> Said the Princess Bink—'O! Yes!
>   I will certainly cross the Channel
> And marry you then if you'll give me now
>   That lovely scarlet flannel!
> And besides that flannel about your nose
> I trust you will give me all your toes,
> To place in my Pa's Museum collection,
> As proof of your deep genteel affection.'
>
> The Pobble unwrapped his nose,
>   And gave her the flannel so red,
> Which, throwing her Beetroot cap away,—
>   She wreathed around her head.
> And one by one he unscrewed his toes
> Which were made of the beautiful wood that grows
> In his Aunt Jobiska's roorial park,
> When the days are short and the nights are dark.[102]

The logic of this first version of the story is highly visual. Princess Bink wears a suggestive beetroot cap through which her head protrudes. The colours lavender, pink, red, crimson and scarlet all make an appearance, alongside yellow and green, and the acquisitive Princess eats 'crumbs and cream', which sounds like 'crimson cream'. There is something inescapably sexual about all this redness: a feeling of blush, of blood rising to the surface and of wrappers (the kind that might protect a sensitive protuberance) being peeled away. The Princess, indeed, with her beetroot cap and protuberant head, seems herself a kind of phallic object that will swallow or displace the Pobble's toes. As in so many of Lear's poems or dialogues of love and courtship, the female takes control while the voluntarily castrated male learns to adapt.

'O Pobble! my Pobble!' the princess exults, echoing Walt Whitman's 'O Captain, my Captain', his 1865 elegy for Abraham Lincoln, which uses the extended metaphor of a boat returning triumphantly, though its captain has died, for the end of the Civil War. Lear was reading 'queer Walt Whitman's' poetry in 1872 with John Addington Symonds (Symonds had written a monograph on Whitman), and his perhaps unconscious transference of Whitman's nautical imagery here is ambiguous. The Princess's tenderness seems to be grounded in conquest rather than submission. She is more of the captain in this relationship than the Pobble is. However, once he has shed his appendages, the Pobble and his mate dance all day long over the hills and dales of Wales.

Daniel Karlin has argued that the change in the Pobble's story from wedding to solitude makes it a 'sadder' sequel, like the second part of 'Mr and Mrs Discobbolos' or the subsequent history of 'The Owl and the Pussy-cat', where the happy-ever-after tale is 'disfigured'.[103] It is undeniably true that marriage in Lear's poems is not the last act. There is always the likelihood of a terrible coda, and this reflects Lear's own feelings about marriage as a state that is as anxious and threatening to selfhood as it is theoretically promising of unity and fulfilment.

However, I would suggest that the version of the Pobble's tale that we customarily read, in which Princess Bink has dropped out of the picture, is actually the version that gets to the heart of what the poem wants to say, and not sad at all. 'The Pobble who has no Toes' is a poem about what one can do without. The Pobble loses his emotional cover, the flannel comforter that protects him from other losses. He is exposed, a word poignantly used in the Victorian period to mean babies who were left outside to die. But he can re-cover. All is not lost. Going back may seem like defeat, but it can be reconceived as a relief. The Pobble who *has* no Toes, is, after all, immortal. Like the zoophyte he continues in an indefinite present tense.

The Pobble and the First Cross-Channel Swim

The story of the Pobble has customarily been read in only one context: that of Lear's personal life. However, there is a likely connection between the poem's narrative and contemporary events that illuminates its preoccupations. It is easy to miss the fact that the Pobble is swimming the Channel when his toes drop off. In Lear's poem it is the Bristol Channel. But attempts to swim the English Channel were very much in the news in the 1870s, and it is impossible that Lear, when he was writing the poem in 1873, would have been unaware of an attempt that failed in a comic and humiliating way.

On the morning of Saturday, 24 August 1872, a crowd of several thousand people gathered at the Admiralty Pier in Dover to witness a peculiar event. The signal that it was about to begin was given by the booming of the band of the Royal Zoological Society. They played a cheerful selection of music to encourage a 'splendidly built' young man of twenty-four called J. B. Johnson, who was about to undertake a wager proposed in his hometown of Leeds at the odds of £2,000 to £60. The arrangements had been made by Mr Frederick Strange, the proprietor of the Surrey Zoological Gardens. At half past ten, the steamer *Palmerston* left the pier with Johnson aboard. The crowd cheered wildly. At twenty to eleven he appeared on the bridge, clad only in a bathing costume, and sprang into the water. The water was 'lumpy' and ferociously cold. Nonetheless, Johnson set out strongly, swimming on his side 'with long, powerful strokes', accomplishing two miles in twenty minutes. The steamer towed a smaller vessel in which Johnson's brother waited, ready to render any needful assistance.

For the first four miles, Johnson swam without resting. But the tide pulled him out between Dover and Dungeness. Those who had planned the attempt had calculated that when the tide turned, Johnson would be swept towards the French coast. If he could only maintain his stroke for around thirty miles, he would become the first recorded man to swim the English Channel. However, after just over an hour, when he had accomplished seven miles of his landmark journey, Johnson wavered. His only fear had been whether he could maintain blood circulation. Now he complained that he could not feel his feet. He rested and wanted to renew his efforts, but the surgeon aboard the *Palmerston* advised him to come out. The bold attempt had failed. Interest in the possibility of swimming the Channel, however, remained at fever pitch in the 1870s following Johnson's failure, and in August 1875 Captain Matthew Webb succeeded, after two failed attempts, in reaching France.

As the Surrey Zoo's involvement in the affair illustrated, the cross-Channel swim was a kind of scientific experiment into the capacities of the human animal. The *Dover Express* commented that Johnson 'seemed as much at home in the water as upon land'.[104] Both at Dover and at Calais, he amused the crowds by performing 'aquatic tricks', and it was said that he had smeared his body in porpoise oil. Moreover, the journalist speculated, 'it would be interesting to match a civilised European like Johnson with some of those savage islanders who seem almost to half live in the sea. . . .' Could Johnson compete against a Kanaka Indian? These comments implicitly raise the possibility that man began his evolutionary existence in the water: Johnson seems as 'at home' there as upon land. More explicitly, they raise the question of whether 'civilised European' man in his process of development has lost aquatic hardiness more obviously pronounced in 'savage' races. The Channel crossing, the *Express* concluded, was probably impossible, 'since Science has not yet invented a stove that could be tied to the feet of a swimmer, and so warm him on his "dim and perilous way"'. The portable foot stove to combat aquatic hypothermia is an invention that itself seems to belong in the realm of nonsense.

The failed cross-Channel swim attempt was both serious and irresistibly funny. The fact that the young champion had been halted by numb toes presented a picture of spectacular virility compromised by a complaint of a familiarly domestic, even feminine, nature. The bathos was delightful, and the punning possibilities of the 'feat' that had been defeated by the protagonist's cold feet were legion. It was not long before a comic song was in circulation.[105]

Lear had already conceived the idea of a Pobble without toes in May 1872 when he drafted 'The Quangle Wangle's Hat' and made the Pobble one of many creatures on its brim, though the Pobble in that picture looks like a quadruped. But when in early 1873 he gave the Pobble his own story and needed a mechanism by which it had lost its toes, I believe that the cross-Channel swim floated into his fantastical imagination. The connections are compelling. Lear would have seen the story in August 1872, if he didn't already know about it through his zoological connections. His nonsense poem features a creature who tries to swim across a Channel, who is threatened with his toes dropping off but who is rescued and reassured that going home empty-handed does not constitute failure. Like Johnson's experiment, it also implicitly raises the question of man's relationship to other aquatic creatures, his putative ancestors. The writings of Darwin and Huxley had argued that the process of evolutionary development involved cul de sacs, where one species adaptation flourished and another failed. The corollary was that man was not the end of creation, but a branch in a line that might be 'gradually extinguified', continue in different form or reverse its tracks. Involution and evolution might, in the grand narrative of deep time, be difficult to distinguish from one another. This thought is potentially troubling, but also potentially consoling, from a personal and from a biological perspective. 'The Pobble who has no Toes', like 'The Jumblies', is a classic Lear poem because it is circular: we are allowed simultaneously to have the flow of progression and the comfort of return. In Lear's imaginative world a state of perpetual betweenness answers a very deep psychological need to resist finality, to remain forever in play.

Nonsense and Progress

Its narrative of losing one's toes in the water connects 'The Pobble who has no Toes' with a little-known poem that Lear wrote for his friend the clergyman and headmaster Edward Carus Selwyn in 1884.

> . . . His house stood on a cliff,—it did,
>   Its aspic it was cool;
> And many thousand little boys
>   Resorted to his school,
> Where if of progress they could boast
>   He gave them heaps of butter'd toast.
>
> But he grew rabid-wroth, he did,
>   If they neglected books,
> And dragged them to adjacent cliffs
>   With beastly Button Hooks,
> And there with fatuous glee he threw
>   Them down into the otion blue.
>
> And in the sea they swam, they did—
>   All playfully about,
> And some eventually became
>   Sponges, or speckled trout. . . .[106]

Lear imagines Carus Selwyn's recalcitrant pupils meeting a fate that most teachers have, in the privacy of their own minds, visited upon their most annoying students. The master pushes them off a cliff and they are swept out to sea, never to be seen again. This verse contains parodic echoes of Thomas Hood's 'The Dream of Eugene Aram', a poem famous in the nineteenth century about a real-life schoolmaster who was also a murderer, which also influenced Lewis Carroll's 'The Walrus and the Carpenter'.

What is interesting is how the children in Lear's Dingle Bank poem adapt. The boys who can't boast of 'progress' with their book-learning evolve or are reborn in reverse, becoming fluid creatures swimming 'all playfully about'. Their punishment turns into a release. Indeed it playfully suggests a redefinition of what 'progress' for children might actually amount to. Perhaps the cool 'aspic' of the house ('aspect', but also a jelly for preserving food) is holding them into a shape that confines their movements, just as buttons confine us in our clothes. (Contemporaries remarked that Lear always wore loose clothes; his skin and his mind were both easily irritated by confinement.) Lear's poem hints that children may sometimes be better off finding their own adaptive pathways, refusing the schema of academic progress that human society prizes. Just as the Pobble loses his toes and finds he is much happier without them, the boys thrive when they regress into more primitive forms, freed from the beastly B[utton H]ooks of formal education.

As Sally Shuttleworth has explored, evolutionary progression from primitive organisms to higher animals and the child's progression from babyhood to adulthood were routinely compared in the late Victorian period. Ernst Haeckel in 1866 formulated the influential principle that 'ontogeny recapitulates phylogeny': the individual's life plays out the same developmental stages undergone by the race; childhood thus reenacts the forms of animal or 'savage' life.[107] These theories had implications for how children should be treated. Sydney Buckman, a palaeontologist, suggested that stealing fruit, for example, was a natural instinct for children. In a discussion of disciplining children's sleeping habits, he commented that it was remarkable 'how much unnecessary suffering is inflicted on infants and children because parents fail to recognise the ancestry from "animals", and consequently the instincts, different from those of adults, which children have inherited'.[108] George J. Romanes in *Mental Evolution in Animals* (1883) produced a chart suggesting that on the psychological scale, human infants were at seven weeks equivalent to molluscs, at twelve weeks to fish, at four months to reptiles and octopi, at eight months to birds and at twelve months to monkeys.[109] I am not suggesting that Lear subscribed to these views regarding child psychology, merely that he produced his later nonsense in a climate where there was frequent comparison between theories of animal-human evolution and of child-adult development. Such ideas influenced other literary works, including Tennyson's *In Memoriam*, which Lear knew by heart, and Charles Kingsley's *The Water-Babies: A Fairy Tale for a Land-Baby* (1863), which Lear greatly admired.[110] Kingsley is not usually thought of as a nonsense author, but *The Water-Babies* contains passages that are recognisably nonsensical, and this work—which features both a mad March hare and an otter grinning like a Cheshire cat—was a significant influence on Lewis Carroll as well as Lear.

Significantly, Lear's Dingle Bank poem promises both adult and child the pleasure of regression. It is written for an adult as part of an affectionate correspondence that traded in nonsense humour on both sides. The schoolmaster is permitted the 'fatuous glee' of acting out violent impulses. But the boys are permitted to regress indefinitely, to become marine life forms. The characters Mr Lear, the Polly and the Pusseybite in Lear's 1866 story fall into the water and are dashed to 'atoms', which can be reconstructed into different, composite creatures. But 'some' of the Dingle Bank boys change 'eventually': a process that sounds much more like real evolution. The fact that they become 'sponges and speckled trout' is fascinating. Some of them are—as Lear had in 1859 imagined himself doing—changing into zoophytes, forms of life that hover between the animal and the vegetable. Darwin had identified sponges and an early fish-like creature as the kind of multicellular organisms from which all mammals, including man, evolved.[111] Lear's Dingle Bank schoolchildren are becoming primitive life forms.

Kingsley's *Water-Babies* had also explored the possibility of a child regressing into an aquatic being. In this strange fiction, Tom—a young chimney sweep, grimy with soot and neglected by society—dies in the early pages. He is reborn as a tiny water creature, grows gills as an eft and must swim down the river to the sea. On this journey Tom encounters speckled trout and enjoys playing with these primitive creatures who have not evolved significantly from their early biological niche. They are patronised by their patrician relatives, the salmon. As Kingsley notes:

> For you must know, no enemies are so bitter as those who are
> of the same race; and a salmon looks on a trout, as some great
> folks look on some little folks, as something just too much like
> himself to be tolerated.[112]

The expressions 'great folks' and 'little folks' here are ambiguous: Kingsley alludes to class warfare, but also to the relationship between adults and children. Adults in his text often *do* despise (and maltreat) children, and the hint that they do so because they are too closely related for comfort takes us a step towards a profound psychological insight. Adults often fear what children reveal to them about the persistence of the child-within-the-adult who has not evolved. The child and the adult may be different 'species', but also too closely related for comfort.

Kingsley's awkward but powerful text struggles to fuse his interest in Darwin's theories of evolution, his Christian faith and a Wordsworthian view of childhood (in turn derived from Rousseau) that sees the child as closer to Nature than the adult. Tom's fluid journey along the river from eft to water-baby and eventually to spiritual manhood on the island of St Brendan mimics the pattern of Darwinian evolution from primitive aquatic life-form to *Homo sapiens;* but Tom's is also a story of moral regeneration, where being reborn 'as a little child' is the path to salvation. The water into which Tom falls when he dies and begins his rebirth at the start of the novel is ambiguously that of protoplasmic sea life, amniotic fluid and the baptismal font. Elsewhere in *The Water-Babies,* Kingsley worries about the possibility of human involution: he imagines men reverting to a society of apes, based on aggressive competition and moral degeneracy. Tom's journey is, saliently, like the Pobble's, a way of going forward and going back at the same time. One can see in Lear's incorporation of ideas from *The Water-Babies* into his Dingle Bank poem, a similar desire to reconcile evolutionary ideas about man's emergence from aquatic life forms with a lingering sense of child-hood as better aligned with the 'natural' before social pressures, inscribed within the educational system, produce alienation.

Indeed, one of the functions of nineteenth-century nonsense literature is to interrogate the idea of progress. Jean-Jacques Lecercle has argued that nonsense emerges in the mid-nineteenth century in response to the debate about whether there should be universal public schooling and, if so, what form it might take. This debate eventually resulted, in 1870, in the provision of free schooling in Britain for boys and girls. Lecercle concludes that 'non-sense as a genre is a by-product of the development of the institution of the school. . . . The texts provide an imaginary solution to the real contradiction between the urge to capture an ever wider proportion of the population for the purpose of elementary schooling and the resistance, religious, political and psychological, that such a cultural upheaval inevitably arouses'.[113]

It is certainly true that many nonsense texts were written by educators and that they contain humorous criticism of the Victorian schoolroom. *Nursery Nonsense or Rhymes without Reason* (1864), written by D'arcy Thompson, a professor of Greek at Edinburgh University, includes a poem, 'Dr Bray', in which various animals send their offspring to a school run by a donkey. Of course, he can't teach them anything useful. He is, after all, only able to bray, and they need to learn to bark, miaow and cluck.[114] If they mind what he says they will 'grow up little asses'. The punning satire is pointed. The real-life Dr Bray was a prominent educationalist who set up Sunday schools in Britain and in India. Dumb clucks won't benefit from the attempt to educate them collectively. Lewis Carroll's *Alice in Wonderland* (1865) also makes satirical points about the Victorian day school. The Mock Turtle explains that his master was a Tortoise ('because he taught us'), but, one suspects, equally because tortoises are notoriously slow. The school offered 'lessens' that got shorter every day. There is a broad hint here about the diminishing returns of conventional primary education. In Charles Leland's *Johnnykin and the Goblins*, a now little-read but fascinating nonsense text of 1877, Johnnykin is bullied by his fellow schoolboys. When he saves a stone goblin in the churchyard from being destroyed by his oafish classmates, the goblin saves him from the miseries of school. He transforms a donkey into a substitute Johnnykin who, being hay-brained and keen on sports, will satisfy his teachers.[115] Meanwhile the real Johnnykin escapes school forever; he enters the adult world as an artist, bypassing the asinine system of education that was thwarting his natural talents. Lear's private nonsense poem about the Dingle Bank schoolboys seems to fit into this pattern of nonsense joking about the limitations of school, using the animal kingdom to convey the natural life within the child that conventional education suppresses.

However, Lear's published nonsense has nothing directly to say about school. It forms a subtler intervention in the debate about what children ought to be reading. Early guns in this war of words were fired by Charles Lamb, who in 1802 famously wrote to Coleridge objecting to the trend towards what he thought of as science rather than poetry in children's books:

> Mrs Barbauld's stuff has banished all the old classics of the nursery; & the Shopman at Newbery's hardly deign'd to reach them off an old exploded corner of a shelf, when Mary ask'd for them. Mrs Barbauld's and Mrs Trimmer's nonsense lay in

piles about. Knowledge insignificant & vapid as Mrs B's books convey, it seems, must come to the child in the *shape of knowledge*. . . . Science has succeeded to poetry no less in the little walks of children than with men. ———— Is there no possibility of averting this sore evil? Think what you would have been now, if instead of being fed with Tales and old wives fables in childhood, you had been crammed with Geography and Natural History?[116]

In the opposite trenches, Priscilla Wakefield, author of many successful works in natural history, threw a grenade in her preface to *An Introduction to the Natural History and Classification of Insects* (1816), asserting that:

Nonsense has given way to reason; and useful knowledge, under an agreeable form, has usurped the place of the Histories of Tom Thumb, and Woglog the Giant. No branch of science seems better adapted to this important purpose, than natural history. . . .[117]

Nonsense in these various sorties by children's authors is a term of abuse. Lamb claims that science is nonsense and that fairy tales are what children need to thrive intellectually and emotionally. Wakefield argues that fairy tales are nonsense and that science is its opposite; advances in children's literature towards reason and useful knowledge have happily usurped more primitive works such as *Tommy Trip's History of Beasts and Birds* (1767), which included the history of his dog Jowler and of Woglog the Giant.

Lear's *A Book of Nonsense* (1846) released into this atmosphere was a small smoke bomb, and his *Nonsense Songs, Stories, Botany and Alphabets* (1871) queered the battlefield. Rather than claiming that what he wrote was what children *should* be reading, Lear was happily proclaiming in his titles that his books were just the sort of absurd stuff that others said children should *not* be reading. He recoups *nonsense* as a term of commendation. By including 'nonsense botany' and 'nonsense alphabets' with his poetry and songs, Lear, who had been professionally engaged in both science and poetry, played hopscotch with these categories as putative opposites. His nonsense rejects the terms of engagement under which the contest over children's minds was being fought.

Since natural history was a hostage in the battle over what children ought to read, Lear's 'Nonsense Botany' is of particular interest. It is, as Lecercle suggests, a 'spoof' of botany as an academic discipline; yet it is also a playful exploration of natural forms that investigates the similarity of natural and man-made objects, and how animal, bird and vegetable shapes resemble or echo one another in part or in aggregate. Lear introduces his first published 'Nonsense Botany' (in *Nonsense Songs, Stories, Botany and Alphabets*) as the work of 'Professor Bosh', a 'valued and learned contributor' to the *Nonsense Gazette,* 'whose labours in the fields of Culinary and Botanical science, are so well known to all the world'.[118] Compared with the asinine Dr Bray or Kingsley's murderous Professor Pttmllnsprts, Bosh is a delightful crank. Lear enjoys guying the bumbling academic as a figure of fun. But in real life he admired and consulted such men. It is noticeable that he affixed botanical labels to the plants in his garden in San Remo and waxed wrathful when 'horrid' children pulled them out: 'so Botany is confounded dismally and abysmally'.[119] He also, however, sometimes wrote the plant names backwards to confuse and amuse the young Hubert and Arnold Congreve.[120]

The impulses to order, to study and to educate are strong in Lear. He often lent works from his own considerable library of natural-history books for children, friends and servants to peruse. Lear taught art to both adults and children for much of his life. His pupils ranged from Queen Victoria to Dimitri Kokali, the son of his servant, Giorgio, to whom he voluntarily taught reading, writing and arithmetic, an unusual and considerable service for an employer to bestow on the child of an employee. Lear's friends included the Liberal minister Henry Bruce, who in the 1860s was a significant advocate for a universal, nondenominational system of education that would encompass the majority of children who were not yet in school. He was also close to Anthony Mundella, who ran Board Schools that in 1884 taught 1.3 million children who, Mundella claimed, arrived 'wild, almost barbarous, unclad, unfed, filthy, ignorant, neglected' and are 'sitting clothed in their right minds to-day'.[121] Education could clothe children literally and figuratively, offering them a way to know their own minds. Lear sometimes regretted that he had not benefited more from formal education and artistic training; in 1863 he commented in his diary, 'at times I say—would I had been educated—but that is folly'.[122] He valued knowledge and those who possessed it.

However, the impulses to disarrange, to play and to feel glad about skipping formal education are also prominent in his lexicon of feeling. Contumaciously, he once commented that he was glad he had escaped formal education, as those who received it become 'cut and dry'—like biological specimens—whereas he remained always 'on the threshold of knowledge'.[123] In 1885, in a letter to the Mundellas, he conceived a 'Bored School' trip during which eighty-three students were eaten by polar bears, leaving only a ring of tombstones to commemorate the 'History fact that so large a number of deservingly aspiring British scholars suddenly by Polar Bears devoured were, leaving nothing but a posthumous howling of disconsolate tears for the consideration and contempt to posterity. . . .'[124] Scholastic outings in Lear always have the potential to end in bears. He does not want children, or the child-within-the-adult to whom he speaks with equal attentiveness, ever to be bored. Better to be gored, so long as the attack is funny. Natural appetite has its revenge on human reason in this wild assault, which is a blackly comic version of the fate of the Franklin polar expedition. Imagining being 'extinguified' here, as in the 'Seven Families of the Lake Pipple-Popple', can be liberating. It relieves humans of the responsibilities of 'aspiring'. A 'polybingular' monument is all that will remain of them.

Lear's Nonsense Botany is delightful for many reasons. One is the sense of imaginative abundance it conveys. Lear liked to quote the old nursery rhyme: 'if all the world were apple pie / and all the trees were bread and cheese'.[125] His botany conjures a kind of Golden Age where not only do plum buns grow on trees, so do kites, kettles and pocket watches. Everyone has heard of a man-made 'boot tree', but Lear's Shoebootia Utilis, from which boots stick out, ready for the passerby to help himself, is an efflorescence of wish-fulfilment. Just as his zoological and ornithological paintings dramatise individual species, so his imaginary plants are graphically arresting, their odd blooms often deliberately loud (Barkia Howloudia, Tickia Orologica) or large (Washtubbia Circularis) or both (Stunnia Dinnerbellia). These plants convey infantile delight in being able to grasp buns while also offering the intellectual pleasure of being able to grasp visual and verbal puns. As contemporary readers noted, it is often clear what genus of plant Lear's imaginary species belong to. For example, Armchairia Comfortabilis looked to a reviewer in the *Examiner* like 'a noble species of arum', whereas Queeriflora Babyoïdes 'seems allied to an hibiscus'.[126] Another identified Manipeeplia Upsidownia, a plant in which lots of tiny human figures are dangling by their ankles from the stem, as a kind of fuchsia. The fruits of Plumbunnia Nutritiosa resemble strawberries, while the Tigerlillia Terribilis has petals that are a cluster of real tigers; the petals of Pollybirdia

Fig. 3.15a **Bluebottlia Buzztilentia,** *Laughable Lyrics* **(1877)**

Fig. 3.15b **Crabbia Horrida,** *Laughable Lyrics* **(1877)**

Singularis consist of a clutch of parrots. Anna Henchman helpfully notes that Lear's botanies 'inspire . . . reflection on what constitutes a part, what constitutes a whole, and the strange underlying process by which a single organism can reproduce and turn one into many. . . . Taxonomies assert both an organism's unique particularity and its close relations to others it resembles'.[127] The Pollybirdia Singularis might thus be seen as a type for Lear's nonsense botany in that it contains both literal 'pollys' (parrots) and figurative polymorphosis; it is 'singular' (odd) and plural at the same time. The implicit oxymoron expresses a formative truth about biological identity.

Lear's system of naming burlesques the system of Linnean taxonomical classification. Normally such names require a classical or botanical education to decipher. Lear's, however, are comically transparent. Nastikreechia Krorluppia, bearing a procession of caterpillars along its stem, is a phenomenon depressingly familiar to all gardeners. Gardening has traditionally been an amateur pursuit, and Lear's nonsense plants restore botany to the common or garden ground of universal legibility. But the humour nicely balances anti-academic and intellectual jokes. The appreciative reviewer who described Lear's work as 'The Science of Nonsense' dismissed the nonsense cookery as something that was too close to the 'animal spirits' of children, whose minds were, like the soles of their feet, too easily tickled. He preferred the cleverness of the nonsense botany. It was not only about science, but in its own way scientific. Indeed such fine nonsense, he argued, could only have been produced by one of the 'higher animals'; nonsense thus, strangely, becomes a proof of man's evolutionary development into an apex species.[128]

According to a letter Lear wrote to Mrs Bellenden Ker in 1870, some of his fantastical flowers are to be found 'in the Jumbly islands'.[129] This is a nonsense destination, yet as Lear's illustrative work on *Captain Beechey's Voyage* and his reading of Darwin would have made him acutely aware, islands such as the Galapagos were precisely the places where new species did evolve. Lear had in the 1830s and 1840s enjoyed playing with the hybridity of the Hippopotamouse Rabbitte, the Froglodytes, the Owly-Pussey-catte and bullfrogs who have the heads of bulls and the tails of frogs. In his nonsense botany of the early 1870s, humans, animals, birds, insects and molluscs, in addition to many objects of human utility, are all to be found in flowering plants. There is a certain visual and biological truth in this. In 1872 Lear noted that one of the many unusual plants he cultivated in his San Remo garden, *Clyanthus puniceus,* had red flowers 'like lobster's claws———4 bunches of them'.[130] This was a New Zealand plant grown from seed sent by his sister Sarah Street. The Crabbia Horrida in his nonsense botany is an imaginative outgrowth of this real observation. Lear's reading of work in natural history would also have reinforced the idea that 'higher' forms of life do derive from common ancestors such as zoophytes that show the inseparability of animal and plant origins. Naturalists looking at marine invertebrates through a microscope were apt to see in these tiny creatures forms that apparently replicated those of 'higher' mammals. Kingsley noted that zoophytes resembled squirrels' tails and lobsters' horns; that sea urchins were 'babies heads'; that polype cells were edged with spines 'and on the back of some of them is—what is it but a live vulture's head, snapping and snapping?'[131]

In 1864, E. W. Cooke, a Fellow of the Royal Society, while attending a meeting of the BAAS, used the breaks between scientific meetings to walk on the beach. Like Lear, he was a skilled artist, and he found himself drawing pictures in which fossils and marine animals he had studied under the microscope combined with anatomical parts of other creatures to form 'grotesque animals'. The first was an ammonite combined with a crested cockatoo. Cooke explained, 'One of the great physiologists and naturalists of the age, on looking at these drawings, quaintly remarked, "How all the parts of the animal kingdom fit each other!" and it constantly occurred to the Author that the most diverse genera and species, when shuffled together, might again be united like *dominoes*, with a kindred aptness, and, in some instances, even of gracefulness. . . .'[132] Cooke's kindred unions of organic parts and analogous structures are not advertised as 'nonsense', yet they bear comparison with Lear's 'nonsense botany', where the Cockatooca Superba is the avian inflorescence of a strange plant, or with Lear's drawings of the Scroobious Pip as a creature that combines the characteristics of an echidna, a human, a peacock and a fly. Cooke's *Grotesque Creatures* was published in 1872. He reflected that 'my partnerships are not "Limited", for . . . in the dark depths and caverns of animal life, there may still exist endless stores of new Birds, Beasts, and Fishes'. D'arcy Wentworth Thompson, the biologist son of the author of *Nursery Nonsense*, would explore the reasons for the similarity in shape between creatures of different species in his seminal study, *On Growth and Form* (1917), in which he demonstrated the identity between the morphology of a marine shell and an animal horn as products of the same mathematical parameters. Thompson would show via 'transformations' how variations in form between related species could be modelled visually by mapping one onto a sheet and then stretching it in a particular pattern. Artistic extrapolation on sheets of squared-up paper (the kind of tracing Lear did when transferring sketches to larger canvases) and imagining scientific processes of cellular growth turn out to be very similar occupations. We see here how 'nonsense' and science in the late nineteenth century are, in fact, kindred disciplines in their imaginative interest in likening form between species and conceiving its possible outgrowths and sports.

Fig. 3.16 E. W. Cooke, *Grotesque Animals* (1872)

Lear's ideas gave rise in turn to other nonsense botanies. Marie Duval, the actress and cartoonist, published in 1877 a *Calendaria Botanica Ridiculoso*. This botany has not previously been attributed, but its similarities to her other nonsense make its authorship transparent. Her reimagining of nonsense botany has a distinctly female viewpoint. Duval's plant for the month of February is Cupido Wiltrapia. This has the form of a Venus flytrap *(Dionaea muscipula)*, a carnivorous plant so named because its hairy terminal lobes resemble the female genitalia. Traditional botany identifies in this fly-eating wetland plant a vagina dentata. Duval's specimen, au contraire, is trapping women. They are reading valentines or love letters written on its open leaves, which then abruptly shut, ensnaring them, leaving their heads and legs sticking out. Her botanical 'discovery' identifies with women.

It draws a critical connection between the kind of cultural leaves we read and the plant leaves to which we give scientific nomenclature that reflects society's sexual prejudices. Duval's Bluebottlia Episcopalia takes Lear's fly-plant, the Bluebottlia Buzztilentia, in a new direction, as each flower has petals formed of bishops wearing blue copes. Blossoms are usually identified with femininity; Duval makes her bluebottles, which resemble both petals and flies, male yet florid. *Bluebottle,* as we have seen, was a word for a cornflower that became a word for any official in blue uniform and hence an annoying fly. Duval traces this etymology backwards in a picture that mimics biological involution: from man, to fly, to flower. Male bishops may be at the head of a social hierarchy, but at the daisy end of the evolutionary chain. Her designs respond wittily to Lear, playing with similarities between zoological and botanical forms while exercising her newspaper cartoonist's flair for social commentary.

In Lear's art, the persistent likening between human and nonhuman species is always a product of both liking and kenning, in the sense of knowing through time. Visual recognition is a form of sympathy. In fact, its revelation of the likeness inherent in form suggests that we may be intimate even with creatures that at first appear strange. The emotional logic of Lear's work and its visual attention to the life of creatures are thus impossible to separate. It creates the conditions for intimacy by depicting the primacy of the body and of physical behaviour—exuberant, dramatic, desiring, social yet wary—that humans share with other animate life-forms.

Walter Savage Landor had written in *Imaginary Conversations* (1846) that 'children are not men nor women: they are almost as different creatures, in many respects, as if they never were to be the one or the other: they are as unlike as buds are unlike flowers, and almost as blossoms are unlike fruits'.[133] Natural history in the nineteenth century offered models for thinking anew about the alterity of childhood, its distinct subjective drama and its often-silenced perspective. However, thinking about humans as a species within an evolutionary paradigm where change was possible from 'higher' forms to 'lower' ones also tended to suggest the possibility of regression from adult to child, and from human to animal, bird, fish or even plant. This is the direction that Lear's nonsense primarily takes. It speaks to a deep desire for return. Often telling stories of involution rather than evolution, it explores the peculiarities of being a 'humanbean' through the possibility of abandoning human forms and norms to roost in a tree, swim in the sea or fly out of sight. Nonsense, indeed, opposes the tyranny of 'progress' considered

Fig. 3.17a Marie Duval, *Calendario Ridiculoso* (1877)

Fig. 3.17b Marie Duval, *Calendario Ridiculoso* (1877)

as a one-way street towards growth or education; in it, supposedly 'higher' forms of knowledge are often relegated to supposedly 'lower' forms of knowledge—such as the instinct to play—that are equally vital to our emotional lives and creative capacities.

'I am a queer beast to have so many friends', Lear wrote to Lady Waldegrave in 1867.[134] Lear's nonsense allows us to acknowledge that humans are all queer beasts, who contain aspects of the child and the adult, the animal, the bird and the fish; we are beings in development, whose physical shape often feels awkward, compromised, odd. His jumbly, mixed-up creatures are entities in which adult and child can coexist; where 'class', like 'species', is ambiguously a fact of identity and a fluid construct, and sexuality is polymorphic. Coming to terms, in the sense of inventing words and forms— as Lear perpetually does in his poems and illustrations—and coming to terms emotionally with this inchoate reality are linked. In the jumbliness of Lear's nonsense we can see reflections of our own perpetually unresolved nature, with delight rather than dismay.

4

DREAMWORK
Lear's Visual Language

I was once a bottle of ink
    Inky
    Dinky
    Thinky
    Inky,
Blacky Minky
Bottle of Ink![1]

L EAR very rarely dreamed. At least, he did not have conscious access
to the narratives formed by his unconscious mind during sleep. It was
an oddity he remarked: 'When I woke—one of those absurd ideas which
are the nearest approach I ever have to dreams, and which comes as I wake
in fits of laughter,—presented itself'.[2] It is striking that his closest approach
to dreaming comes in the form of an 'absurd idea' that stimulates laughter.
In this case it is a dream of wish fulfilment regarding artistic success, that
people will come in droves and buy his pictures, but the dream is not 'fool-
filled'. The diary entry passes lightly over the fullness and fooliness that
dreams offer us. But there is something important here, in the relationship
between the absurd and desire, that is characteristic of Lear's artistic vision.
His art deals in the 'foolfillment' of wishes, often conjuring plenitude and
illusion at the same time. One can imagine why direct communication between Lear's sleeping and waking mind might have been difficult. There
was a wealth of what he called 'physical and psychical' trouble in his past,
of whose effect on his current mental life he was acutely aware. He claimed
(not wholly accurately) to have total recall of everything that had happened

to him since he was four years old. His missing dreams together with the obsessive recollection of actualities suggest that Lear's mind policed its boundaries with a zeal that forced its 'absurd ideas' into waking forms.

Where did Lear's capacity for dreaming go? The almost too-obvious answer is into his art, which so often has dreamlike qualities: a combination of extreme strangeness and familiarity, a sense of existing simultaneously in the moment and out of time. As Freud notes, the process of dreamwork is regressive, it takes thought-material on a path 'in the reverse direction to that taken by the development of mental complications' towards 'a pictorial character'.[3] As verbal thought renders itself into dream-image, it condenses and transposes material from the waking mind, making it unreal, sometimes absurd, so that it can be viewed by the dreamer with relative equanimity. It often seems that Lear's nonsense makes visible this aspect of dreamwork: his limericks throw up in the air images whose calmness is at odds with the severity of the actions and consequences narrated in the verse.

> There was a young person of Janina,
> Whose uncle was always a fanning her;
> When he fanned off her head, she smiled sweetly, and said,
> 'You propitious old person of Janina!'[4]

There is pleasure in the possible detachment of word from image, and in registering the gap between the impressions they convey, that is similar to the pleasure in acknowledging the difference between the head and the body, or the conscientious superego from the licentious id. Many of Lear's early cartoons depend upon the comic energy generated by this split. His limericks can allow us to view our own emotional detachment with delight.

However, as an artist-writer Lear is also peculiarly alert to the dreamlike way in which word and image are not necessarily discrete or distinct forms. Like twins in the womb of expression, they share the same constituent matter; they can play with and shade into one another. Tellingly, most of the books Lear recalls as making a significant impression on him in childhood and young adulthood are illustrated volumes: a picture Bible; the Boydell Shakespeare; the Comte de Buffon's *Histoire Naturelle;* Thomas Stothard's illustrations for *Robinson Crusoe;* Turner's illustrations for Samuel Rogers's poem *Italy.* These were the books that fired his imaginative process, giving him a sense of the porousness of text and picture that would permanently shape his creativity. Words become worlds via the physical space they occupy and their expressive capacity to create pictures, which resides as much in their immediate shape to the eye and ear as in the more abstract idea of meaning. We first receive written language as image, a gift that Lear replicates over and over in the more than thirty picture alphabets he drew for friends' children. Picture alphabets appear in all three of Lear's later nonsense books. They have not been much discussed, but to me they appear foundational: they communicate Lear's perception of language as living form. For Lear the letter as a sign always retains the potential of the pictogram. In 1868, he wrote to Anne Scrivens:

> I have burst out in a new place a making monograms: several
> are much admired:—I make the initials into some object or
> other—sometimes appropriate at others merely pretty. Here's
> an ancient Lamp with a border.[5]

Lear enjoyed transforming his friends' initials into pictures. Emma Elizabeth Munro Ferguson became an Aladdin's lamp with a design running round the edge. Anne Glass became a champagne flute. Louisa Isaak was represented in the form of a nose and an eye: L^I. The fact that an I, in Lear's imaginative world, can become an eye and that his own interwoven initials can become an ear demonstrates the way in which the senses are, for him, intertwined.[6] When we view marks on the page, they can be seen, read and 'heard' in ways that emphasise the synaesthesia inherent in language and its ability to conjure simultaneously aspects of the inner, perceiving self and the perceived outer world: their osmotic relationship.

In Lear's landscape paintings, as in his nonsense, the relationship between word and image is dynamic. It is not simply that image illustrates word, or that the notes Lear writes on his sketches as aide-mémoires on colour and scenery are gradually replaced by pictures of the scenes he remembers. Rather, word and image are constantly in dialogue that limns the qualities of landscape as itself an intertext where personal experience, literary allusion, history, myth and previous visual representations meet. Many of Lear's notes on landscape read like tone poems; they reveal the mingled qualities of place as a 'poetickle site': something that might be a sight to paint or to conjure in poetry, or that might be ticklishly poised between these two modes of representation. Lear's appreciation of the confluence and dialogue between word and picture is one of the factors that makes him so sympathetic to Pre-Raphaelitism and I want, toward the end of this chapter on word

and image, to think about Lear as a self-declared Pre-Raphaelite painter, relating the boldness, interdisciplinarity, colour and drama of his painting as a
member of this movement to the qualities we admire in his nonsense.

Moving Images

Lear's gift for conveying visual drama powers his simultaneous development
as an artist and a writer. In an extraordinary letter from summer 1835,
written at Knowsley Hall to his friends George and Fanny Coombe, he
describes a cricket match on the lawn on a hot day that involves both aristocrats and servants (although Lear shrewdly notes that the servants don't
get to bat). The cricket match is disrupted when the kitchen of the stately
home catches fire and everybody has to participate in a more serious kind of
game, fetching and passing water to quench the flames. The letter proceeds
by fits and starts, as if Lear were commenting in real time:

> Fire! fire! fire!—Engines!—Water. God bless us—the noise
> increases & all the cricketers are rushing toward the outbuild-
> ings across the lawn: I smell smoke—a chimney on fire I dare
> say—must go and see—variety is delightful. . . . 4 o'clock I
> date from Knowsley now—but before you get my letter I sadly
> fear Knowsley Hall will have ceased to be. . . . The engines are
> playing—but can do little execution—the fire is so central—
> they are unroofing the house. . . . Water—water is the
> universal cry——the dignities are done away with—we are
> all in shirts & trowsers & perspiration—the grand staircase is
> covered with humanbeings—to & fro—jugs—tubs—
> buckets—barrels—everything that can carry water.[7]

Lear writes that he is violently sick and faints, but he can't resist continuing
to report:

> A long line of a 100 people or more convey filled & empty
> buckets from & to the horse ponds. Grooms—ladies—Lord
> Derby & the Lord knows who—all take a part. Lady
> Charlotte Penrhyn & her beautiful daughters—3 footmen—10
> housemaids—& the fat coachman are all drawing buckets at
> the tank—the French governess & Sir John Shelley are

> tubbing it—the Rev Hopwood—Lady Elinor & 20 Gardeners
> command a regiment of watering pots. Lady Shelley keeps
> poking about with a leaky washing bucket. Some right
> honourable children who can do nothing else are sounding the
> alarm bell. . . .

Did Lear really take a break of a few minutes from firefighting to continue his letter? We will never know. But a gift for black comedy infuses the whole missive with an energy that teeters deliciously between alarm and hilarity as the house is unroofed and the occupants are undressed. Lear's sequences of words convey an animated visual picture that could easily form the basis for a strip cartoon or film sequence. The regiment of watering cans is almost a nonsense proposition. Similarly, one visualises the French governess and the knight 'tubbing it', literally joining one another in a tub, like the butcher, the baker and the candlestick maker of nursery rhyme. The conflagration kindles the mixture of delightful and dreadful so characteristic of Lear's limericks. The reams of long dashes conjure the chain of humanbeings who are passing buckets to one another. They also act in the manner of filmic jump cuts, to convey the speed of events and the way that our attention registers different sensory impressions: hearing the cry of 'Fire!' and the alarm bell, smelling smoke, viewing the different classes of people in motion. Lear's visual language emphatically includes his characteristic punctuation: the long dash, which acts rather like the successive frames of his storyboards, and the exclamation mark, which like an inverted champagne bottle going 'pop' insists that we attend to the physical drama of utterance. On one occasion he marshals twenty-seven exclamation marks to express his delight at a fine day.[8]

The earliest of Lear's cartoons that have survived date from the early 1830s, when he was beginning to make a name for himself as a natural history painter but was also leading the social life of a young man eager to meet people and to entertain them with comic songs, rhymes and sketches. Lear in this period was highly mobile, travelling the country and regularly meeting new people. His cartoons are also mobile, conveying wit as a happening, a performance. Lear often drew sketches as a way of entertaining others in real time. Frequently, they take the form of a cartoon sequence. He imagines events taking place in stages or scenes, with distinct pictures for different phases of the action as they occur. A good example of this is his approach to a preexisting limerick, from *Anecdotes and Adventures of Fifteen Gentlemen* (1822), which he dramatised visually in two parts.

There was an old soldier of Bicester—
Who went walking one day with his sister—

When a bull with one poke—
Tossed her into an oak—Before the old gentleman missed her.[9]

In the tiny book from which Lear takes this verse, there is only one picture illustrating it, and it is comparatively tame.[10] The artist, probably Robert Cruikshank (elder brother of the more famous George), depicts the sister being tossed into a tree in one direction while her brother walks in the other. In creating a separate 'before' and 'after' scene, Lear makes the scene much funnier. Both the soldier and his sister look pompous, with their identical aquiline noses in the air. The snooty sister, walking behind her brother, is portrayed on tiptoe with a plumed hat and a parasol, as if she scarcely deigns to touch the ground. It is therefore no more than poetic justice when the bull—with a knowing, indeed conspiratorial, look to the audience—tosses the sister into a tree, without the brother perceiving that anything has happened. He strolls on regardless. The fact that there are inconsistencies between the first and second drawings (for example, the soldier has no spurs in the second picture) suggests that Lear made them quickly. Predictably, commas in the original poem have, in his rendition, become long dashes—conveying a visual impression of headlong travel. The speed of the movement of his pen enters his depiction of the vault into the oak tree. This could be the premise for an animated cartoon of the kind where Tom and Jerry are thrown skywards and Tom does a double-take and begins to fall only when he suddenly realises that there is no ground beneath his feet.

The early 1830s saw the invention of a number of devices that became part of the early history of animation. The zoetrope was a circular mechanism with slits, through which a child could watch a sequence of drawings that spun around, creating the illusion of motion—a galloping horse, or a leaping frog. Lear's two-part drawing could easily form the basis for such an animated cartoon, where the old soldier's position in the frame is unaltered, but we see the sister tossed into the tree over and over again. One of the things that makes such sequences so satisfying is their infinite repeatability. The limerick lends itself to this, with a short dramatic structure defined by a turn. It can be treated like a flip book or a zoetrope ribbon, as an image that leaps afresh on each new viewing. We do not know if Lear ever encountered a zoetrope. He certainly saw a magic lantern,[11] and given his

There was an old soldier of Bicester

Was walking one day with his sister;

A bull, with one poke,

Toss'd her into an oak,

Before the old gentleman miss'd

her.

Fig. 4.1 There was an old soldier of Bicester, *Anecdotes and Adventures of Fifteen Gentlemen* (1822)

Fig. 4.2a & b **Lear's version of 'There was an old soldier of Bicester'**

Fig. 4.2b

frequent visits to toy shops and his interest in mechanical toys—such as a bird he bought for Edgar Drummond's child that could be screwed to a table and, when knocked, would 'wag his tail & nod his head with vivacity or solemnity'—it would not be surprising if he had.[12] The point is rather that Lear as an artist has a facility for imaginative projection, which often results in images that dramatically project their subjects into physical space.

It is fascinating that Lear's first approaches to comic illustration often produce a cartoon storyboard, a highly unusual form in this period. William Hogarth had led the way in producing narrative sequences of pictures, typically illustrating a tragicomic downfall. The Cruikshank brothers drew 'before' and 'after' cartoons. The Swiss artist Rodolphe Töppfer is usually regarded as the inventor of the cartoon sequence in the 1830s, but Lear might well have seen work by, for example, Joe Lisle who, around 1832, illustrated the song sheets for 'The Cork Leg' with a storyboard.[13] Still, this was fresh ground. The term *strip cartoon* was not coined until 1916; indeed, *cartoon* became current as a word to describe comic designs only in the 1840s. Much of the comic illustration that Lear would have grown up with had emblematic qualities, as befitted the finicky process of engraving; it preferred to investigate a social or political scene through a detailed focus on characters and situation. Lear's cartoons, instead, make play of their own improvisational sketchiness. Lear relishes the way that a sequence of images, offset by text, allows us to see time happening dramatically. Characters are often literally or figuratively 'up in the air'. Our successive windows into the comic narrative constitute a theatre of consciousness where we can appreciate the contrast between the ignorance of the cartoon character, who is not privy to the knowledge of what will happen, and our own knowing overview.

The juxtaposition of text and image, through the subtly or radically different information they can convey, permits us to appreciate and relish potential inner discrepancies in our feelings about physical and emotional violence or excess, externalising an internal conflict between decorum and unruliness. The early limerick about the soldier of Bicester is particularly satisfying because its internal dynamic replicates the reader's own process in appreciating the joke. The soldier doesn't 'miss' his sister. Literally, he doesn't notice she is gone. But figuratively, we may also suspect that he doesn't 'miss'—doesn't regret—her absence. He doesn't give a toss. That's the bull's remit. The picture hints that the bull and the soldier are standing in for one another: the two outthrust points of the soldier's moustache uncannily resemble the bull's horns, and the sharp point of the soldier's umbrella reinforces their shared capacity to poke. The id acts out its subconscious sexual aggression (in the form of the bull), while the respectable ego (the soldier) proceeds with its conscience inviolate. We as readers conspire in this guilty pleasure. We enjoy the sudden act of violence.

Although subsequently in Lear's published work he created a single picture for each individual limerick, the feel of the cartoon-in-motion is retained in his nonsense books. Each limerick contains the basis of a 'before and after' story. Traces of the storyboard are especially evident in limericks such as 'There was an old person of Diss', where the old person jumping into a ditch is rendered in three frames within one picture. Modern imprints of the limericks often feature several on one page. This falsifies the experience of *A Book of Nonsense,* which, like a flip book, depends on the energy detonated by the movement from one outrageous image and its accompanying limerick to the next. By turning each page, we become partly responsible for the projection of characters, for their extraordinary leaps and wayward acts, which in turn allow for the projection of mixed emotional reactions on the reader's part.

Among the liveliest of Lear's cartoon storyboards is a series of pictures of himself on horseback that he produced on a tour with Charles Knight in Italy in 1842.[14] In this sequence of equestrian disasters, which sees him, long-legged and bespectacled, bouncing about on the wrong side of the saddle or clinging to the horse's neck, halfway through a thornbush, confronting an 'irascible ox' (which wears glasses similar to his own) or being pitched into the air by his rearing steed, Lear becomes a cartoon character. His serial haplessness is endearing, like that of Buster Keaton or the bespectacled Harold Lloyd in a silent film. Even as one laughs, one cannot help but sympathise and admire the brio with which Lear renders the horse's bad behaviour and his own ineptitude. Again, one can easily imagine this sequence of drawings as a flip book or the images on a zoetrope ribbon; the horse prances and kicks, and Lear is thrown into ever new and awkward positions. Lear may well have come across *Horse Accomplishments* (1799), a set of cartoons by Thomas Rowlandson and George Moutard Woodward in which horses are shown doing ridiculous things to their riders. In 'The Vaulter', a horse projects its rider into a bush, while in 'The Astronomer' the horse is sky-gazing, to the discomfiture of its supposed master. Hablot K. Browne's illustrations to Dickens's *Pickwick Papers* also depict equestrian mishaps; urban men unsuccessfully attempting country pursuits were a staple of 1830s humour. But Lear's images have a sketchy, perpetually inventive

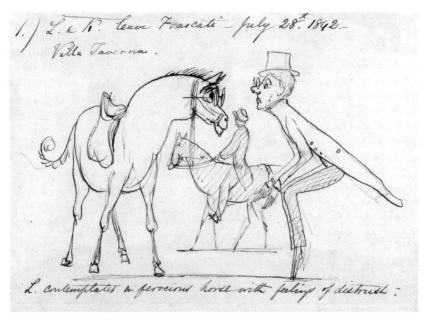

Fig. 4.3a–d **Lear's cartoons of himself on horseback (1842)**

Fig. 4.3b

Fig. 4.3c

Fig. 4.3d

energy that locates the comedy in the present continuous tense. They form
a long sequence of over twenty cartoons featuring the same characters that
can be 'read' in quick succession as if the pictures themselves were travelling like the horse and rider. The lines of text beneath each image act like
the intertitles in silent cinema; they politely understate the misadventures
that we can see occurring in the pictures, adding to the fun. The caption
'L. declares that he considers his horse far from tame' sits beneath an image
in which rider and horse are caught in midair like a Catherine wheel, with
all eight limbs flying in different directions. In these sequences, Lear shows

Fig. 4.4 'An Astronomer!!' from *Horse Accomplishments* (1799)

himself to be one of the grandfathers of the visual animation that would, in the 1890s, become what we know as cinema.

The technique he employs here of comically offsetting image and text is vital to Lear's later nonsense. It is a technique he mastered in adolescence and never forgot. In 'Miss Maniac' (circa 1829), a cartoon storyboard Lear produced for Fanny Drewitt before her marriage to George Coombe, he 'illustrates' a sentimental poem about a woman who is betrayed by her lover and, evicted by her father to sleep rough with her baby, descends into madness. Lear's images, however, deliberately undermine the tragedy of the narrative, reframing it as comedy. The source of the poem has not been traced, but it likely came from a periodical, perhaps one of the sentimental annuals that Lear shared with the Drewitts in the 1820s. His visual spoof is long, elaborate and highly entertaining in its exploration of the clichés of melodrama, which are both literary and visual.[15] The figure of the female maniac maddened by lost love was usually portrayed amidst the wild outpourings of nature: by water, at night, and with her loose hair blowing wildly as she wandered. In James Stuart's 'The Maniac' (1811), the beautiful heroine is introduced:

Hah! who is she with folded hands
   That gazes on the stream,
And wrapt in melancholy stands,
   Beneath the lunar beam?

   . . .

Her auburn tresses wildly flow,
   Dishevelled in the air,
The image she of heart-struck wo,
   Sublimed into despair.[16]

Lear chooses to portray similar lines in 'Miss Maniac' in ways that expose and undermine convention. Thus, 'I listen to the stream that dashes far below' is illustrated in an urban street, where the 'stream' comes from someone using the public water pump. The heroine's hair is loose because it is artificial—we see it and various combs fall off her head, so when she 'awakes to shame', it is ambiguously sexual or aesthetic. She is, in any case, startlingly ugly, which makes the idea of her seduction seem inherently absurd. Her illegitimate baby has a comic copy of its roguish father's face, not a child's face at all—rather like the prolific illegitimate babies of the local milkman, Pat Mustard, in the television comedy series *Father Ted*, who all have his moustache. When Miss Maniac ends up by the lake, reflecting on how terrible it is 'to mourn—and mourn alone', the crescent moon forms a smile, and the baby pops laughing out of her box of 'caps and laces', while the inevitable parasol floats in the water. Lear calls out the clichés by literalising the figurative lines. Miss Maniac's metaphorical complaint—'There is a chain about my brain'—becomes no more than the truth: the heroine wears an iron fetter around her head, while 'a consciousness of unknown things' is illustrated with concrete problems, such as 'a way to pay the national debt'. The ineffable sublime becomes a kind of literal arrears. The pictures form a comic critique of the rhetorical idiom of the original. They highlight its aspiration to tragic performance and make the protagonist a bad mime, whose immersion in her own overheated sentimental feelings seems to prefigure, even deserve, her final descent into the burning passion of madness. Lear's teenaged aesthetic vision is, by contrast, ice cool. The cartoon storyboard explores the possibility of detachment from the sentimental workings of the text.

Fig. 4.5 A
scene from
'Miss Maniac'

Lear appreciates that, in cartoon, image is never merely an illustrative servant to writing; rather, it asserts the primacy of viewing. If we are in doubt, we believe what we see rather than what we are told. The visual cartoon can thus elicit meanings that are submerged or absent in the verbal text, investing the partnership with the frisson of doublespeak. In another early cartoon, the line 'Oh! Bee!—leave me!', which Lear describes as an 'address . . . in the imploring accent of a distracted lover', becomes an imprecation to a bee that has landed on a man's enormous nose.[17] What might seem in one context to be a Romantic plea for faith (Byron's motto was 'crede me!') appears in another to be a request to buzz off. The joke is that we can't necessarily *believe* words that we hear or see, for all are capable of interpretations that recast their meaning, or at least alter their emotional tone. Lear's early nonsense interrogates the earnest self-absorption of sensibility, partly through picturing its protagonists as they cannot see themselves.

'A moving spectacle', a sketch from the 1830s, when Lear was in his twenties, is a picture of a young woman Lear spotted in Prescot, the town nearest to Knowsley, with a plumed hat so huge that it looks like a swaying Fabergé egg atop her highly wrought hairdo.[18] Lear favoured simple dress in women and liked to caricature grandiose hats, elaborate hairstyles and fancy trains on dresses. The pun is instructive. The lady believes that she 'moves' spectators to admiration. But all that is moving is the hat, which wobbles as she walks. The transitive and intransitive senses of the verb *move*, here deliberately confused, neatly convey the gap between subjective and objective state; the static cartoon underlines this disparity, and we can take pleasure in being unmoved by it. In another cartoon from this period, Lear illustrates the line 'he threw both of his eyes up to heaven' with a sketch in which a man tosses his eyes into the air and another gentleman catches them.[19] The line resembles one from a sentimental scene in Tobias Smollett's *Sir Launcelot Greaves* (1760): Captain Clewline has been imprisoned for debt in the King's Bench Prison. His young son, Tommy, visits him there, which leads to the child being fatally infected with smallpox:

> He would snatch up the boy in a transport of grief, press him
> to his breast, devour him as it were with kisses, throw up his
> eyes to heaven in the most emphatic silence; then convey the
> child hastily to his mother's arms, pull his hat over his eyes,
> stalk out into the common walk, and, finding himself alone,
> break out into tears and lamentation.[20]

The passage, full of the sensibility fashionable in the late eighteenth century, might suggest that the captain is a Man of Feeling; it might alternatively suggest the egotism of his performance of his own emotions. As Jeremiah Lear had been (Lear believed) imprisoned for fraud and debt, this topic cut very near the bone of Lear's early emotional life.[21] Like 'Miss Maniac', the passage from Smollett involves an adult who neglects their child, falling into the bog of self-pity. Lear invites us to mind the gap between the emotive rhetorical figuration of eyes and their reality as immovable organs. What we see trumps what we say, which is often specious or affected.

These early cartoons are helpful in demonstrating the critical process through which Lear arrived at the more familiar style we know from his limericks and his mature nonsense work. It is not a naïve style. Rather, it rejoices in characters who perform their emotional desires, often with consequences that are physically disastrous. In some of the early limericks we can see traces of the critique of sentiment that is present in Lear's youthful cartoon sequences. In 'There was an old man of Lodore', for example, the man 'who heard the loud waterfall roar' has tumbled into the very water whose sound attracted him:

> There was an old man of Lodore,
> Who heard the loud waterfall roar;
> But in going to look, he fell into a brook,
> And he never was heard of no more.[22]

This is a sly limerick. The waterfall of Lodore, near Derwent Water in the Lake District, was famously celebrated by the Romantic poets. In Robert Southey's 'The Cataract of Lodore' (1823), which Lear must have known, Southey answers his children's request to tell them 'how the water/comes down at Lodore/With its rush and its roar'. The poem is remarkable for the way in which it re-creates the waterfall visually, as well as aurally, on the page, with lines that grow longer as the waterfall swells from a small stream into a cataract:

> And curling and whirling and purling and twirling . . .
> And thumping and flumping and bumping and jumping,
> And dashing and flashing and splashing and clashing,
> And so never ending, but always descending,
> Sounds and motions for ever and ever are blending,
> All at once and all o'er, with a mighty uproar,
> And this way the water comes down at Lodore.[23]

Lear's own play with the visual aspects of the physical text is indebted to such experimental poems. In this limerick, however, he invites us to imagine the comic consequences of lyrical immersion in nature. The old man of Lodore, who may be Southey himself, becomes literally overwhelmed. In the accompanying illustration, the rush and gush of the falls upend him; the fishes stare at him. He looks extremely surprised, with his top hat on and his eyes open even underwater. The Laker disappears up his own celebrated brook and is 'never heard of no more'—a characteristic Lear line, combining a sense of Romantic tragedy with a comic Cockney double negative. 'Going to look', the man unintentionally becomes the comic object of a viewing experience different from the one he proposed.

Lear's cartoon storyboards of songs by Robert Burns and Thomas
Moore similarly involve incongruities between what is said and what is
seen that shift the genre of the lyric from tragedy to comedy: 'ye *little*
birds' in 'Ye Banks and Braes of Bonny Doon' are bigger than the trees
they sit on; the grinning heroine is old and hideous, 'plucking' a rose with
hands like secateurs.[24] These visual-verbal jokes recur in Lear's limericks,
for instance when a 'small' puppy in the text is a huge beast in the picture. In 'There was an Old Man of Peru', the wife is said to bake her
husband 'by mistake' in the oven, whereas in the picture the giant wife is
delivering her tiny husband to the stove with unmistakeably deliberate
glee. She looks uncannily like the virago in 'Bonny Doon'. These similarities point to the shared origins of Lear's limericks in re-viewing the
tradition of sensibility, where the mind and body are seismographs for
extreme feeling. In the limericks, we are frequently invited to laugh at
extreme behaviour, though mirroring within the images also invites sympathetic identification.

Thomas Byrom devotes a chapter of *Nonsense and Wonder* (1977) to discussing the discrepancies between word and image in Lear's limericks. He
observes, 'In nearly every picture poem there is a discrepancy; and when we
look closely we see that, in each, this discrepancy is the key which unlocks
not the whole secret but as much of it as we are allowed to know'.[25] He
notes that the text of Lear's limericks often describes violent and bizarre
events that should create alarm; the images, however, are mostly reassuring. The characters in the drawings do not seem to feel the physical pain
and social indignity to which they are subjected. They are calm, indifferent,
sometimes ecstatic. Byrom concludes that 'the discrepancy has one governing principle: the cartoon expands the sense in the direction of a mysterious happiness at the expense of the intelligibly sensible, and often sensibly
glum, view of life. The motive of the discrepancies is to make life look
strange and more joyful'.[26]

Byrom identifies something important here, which is that the emotional
tenor of the images in Lear's limericks is usually pleasurable, although the
events described in the text may be painful. Yet he also misses a trick. His
focus on mystery and wonder maintains a reverential distance from the *process* by which the discrepancy adds to our yield of pleasure. The limerick we
first looked at concerning the soldier of Bicester is helpful here, in that it

allows us to identify a punning association that is also a disassociation—between 'not missing' someone (not noticing their absence) and 'not missing' them (not caring about their absence). The 'gap' between text and image realises the inner discrepancy between our consciously policed view of violence, strangeness, excess and our secret relish for them. The image tells the truth of what is unspoken.

Lear's visual renderings of the limericks are like dreams: sometimes very violent events occur within a dream whose general emotional tenor is not frightened but calm, even amused. As Freud observes, jokes and dreams are very similar in their processes of condensation, substitution and 'representation by nonsense'.[27] In one of Lear's earliest limericks: "There was an Old Man of Nepaul—From his horse had a terrible fall— / —Yet, though broken in two—By some *very* strong glue—They mended this Man of Nepaul."[28] The man in the picture is smiling. The two broken lines of text, resembling the two halves of the man's body, suggest the way that words and images alike can be painlessly separated and reconfigured. The emphatic *very* is a kind of comic adhesive. This limerick is a good example of what Constance Hassett has recently characterised as the 'intermodal' operation of the picture limerick, in which the image can send us back to the text with a new consciousness of visual-verbal associations and patternings, and vice versa.[29]

Sometimes it is good to acknowledge the split between our upper and our lower halves, to celebrate physically the possibility of emotional detachment. In 'There was a young person of Janina', the young lady whose head has been fanned off by her uncle is similarly 'smiling sweetly'. 'Losing one's head' can be fun. Here, the image literalises the text but maintains a figurative distance from its reality. There is pleasurable release in the possible displacement of word from image similar to the release in acknowledging the difference between the head and the body, or the superego and the id. Here, the reader's detachment from the consequences of her own laughter is mirrored in the freedom of the delighted girl, who seems to levitate from her couch. The dreamwork of the limerick image pictures the temporary liberation of the subconscious.

> There was an old person of Stroud,
> Who was horribly jammed in a crowd;
> Some she slew with a kick, some she scrunched with a stick,
> That impulsive Old Person of Stroud.[30]

There was a young person of Janina,
Whose uncle was always a fanning her ;
When he fanned off her head, she smiled sweetly, and said.
" You propitious old person of Janina ! "

Fig. 4.6a The young person of Janina, *More Nonsense* (1872)

There was a young lady of Firle,
Whose hair was addicted to curl ;
It curled up a tree, and all over the sea,
That expansive young lady of Firle.

Fig. 4.6b & c Limericks from *More Nonsense*

There was an old man in a tree,
Whose whiskers were lovely to see;
But the birds of the air, pluck'd them perfectly bare,
To make themselves nests in that tree.

Fig. 4.6c

In the picture, the woman wears a large hat that obscures her face as she belabours the crowds of smaller persons around her. The image grants her murderous rage a kind of impunity, not least because its own quality of movement is quick, impulsive. Her stick is not unlike the pen with which the image is drawn. The wilful subject demands its own unreasonable space, which Lear's cartoons, so large relative to the verse, project onto the physical area they occupy.

> There was an Old Man of Kildare,
> Who climbed into a very high chair;
> When he said,—'Here I stays,—till the end of my days',
> That immoveable Man of Kildare.[31]

The limericks embrace a pleasurable regression, which is often simultaneously a regression of old person towards infantile behaviour (such as screaming or staying in a high chair) and a pleasurable regression of figurative language towards the literal qualities of image. The old man of Kildare is literally 'immoveable'. In his high chair, he resembles an overgrown toddler with a pipe.[32] The old person of Pinner is literally 'elastic': rolled up like a coil of rubber. It is a social skill to be figuratively 'expansive' (outgoing), but the young lady of Firle is literally so, like a baby in the womb, or a fast-growing ivy:

> There was a young lady of Firle,
> Whose hair was addicted to curl;
> It curled up a tree, and all over the sea,
> That expansive young lady of Firle.[33]

This happy person is an acted doodle. Lear explores the way in which an identical curling line can become a tendril of creeper winding round the tree, or a wisp of cloud or smoke over the horizon. The curling lines are similar to practice handwriting; they demonstrate the process by which text can return to the free play of image, before it is securely defined as representing one thing or another. The visual doodle and the verbal pun both point towards a multiplicity that is within us, as it is in the world around us, offering a form of release from the singularity of self. In Lear's work this flight is frequently in the direction of infancy or animality, or both. The 'old man in a tree,/Whose whiskers were lovely to see' has birds streaming from his head like rays of sunshine. They are plucking his face bare in order to make nests. But the activity strikes the viewer as benign because the shape of the whiskers already resembles that of a nest, with the man forming the shape of a contented egg inside it. The birds are returning him to an infant state—the covert goal in much of Lear's poetry—so their apparent depredations are in fact solicitous, parental.

Daniel Fowler admired the 'intentional bad drawing' of Lear's cartoons.[34] Nineteenth-century critics frequently commented that Lear's nonsense drawings resembled the work of a 'clever child', that they were 'childlike'.[35] The critics are suggesting that in some way Lear is not only appealing to children's taste or humour; artistically speaking he is *ventriloquising* childhood, expressing the world as if seen from a child's point of view and drawn with a child's limited but energetic capacity. This is significant. It expresses a sense that Lear is actually performing quite a complex manoeuvre in the illustrations to his nonsense. He is performing a less inhibited style, entering into the way a child might communicate visually, but doing so with the skill of a professional artist and the knowing self-awareness of an adult. He is, then, expressing what it might be to see things as a child and as an adult simultaneously.

Lear's nonsense was read by adults as much as by children. On holiday he repeatedly came across medical doctors, army men and governesses who repeated his limericks back to him. Reviewers noted that he 'raises many a hearty laugh from the grave divine and the lawyer, as well as the little children for whose amusement it is professedly written'.[36] One admitted that the limericks had led to evening amusements in which young and old members of a house party had invented limericks for all the stations on the South-Western railway line.[37] Another affected to complain that his review copy of Lear's nonsense had been 'nearly every day stolen out of the study in order that it might be devoured in the nursery'.[38] Lear's nonsense also permits adults, figuratively, to steal out of the study and into the nursery. His work is a vector across which old and young persons can pass to and for one another. Byrom is right that the effect of the pictures is to soften the text. He calls them 'transcendental—if that is the right word'. But another way to look at this is that the limericks are bifocal; they are a kind of dreamwork that allows us to perceive our own inner discrepancy—between the primacy of infantile desire expressed in the image and the conscious absurdity expressed in the verse—and temporarily to resolve it.

Alphabets

Images are essential to the gift that Lear makes of language and to the way in which he invites readers to see its continuity with living form, its inherent play, in the sense of both mobility and comic potential. From 1846 until his death, he was in the habit of making alphabets for his friends' children. These were important gifts, though also ones that he could make cheaply and relatively quickly. Lear explained with mock gravitas that half hid real emotional investment that they were 'libraries of letters' and could be given a longer life by pasting the paper onto linen and sewing the pages together to make a book.[39] Each of the thirty or so alphabets was different, and Lear experimented with various styles—some based on extensive alliteration, some involving multiple rhymes on the same syllable, some constructing a chain narrative that joined all the letters together. They explore pattern as something that is both visual and verbal. Indeed one might compare them to illustrated sonnet sequences in that they collate ephemeral moments to create a lasting monument, celebrating the potentially contradictory qualities of poetry as tangible content and decorative frame. Both Lear's paintings and his nonsenses were frequently produced as sequences. The repetition of form, with difference in substance, offers a way for the mind to travel, rather like glimpsing changing scenery—as Lear so often did—out of the frame of a railway carriage window. Lear's love for alphabets, like his love for limericks, is rooted in his restless pleasure in momentum, in repeated order that can also express variety and drama:

> T was a Tadpole
> Who lived on a log,
> And all of a sudden
>   Turned into a Frog.[40]

The freehand line-drawn alphabet shows the capital and lowercase *T* and *t* of type becoming the flowing letters of copperplate: *T* has four distinct forms. Like a tadpole, *T* is not one thing; it has many phases. The anthologies of Lear's work that reproduce his alphabets entirely in type lose a great deal of the originals' charm. Lear's hand-drawn alphabets delight in the continuity between, for example, the four kinds of *S* and the twisty lines of a snail's shell: 'S was a Snail, / Who crawled up a wall, / And crawl'd down again, / Crawly, crawl, crawl, crawl'. Lear makes the child see and feel the similarity between crawling and scrawling, between seeing a snail and being one, that writing illuminates.

Each alphabet becomes for each special individual child of his acquaintance a carnival of animals and objects that commend the letters as agents with individual identities and dramas. Again and again, one is struck by the mobility of Lear's line, in text and in image, and how he uses these to convey excitement.

> C was a Cobweb
> Which caught a small fly,
> Who tried to escape,
> From the Spider so sly!
>   **c!**
> Cobweb and Fly!

Lear's use of exclamation marks, which exceeds that of any other author I have come across, is a verbal trait that is also an exuberant visual cue. 'c!' 'See!', he seems to exhort us when he places each letter centre-stage. Behold! Both the symmetrical layout of the cobweb with its bull's-eye spider

S was a Snail,
    Who crawled up a wall,
And crawl'd down again,
    Crawly, crawl, crawl, crawl

Fig. 4.7 'S was a Snail' (c. 1880)

and the balanced layout of the rhyme with its defining letter successfully capture our attention. Again, when Lear points to the letter *e* in this alphabet, he directs us to look not only at the conventional elephant but specifically at 'squinny' (partly closed, peering) 'Elephant's eyes', drawing a connection between the shape of an eye and the letter *e*, but also implicitly linking the act of writing with attentive, appreciative looking. Lear's confident and bold eye for graphic design is inseparable from his use of language and his sense of letters as vibrant subjects within our visual field.

All languages in their beginning are mimetic. The first letter or sign in Semitic script, *aleph*, is based on an Egyptian hieroglyph depicting an ox's head: this gave rise to the Greek *alpha* and thus to our own first letter, *A*. The child's alphabet, teaching the form and use of individual letters by presenting each one linked to a representative object, thus takes us back to an apprehension of language and its origin that is rich in primal association. It allows the child to see signs as the things they represent. *G is* a goat. Lear, consciously or unconsciously, often inscribes the letters he is communicating within the forms of the images he chooses to represent them. Thus, in the

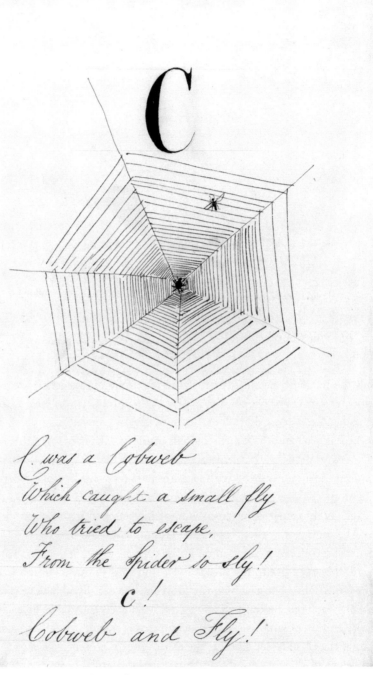

Fig. 4.8 'C was a cobweb' (c. 1865)

alphabet he made for Gertrude Lushington in 1867, the letter *G* is clearly visible in the curl of the goat's horn. Less obviously, *B* is in the wing of the butterfly, *I* in the ice with a spoon standing in it, *O* in the eyes of the owl, *U* in the urn, *Y* in the trunk and branches of the yew tree, *Z* in the jagged edge of the piece of zinc and *X* in the splayed limbs of King Xerxes.[41] Like a linguistic form of natural theology, this visual discovery of language in the natural world emphasises its availability, its continuity with the living forms of which we all are part. The symmetry of Lear's patterned rhymes often echoes symmetry in nature; the forms of creatures and of letters unfold to disclose their natural beauty:

> B was a Butterfly,
> Purple and green,
> A more beautiful butterfly
> Never was seen.
> ## b!
> Butterfly bright!

An insightful article by H. A. Page called 'Child-World', which appeared in 1869 in the *Contemporary Review*, noted, 'Words to the child are nothing less than the animated bodies of living things, which, to his excited imagination and memory, jostle each other in the confused procession of being'. Page recounted seeing a little boy whose father was 'making names': 'On "TO" being made, they were at once identified as a tree and a hoop; the next word beginning with "I," it was put down as the stick; and as much joy was exhibited over them as though the boy had come into possession of the real objects'.[42] Page suggests that, to the mind of the child, letters are playthings; they have a living reality. Lear's alphabets engage the child at this level of magical thinking. Just as his poker and tongs, broom and shovel are animated characters with heads and arms, so the letters, despite what Lear elsewhere punningly calls the 'despotism of Type', have individual identities and adventures.[43] They are envoys of the intimacy of gift exchange that Lear's communication, whether handwritten or typeset, always seeks to establish. His alphabets are fascinating for the way in which they both draw on very old models of children's alphabet and introduce inventive twists.

Alphabets for children that aim to teach the different letters by assigning each a representative object have been current in Britain since the seventeenth century. *Orbis Sensualium Pictus* (Visible World in Pictures, 1658),

Fig. 4.9a 'G was a Goat' (c. 1865)

Fig. 4.9b 'X was King Xerxes' (c. 1865)

by Comenius, which enjoyed lasting popularity, contains an early picture alphabet. Fascinatingly, this alphabet is also a phonology: it emphasises learning sounds made by living creatures. *U* is the owl's hoot, *S* the serpent's hiss, *Z* the bee's buzz. When Lear produced his 'B was a lovely Bee,/It flew about a flower/And sang aloud, "a-buzz", "a-buzz"/For more than half an hour', he was harking back to a very old tradition in children's alphabets of aligning sound with letters as well as visual form.

By the eighteenth century three major kinds of pictorial alphabet had emerged. The first was the 'swallow alphabet'. The most famous of these was *The Life and Death of a Apple Pye*, in which *A* was the apple pye, *B* bit it, *C* cut it, *D* dealt it and *E* eat it. A 'pie' was, in the fifteenth and sixteenth centuries, a book of directions in Latin for saying the church service, and a 'pie book' was an alphabetical index to rolls and records—so there was a very old pun embedded in the swallow alphabet linking literacy and consumption. The second kind was the 'body alphabet', in which the alphabet was visually anthropomorphised, with persons standing for the letters. This often featured trades. Thus, in *The Pretty ABC* (1812), a tiny book of four inches high by two inches wide featuring very primitive woodcuts, 'A was an Admiral, looking out for a fleet/B was a beggar, that begg'd in the street' and 'C was a cobbler, mending a shoe'.[44] In some body alphabets, human figures were shaped into the twenty-six letters—sitting down to make an *L,* thrusting arms out on both sides to make a *T*—turning each letter into an acrobatic pose. In a variation of this practice, *The Invited Alphabet* (1818), by the Quaker publisher Darton, showed pictures of children using sign language to finger-spell each letter, a practice that (as Lear knew from his friendship with Constance and Arthur Fairbairn) enabled the deaf to converse, but was also, Darton suggested, 'a mode already well known to many children', who used it for silent, private conversation.[45] The third type of alphabet was the 'worldly alphabet', which focussed on commercial objects.

As Patricia Crain has discussed, there is a battle continuously visible in children's alphabets throughout the seventeenth, eighteenth and nineteenth centuries between religious and secular governance of language acquisition. There is also a more good-natured struggle between 'high' and 'low' discourses, with alphabets (which were cheaply produced alongside chapbooks, broadsides and almanacs) often scavenging 'from such visual artifacts as tavern signs and such oral/aural artifacts as folk rhymes, rhyming slang, & popular broadsides the materials of literacy'.[46] Lear's alphabets participate in this ongoing debate about how letters should be taught, which involved visualising the iconography of language itself. In general they are on the side of the old, the low and the secular—but most essentially, as with his limericks, their visualisations enable the reader to see, even in the abstraction of idea that is text, the primacy of the physical body and its claims.

Lear must have been acquainted, probably from childhood, with alphabets of various kinds, for in making his own he weaves in and out of the different traditional forms. He produced his own version of the traditional 'swallow alphabet', 'A was an Apple Pie'. In another of his rhyming alphabets,[47] he begins with the traditional opening, 'A was once an apple-pie', then goes on unconventionally to scat on the sound of *pie*, making a sequence of rhyme words that suggest baby talk:

> A was once an apple-pie,
> > Pidy
> > Widy
> > Tidy
> > Pidy
> > nice insidy
> > Apple-Pie

Lear re-creates the 'body alphabet' in his repeated rendition of *X* for Xerxes and of *Y* for Youth—both extremely common subjects in early alphabets. Elsewhere Lear pictures objects, as in a 'worldly alphabet', such as *D* for doll, *F* for fan, *V* for veil and *H* for hat.[48]

Lear's alphabets advertise the pleasure inherent in language by presenting large pictures that offer immediate sensory rewards to eye and ear.

> A was a lovely Apple
> > which was very red & round
> > ————————It tumbled off an Apple tree
> > And fell upon the ground.

In this model of language, the fruit of the tree of knowledge is a delightful windfall, plump and colourful, that tumbles—via Lear's gift of the alphabet book—into the child's lap.[49] This story-within-language contrasts with the punitive tale inherent in many moral alphabets, where *A* is for Adam: 'In *Adam's* Fall / We sinned all / Thy life to Mend / This *Book* Attend'—a formula that dates from 1690 but was still current in 1820.[50] In *The Amusing Alphabet for Young Children Beginning to Read* (1812), a primer whose persistent harangue strikes the modern reader as far from amusing, *A* is an Apple that a boy took without Mamma's leave. It is eaten by a pig. The child is warned that stolen fruits will always be confiscated.[51]

Lear's language is delectable: *J* for jujubes and *O* for oysters call attention to similarities between the visual and oral aspects of reading and speaking, viewing and eating. Daisy Terry recalled that she and her brother Arthur, on holiday in the mountains south of Turin in the summer of 1870, descended to the dreaded table d'hôte at their pension each day to discover a delightful surprise:

> I still have a complete nonsense alphabet, beautifully drawn in
> pen and ink and delicately tinted in water colors, done on odd
> scraps of paper, backs of letters, and discarded manuscript.
> Every day Arthur and I found a letter of it on our plate at
> luncheon, and finally a title-page for the collection, with a
> dedication and a portrait of himself, with his smile and his
> spectacles, as the 'Adopty Duncle'.[52]

Lear was conveying his art of language as consolatory feast, with himself at the head of the table. When in 'The Jumblies' Lear conjures the treasures that these brilliantly coloured creatures buy in their 'land all covered with trees', the words, colours and eatables are all one:

> . . . a pound of Rice, and a Cranberry Tart,
> and a hive of silvery Bees.
> And they bought a Pig, and some green Jack-daws,
> And a lovely Monkey with lollipop paws,
> And forty bottles of Ring-Bo-Ree
> And no end of Stilton Cheese

In this dreamlike country of capitalised nouns, Bees are silvery (perhaps their sound, perhaps their colour) and Monkeys' lovely paws have become 'lollipops' and Jack-daws are green. Lear's visual approach to language explores the simultaneous abundance for the eye, ear and palate that words can embody. 'No end of' is a favourite Lear expression. Its informality beautifully expresses the joy of infinity.

Nineteenth-century alphabets were often prim about the kind of low and disreputable material from earlier eras that they were replacing with educational improvements. The author of one alphabet of 1879, which linked every letter to a biblical text, was self-congratulatory:

> Having observed what utter nonsense is put into the mouths
> of children, and the firm hold it takes on their memories,
> (I refer to 'A was an Archer that shot at a frog', etc) I have
> ventured to compose, in simple rhyme, what I will call 'THE
> CHILDREN'S MORAL ALPHABET', with the hope that
> it may as easily, and as permanently, lodge in the mind a few
> grains of truth which shall germinate, & even bear some
> fruit, in the future.[53]

It is important, I think, to see Lear's self-advertised 'nonsense' alphabets as a raspberry blown at this kind of alphabet, in which verses are made to carry a representative burden, like Neddy the Ass who *stands for* A'. Lear's alphabets present language not as a substitutive moral system of representation but as a shared sensorium where content naturally resides in form. In this model, 'nonsense' is rehabilitated as a meaningful mode of language acquisition, its patterns as relevant to the associative web of perception and oral consumption (what is 'put into the mouth') as any more pointedly wholesome 'grains of truth' would be. The 'nonsense' of 'A was an Archer who Shot at a Frog' was a long-lived alphabet rhyme already extant in 1742 as *The Child's New Play-Thing* and still current in the nineteenth century.[54] The debate about 'nonsense' in children's literature in the Victorian period is, fascinatingly, partly a debate about the survival of such ancient rhymes and whether they should remain part of children's educational ambit.

Lear resists modernisation for its own sake. In an alphabet of 1880:

> J was a small jackdaw
>   He lived on the top of a mill
> And if he has not flown off
>   He probably lives there still.

Lear plays here with a nursery rhyme, first printed in 1714 but probably a century older, that runs, 'There was an old woman / Liv'd under a hill, / And if she be'nt gone, / She lives there still'.[55] The letters of Lear's alphabets enjoy their existence within a familiar space that celebrates timelessness. This contrasts with those commercially minded Victorian alphabets that endeavoured to be contemporary by offering *V* for Victoria, *W* for Wellington, *D* for Diamonds and *G* for the Great Exhibition.[56]

King Xerxes had featured in *Finch His Alphabet* (1630) as Xerxes 'who for his beastliness . . . had great blame'.[57] Lear's alphabets are traditional in featuring Xerxes but, by contrast with earlier models, invest him with energy and colour that is enjoyably loud and violent:

> X was King Xerxes
> Who more than all Turks is
> Renowned for his fashion
> Of screaming with passion.
> **x!**
> Shocking old Xerxes!

Xerxes in this alphabet is depicted with his arms and legs widely splayed as he waves his sword in rage. The figure of the King thus forms an 'x'. In another of Lear's alphabets he waves a cutlass in one hand and a dagger in the other and his propensity for clashing is emphasized by the vibrant 'Turban of green, yellow, / Purple, and Red' that he wears: 'X! / O! King Xerxes!'.[58] In a third alphabet, where the cross-stroke of the X swaggers down the page:

> X. was once a great king Xerxes,
>> Xerxy
>>> Perxy
>>>> Turxy
>>>> Xerxy
>> Linxy Lurxy
> Great King Xerxes!

Xerxes is presented as screaming with passion, like a child. The mighty king is also a baby whose rhyme words are free-associating babble. Such approaches to teaching language to infants, for whom text and image have not yet established themselves as different in kind, reveal the sensibility at the heart of Lear's power as an author: he revels in the fact that written text

A King from Death
Can't save his breath.

X   Xerxes the Great did die,
     And so must you and I.

Fig. 4.10 'Xerxes the Great . . .', illustration for the letter X, from a *Child's Alphabet . . .* (c. 1820)

is not a simply a code, a set of inert keys that we exchange for items in our store of ideas. Rather, letters (x!) are characters who are powerful and dramatic as entities in themselves, full of expressive potential that resides in their shape on the page, the patterns they make to our eye. They mimic the period of our childhood development when we are passionate kings who scream rather than servants to the work of meaning.

In another alphabet of 1880, Lear gives us:

> K was a very small King
> > Who wore a prodigious crown;
> His cloak was of scarlet velvet,
> > Spotted with blue & brown.

This 'very small King' is also a child. He looks rather overwhelmed by his crown. The underlying tendency of Lear's alphabets, like that of his limericks, is to build reciprocity between the child-self and the adult-self, recognising the persistence of the childish mode of perceiving the world. The child is not waiting to be allured into 'the vestibule of literature', as one contemporary

Fig. 4.11 'K was a very small King' (c. 1880)

alphabet asserted.[59] Rather the rebellious, angry child, like other natural phenomena, is already present in language itself.

> Y was a Youth, who kicked
>   And screamed and cried like mad;
>   Papa he said, 'Your conduct is
>   Abominably bad!'

In this highly unusual alphabet, originally produced for the children of the Reverend Walter Clay and subsequently published in *Laughable Lyrics* (1877), Lear relates each letter to the belongings and wishes of 'Papa'.[60] There is something both thrilling and troubling about the dominance of the father in this alphabet, the alpha male who makes all the letters abet him. He is behaving as a child would, relating the universe to his own needs. He is not very small, yet he uses baby talk: 'Papa he said, "If Piggy dead, / He'd all turn into Pork!"' We are told that he cannot reach *N* (for nut) because the branch is '*much* too high'. Child and adult are conflated, their solipsism like that of the capital letter: inevitable. The tension between whether the alphabet is *for* child or adult becomes more apparent when we learn that:

Y was a Youth, who kicked
   And screamed and cried like mad ;
Papa he said, "Your conduct is
   Abominably bad!"

Fig. 4.12 'Y was a youth', *Nonsense Songs, Stories, Botany and Alphabets* (1871)

S was Papa's new Stick,
   Papa's new thumping Stick,
To thump extremely wicked boys,
   Because it was so thick.

Here is a violence between fathers and sons that is not often acknowledged in Victorian nursery literature. It becomes an internal rebellion within the alphabet itself, where letters (*S* and *Y*) act out a dialogue between oedipal rage and punishment via the objects they represent.

Violence also actuates the following alphabet, the last word in Lear's last published nonsense book, where *A* 'fell down and hurt his arm against a piece of wood'. The other letters all propose remedies, ranging from Violins to double-X ale, but *A* is ultimately captured by *Z* for zinc, who declares:

'We'll shut you up! We'll nail you down! We will, my little master!
'We think we've all heard quite enough of this your sad disaster!'[61]

A is 'shut up' in a box, rather like the mucous membrane in one of Lear's oddest unpublished poems.[62] The end of the alphabet silences its beginning. Nailing things down, which is what language helps us to do in the sense of 'defining' things, can be an uncomfortably literal process. In Lear's expression 'little master', one glimpses ambivalence about the rule, and rules, that learning letters begins to impose on thought. The indefinite article, *A*, is both controlling authority and petulant child. Do we master language, or does it master us? Lear's nonsense, offering us the gift of words that refuse to stay within the lines of dictionary vocabulary, includes alphabets as a starting point for releasing the free association, the word-doodling that language, regarded as image, naturally permits.

One alphabet in particular demonstrates how nonsense can arise from a sensory process of seeing, hearing and feeling our way through language that can be progressive and simultaneously incorporate regressive desires:

J was once a jar of jam,
   Jammy
   Mammy
   Clammy
   Jammy
 Sweety-Swammy,
   Jar of Jam![63]

This word-ladder takes us through words that have a place in the dictionary ('Clammy') and words that don't ('Swammy'). It conveys sensory, oral impressions that we associate with the taste and texture of jam, but also includes a word ('Mammy') whose connection with food is more primal. Lear used to play at 'squaring words'—a game popularised by the inventor of the computer, Charles Babbage—with Emily Tennyson.[64] The goal was to get from one word to a completely different word by switching only a single letter each time. This alphabet is like a word square. One can see its process both as analogous to the early development of computer code and as a pre-Freudian chain of psychological association that can elicit buried relationships.

R was once a little rose,
    Rosy
    Posy
    Nosy
    Rosy
Blows-y—grows-y
  Little Rose!

Of course, roses aren't nosy in the dictionary sense of 'overly curious'. But humans poke our noses into them. The rhyming ladder images a childish continuity between *being* the rose and *seeing* it, smelling it, playing with the 'posy' of sensory associations that the mind rhymes to the idea of roses. Lear enters into the child's mind, its chant, making visible to us the possibility of rhyme as both visual and aural homology and shared associative field. Roses 'blow' (open their buds), but they can also be 'blowzy' (dishevelled); both possibilities are organically open in the imagery this alphabet calls up. In the synaesthesia of this play, we are made conscious of our mixed physical sensations in apprehending and generating language. The word chain can indeed illustrate the liquid process by which thinking turns into writing and drawing: 'Inky, Dinky, Thinky, Blacky minky, Bottle of Ink!' The form of this rhyme as it is arranged on the page resembles an I. And '*I* was once a bottle of ink' could refer to the letter or the self; both are creatively realised when we pour ourselves into word and image. One might identify some of the words in this alphabet as 'nonsense words': *kity* (like a kite), *nimpy*, *flimpy*, *faily*, *pidy*, *widy*, *tweedly* and *threedly* might equally well appear in any of Lear's longer nonsense verses (*flumpy* features in 'The

Pelican Chorus'). Yet in this context, where the chains of association that produce them are visible, they are scarcely nonsensical; indeed one might regard them as multisense words rather than nonsense ones.

In appreciating this alphabet, then, one gains an insight into how Lear's 'nonsense' language arises and how it works. His nonsense is particularly interested in transference of physical sensations from text to reader through language as a visual pathway, as much as a semantic one. In the dreamwork of Lear's nonsense, the constellation of perception and association that is language becomes more apparent. Rhymes and puns are no longer contingent or taboo but all potentially relevant and meaningful. The roles of the visual and oral in shaping language are more prominent. The body of text and its relationship to the physical body is centre stage. And our own feeling for words, the mental and physical sensations they excite in us, are elevated to the status of meaning: our feelings become more meaningful in forming interpretations. The nonsense word reads us. It makes visible the cluster of material—incomprehensible at one level, yet richly significant at another—that might under other circumstances form a dream or an analysis.

From 1867 to 1871, during the same period when he was working towards the publication of *Nonsense Songs, Stories, Botany and Alphabets*, Lear began producing monograms for adults, mostly women of his acquaintance. On 3 September 1867, he was working simultaneously on a monogram (of a Jay and a Bee) for Sissy Baring and on Gertrude Lushington's alphabet.[65] Lear also experimented with letters to friends in which pictures stand in for words: 'catalogue' is an image of a cat and a log; 'dear Lionel' is a deer and a lion with an *L*.[66] One wonders if the hieroglyphs he saw in Egypt in 1867 had any influence on him. Lear was, unusually for his era, able to appreciate ancient Egyptian sculpture, design and drawing as high art and was horrified by the tourist graffiti that despoiled them.

His monograms offer a similar kind of pleasure to the 'child's' alphabets in that they return the word to its beginnings as image, and before that as physical entity: 'A *was* an Apple Pie'. His friend, A Glass, is a glass. Anne Scrivens becomes an egg. Another friend becomes a staircase with a railing. The lighthouse and the crescent moon that Lear chooses to represent Agnes Mary Clark could almost be a tarot card suggestive of multiple meanings: male and female; light and darkness.[67] These emblems, through the potential they reveal for names to be read as fertile imaginative cues rather than genealogical labels, suggest the capacity of the self to flourish imaginatively through letters—which always retain their hieroglyphic power to signify in themselves—beyond the given meanings-by-association of birth and marriage. It is intriguing that it was mostly women for whom Lear invented monograms. Women's names usually reflect those of their fathers' and husbands' families; the female 'line' is conventionally silenced in patriarchal nomenclature. Lear draws out of his friends new possibilities. In his hands, their monograms metamorphose into aspects of the world all around: a lamp, a lighthouse, an eye, a staircase, an egg. All these objects are positively associated with vision or change. One might see, in the lighthouse and lamp especially, a pun on 'illumination', where Lear's play with letter-as-image throws light on the inner world of how we customarily see ourselves and how we might see ourselves differently. There is an aspect of free association in relating letter to person to object, where Lear performs the transformative role of the dream and the interpolating role of the analyst simultaneously. One glimpses here, and in Lear's nonsense letters to fellow adults, the truth that his play with word and image constantly brings the child and adult self closer, acknowledging the space they share and how a return to the perception of self-in-other and the free play it engenders can ease the burden of separation and isolation that is so fundamental to the experience of adulthood.

Porous Language: Inside Out

Lear often uses words that are perfectly intelligible but are either unusual or improvised variants on standard vocabulary. Most are adjectives to describe the qualities of weather ('haily'), persons ('blindy') or landscape ('woldy'). Here is a list of fifty such expressions, drawn from the diaries:

> Peery, swelly, luckiously, wetty, parky, woldy, lany, beamy,
> gleamy, haily, aperiently, abruptious, queery, grovy,
> dimmy, spoony, calmy, soothy, spasmy chasmy, maddy, baddy,
> come-parrot-tifly, equalnoxious, fuddly, shambly, bebothery,
> hurricanious, stunderthorm, groovy, obskewer, moonfully,
> slowy, dampy, unhingy, punty, beezly, dreggy-dismal,
> ablooshious, choliferously, fooly talky, blasty, tipsical, coaly,
> stunny, piny whiny, shrilly-howly, denudaciously, go-ahead-i-
> ally, fleaful dweffle, splendido-phosopherostiphongious.

A few of these words are phonetic renderings that play punningly with dictionary words. The equinoctial gales that Lear hated are 'equalnoxious'; 'fleaful dweffle' is a play on 'fearful dreadful' that expresses the miseries of fleabites; Lear's 'splendido-phosopherostiphongious' evening with Robert Browning is so brilliant that it conjures with a magician's hyperbole the glow of phosphorus.[68] But most are simply formed by adding the letter *y* to a noun, a verb or another adjective. These latter adjectives, like 'widy, pidy, nice insidy' in his nonsense alphabet, are so characteristic of Lear's voice that it is tempting to conclude that he simply refused to abandon the shorthand of baby talk whereby a cage full of lions is 'liony', a pond full of ducks is 'ducky' and a lagoon full of punts is 'punty'. There is, however, more to it than that. Lear's familiarising adjectives communicate a view of the world in which perceptions of the self, the weather and the landscape are so close that they are not discrete. He describes a day as 'soft-soppy-shiny-shivery'. In this compound adjective, the qualities of the damp weather and how it makes him feel are inseparable. His description acknowledges that weather and mood are aspects of the same perceptual field. In the same way that 'silvery' can synaesthetically refer to a quality of sound and of colour, 'soppy' can be a word that hangs in the air between the weather and us. A 'moonful' night, where the moon is literally at its fullest and about to wane, may make us feel mournful, or even lunatic. A 'spasmy chasmy valley' gives one a sense of up and down that is both external and internal. 'Groovy' to Lear means stuck in a monotonous groove, like a cartwheel in a rut. More subtly, a word like 'stunny' (meaning stunned by bad news) conveys a similar sense of the subjective self as vulnerable to feelings produced by the interaction of person, event and environment that become who we are at that time. We may be sunny or stunny as the prevailing emotional weather takes us. When Lear reports that he is 'unhingy', the term feels different from 'unhinged'. Its awkwardness communicates his unresolved sense of being both active and passive in his emotional experience, his mind hanging like a hinge that has come loose from its moorings but may, through careful application to his oils, be made to work smoothly again.

Because of his epilepsy and depression, Lear was constantly interested in his own emotional state and how much he might be able to control it through willpower and how much might be attributed to congenital and circumstantial factors that were beyond his power to change. He might wake 'exhilarious' and acquire the 'dismy dreamal' qualities of a coldy, 'mouldy melancholy' day.[69] Lear's verbal medleys brilliantly convey the real emotional between-states that we experience, usually in response to a mixture of internal and external factors. He called his depression 'morbidiousness'. In this word, too, we get the sense of the soft and damp that may be within us, or may be in the actual and emotional climate around us. The phrase 'emotional barometer' was not current in Lear's lifetime, but he thought of his own inner state in these meteorological terms: 'the moral and mental barometer has gone down today'.[70] Lear's susceptibility to the atmospheric changes within and without, and his acute awareness of the connections between them, enters into his vocabulary as a writer and a painter creating words, and works, that are often so effective because they convey to us a multisensory sensitivity to the porousness of self and place, climate, colour, mood. Seeing and being are codependent activities.

In June 1869, Lear recorded in his diary that he disliked Monsieur Badourdace's trial woodcut made from his vignette of a Corsican landscape. It was 'alack! woundy hard & ugly, though well kept as to drawing throughout'.[71] The 'woundy' quality of this woodcut suggests that he feels the 'hard and ugly' cuts in the wood as cuts in his own skin. Lear was woundy as a person: wounded by his past history and thus acutely sensitive to sound, colour, line, atmosphere, as if his emotional skin were always open to the elements. Colour is emotion in Lear. Good days are 'white'; bad days are 'black'. Depression is 'neutral tint Indian ink spirits'.[72] Pleasure is polychromatic, 'a wonderful parrot-glory of colour', vivid and intense.[73]

It is a moot point whether one refers to any of the creative adjectives in Lear's diary as 'nonsense' vocabulary. They are not part of the performed work of nonsense in his self-described 'nonsense letters' and 'books of nonsense'. Yet Lear was highly aware that his journals were of interest to readers, as some of them had formed the basis of his travel books, and that they might in future be published. Some of the words, such as 'equal-noxious', do occur in letters as well as in the diary. There is no hard and fast barrier between the language Lear deploys in his journals to express himself and what we might term 'nonsense' words.

Many of the words in Lear's published nonsense operate on the same principles. Jumbly, jingly, shingly, flumpy, purpledicular, the Crumpetty Tree, the Bisky Bat, the Attery Squash, the Chankly Bore, the buzz-tilential flies, and the Jumblies' moony song all bear the traces of Lear's characteristic methods of word formation. The 'silvery' light and 'silvery' noise of 'The Dong with a Luminous Nose' fuse in the synaesthetic experience of sound and vision that this moonlit poem conjures. The Jumblies' song is 'moony' both because it is delivered at night and because there is a 'moonful' aspect to it. In this 'nonsense' world it makes perfect sense that the Gromboolian Plain (with its rumble of grumbling) and the Torrible Zone may ambiguously be actual places or states of mind. A 'serious bore' was Lear's usual way of describing things he hated but was obliged to do. It is no accident, then, that the word keeps cropping up in his nonsense in various transmutations, as the Chankly Bore, Borley Melling (Uncle Arly's ancestral home, which isn't 'merely boring' but close to it) or Ring-Bo-Ree, a delicious-sounding drink in 'The Jumblies' that seems a kind of antidote to dullness. The betweenness of Lear's words echoes the perceptual osmosis that he is constantly evoking between the inner self and the outer world.

This osmosis is characteristic of Lear's longer nonsense poems, but also of his landscape painting. Many critics who enjoy the nonsense are less certain in their admiration for Lear's landscapes, especially in oil. Indeed there has been what one might almost call a tradition in literary criticism of addressing Lear's writing without speaking much about his landscape paintings. It is as if the landscape paintings—which Lear produced in large numbers, sometimes embarking on sequences of eighty or a hundred watercolours at once, which he referred to as 'Tyrants'—constitute a day job from which the literary critic has posthumously sought to rescue Lear, liberating the 'night side' of his personality that expresses itself in his free time, in poetry, in letters and cartoons whose quickness of line contrasts with the delicate and often elaborate work of the paintings. Ann Colley sees the nonsense as the 'reverse' or 'inverse' of the landscapes.[74]

But I am going to put my head above the parapet and confess that I love both Lear's poetry and his landscape painting. And that I see in both of them a form of dreamwork in which the porous relationship between word and image mediates the relationship between the self and the world, conjuring the space we inhabit, imaginatively and actually, as a field of association that is always both external and internal.

LANDSCAPE AS TEXT

Lear's feeling for landscape is unusual. Like his description of weather, it embodies his powerful sense of physical contiguity with what he sees and experiences. In June 1875, journeying a very familiar route by rail through Ventimiglia, Mentone and Monaco, he noted, 'all beautiful—yet somehow with scars and seams of matters past and painful'.[75] The 'scars and seams' that one would normally associate with the geology of coastal rock here become scars and seams of memory. Lear's own personal geology and that of the landscape he passes through are indivisible. To look out of the train window is also to look painfully inwards, at the strata of experiences in this region laid down over the years in his own sedimentary layers. Re-viewing the landscape necessitates reviewing his re-viewings of it at different phases of his life, and thus looking at the 'scars' that change has wrought on it and on him. Landscape to Lear is a self-conscious theatre of memory.

'What a mingling of sadness and admiration of landscape botheringly will persist in existing!', he grumbled, conveying with the passive voice a sense of how such feelings were beyond his active control. 'All the unsought morbid feelings . . . of past years crop up at once—such as the Hornsey fields & Highgate archery, & the sad large Thorn tree at Holloway about 1819 or 1820 . . . the Mill at Arundel, or Peppering in 1824 &5———the heights above Plymouth in 1836/7. . . . Civitella 1839 & Nemi——all were with me at once'.[76] Similar outbursts recur again and again in Lear's writing. Lear experiences memory as a montage of landscapes, each imbued with particular meaning as a site where he experienced intense feelings, often of pleasure and of anguish combined. These scenes can all appear 'at once', just as his many different memories of a particular place can all be present to him simultaneously when he thinks of it. Each scene is like the site for an acupuncturist's needle; it triggers a flow of physical and mental feeling that exceeds a thousandfold the scope of the point touched. That point can be as large as a town or as specific as a 'sad Thorn tree', like that in Wordsworth's poem 'The Thorn', which marks the spot where a mother may have buried her child. In Lear's writing about memory, we glimpse an inner/outer landscape everywhere dotted with such markers—not 'spots of time' so much as heavily overscored nodes in the landscape where personal and cultural ley lines repeatedly cross. The past is landscape: in 1859 he reports 'the whole bright stream of (past) life glitters before me as it was in a distant valley, & I can seem to mark all its windings and shadows'.[77] The confluence of images as they assail him echoes the unwelcome confluence of depressive thoughts with happy memories. He tries to 'crush' such morbid thoughts but is aware that 'I crush a good deal else with them'. Lear's creative, artistic recall of landscape and his depressive thoughts are so intertwined that it is difficult to check one without affecting the other; he is 'morbid'—a word that in Italian means 'soft'—and landscape makes an impression in him that is also a dent, a fingerprint.

To a greater or lesser extent, most of us will recognise in ourselves aspects of the process Lear describes. The psychotherapist Christopher Bollas argues in *Being a Character* (1992) that we use objects and places to conjure 'self experience', investing them with significance that enables them as well as offering sensations in the present, to contain episodes in our past, or to project particular aspects of our personality.[78] In this waking dreamwork, the evocative power of the places and things we choose is like that of words whose syntax we arrange to predicate who we are as characters. We may consciously use these places and objects but may also find ourselves unconsciously reaching for them, transformed by them or, on a sudden and unexpected encounter, overwhelmed by the nexus of feeling and prior significance with which they are endowed.

Bollas gives the example of a swing. For him, during a period of early childhood when he was sent away to nursery and was aware of tensions in his parents' marriage, a swing was the object he unconsciously nominated to conserve some aspect of his loneliness:

> I don't know why exactly, but I imagine that this thing which had been so much fun (it is an object for a joyful two-person relation), now empty and unoccupied, signified the absence of such pleasure. Perhaps I located my slight depression in the object. I know that to this day if I see a certain type of child's swing in a playground something of the self experience prevailing at that time is revived.[79]

Lear's lifelong collection and recollection of place is remarkable for its vivid persistence and for the way in which it is always personal. As a painter, spending hour after hour sketching views, he was engaged in the process of making memory, and—in Bollas's parlance—of conjuring the dreamwork of the object, its capacity to contain and evoke aspects of the self. His professional life and his personal life were thus inseparably intertwined; indeed one might argue that Lear chose his profession precisely because of the perpetual revisiting that was so necessary yet painful a feature of his inner life.

Memories might assail him unexpectedly, but one also sees him touching the memories attached to certain places as though they were rosary beads, circling speedily around the most significant moments in his life in a way that was partly weary penance and partly comforting ritual. This process of visiting and revisiting had a literal analogue in his artistic methods as a painter and a writer. He would take notes when he travelled, then write these up in his ordinary diary, then work them into regional memoirs that underlay his travel books. Likewise his watercolours and oils involved a process of 'going over old ground' that could take many years. Lear sketched and painted literally thousands of landscapes. He dated his sketches carefully and arranged them in folders and cabinets where he could access them at a later date. When he returned to a sketch and penned it out in Indian ink, then perhaps worked up the subject into a finished watercolour or oil painting, he was returning to the place concerned with all its associations. All his prior experiences of that landscape were in the work. In addition, the finished painting contained elements of all the places in which he had worked on it. He noted for example that he had begun his major oil of Tomohorit in Albania in 1849, had studied the beech trees at Petersfield near Hastings and had painted the right foreground at Selborne in Hampshire;[80] by the time of its completion in 1872, over twenty years of his life in multiple locations had passed into the canvas. Lear's paintings, particularly the larger commissions, often progressed very slowly, gaining several series of delicate washes and areas of colour. Figures and other additions to the subject matter might be scraped back or sponged out only to be repainted. The business of his landscape painting and writing was travel, but it was also a potentially infinite process of revisiting himself.

In Lear's most successful paintings of landscape, I think we perceive the dreamwork that place accomplishes in his psychic life; this in turn calls upon the viewer's own experience of landscape as a repository of memory and association that includes visual and literary, actual and imagined encounters. Lear experimented with different painting techniques over the course of his life, but it is not difficult to recognise one of his works; in paint as in language he has a signature style. What makes a Lear landscape painting distinctive? There is a combination of dramatic boldness in the choice of subject and evanescent delicacy in the line and colouring that makes his views poignantly atmospheric. They convey simultaneous intimacy and distance.

Fig. 4.13 *Langdale* (1836)

In an early pencil, charcoal and body-colour study of Langdale made on a tour of the Lake District in 1836, Lear has drawn a young woman traversing a stone bridge. This beautiful study is reproduced here for the first time. A gnarled, thick-trunked old tree grows out of the riverbank. To the right, thunderclouds mass over barely sketched mountains. The river flows through the centre of the picture, and our eye is drawn to the dark curve of the inner recess of the old bridge and the reflections below it.[81] In its broad design, this is a traditional English picturesque landscape painting comparable to Thomas Creswick's *The Stile* (1839); Lear admired Creswick's work. But it is distinctively Lear's because of its dreamlike invitation to enter into a narrative of inwardness. The flow of the water towards us suggests time, moving yet arrested. The storm is a drama that lies in the future. The bridge becomes a narrative path that the eye travels, like the indistinct figure, towards an unknown destination. One might think of women who inhabit poems set in this region, such as Wordsworth's Lucy. But the picture offers us no concrete markers of character or mission. The tree, the bridge, the mountains are hypnotic objects that figure an ever-incomplete journey of our own.

In another accomplished early work, from 1838, Lear has drawn Amalfi, a town in southern Italy that is stuffed into a cleft in the rock like a hoard of Byzantine treasure. Lear chooses a dramatically low angle and vanishing point, so that the vertiginous rock hangs in front of us like a theatre curtain partly obscuring a panorama. The houses grow out of the cliff, stark white light catching their bare facades; the steep mountains pile and range like the clouds above. We are on the twisting coast road, where an anonymous group of women gathers. One of them carries a bundle on her head. Her figure echoes the form of a far distant convent, perched high above the precipice. Lear would have been acutely aware of Turner's view of Amalfi, for Samuel Rogers's *Italy*, which was taken from the sea. He brings his own interest in comparative organic form to a picture that is conscious of predecessors but finds its own pathway between the quietness of detailed attention to rock and buildings and the internal drama that a landscape associated with the Gothic novels of Ann Radcliffe might suggest. Again, this 'poetical topography' is broadly accurate (one can recognise the view today) and yet also finds something in the landscape that is fantastical, where house, rock and person are outgrowths of the same psychogeography.

Tennyson famously paid Lear the compliment of writing him a sonnet, 'To E. L., on his travels in Greece', which declares:

> . . . all things fair,
> With such a pencil, such a pen.
> You shadow forth to distant men,
> I read and felt that I was there:[82]

This may be true of Lear's travel writing. However, in his landscape paintings, it seems important to the power of their spell that, as in a dream, we feel we are *not* there. Rather, the landscape hovers before us with lucid intensity. There is an evocative stillness in these works, a sense of time arrested. It is sometimes reminiscent of glass slides overlaid to produce a composite picture of strange intensity that comprises the sum of multiple impressions viewed at a distance of time and space. In *Kasr-es-Saad* (1877), for example, the cliffs that fade into light on the right-hand side are subtly at odds with the left-hand foreground that fades into darkness. A flight of tiny birds wafts up like smoke from the spit of land as it touches the Nile; they are a kind of genii escaping from the bottle of time, an evocation of ephemerality and suddenness that conflicts with the immemorial quality of the backdrop, creating a productive tension.[83] In *Pyramids Road, Ghizeh* (1873), Lear has

Fig. 4.14 *Amalfi* (1838)

created a hypnotic visual tunnel of consciousness, a painting that images
the mind itself travelling—something that can happen in a moment when
the body is still. The camels and foot passengers under the cavernous foliage of regularly spaced trees are so far divorced from the pyramids and
flat sands outside the tunnel, which are faintly rendered in light wash, that

the dreamlike passage of humans and animals, whose faces we cannot distinctly see through the dark arch of interlacing boughs, hovers between memory and metaphor.

The objects of distant vision, in this present that is also out-of-time and hence consciously unavailable, are imbued with a particular emotional colour. The hepatica-blue sea—so characteristic of Lear's faraway coasts—the cliff-perched monastery, the sunset-washed rocks that are about to be obscured by darkness are neither strictly realist in their representation nor strictly symbolic; rather they suggest the ability of landscapes in dreams to be both, to be pregnant with multiple meanings that are not fully available to the dreamer in the moment of dreaming. One might argue that this quality of ineffability, of glimpsing what can never be reached, is the sublime.[84] But Lear's is not a Burkean sublime of terror and power. In fact Lear much more commonly used the word *picturesque* for his landscapes, the quality that Burke sees as the feminine counterpart to the sublime. There is a delicacy to Lear's painting even when portraying the ruggedly towering or dramatically vast scene. Citing the defining qualities of his work, he noted 'delicacy, and individuality'.[85] His inaccessible, clifftop monasteries float in the aether of imaginative space. Lear's preference in zoological art for drawing hedgehogs over tigers finds its way into his landscape painting as a preference for communicating inward drama rather than outward potency.

In one of his diary entries he refers to 'torrents of stone', a clue to how he sees the organic flow of water even in the apparently solid form of rock. Lear disliked 'hard' qualities in painting.[86] His most successful mountain landscapes more often have a V-shaped composition than a phallic one, subtly mimicking a feminine rather than a masculine sexual geography.[87] For example, in Lear's *Kangchenjunga* (1879), now in Yale's Center for British Art, the vines and tree ferns rather than the Himalayan peak are the true stars of the painting; creepers stream from the treetops like Rapunzel's hair, echoing the flow of the central chasm, with its hazy waterfall of light. Similarly, in his *Marble Rocks, Jubbelpore* (1882), paint seems almost to drip down the canvas, making drapery of the shining rocks, the bright light and the water into whose translucent depths they plunge. I find this picture mesmerising.

Where language is in dialogue with image, its commentary can be playfully ironic or a meditation on form that allows these competing methods of representation to slide into one another, like ice into water, revealing their shared molecular basis. Lear's annotations to his sketches respond to the 'po-etickle' landscape in ways that foreground these ambivalent possibilities.

Lear annotated his sketches profusely, writing not in the margins but di-rectly on the images, scattering words amongst the hills, trees and waves. Most artists make notes for themselves, but Lear's are in the familiar lexis he favours—'rox' for 'rocks', 'sno' for 'snow'—and contain observations on colour, vegetation and the inhabitants of the landscape that are personal and playful. Mentone is 'urby & piney'. Metzovo has, on a distant hill, '10000 sheep'. Lear loved to exaggerate and here makes a tiny joke for his own re-turning eyes. In a sketch of Corfu, he has immortalised 'moose Katoes or Natts', which doubtless landed on his paper. He experiments, here as in his nonsense writing, with different ways in which words can be visually ren-dered: 'Euphorbia', 'youforbia', 'U.4.beer'.[88]

The mix-tone compound adjectives he creates to convey what he sees are often beautiful in themselves: 'ochry white sand', 'houses all ruined gray with green shrub', 'stems bluegray', 'all the tone of the hills more washwatery & gloomier'. Indeed, some of his notes if written out separately could form an imagist tone poem or haiku:

> arum—lilac shadow on white
> storks on castle red-ochre & bluish gray
> greeny
> bare
> old walls[89]

In a painting of Corfu that he worked at on two separate days in 1864, he identifies 'anemones', 'reeds, canes & cactus' and then 'cliff-pale, grass-gold, green shale green, far down'.[90] This could almost be a line from Gerard Manley Hopkins. Lear's notes convey the way in which landscape strikes our eyes before our impressions are mediated by the spatial and syntactic structure of a conventional sentence. In the same sketch, Lear writes 'pome' as shorthand for 'pomegranate'; elsewhere in his letters and diaries he uses 'pome' to mean 'poem'. These landscapes are full of pomes, in both senses. Sometimes in his painting notes he quotes snatches of Tennyson—'All hardly differing from the sky—a little greener. Break,—break, break!' Or he embarks on an irritable rhyme of his own: 'O! ye crows of Malibar / What a cussed bore you are!'[91] The intertextual mixture here of humour and evo-cation of beauty is utterly typical of Lear. Sometimes a cartoon pops up from behind a rock: in one sketch of Kithira a tiny Venus rises from the sea.[92] The effort towards transcendence is comically doomed. Desire and its absurdity turn out to be aspects of the same dream.

In a sketch of Suli from May 1849, now in the National Gallery of Scotland, Lear has written 'immense!' and 'all immense' above the cliffs. A couple of men are perched looking into the scene towards the water. Lear records, 'dark greens and grays', 'dark grey rox', 'deep dark brown', 'ilex', 'ruins', 'palest blue water', 'pink', 'very pale; in light', 'thick woods', dark blue', 'very dark purple', 'path'. The size and trajectory of the handwriting varies with that of the landscape features. So the biggest 'immense!' is over the mountains to the right; 'dark greens and grays' plunges vertically into the abyss; the word 'path' is as tiny and faint a line as the path itself.[93] In a painting of Karyes, in Greece, the word 'stream' flows along the current, while 'wall' is inscribed in tall vertical letters into the form of the wall. Elsewhere, the word 'ilex' curves like a creeper around a holly, and the phrase 'sloping green sward' suits the action to the word.[94] This is yet another example of the way in which writing and drawing are inextricably linked for Lear as ways of perceiving and recording the world: prose becomes image, morphing into the landscape itself, just as letters become images in Lear's alphabets and monograms.

The most surprising thing about Lear's annotations is that he often didn't remove them when he began to pen in his sketch with Indian ink and to paint over it with washes of watercolour. The words remain as strata in the geology of the painting, just as Lear's own multiple experiences of the landscape remain as strata in the geology of his memory of that place. In fact, Lear sometimes *pens in* the words. They become, at this point, something more than an aide-mémoire for the artist trying to recall the colours and features of the landscape in his studio at home. Language is acknowledged as being inevitably present within the scene of encounter and of memory. Once we are literate, we cannot see a tree without thinking 'tree'. Lear's paintings hint at this subconscious truth with their words that are still partially visible beneath the surface of all we see. Once you become aware of the presence of words in Lear's watercolour sketches, you begin to see more of them, rather like a naturalist who has become attuned to the presence of birds and insects in every tree and bush. A sketch of Constantinople from Ayoub, now in the Ashmolean Museum, is typical in this regard. We are gazing down towards the sea from the high vantage point of a graveyard bordered with cypresses. Tombs lean at crooked angles. Only after a moment

does the eye discover a few human figures turned away from us, as anonymous as the stone slabs and similarly shaped. The notes read 'many old
tombs—turbans fallen off onto ground', 'path', earth', 'blue & gold'. Only
with patience does one descry that there are also words in the distant sea and
sky. These fleeting marks, which might from afar seem to be lines of cloud or
wave, suggest the transience alike of human and other natural forms. The
word 'turbans' draws attention to the fact that the graves resemble people;
some have shoulders and round 'heads'. We cannot read what is written
on the individual tombs, but Lear's conflation of word and image reminds
us that all landscape is both a nest and a graveyard, full of buried character
and utterance.

Lear's paintings are often praised for their topographical accuracy, but
they are not merely depictions of a place as a geographical reality; they convey
a sense of place as a crossing point where personal memory, imagination,
historical record and legend meet. The best of them are dreamlike in a positive sense. They reflect Lear's self-awareness that, in them, looking is also
re-viewing, that we are seeing something that is replete with meaning that
is both inherent and imported. They are delicate, careful in their finely drawn
line and colour, yet also bold in capturing the drama of scenery and how it
can affect us as an internal drama. The relationship between word and image
is an analogue for the porousness of perception and how it involves perpetual
mediation between what is seen now and what has been seen and thought
before.

The interplay of word and image in the fabric of Lear's paintings and his
literary productions meant that he was extremely well placed to understand
and to join an artistic movement that was also an assertion of the essential
interdisciplinarity of art. This was, in Britain, the most influential artistic
group of the early nineteenth century, and Lear's place in it has been largely
ignored. I would like, in the final section of this chapter, to think about Lear
as a Pre-Raphaelite and to draw a link between his paintings in this mode
and his visual poetry.

Edward Lear, Pre-Raphaelite

Lear was a self-elected Pre-Raphaelite. This fact is not widely known and
deserves further consideration than it has yet received in art-historical and
literary criticism. Lear was a relatively late adopter of Pre-Raphaelitism. He
became friendly with William Holman Hunt in 1852, after Hunt visited

his London studio at Stratford Place. Lear was forty, Hunt only twenty-five—yet it was evidently Lear who was on the back foot, exhibiting his sketches nervously to an artist who had begun his studies at the Royal Academy in 1844, who was known as one of the leading figures of the Pre-Raphaelite Brotherhood and who painted controversial works that sold for up to 300 guineas a canvas. Hunt was not immediately impressed with Lear's painting but liked him well enough to offer artistic advice, recommending that he should attempt to produce oils *en plein air*. If Lear cared to join him at a painting retreat in the country, Hunt would permit him to observe his working methods and to learn Pre-Raphaelite painting techniques. Lear accepted the offer, renting Clive Vale farm near Fairlight in Sussex for the two to share. After some initial anxieties, largely due to Lear's worries about personal space, the working party-cum-holiday was a great success. William Rossetti joined them for a time, as did John Everett Millais, who Lear joked might usher in a new 'Milllaisnium' in art. Lear studied Hunt as he painted the cliffs that form a backdrop to *Our English Coasts 1852*. In the evenings Lear made notes in 'Ye Booke of Hunte' (now sadly lost). Hunt later remarked that Lear 'took down my answers to inquiries as to the pigments and system I should use in the different features of a landscape'.[95] Lear worked on the painting that became *The Quarries of Syracuse,* using the Sussex cliffs to stand in for the Sicilian limestone. He began to refer to Hunt as 'Daddy', an ironic moniker given their respective ages, but one that paid playful homage to Lear's debt to Hunt as an artist. He taught Hunt Italian. They remained close friends for the next thirty-six years, until Lear's death, often consulting each other about their respective paintings and more personal affairs. Indeed Lear thought at one time that Hunt and he might live together. Lear became part of a social and creative circle of artists that included all the then-current members of the Pre-Raphaelite Brotherhood. He knew the sculptor Thomas Woolner ('Uncle Tom') well, and was also familiar, though less intimate, with John Everett Millais, Dante Gabriel Rossetti and Frederick Stephens. Other associates of the brotherhood whom he counted among his friends were Thomas Seddon, Robert Martineau, Augustus Egg and Ford Madox Brown, whose work Lear valued highly and of whom he significantly wrote, 'after all he is the real first P.R.B.'[96]

In 1852 Lear was an established, middle-aged painter who had lived and worked in Rome in the artists' colony for over a decade; he had a solid if narrow base of clients for his paintings amongst the 'upper 10,000'. One is tempted to wonder why he was drawn to join the Pre-Raphaelites. Founded in 1848, they were the most controversial group of the era. Their antiquarian title (alluding to their admiration for mediaeval and early Renaissance art) is partially misleading, in that their techniques and social subjects were boldly avant-garde, offering an explicit challenge to the methods, hierarchies and aesthetic values of the Royal Academy. The answer to the question of why Lear became a Pre-Raphaelite is complex. Lear was an inventive artist, always interested in new ways of producing images; his natural-history painting had predisposed him to the detailed study of nature. He was also frustrated. He had not had the benefit of early training in the Royal Academy Schools, and his belated attempt in 1849 to study at Sass's, the entry point for the Academy, had led him to withdraw after less than a year. He did not command the kind of fame and prices as an oil painter that he craved. However, these facts in themselves are insufficient to explain Lear's attraction to Pre-Raphaelitism. The movement chimed with him at a deeper level. Its bold, confrontational use of colour and its dramatic subjects stood out against the dull palate of many conventional oils of the period. Its rebellion against the coterie votery of the Royal Academy and the wider political illiberalism the Academy represented spoke to the angry nonconformist in him, personally and politically.[97]

Further, the idea of a collaborative brotherhood was a charm well placed to win Lear, whose own art was so twined with gift-giving and performance within a social network of shared creativity. Lear wrote to Hunt in 1882, 'except you and Johnny Millais . . . is not "the whole round Table" of the Preraphaelite period "dissolved"?'[98] Lear's powerful conception of the brotherhood as a 'Round Table' links the mediaeval motifs prominent in the group's early subject matter to a broader sense of the chivalry and idealism embodied in its refusal of traditional hierarchies. He described the P. R. B. to Hunt not as a 'School' but as 'a College'.[99] Lastly, one of the driving forces of Pre-Raphaelitism was its fascination with literature, particularly poetry. At the beginning of the movement Keats was the lodestone of its members' artistic ideas; Tennyson soon became an equally powerful magnet. Word-painting and the potentially hypnotic concentration of sensory stimuli within a limited frame link the art of poetry with the intense gaze that Pre-Raphaelitism embodies and solicits. Often poems were inscribed in the frames of the Pre-Raphaelites' paintings or acted as a direct inspiration for their subjects. Elizabeth Prettejohn has persuasively argued that Pre-Raphaelitism may be 'best understood as an attempt to break down the boundaries between the arts. . . . Pre-Raphaelitism was both a literary and

an artistic movement; or perhaps it would be better to say that it was neither, in that it refused to recognise the difference as meaningful'.[100] Lear's
naturally intertextual practice as an artist who was also a writer and a musician dovetailed with the concerns of a group whose paintings so often express a desire to be read.

Shortly after their working holiday together in 1852, Lear sent Hunt a
gift of his own books. He also proposed that Hunt tackle subjects from
Welsh ballads, a suggestion that Hunt embraced in a letter that also ven-
tured a few words in Italian: 'I am very glad to know of the Welch ballads.
I should think that they would be sure to contain some good subjects, and
in hopes of this and for the mere pleasure of reading the quaint things, I
will certainly procure them'. I have found no evidence that Hunt painted
from these ballad subjects. However, the correspondence shows how Lear's
reading and cultural influences affected Hunt at a personal level. Hunt felt
his lack of early education and family support for his artistic career bitterly
and later expressed to Lear 'how much I am indebted to you for the amount
of culture that I have got since the time I first met you'. In one of Hunt's
early letters to Lear, he attempts to convey the howling of the wind as a
stave of musical notes; in another he includes a cartoon of himself lying su-
pine on the floor with a palette in one hand and Cadmium his cat sitting
on his chest. Lear's musicality and his gift for cartoon brought out a private
side of Hunt that was playful and less dour and dogged than the character
of Hunt's public paintings, which are so often preoccupied with struggle
and temptation.

One of the pleasures of reading a Pre-Raphaelite painting with knowing
eyes is to detect warm currents of sociability beneath the surface tension of
the subject matter. Millais's *Isabella* (1849) is both a portrait of a predatory
society dominated by money in which murder is being contemplated, and
an affectionate tribute to Keats and to members of the Pre-Raphaelite
'family' who sat for the figures around the table. Lear knew this painting
well and sketched its outline from memory in his diary. He commented in
1869:

> My uncle Tom [Thomas Woolner] has bought no end of
> Turners and other pictures, among the rest the early Millais,
> the dinner scene with Isabella and the Brothers—to me the
> best of all Millais ever did—for finish, drawing,—& expres-
> sion it beats all his later works out & out.[101]

This analysis demonstrates both the sharpness of Lear's critical eye and how the Pre-Raphaelite circle outlived the period of its initial celebrity, continuing to weave artistic and social bonds. One can imagine Woolner and Lear at lunch reprising Millais's dinner scene of twenty years before.

Similarly, Holman Hunt's *The Awakening Conscience* (1853) is both a startling approach to depicting the 'fallen' woman and a painting that affectionately inscribes male friendship and influence in its circle of visual symbols. It is one of the most famous of Pre-Raphaelite paintings, and Lear is in it, although not immediately visible. The focus of attention is a kept woman, a rich shawl draped suggestively around her hips, who jumps up from her lover's lap as they canoodle at the piano. Thomas Moore's song 'Oft in the Stilly Night' has touched a chord in her, causing her to feel a pang of remorse. The oppressively ornate sitting room is full of objects that signify the trap she is in. A cat pursues a bird. Tangled embroidery threads and a dropped glove symbolise sexual losses and errors. In the left foreground lies a copy of Lear's published song-setting of Tennyson's poem 'Tears, Idle Tears', from *The Princess* (1847). Lear's name is clearly visible on the title page. Indeed, Hunt has given us the words 'Songs', 'Tennyson', 'Lear' and '[Id]le Tears', so that the page within the canvas becomes a setting in which Lear and Tennyson's names are visually blended. Tennyson's *T* springs out of 'Lear's' lap, so we have a teary Lear, which seems apt, given the emotional qualities of Lear's songs. Thomas Seddon posed for the male figure and Annie Miller (Hunt's fiancée) for the female figure, reflecting Pre-Raphaelite collaboration. Art, literature and music form a benign circle that has the potential to release the fallen subject from the web of contemporary social evils. Emily Tennyson recorded that Lear in November 1857 sang his settings of Tennyson's songs to an audience that included Holman Hunt, Dante Gabriel Rossetti and the poet and dramatist Henry Taylor alongside the Tennysons—'all pleased with Mr Lear's singing'.[102] This was the year of publication of Edward Moxon's now-famous edition of Tennyson's poems with illustrations by, among others, Hunt, Millais and Rossetti. Lear was part of the wider collaborative structure of this group; he formed one of several bridges between Tennyson and the Pre-Raphaelites, both socially and artistically.

In Lear's own Pre-Raphaelite paintings we see both the influence of Pre-Raphaelite ideas concerning light, colour and space and the allusive significance that energises Hunt's work. Lear's *Quarries of Syracuse*, whose full title is *The City of Syracuse from the Ancient Quarries Where the Athenians Were*

Imprisoned BC 413, is a strikingly experimental painting. Rarely seen or reproduced, this is one of the most important of Lear's oils: its P. R. B. methods may require some commentary to elucidate the boldness of their manoeuvres. The midday light in this picture is sharply confrontational; its high, flat horizon draws the eye upwards, across the bare rock of the quarries with their vertiginous drop, towards the distant city of Ortigia, which hovers like the floating island of Laputa above a hepatica-blue line of sea. The scene is apparently peaceful. To our left, a man lies on a rock ledge above the quarries, gazing towards infinity. Some jackdaws and a fig tree give a crisp present-tense vividness to the foreground; an iridescent bird, a roller, flies out over the quarries, its wings in motion. But, as in so many Pre-Raphaelite paintings, there is a focused air of dramatic tension that is discomfiting. The angles are vertiginous. The bird hangs in space. It seems as if the figure of the spectator, which juts out awkwardly into the visual plane, might at any moment slide off and plunge hundreds of feet into the quarries, where trees crowd, recalling the prisoners of ancient times. The classical historian Thucydides had made the quarries famous as a kind of early concentration camp. This was a place of human horrors. Following a disastrous Greek attack on Sicily during the Peloponnesian war, seven thousand men were imprisoned there for eight months, suffering from exposure, hunger, thirst and disease as they slept among the rotting corpses of their friends. Those who survived to be sold into slavery would have looked out towards the horizon with terrible longing. This context charges Lear's painting with the force of contrast between idyll and horror, a contrast embedded in the strata of the rock that have been chiselled out of the quarry and in the terrible gulf it opens up.

In Lear's painting no detail is allowed to escape. The middle ground does not subside into a graceful blur but remains confrontationally loud and photographically sharp. The bright, direct midday light strikes the rock pillars on the further edge of the quarry, highlighting the steps cut into them in ancient times, so that they resemble failed exit routes. Lear's uncharacteristic long title is itself an experiment in relating text to image, an instruction to the viewer to consider the past in the present. Landscape is set within a historical and political framework of threatened freedom. Contemporary viewers would have been aware of modern Greek struggles for independence and of battles that continued to be fought over the governance of both Greek and Italian territory. Lear may well have seen Ford Madox Brown's *An English Autumn Afternoon* of the same period (1852–1854), in which two viewers

on the left-hand side gaze out over a north London scene undergoing urban
development. In Brown's painting, too, a bird in flight measures the distance between foreground and distance. In both paintings we are invited to
look carefully at a view both serene and threatened, fraught with evidence
of change. In the context of the Athenians' imprisonment, the bird's freedom
to cross the gulf to Ortigia emphasises the historically contingent nature of
human liberty.

Some critics were impressed by the *Quarries of Syracuse,* 'a fine painting . . .
of a bold and novel description'.[103] Others loathed it: 'The Syracuse stone-
quarries is a most unpromising subject, and as might be expected when
worked out into a picture is perfectly hideous. We saw it this summer at the
Royal Academy and could only suppose that some very strong classic association indeed could have induced the Hon. F. Lygon to give a quarter of
a thousand pounds for such a *thing*'.[104] In fact, Lord Lygon had originally
wished for Holman Hunt's *Our English Coasts, 1852,* but was persuaded by
Hunt to claim Lear's painting as his Art Union prize instead. The willing
substitution of Lear's painting for Hunt's points to shared qualities in two
coastal views, painted in the same place and at the same time, whose pre-
carious landscapes contain implicit political drama.

Lear made the Tennysons a present of a smaller painting of the same subject matter. He explained:

> I hope you & Alfred may like the little picture: I wish he
> would take up the subject for a poem:—turn himself into one
> of the Greek soldier & sailor captives, & write a million of
> lines. Why not the whole siege, with episodes of love madness
> melancholy &c &c—at his own pleasure?—The best modern
> account of these events by the bye is in Grote:—& by the bye
> also some of the captives certainly sung & were poetical—
> since someone was set at liberty for so doing.[105]

As far as we know, Tennyson did not embrace Lear's suggestion that he
should compose a poem on this topic. Had he done so, Pre-Raphaelite influence would have come full circle, with Lear's art, inflected by Hunt's
criticism, producing work that in turn inspired further poetry from the laureate. It is nonetheless significant that Lear envisioned his painting as a potential source for a classically inspired long poem with an epic scope that

could self-referentially allude to the Athenian narrator's own liberty as won through song. Lear often made reference to his own visual artworks as 'poetical' topographies or 'poeticle landskips'.[106] This can be understood in multiple ways. Lear wanted his paintings to be poetic, communicating emotionally and rhetorically in the manner of literature; he also depicted landscapes that draw on literary sources and invite literary responses. Lear, as we have seen, nurtured from the 1850s until his death a never-completed project of illustrating Tennyson's poems with scenes Lear had viewed during his own travels. One of the many reasons why this project was never satisfactorily completed is that its power dynamic was wrong.[107] Lear didn't really want to illustrate Tennyson. He wanted to reply to the stimulus of Tennyson in a way that would tempt the laureate back into artistic conversation with him. While the chiaroscuro vignettes Lear mostly produced as Tennyson illustrations do not achieve this goal, the striking oils of the 1850s and 1860s that engage Tennyson are much more successful flags for Lear's true ambition.

Again in his Pre-Raphaelite painting of *Thermopylae* (1853), which was famous as the site of an unequal battle between King Xerxes and the Spartans, Lear harnesses the drama of intense colour and crisply focused distance in a way that refuses to allow landscape to subside peacefully into a backdrop. The intensity of the Pre-Raphaelite gaze calls to mind the many different senses of the word *focused:* rapt, engrossed, sensuously absorbed, but also dogged, driven and resolute. The mountains are indigo, the sea is turquoise, the figures in the foreground wear scarlet, the Spartan colour. There is a memory of battle in the air. It woke up the critics who saw it at the British Institution and responded to its drama. Lear passed on the compliments to Hunt: 'all the praise of colors, & its adaptation was wholly owing to you Sir. . . . Not but that I dare say 99 out of a hundred will blame & not praise the color—how green! how blue! how queer!'[108] Lear enjoyed the idea of challenging the viewer with eye-popping colour. Letters show that Lear helped Hunt, while the latter was in the Middle East, by supplying him with the German paints he preferred. Collapsible tin tubes of metal oxide paint in shades such as emerald green and cadmium yellow were new in the nineteenth century, and many of these arrestingly bright pigments were developed in Germany.[109] The Pre-Raphaelites became particularly associated with purple and green. When the Jumblies, whose heads are green and hands are blue, sail away in their sieve with a pea-green sail, despite the warnings of a fatuous public, they embark on a Pre-Raphaelite voyage.

Lear also embraced the critical language of Pre-Raphaelitism. Holman Hunt was in Jerusalem in the spring of 1854, so Lear reported to him about the defects of that year's Royal Academy exhibition:

> The Academy exhibition is unusually bad. Sir Charles has a 'Giorgione & water' female head,—more like a piece of boiled veal than a woman. Maclise's immense picture wants nature and variety to me. . . . Boxall has a Lady Eastlake dipped in treacle—Landseer a huge canvas full of slosh—melancholy to see when one thinks of what he could do if he liked.[110]

Lear's criticism of subject matter, colour and composition meld with implicit criticism of the complacent attitudes and modes of viewing that these pictures embody and endorse. Sir Charles Eastlake, a member of the Royal Academy and later the first director of the National Gallery, painted idealised female portraits, which Lear here dismisses as 'boiled veal'. 'Veal' (a calf fattened for consumption) was Pre-Raphaelite slang for a patron, so the implication here is that flattery as well as second-rate historical imitation is involved. William Boxall, an associate of the Academy, has painted Sir Charles's wife—another indication of the closed circle of Academy patronage—'dipped in treacle'. This double-edged complaint (too saccharine, too dark) echoes the PRB conviction that the Academy fostered pictures whose want of brilliant pigments and detailed labour-intensive brushwork was a legacy of dull and lazy habits of painting ('slosh') compounded by cronyism.

Lear's painting of 1854 for the Earl of Derby, *Windsor Castle*, also bore clear evidence of his colour experiments with Hunt. Lear worried a great deal about it, having asked the earl for special permission to live by the castle to enable him to put in the hours of work necessary to get it right. He was, however, satisfied with the result. He told the earl he was 'obliged to confess after all my growling, that I am greatly pleased at the effect it has produced on those who have already seen it. J. Millais & Frith consider it the best thing I have done by far'. Lear reported:

> The first impression I find of those who see it is
> O how *green!*——
> But by the time that visitors have sate before the picture some time,
>   I find they discover feelings just such as I wished to create. . . .[111]

The dramatic effect was important to Lear. One recalls the alphabet in which King Xerxes stands in his purple, green, red and yellow turban brandishing cutlass and dagger. In his landscape painting in oil he wanted to elicit a similar surprise. Colour could be felt in italics. It would be followed by the 'discovery of feelings' Lear had engineered like an impresario: the reluctant acknowledgement that England could sometimes be so vividly green and that truth to nature was different from convention: 'Though of course there are many who think that trees should never be painted green, (because they *are* so), & that all Landscape should be filled up with trees like Claudes,— (because they *ain't* so). To such, strict copies of nature are odious'. Lear in fact respected Claude's work and had learned substantially from it, but he had moved on. Here he scolds the laziness of looking through the Claude-glass of convention rather than directly with open eyes. In Lear's *Nuneham* (1860), which bears comparison with Madox Brown's *The Hayfield* (1855–1856), the immersive greenness of grass and trees is the true subject of the sheep-strewn landscape.

The vivid colour in Lear's oils of this period, like that of his PRB col-leagues, is not merely actuated by a desire to produce a 'strict copy of nature'; it has a political dimension. He often reflected that England was 'filthy'. Rain, dirt and pollution prevailed. Chocolate-coloured fog smeared the lens of London. In 1853 Dickens's novel *Bleak House* was published, commemorating forever the rolling sea of fog that mired the capital in cor-ruption both atmospheric and moral. Lear's desire to render Windsor in pure, pristine colour, at the height of summer, was both wishful and con-frontational. He wanted Britain to be more like his *beau idéal* of it. In liber-ating landscape from the 'slosh' and 'treacle' of the Royal Academy, the Pre-Raphaelite Brotherhood were challenging historically sanctioned modes of oil painting and simultaneously painting a lighter, brighter vision of England that dazzled with its insistence that it could be a green and pleasant land if freed from what Lear called the 'filth Anglosaxon' that clogged it.

Several critics have downplayed Lear's Pre-Raphaelitism as a brief ex-cursion into new technical territory followed by a hasty retreat into his pre-vious working methods. Allen Staley declares, 'It cannot be said that the tutelage . . . of Hunt had much lasting impact on Lear's art'.[112] Peter Levi claims that Hunt 'led Lear a long dance'.[113] Levi argues that Lear should instead have been studying the work of Turner, whose Folkestone notebook would have 'blown Hunt's small portion of brains' and 'shown Lear exactly what he needed to be shown'. The judgement patronises both Hunt and Lear, who studied Turner's work repeatedly and closely all his life. In San Remo he had Thomas Underhill's engravings of Turner's paintings, which he had personally commissioned, constantly before him. Diary entries show him consulting Turner's seascapes directly before embarking on his own.[114] If he was painting as a Pre-Raphaelite it was because the movement spoke to him differently. Although his feelings about individuals within it waxed and waned, Lear's allegiance with the group was lifelong, and the influence of Pre-Raphaelite thinking on his art was lasting. In 1871 he wrote that he 'Worked . . . off and on—at Corfu Citadel, Ventimiglia, Lerici, Megaspelion, Palermo: blue pink & yellow—a la Holman Hunt'.[115] Travelling in India in November 1874 he recorded that his bungalow was quiet and had a huge pipal tree nearby: 'So I could very well work out my Preraffaelite ideas of my "tree fern"—a branch of which I had brought back:—this occupied till 6 or dark'.[116] This implies that he was not only painting minutely and protractedly from nature but was 'working out ideas' in a way that was specifically indebted to Pre-Raphaelitism. He may have been observing the effects of light on colour, which he explores in the same diary entry. Lear dubbed Holman Hunt 'one of the greatest of mental painters':[117] the ideas and narratives conveyed in Hunt's work were of great interest to him. He did not always agree with Hunt's iconography, but from his exposure to the Pre-Raphaelites and the wider circle that included Ford Madox Brown, he gained confidence in the ability of his painting to make a contemporary statement.

This is nowhere more apparent than in his paintings *Beachy Head* and *Philae,* a pair of oils commissioned by the banker Henry Grenfell in 1862. This 'double-work', comparable to Dante Gabriel Rossetti's double works of the same period (such as *Soul's Beauty* and *Body's Beauty,* begun in 1864), is especially intriguing for the way that it deploys verses by Tennyson, painted on the frame of each picture. *Beachy Head* is one of the most remarkable of Lear's mature paintings yet has received very little critical attention, partly perhaps because it rests in private hands and therefore has only been seen by the public on the rare occasions when it has been exhibited. It is an extraordinarily atmospheric painting. The cliffs of Beachy Head are, at over five hundred feet, the tallest in Britain and were renowned even in the nineteenth century as the site of accidents and suicides, though also as a beauty spot. Lear depicts them gleaming in the moonlight. The composition is diagonal, dramatically veering from the dark beach and stormy clouds on the left to the luminous sweep of the rock face on the right. The viewer's perspective places her on the cold beach in the foreground, amongst slippery black stones, while her eye is drawn to the exposed strata of the rock as it curves away. The cliff, which rears up on the right of the picture, is like the looming rampart of a ghostly castle with distant seagulls swooping around it. Purple bruises the sky and suffuses the sea, contrasting with acid green in the band of seaweed along the shoreline. These complementary shades invoke conflict underlying a scene of mysterious, dreamlike beauty. Lear delighted in advertising to his patron the sensations that the painting would produce:

> I am very glad you know the place—which it has been my aim
> to render in its coldest & uncomfortliest phase. Some who see
> it say it is necessary to look at it from below an Umbrella—&
> with thick boots on: while others are pained by a sensation of
> sprains in the ankles when they look at the round black
> stones:—of these last are Archibald Peel & W. Lushington
> recognizes personal points & peaks which nearly destroyed
> him once when he fell down half the cliff.[118]

It is typical of Lear that he imagines his viewers being 'in' the painting, under an umbrella, and suffering from painful feet. He wants the cold atmosphere to be palpable. He has even invented an odd superlative, 'uncomfortliest', to suggest the awkwardness of being uncomfortably cold, a state he himself abhorred. The picture, in Lear's description, is a dramatic panorama that the viewer enters, inhabiting its virtual reality and feeling its chilly mental and physical effect.

Both Holman Hunt and Frederic Church sometimes toured large paintings in the manner of a cinematic IMAX experience today: viewers paid for a ticket to see the individual picture and experience the dramatic sensation of entering its landscape. Lear did not do this, but he liked to think of his major oils in similar terms, as able to transport the viewer beyond the frame. Of his large and splendid *Kinchinjunga,* he issued a comic warning:

> All I beg of you particularly is this,—that if it stands on
> the ground, you will put up a railing to prevent the
> children—particularly the twins, from falling over the edge
> into the Abyss. Any slight wire fence will do.[119]

This kind of synaesthetic experience—potentially funny, potentially deep—
is vital to Lear's art, where infinity is always haunted by levity. He values
the personal identification that fuses an image with memories or imagin-
ings of a real place, bringing a kind of 'recognition' to the picture that is
multilayered. There are 'personal points & peaks' in its composition that
speak to the viewer's inner world through the outer world of shared perspective. The painting, like a conversation poem, includes its audience in its
projected vista. Beneath *Beachy Head* are two stanzas from Tennyson's poem
'You ask me, why, though ill at ease'. The position of the words on the gold
frame is unusual: they are in black capital letters, and the two stanzas are
side by side, symmetrically balanced beneath the shimmering landscape of
moonlight, stormclouds, shining white cliffs and water.

> You ask me, why, though ill at ease,
>   Within this region I subsist,
>   Whose spirits falter in the mist,
> And languish for the purple seas:
>
> It is the land that freemen till,
>   That sober-suited freedom chose.
>   The land where, girt with friends or foes
> A man may speak the thing he will;[120]

Tennyson's poem itself buttonholes the reader, suggesting that he or she has
asked a personal question to which the poet offers a response. As with so
many of Tennyson's poems, however, this dialogue reveals itself as internal.
The sentiment is apparently patriotic: Britain is the land of intellectual liberty and free speech. But it is hedged around with doubt. Tennyson wrote
this poem in 1833, during the controversy over the passing of the 1832
Reform Bill, but it was not published until 1842. It bristles with internal
conflict, between pride in the British tradition of political liberalism and
democratic freedom and a more conservative sense that this tradition is the
result of gradualism rather than sudden change by 'faction' or 'banded
unions'. Freedom 'slowly broadens down from precedent to precedent' and
new thoughts 'diffuse' themselves by degrees to fullness, within a land of
'settled governance'. The speaker 'subsists . . . ill at ease', while his spirits
'falter in the mist and languish for the purple seas'. It is a poem of mixed feelings about Britain as a political home. And, significantly, it was a work Lear

couldn't let go of: he produced no fewer than twenty-three illustrations to it in addition to his oils. In the final stanzas, Tennyson proclaims:

> Should banded unions persecute
>   Opinion, and induce a time
>   When single thought is civil crime,
> And individual freedom mute;
>
> Though Power should make from land to land
>   The name of Britain trebly great—
>   Tho' every channel of the State
> Should fill and choke with golden sand—
>
> Yet waft me from the harbour-mouth,
>   Wild wind! I seek a warmer sky,
>   And I will see before I die
> The palms and temples of the South.

This 'wild wind' echoes the famous opening line of Shelley's 'Ode to the West Wind' ('O wild West Wind'), in which the anarchist Shelley implores the wind to sweep him up in its prophetic breath, 'to quicken a new birth' of global revolution. But Tennyson asks the wind more ambiguously to carry him away from Britain if, in future, individual freedom is suppressed and opinion persecuted. He imagines a country more powerful but more corrupt, its channels of state 'choked with golden sand'. The poem is a statement of national identity that is also a threat to leave.

Lear chose the subject of *Beachy Head* himself; he did not know if Henry Grenfell had ever been there. His double work engages personally and politically with the mixed feelings of Tennyson's verse. Lear depicts the edge of southern Britain as if from the perspective of someone who may be admiring its strength or leaving its cold defences behind. He recalls this early poem at a time of disunity in the Liberal Party, when 'faction' was threatening to tear it apart. Grenfell was a prominent Liberal, and Lear felt confident in addressing him on political matters, expressing for example a mutual dislike for Joseph Chamberlain, a screw magnate from Birmingham who opposed the Universal Education Act and whose radical platform would in the 1880s undermine the Liberal Party from within. Vivien Noakes has characterised *Beachy Head* as a 'straightforward topographical picture',[121] but in this instance I cannot agree with her. It is not as explicitly political as Holman Hunt's *Our English Coasts, 1852* or Madox Brown's *The Last of England*, but it shares the same visual territory. One is reminded of Matthew Arnold's poem 'Dover Beach', written in the 1850s but not published until 1867, in which he evokes the poignancy of the bare beach by moonlight, his thoughts drifting to the 'naked shingles of the world', in which religious doubt and conflict are ascendant. *Beachy Head* would be Lear's last English oil painting, and it has the ambiguous wave of a farewell gesture.

Two important features of Lear's painting are not well known. Firstly, Lear conceived *Beachy Head* and *Philae* as 'the *North* & *South* pictures'. Echoing the title of Elizabeth Gaskell's political novel of 1855, Lear sets these different paintings against one another in deliberate conversation that implies competing values. Secondly, it has not before been realised that *Beachy Head* is a close visual response to a painting of the North Pole, *The Icebergs*, by the American artist Frederic Church. Lear admired Church's paintings greatly. He wrote to James T. Fields in January 1880:

> Church the Landscape painter . . . I consider the greatest
> Landscape Painter after Turner;—& one of his works, 'The
> Heart of the Andes' hangs always before me. I have heard
> Church's works decried as wanting in certain technical qualities,
> & conditions of art:—yet he is not the greatest Orator, it seems
> to me,—who can speak with perfect fluency & charm of
> rhetoric on one or two subjects,—but rather he who with less
> power of eloquence or popular persuasiveness can bring home to
> the hearts and minds of his audience convictions on a multitude
> of different subjects with unfailing force.[122]

Lear here compares visual and verbal rhetoric. The technical quality of painting is secondary to its power to communicate. Through his forceful eloquence Church succeeds, in Lear's view, in 'bringing home' to his audience's 'hearts and minds' subjects including the Arctic and South America. This makes him a greater visual orator than an accomplished genre painter of narrower scope would be. Lear was fascinated by the scale of American art and the new worlds it opened up. He especially admired Albert Bierstadt's *The Rocky Mountains, Landers Peak* (1863), which he saw at Thomas Maclean's gallery in 1866. 'What a picture was that of the Rocky Mountains', he reflected, 'extremely beautiful, and far beyond what anyone here can do'.[123] He echoes its composition in his own grand vistas of Kinchinjunga in the Himalayas. Frederic Church's work was at this time more highly prised in Britain than in his native America. Knowing this, Church toured his 'Great Pictures', hoping to increase their renown and to find a prominent bidder for canvases priced at sums few could afford. *Niagara* had come to London in 1857 and *The Heart of the Andes* in 1859. *The Icebergs* travelled to Britain in June 1863. It was displayed at the German Gallery in New Bond Street and received glowing reviews in the press.[124] Its subject, an Arctic scene of menacing beauty, resonated with a British public still in shock at the loss of the Franklin Arctic expedition in 1845, in which all 129 men perished. Church's painting had originally been titled *The North*, and its icebergs, during this period of the American Civil War, were seen as representing the uncompromising strength of the Unionist position that Church supported. However, when the painting failed to find an American buyer, Church altered the name to *The Icebergs* and added drama by including the broken mast of a ship in the foreground. This detail emphasised man's comparative powerlessness in the face of nature's extremes. Lear records in his diary that he went to view *The Icebergs* on 23 July, but found the gallery shut. He must nonetheless have seen the painting in actuality or in reproduction. Chromolithographs, then the most advanced method of colour reproduction, made it a talking point in London that season. Among the works it inspired was Edwin Landseer's *Man Proposes, God Disposes* (1874), a version of the icy scene in which two polar bears are feasting on human remains at the site of the shipwreck.

In *Beachy Head*, Lear directly recalls the dramatic composition of Church's *The Icebergs* in a way that is immediately apparent when one sees the two images side by side. The left foreground is a dark and cold foreshore; the sea occupies the middle distance, flowing into a curved bay. But the focus of both paintings is the luminous white expanse of rock / ice that rises sheer in the upper right of the picture, suggesting both the beauty and the harshness of 'the North', a title Lear also entertained for his work. It is fascinating that Lear chose to portray the south coast of England as if it were an Arctic landscape. One could see this as a domestication of the Romantic wilderness. However, the opposite is also true. Lear dramatically alienates England in this picture, representing it at its extremity as a strange, cold place whose eroded cliffs are as forbidding as they are impressive. In his diary for 1869, Lear reflected, 'The long line of Beachy Head is so beautiful! & what places between Hastings & Eastbourne might be lived in happily, were one in any other country—less venal & odious & revolting!' Then, a week later, 'How dreary & frightful does all this country seem now—& how one wonders that one had thought at all of living in it!'[125]

Lear's art is energised by the emotional boomerang-twang of somebody for whom 'belonging' was a state of rest between 'being' and 'longing' that was neither sustainable nor, were he to confront the truth of the matter, actually desirable. He may not have been bipolar in the modern medical sense, but the momentum of his creative pendulum always involved periods of intense happiness and productivity followed by periods of intense despondency and gloom in which he questioned all his previous choices and expressed weariness with being wherever he was. He had to keep moving. Physical activity and stimulation kept his epilepsy and his depression at bay. Lear's incessant toing and froing were demanding for those of his friends and servants who had to endure the sudden geographical and emotional reversions they occasioned. But these reversions are also essential to what makes Lear's art feel alive. The pairing of *Beachy Head* and *Philae*—with each other and each with its ambivalent verse— is emblematic of Lear's habitual process in playing the attractions of one place off against another. The dialogue between image and text serves to emphasise a wider dialogue that is both internal and external: a dialogue between competing visions of landscape that is also a dialogue between the competing social, political and aesthetic values that north and south embody.

In *Philae,* the companion painting representing 'the South', Lear portrays the Temple of Isis at sunset on its sacred island, which greeted travellers as they sailed up the Nile as Lear had done in 1854 and would do again in 1867. The colours are appropriately warm and spicy: ginger, cinnamon, saffron, with hints of chili and violet. Lear, however, reported to Grenfell that he had been in an argument with a Royal Academician who refused to believe that such colours existed in nature:

> [he] . . . contended that such & such colours were impossible, until silenced by the testimony of many who knew the places, & whose judgement he was obliged to respect. 'Then'—said he—'I thank God I never saw such, & I hope I never may.'— in which sentence the Academic or out & out Tory spirit is very beautiful.[126]

One both hears and sees Lear's rebelliousness, which animates this painting as it does his nonsense. His bold use of colour challenges the assumptions of members of the Royal Academy. Such people are 'Tories' in spirit because of the literal and figurative narrowness of their viewing spectrum. They prefer an 'Academic' approach—for which I think we can read both 'an approach sanctioned by the Royal Academy' and 'a vision based on theory rather than practice'—to the evidence of their senses and the claims made by others' experience. In 1875 he grumbled, 'The conversation of RAs is I must say generally odious'.[127] The continued influence of 'Pre-Raphaelite ideas' in Lear's aesthetic politics is apparent. The double work *Beachy Head* and *Philae* explores Lear's ambivalence about where he is situated in relation to England. He values Britain's democratic history and the legacy of free speech. But that history is threatened by mists and darkness. His own artistic and personal liberty is located in the warm south, where 'impossible' colours are both possible and tolerated.

Impossible Colours, Nonsense Words

Critics of Lear's work commonly did find his use of colour 'overcharged'; a critic in the *Illustrated Times* of March 1867 complained, 'To English eyes many of his works will seem utterly impossible in colour. . . .'[128] There is an intimate relationship between the 'impossibility' of Lear's nonsense and of his use of colour in painting. Both challenge the limitations we impose on credibility, opening up a space of imagined freedom from, respectively, the viewing constraints of the English language and Englishness.

Lear mixes words in the same way that he mixes colours as an artist. He refers to a 'parrot-green-prickly oak'. This, one of many invented compound adjectives, conveys an idea of bright colour and tactile spikiness that we feel simultaneously as sharp to the eye and the skin. Expressions such as 'grape-purple water' and 'bare mangy fox-skin hills' likewise suggest how alive his visual impressions of landscape are, by allusion to other living forms.[129] Waves are 'deep blue-black, with silver crests—valley-making, gulfing—vast, forcible, opal-vitriol hued above, solemn inky below,—gull-abounding, ever-moving terrible'.[130] One hears the influence of Lear's reading of Greek in his invention of compound adjectives that sound like translations from Homer and that capture the sound and motion of the sea as well as its complex blend of colours. He is excited by the way we pinch our senses awake when we take existing hues or verbal cues and alter them, making shades that are greeny, okry, rusty, dimmy, gleamy, jumbly.

Lear wrote teasingly to his good friend Lady Wyatt in August 1871 about an experience while travelling in Tuscany:

Meanwhile I had a short interview with Titian's ghost near
Cenaia: he asked after you and Digby, having observed you to
be fond of his pictures: he said that all of the colouring of the
hills about Bellurio & Cenaia was exactly what he had copied
over & over again, which I do not doubt was true, as every
part of the country reminds you of his backgrounds. He asked
me if I would supply him with any new pigment made from
stewed carnations & smashed cherries, But I told him I could
not, & expressed wonder that he should bother himself about
such things. On which he gave a snort & disappeared.[131]

Lear imagines the old master avidly pursuing new pigments, as he himself
did. His imagined red made of stewed carnations and smashed cherries
comes close to Lear's nonsense cookery. But it also suggests the way in which
reaching for new verbal compounds and mixing new colours is a similar process. After all, we can see the red Lear imagines in our mind's eye. As is so
often the case in Lear's writing, the imaginary colour has a smell (of pinks)
and taste (of cherries) that makes it synaesthetic. The contrast between the
traditional idea of a ghost and the physicality of Titian's snort highlights
the awkward but funny dialogue between the intangible ghost of an idea
and the physical reality of language.

Lear remarked when on a trip up the Nile that one could 'learn colour'
in Egypt,[132] exclaiming, *what positive color!* Orange—blue, green. . . . The
color (on the west side) of the sands is absolutely apricot—(or salmon color
azalea—) with the bloom on too, a sort of blush delicate pink'.[133] One feels
here the precariousness of Lear's excited effort to capture his shifting perception of colour in language that is barely equal to suggesting the gorgeous
effects of light. These colours are delectable, like scented flowers or foodstuffs.
Lear refers to the baked Nile mud as 'like chocolate cake',[134] the sands as 'yolk
of egg color or rather apricot', the 'gorgeous cadmiumism' of the sands, and the
'white mosk tops or Sheik's tombs . . . like poached eggs against the sand cliffs'.
Elsewhere he describes 'odious sandy pudding hills'.[135] Landscape often strikes
Lear as good enough to eat. In *Views in the Seven Ionian Islands*, he describes
the 'Food-landscape' of Zante, where currants are grown, as 'one unbroken
continuance of future currant-dumplings and plum-puddings.[136] Indeed, the
edibility of colour and of landscape to Lear's hungry eye constantly suggests
both dreamlike satisfaction and absurdity that presages infinite thirst. Azalea
sunsets meet poached-egg mosques and chocolate-cake mud. His word-

painting habitually combines the lyricism of verbal rapture and comedy. The sublime is the ridiculous. This ever-present Janus-faced self-identity between fulfilment and foolfillment shapes Lear's landscape paintings and his nonsense poetry, which both, at their best, glory in the precariousness of human vision, its evanescent wishfulness, which is also wistfulness for something that cannot be described except through juxtaposition and absence.

Lear's nonsense works bring his painter's eye to bear on language; they are unusually full of words describing colour. As we have already seen, 'The Story of the Pobble who has no toes, and the Princess Bink' is an excursion in shades one might associate with spring (yellow and green) and with blushing and rising blood in sexual parts of the human anatomy (pink, scarlet, lavender, crimson, beetroot). 'The Pelican Chorus' deploys an even wider palette of nine colours: yellow, brown, purple, ivory, black, scarlet, blue, pea-green and white. It also plays on the aesthetic value of tonality, using 'dark', 'dim' and 'twilight' to evoke the shades of the banks of the Nile where the pelicans dance and sing. Lear's visual inspiration for this song was the scenes he had witnessed when travelling in Egypt. He had painted many landscapes, so the colours must have been vibrantly present to his mind's eye; he had observed them closely, written them in his sketches and diaries and re-created them in his studio.

> We live on the Nile. The Nile we love.
> By night we sleep on the cliffs above;
> By day we fish, and at eve we stand
> On long bare islands of yellow sand.
> And when the sun sinks slowly down
> And the great rock walls grow dark and brown,
> When the purple river rolls fast and dim
> And the Ivory Ibis starlike skim,
> Wing to wing we dance around,—
> Stamping our feet with a flumpy sound,—
> Opening our mouths as Pelicans ought,
> And this is the song we nightly snort;—
>   Ploffskin, Pluffskin, Pelican jee!
>   We think no birds so happy as we!
>   Plumpskin, Ploshkin, Pelican jill!
>   We think so then, and we thought so still![137] ♩

♩ Listen to musical link # 11 at edwardlearsmusic.com/audiotrail/#pelicanchorus.

This is a painting in words set to music. The landscape is lyrical. The 'great rock walls' recall the Akrokeraunian walls in Tennyson's 'To E. L., on his travels in Greece', which Lear was in the process of illustrating at the time when he was composing 'The Pelican Chorus'. The 'islands of yellow sand' and the 'purple river' also dimly recall the river isle and purple night of Tennyson's 'Lady of Shalott', a poem to which Lear frequently returned, quoting it both seriously and in parody form. In 'The Pelican Chorus', too, absurd and lyrical aspects coexist. It has some of the ungainliness fused with grace of the Pre-Raphaelite painting.

The pelicans, with their leathery throats and 'flumpy' feet are comically ungraceful. 'Flumpy' is an onomatopoeic word, unique to Lear, but it also visually suggests 'frumpy' and 'lumpy'. 'Nightly snort' is difficult to enounce, even if one does gape like a pelican. The odd, misaligned tenses of the recurring chorus 'we think so then and we thought so still' parody a line from Lord Mansfield's speech of 1770 on a bill against delays of justice caused by claiming Parliamentary privilege. Lear doubtless learned this speech by heart as a child. It was reprinted in Lindley Murray's *English Reader,* a ubiquitous primer in nineteenth-century children's education. Mansfield argued persuasively that 'true liberty . . . can only exist where justice is equally administered to all—to the king and to the beggar'. Mansfield declares the idea that privilege protects members even from criminal prosecution an 'abominable doctrine': 'I thought so then, and I think so still'.[138] It is a nice example, for teaching purposes, of the balanced rhetorical trope of parison. Lear recalls the quote in a diary entry for January 1871.[139] By 1877, it has been decanted through the filter of nonsense and transformed into something new. The transposition is a little like that of some of Lear's spoonerisms ('stunderthorm') or portmanteau words, in which elements are moved around ('dismy dreamal'). Its effect is awkward and moving. Indeed it is moving in its awkwardness. We have all, I suspect, experienced the dreamlike sense that we are present in the past and absent in the present. The pelicans, who are trying to be happy for the daughter they have lost to marriage, shed light on a nonsensicality that is also emotionally true. We cannot help being ridiculous in our longings.

> And far away in the twilight sky,
> We heard them singing a lessening cry,—
> Farther and farther till out of sight,
> And we stood alone in the silent night!

Fig. 4.15 *Kasr-es Saad* (c. 1884–1885)

The moment at which the Ivory Ibis turn into stars that skim across the sky
is especially beautiful. It recalls Ariadne in Titian's famous painting *Bacchus and Ariadne*—an artistic touchstone for the Pre-Raphaelite movement—who is escaping from Bacchus by leaping into eternal life as a constellation in the heavens. The music happens at sunset. And Lear's
masterstroke is to orchestrate a 'fade to dark' that is also a 'fade to silence',
as we both hear and visualise the Pelican king and queen singing of their
departed daughter, who left them in an operatic flight 'of endless birds in a
lengthening cloud'. As we can see in *Nuneham* and *Kasr-es-Saad*, and also
in his illustrations for 'Calico Pie', Lear often uses the motif of a skein of
distant birds in his landscape paintings to connect the land to the sky. It is
a way of sketching a line towards the infinite. The 'lengthening cloud' and
the 'lessening cry' suggest a more that is also less, a 'no end of' that is fulfilment and loss at the same time. The king and queen lament of their lost
child that they probably 'never will see her more'. The song evokes the vanishing point as it exists in visual art and in music, where we see the far blue
of the horizon or hear the last note hang in the air before it is quite gone
from us. The intertext is well placed to suggest what cannot be written,
what eludes any single medium but can exist in the space between poem,
painting, and song that their dialogue limns. Being neither here nor there

in Lear's dreamlike works, which so often highlight the transient or the notionally inconsequential, can offer us a powerful experience of emotional landscape, of the porousness of our senses as they apprehend both what is within us and what is beyond us and of the intense yet intangible colours of feeling.

Fig. 1 Ann Lear, *Edward Lear*, aged nine (c. 1821)

Fig. 2 Edward Lear, 'Malayan Giant Squirrel' (1836)

PSITTACUS ERYTHACUS.
Ash-Coloured or Grey Parrot.
Native of W. Africa.

Fig. 3 Edward Lear, 'Ash-Coloured or Grey Parrot', *The Naturalist's Library* (1836)

MACROCERCUS ARACANGA.

Red and Yellow Macaw.

Fig. 4 Edward Lear, 'Red and Yellow Macaw', *Illustrations of the Family of Psittacidae or Parrots* (1832)

Fig. 5 George Cruikshank, 'C Chimpanzee', *Comic Alphabet* (1836)

Fig. 6 Edward Lear, 'Anthropithecus Troglodytes' (c. 1836)

Nyctipithecus felinus, Spix.   *South America.*

Fig. 7 **Edward Lear, 'Vitoe Monkey' (1835)**

Fig. 8 Edward Lear, 'Toco Toucan', *A Monograph of the Ramphastidae* (1834)

Fig. 9 Edward Lear, 'Whiskered Yarke' (1835)

Fig. 10 Edward Lear, *Karyes, Mount Athos* (1856)

Fig. 11 Edward Lear, *Suli* (1849)

Fig. 12 Edward Lear, *Nuneham* (1860)

Fig. 13 Edward Lear, *Quarries of Syracuse* (1853)

Fig. 14 Edward Lear, *Beachy Head* (1862)

Fig. 15 Edward Lear, *Philae* (1862)

Fig. 16 Edward Lear, *The Marble Rocks, Nerbudda Jubbolpore* (1882)

Fig. 17 Edward Lear, *Kangchenjunga from Darjeeling* (1879)

5

INVENTING
EDWARD LEAR

'You see, there is & must be a great drawback in *My* writing
which yours on a similar subject would not have:—& this is,
that whatever *I* write would be Edward Lear—egotistical &
unmitigated—fanciful—individual—correct or what not—
but nevertheless always *Edward Lear . . .*'[1]

IN 1876 Edward Lear wrote to his friend Lee Warner congratulating
him on his marriage. He invited the newly-wed Mr and Mrs Warner to
visit San Remo and concluded, 'if the lady sees and criticizes my spelling,
you will tell her I am the "Book of Nonsense" and rather crazy'.[2] When I
first read this I assumed it was a mistake—Lear must have meant to write,
'I am the *author* of the Book of Nonsense and rather crazy'. Then I noticed
that in July 1884, at the age of seventy-two, while on holiday in Recoaro,
Lear reports in his diary, 'I introduced myself as the "Book of Nonsense"—
whereon gushings of delight & rappchers'. Later in the same trip, 'various
people English speaking—hailed me as "Book of Nonsense"—a bore'.[3] Lear
identifies himself with his nonsense and comes to be publicly identified by
strangers *as* his most famous book. As Lear himself notes, this can be a delightful form of recognition, producing instant familiarity, but it can also
be troublesome. Where does the craziness of the *Book of Nonsense* stop and
that of Edward Lear begin?

Both in his published nonsense books and in his private letters, Lear performs the role of a figure who entertains us by behaving in a ridiculous
manner. In a letter of 1866 to George Scrivens, Lear pretends to be the
'Stratford Place Gazette' reporting an 'Alarming and Horrible Event'. He

Fig. 5.1 **Lear committing 'sukycide' (1866)**

regrets that this afternoon 'the well known Author and Landscape Painter
Edward Lear committed sukycide by throwing hisself out of a 5 pair of stairs
winder' following the embarrassment of discovering that a book he had requested Scrivens to return was actually in his possession all along.

> On this day . . . the said book tumbled spongetaneously out of
> a coat which had not been opened or shaken or craxpaxified in
> any way whatsoever; on seeing which the unfortunate Gen-
> tleman tore his hair promiscuous, & bitterly reproached his
> self with the trouble he had given to Mrs and Mr G.
> Scrivens . . . & finally giving way to dishpear, opened the
> window & leaped 4th into the street—to the extreme surprise
> & delight of some little children playing on the pavement. . . .[4]

Lear's projected demise becomes a piece of comic theatre. In the accompanying cartoon, the bespectacled, rotund Lear has thrown the offending volume, 'The Goth and the Un', ahead of him. The letter and the book thus become props in a faux-classical tragedy: instead of falling on his sword, Lear falls on his word.

In another epistolary cartoon series of 1871, the comic figure of Lear has furiously sent away an unstamped letter by Marianne North, then belatedly realises that the handwriting is hers, stamps 'with remorse and rage' and makes a 'Stampede' to the post office to reclaim it.[5] Once there, he 'delivers an extampery and affecting discourse' to obtain the letter, then 'stamps and dances for joy' on securing it. Lear lampoons his mistakes and his emotionalism. But he also dramatises the high value of the emotional and physical exchange that writing represents, implicitly including his own gift letter in the transaction. If Scrivens has been short-changed in being accused of keeping Lear's book, Lear repays him with an over-the-top imaginary sacrifice; if Marianne North has failed to pay sufficient postage, Lear will overcompensate by punningly generating more verbal and physical and emotional 'stamps' than any other person could conceive. Part of the pleasure of these cartoons is that they include the reader as co-creator of the comic situation with its accidental omissions, which Lear rectifies by substituting his own cartoon body in their place. You are not only the audience for Lear's antics; you are part of their narrative. He leaps and stamps for you. The verbal and physical excess of his cartoon avatar redeems all possible shortcomings. Lear offers himself as a character who solicits affection by putting himself personally into the reader's hands. Although these are private letters, the intimate nature of the gift exchange they conceive, with Lear's awkward but exuberant body at its centre, informs all his published work.

This is an important difference that distinguishes Lear's nonsense from that of his rival nonsense author Lewis Carroll. Carroll's nonsense has a more pronounced 'inside' and 'outside'. The theatre of his writing has curtains. Alice in Wonderland's journey is carefully revealed at the end of the tale to have been a dream, where objects in the 'real' world have given rise to their imaginative equivalents. Moreover, Carroll policed the boundaries between his professional academic identity and his nonsense writing very carefully. Readers of the 1871 edition of *Alice in Wonderland* would have discovered a Christmas homily in a leaflet within it, which began, 'Dear Children, At Christmas-time a few grave words are not quite out of place' and concluded by urging them to make each Christmas season bright 'with

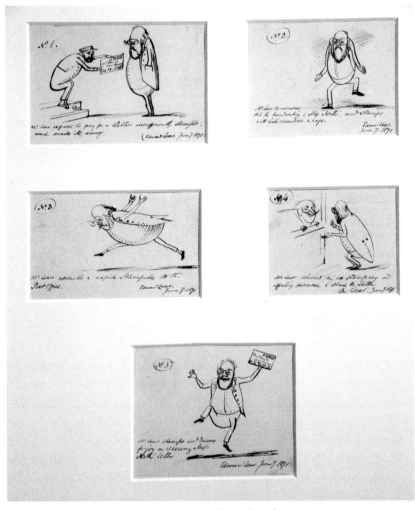

Fig. 5.2 **Storyboard in a letter to Marianne North (1871)**

the presence of that unseen Friend, who once on earth blessed little children'
and 'beautiful with memories of a loving life' which has sought and found
'the happiness of making others happy too!'[6] Such a didactic message was
appropriate from Dr Charles Lutwidge Dodgson, who taught mathematics
at Christ Church College and had taken deacon's orders in the Church of
England. His 'unseen' friendship with children could call on the example
of that of Christ himself. Carroll had a position to keep up. Although he
wrote nonsense letters to his child friends, he refused altogether to accept

letters sent by members of the public addressed to Lewis Carroll. The child actress Isa Bowman remembered that as a girl she once drew a caricature of him. When Carroll caught her doing so, he 'got up from his seat and turned very red, frightening me very much. Then he took my poor little drawing, and tearing it into small pieces threw it in the fire without a word'. Afterwards he caught her up in his arms and 'kissed me passionately'—a reversion of temper that sounds as distressing in its assertion of power as his original fury. Another little girl made the mistake of calling Carroll 'Goosie'. She recalled later that he 'pulled himself up, and looked at her steadily with an air of grave reproof' until she substituted 'a very subdued "Uncle"' instead.[7] Children who mistook Carroll's work as an invitation to regard him as a figure of fun soon learned that they had made a category error.

In marked contrast, Lear delighted in portraying himself as a goose, both figuratively and literally, and indeed as an owl, a bee and a snail. Carroll was five foot nine and always drew himself up to make himself look taller. Lear was a tall man, but in cartoons deliberately belittled himself. From a young age, Lear specialised in self-caricature. He created a distinctive persona that allowed him to dramatise and mediate himself to different audiences, winning their affectionate regard and disarming any criticism that might be levelled at him. This chapter considers that process and how it has affected and continues to affect how we view Lear and interact with his work. Lear's self-fashioning is insistently performative. In it, self-assertion and self-deprecation are intimately linked. Lear demands that we don't take him entirely seriously, but equally demands that we requite what Emily Tennyson memorably called his 'cheerful grumbling' by caring for him. He invites us to participate in the gift exchange of his play and to sympathise with the cartoon Lear, who appears to lack self-awareness (he peers out from behind his spectacles), yet whose antics prove the author's acute consciousness of how he may be viewed. The relationship that readers develop with Lear is something that he carefully curates.

In his teens, Lear wrote letter-poems to his sister Ann and his Sussex friends in which he conveyed news and revived pleasures shared with the addressee. The letter-poem mimics the social rhythm of conversation. Lear never really abandoned the form; his later nonsense often recalls aspects of its imagined dialogue. A striking feature of these early epistolary poems is how often Lear compares himself to food in them. In one, he is as 'black and blue/As a spoonful of milk in an empty plate', and his limbs are 'stiff as a lobster's claw—wot's tied'.[8] In another, he is 'nervously warm—like a

dish of stewed curry', has a face 'like clarified batter' and is 'as pale as a
sucking pig recently boiled'.[9] All these similes are unusual and physically
uncomplimentary to Lear, though they also display his inventiveness. Even
at this early period Lear produces images that are visually arresting. The
uncanny thing about food is that it is a subject that has become an object:

Fig. 5.3a **Lear self-caricature (1840)**

the boiled pig and the curry no longer have agency, yet there is a memory of agency in them that belonged to their living constituents when they were alive. Thus it is absurd to talk of a curry being 'nervously warm', but it is a kind of absurdity that touches a nerve. When we think about our own limbs being like tied lobsters' claws or of being semi-transparently black and blue,

Fig. 5.3b **Lear self-caricature (1840)**

like a bruise or a spoonful of milk in an empty plate, we shift to a place of consciousness that is grotesque because we are unwillingly half-thinking of the objects all our bodies will eventually become. In presenting himself as a consumable, Lear does something clever that his subsequent letter writing will also do. He offers his physical body up to us like a dish, proclaiming simultaneously that he is very unappetising (pale, sweaty, corpulent, stiff) and commanding our sympathy because of his impotence. After all, a curry can't help being hot, and a lobster can't help its claws being tied. They require to be helped and invite others to help themselves to them.

In his twenties, Lear drew himself into his letters to friends. He complained in a letter to the Coombes from Rome that 'my nose is extremely enlarged—& my back very much bent'.[10] A grinning grotesque face, half in shadow, with a bulbous nose and spectacles that conceal its expression is furnished with the caption 'this is my full face & very like'. Lear would joke in letters for the rest of his life about how accurate a likeness his self-caricatures presented. Another cartoon in the same letter shows a very tall young man of twenty-seven who is behaving like an old one. He has long spindly legs, his shoulders are stooped, he is leaning on a cane and his spectacles are so far forward on his nose that they resemble snowballs sliding down his profile. In the text of his letters, too, Lear swings from an energetic and hopeful account of his activities and prospects to more dismal reflections. Comfortably ensconced in the luxury of Knowsley Hall aged twenty-five, Lear nonetheless informed George Coombe that he was lonely and 'morose', and complained of having received no letter from Coombe, a wail of abandonment that becomes familiar to anyone who reads Lear's letters and diaries:

> As for my letter's contents, or rather its discontents—they
> were highly abusive of you on account of your never having
> written. . . . No one is here; Robert Hornby comes on
> Tuesday—& sundry zoologists about the same time. Till then I
> shall feel rather lonesome, as the crocodile said when he was
> dancing a pas seul;—but one cannot be always equally happy. . . .
> I must tell you that I expect to be confined while I am here;—do
> not I beg misinterpret my phrase—altho' I confess I have some
> silent misgivings lest I actually produce a calf;—I mean, I am
> about to be vaccinated, & I am all over nervous & horrible about
> it—*cowed* enough already as far as that goes.[11]

Lear's letters' contents always are discontents, even at this young and promising age, when he was evidently enjoying himself a great deal. That is a large part of their charm. Moaning is to the British what cheering is to the Americans; indeed it *is* a form of cheering. It creates empathy from the base line of admitting the shared experience of intense dissatisfaction in oneself and others. Lear's image of the crocodile dancing a *pas seul* is self-ironising. This is a crocodile whose tears may be faked but who persists with his solipsistic ballet. The succeeding image of Lear expecting 'to be confined' (i.e. pregnant and about to give birth) is still more intriguing. Lear was going to receive the cowpox vaccine against smallpox: he imagines the injection as akin to an ejaculation that will cause him to give birth to a calf. He is *cowed*. He may well have known James Gillray's 1802 cartoon 'The Cow-Pock—or—the Wonderful Effects of the New Inoculation!', in which the bodies of recently vaccinated men and women sprout cows from every part of their anatomy.

Like his later dialogue between the ox and the cow, which he wrote for Chichester Fortescue in the 1840s, this letter of 1837 plays with the idea of losing one's masculinity as well as one's human form. This is not the only moment when Lear hints at a feminine aspect to his character. In his diary, he often performs a comic version of Tennyson's Lady of Shalott or Mariana: 'he only said—"my life is queery—It's very queer he said'.[12] In one extraordinary diary entry of 1860, he refers to himself as 'she', using spoonerism to experiment with a form of linguistic inversion that mirrors his momentary play with gender inversion: 'Waking, she found it was too late to go to Brompton, so she painted for an hour, & then, sending for some bold ceef & bable teer,—she dined'.[13] Cold beef and table beer, via the Babel of nonsense reassignment, can become bold and queer; Lear's identity in nonsense is also freed to experiment with different possible formations. Like the nervously warm curry, or 'The Nervous Family' (a song Lear performed at Knowsley whose musical joke lies in its perpetual *tremolando*), the 'all over nervous' Lear of 1837 trembles on the edge between real anxiety and something that is performed for comic effect. Lear, his early letters tell us, is wary of 'egotism' and its alienating qualities.[14] One way around this conundrum is to perform a version of the self that is knowingly absurd. The *cowed* Lear is such a creation, and he milks it freely.

If one aspect of Lear's self-fashioning as a comic figure is his impotence, another is his excess. He enjoys representing himself as impetuous, intemperate, with verbal exaggeration that becomes part of the fun and acted truth

of the self-portrait. His multiple exclamation marks and underlinings help
to convey his delight in immoderation. Lear reports to George from Knowsley how much he enjoyed 'a gipsy party to Beeston Castle—sublime old
ruins from whose towers 300 feet high one might break one's neck really
with satisfaction—the lovely rides you may very well conclude I enjoyed,—but
above all I put the glorious *Raspberry beds,* at Tabley Hall!—How I did stuff
& cram—they called me "raspberry Lear".[15]

Lear loved to eat well; it was a form of oral pleasure that embodied the
comfort of being given to abundantly. His diaries recall many delicious re-
pasts. The image of 'raspberry Lear' is, however, one of childish happiness,
of stuffing and cramming with one's hands as little boys do. As a result his
body itself might become full and round like a fruit. In the same letter he
evokes the potential embarrassment that lurked around eating formally in
aristocratic circles. Like many middle-class men of his era, he had a horror
of being asked to carve at table. He had to peel his peaches with a knife,
and suffered proto-Prufrockian anxieties. He noted that 'Mrs Penrhyn upset
a dish of truffles—if it had been me I should have burst instantly'.[16] Bursting,
like breaking one's neck with satisfaction, is a form of self-annihilation as
pleasure—or pleasure as self-annihilation—that is very suggestive. Lear becomes like 'the bubble pleasure' in 'Miss Maniac', which inevitably precedes a pop. In his later cartoons of his adventures, his spherical body literally resembles a bubble and will, on occasion, blow away. Lear knew that
his emotional tendency was to shift rapidly from exultant happiness to bleak
depression. He dramatises this sudden reversion within his comic prose,
imagining bursting with embarrassment, the 'satisfaction' of suicide from
the sublime towers of Beeston Castle or (much later) of 'sukycide' from a '5
pair of stairs winder'. Lear's letters often drive toward the extreme, simultaneously embracing and mocking it, just as they simultaneously embrace
and mock Lear's persona, which acts out excessive reactions, promoting itself in the act of imagined self-annihilation.

In Lear's cartoon series during the 1830s for the Hornby family (close
relatives of the Earl of Derby), elements of his early physical self-caricature
become well established. One series depicts his adventures in Greenwich
as he goes to meet Captain Hornby at the docks. Lear is excessively tall and
thin, with his hands thrust into the pockets of his coat, which is so long
that it has some twelve buttons and sticks out behind him like a blackbird's
tail. His spectacles dwarf his eyes and his nose dwarfs his mouth. The
fact of the hands being semi-permanently stuck in his pockets suggests

Fig. 5.4 **Lear daguerreo-type (mid-1840s)**

awkwardness—reticence, perhaps even the self-abuse of the habitual mas-turbator. Yet he engages our attention and sympathy in this series of car-toons through his frustrated, forward-leaning, myopic attempts to locate Captain Hornby and the ignominious way in which he suffers various mis-haps and mistakes along the way. The physical comedy of each scene is its chief pleasure. Lear is dragged out of a sentry box at bayonet point; a po-liceman forces him to sign his name with an absurdly long quill that towers above his gangly frame. Both of these phallic objects act as awkward ana-logues to Lear's body, which he described in a letter to Ann as 'ensiform' (sword shaped), like a botanical specimen with very long leaves. Lear por-trays himself not as the virile swordsman but as the string bean who is threatened at sword point; his masculinity is a comic proposition, something that sticks out but is not under his own control.

Lear's legs in these cartoons are also always in an awkward position. Either they are stuck out in front of him, pressed defensively tightly together at an unnatural angle, or they are splayed like the legs of compasses, as if Lear were striding forward with improbably long steps. Some readers would have recognised the latter theatrical pose as that of the pantaloon, a comic old man whose antics derived from those of the commedia dell'arte figure

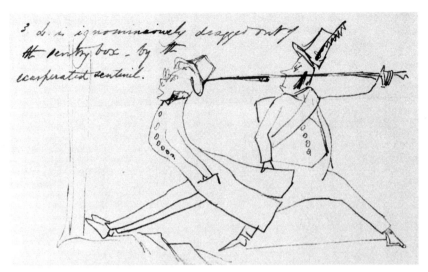

Fig. 5.5a In a cartoon for the Hornbys, Lear is ignominiously dragged out of the sentry box by the exasperated sentinel

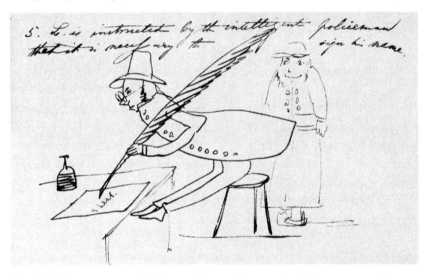

Fig. 5.5b Lear is instructed by the intelligent policeman that it is necessary to sign his name

Pantalone. Pantalone is an old man, tall and skinny, with a cane, a long gown, a prominent nose and often spectacles, which complete his traditional mask. He represents the follies of age: avarice, frustrated sexual desire, and a habit of slipping into emotional extremes when things do not go his way. He cannot control his wandering hands, so they must be kept under his cloak when not in use; his stooping gait involves exaggerated leaning forward or back. Lear's self-portrayal as a pantaloon is obviously ironic given his youth, social gifts and considerable energy at this age—and indeed throughout his life. But in a self-deprecating manoeuvre that also asserts his power to define how he is read, Lear always insists upon his physical unattractiveness. Rather than act the romantic protagonist, he casts himself in a character role. In his drawings he portrays his body as inherently comic. He adopts the physical-comedy techniques of the stage. In his cartoons for the Hornby family, dating from the mid-1830s, Lear presents his character as always getting into physical scrapes.[17] His head disappears inside the sentinel's box, leaving his long body sticking out behind. He peers into a soup basin, having apparently misunderstood Captain Hornby's clerks, who told him that Hornby was at a basin (a dockyard) and not in his office. In these early sketches, Lear cements a view of his comic persona—absurd, ungainly, unconscious—while also proving that as an author and artist he is quite the opposite: dextrous, witty, self-aware.

In a series of eight comic drawings from February 1842, when he was in Rome, Lear again depicts himself getting into amusing physical difficulties. He 'sets out for a walk—but is amazed at the high wind'.[18] Once more the bespectacled Lear is striding forward at a vaudeville tilt, checked trousers splayed fore and aft. But here his arms, which clutch an umbrella, actually seem to be on backwards in a physically impossible conjunction, so they are pointing in the opposite direction to his feet. In the next frame, 'Mr L. loses his hat and contemplates the flight thereof from a serene staircase'. The stair is surmounted by a long thin obelisk. Lear has transposed the adjective 'serene' from himself to the staircase, in a way that will become characteristic of his nonsense writing, in which adjectives, like hats or umbrellas, are always getting separated from appropriate owners and end up alighting on unexpected nouns. The phallic obelisk, like the enormous quill and bayonet of the Greenwich cartoon series, serves to accentuate Lear's comic impotence. He isn't in control. Subsequent frames show him being carried by the wind, sailing along with his inside-out umbrella as a parachute, then flying with some 'familiar and affectionate jackdaws' with whom he converses and rests in a tree. His airborne figure, coattails billowing in the wind, resembles that of the birds he meets. If birds of a feather flock together, Lear is an intelligent kind of crow, of a sort sometimes adopted in the Victorian period as a pet. When he finally reclaims his 'lively hat' it has a hole in it, so that he ends up wearing it like a skirt, jumping along the road in a 'superfluous and unsatisfying manner', as if he were on a pogo stick, a vehicle appropriate to a modern clown. The fact that the jackdaws are 'familiar and affectionate' is charming. This cartoon series explores a series of transferences: hats are alive; birds talk; Lear flies. Lear cannot politely express his own familiar and affectionate status in words, but through his kinship to the birds he can do so. *Familiar* has a variety of meanings: 'on a family footing; extremely friendly, intimate', 'of animals: accustomed to the company of men; domesticated, tame'; 'of persons: affable, courteous, sociable'; 'free, as among persons intimately acquainted, unceremonious'.[19] Lear's affectionate and familiar relationship with the jackdaws, which extends to his looking and behaving like them as well as their being accustomed to his company, places him in the realm of animal and human, dependent and independent, domesticated and free at the same

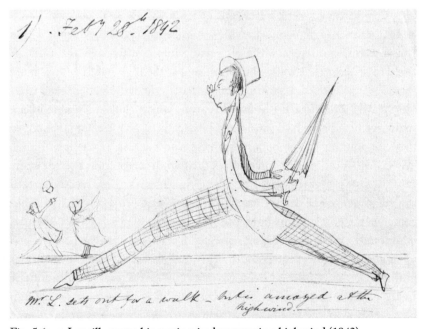

Fig. 5.6a–c **Lear illustrates his comic misadventures in a high wind (1842)**

Fig. 5.6b

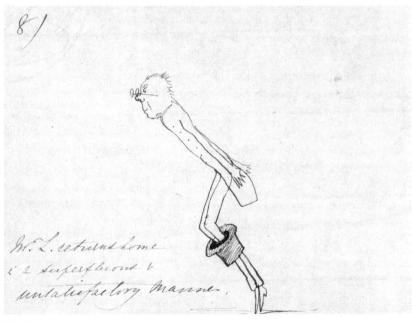

Fig. 5.6c

time. Lear's familiarity plays a vital role in his relationship with the audiences for whom he writes and draws, both private and public; indeed his familiarity cleverly transcends conventional boundaries between the private and public sphere and allows him to fly over class barriers.

Lear's imaginary narrative of being swept away by a high wind will recur eighteen years later in his cartoon series of 1860 for Bernard Husey Hunt.[20] By that time, Lear's caricature-self is small, bearded and globular, but the essential drama is the same. Lear sometimes compared his own journeys to those in the *Adventures of Baron Munchausen,* whose protagonist in one episode of the fantastical narrative is carried away by birds.[21] He also grew up with the story of Sinbad, who is swept off by a giant Roc, and *Gulliver's Travels*—a key text of his childhood—in which the diminutive Gulliver in Brobdingnag is carried away. In his own cartoons, Lear likes to show how being swept up by larger forces can be fun as well as funny. In a letter to Nora Decie of July 1864, the tiny Lear hangs on to the horns of a mouflon (a wild sheep) and is thus enabled to 'ascend some of the highest tops of the Mountains of Crete'.[22] In *A Walk on a Windy Day* he again joins a flock of birds, which he resembles as he flies. There is something liberating as well as self-effacing about his blowing away, getting tinier and tinier until the imagined viewer requires a telescope to see Lear as a speck in the sky. This regression towards smallness is similar to the narratives of involution in 'The Pobble who has no Toes' and 'He Lived at Dingle Bank'. One thinks of famous images in later children's literature—of Winnie-the-Pooh (whose formal name, suggestively, is Edward Bear) attached to the string of a balloon and drifting past clouds, or of Mary Poppins flying with her umbrella. In inventing himself as a cartoon character, Lear anticipates iconic twentieth-century texts in which the child reader has a beloved intermediary whose drift skyward reflects their ability to cross the boundary between magical thinking and physical reality. These are images of dreamy wish-fulfilment as well as uncertainty, a kind of dependency (like that of a baby in utero) where being borne is pleasurable. They combine childlike delight in being carried with a more adult desire for escape.

In his wonderful Italian series of cartoons of himself on horseback, from July 1842, Lear equally enjoys the thought of physical life, in the shape of the horse, running away with him. It is as if he has outsourced his impetuosity to the animal. They get entangled in an obstructive olive-tree, are immersed in an indefinite quagmire, are chased by an irascible ox and the horse ends up wearing the thornbush they have plunged through, like a skirt.

Fig. 5.7 A Walk on a Windy Day (1860)

This is very similar to the image of Lear wearing his hat around his ankles. Lear plays for laughs his Cockney inexperience of horsemanship. But what is really at stake here is movement and desire. The comic vision of self, moving rapidly and static at the same time, is caught in a moment of what Lear calls 'spongetaneous' action that is both dynamic and thwarted, whether by internal circumstance or simply by the fact of there being no further frames, no place for the represented energy to go. This is funny and sympathetic. The speaking silence of the cartoon Lear, like that of a child or an animal, is powerful precisely because it is silent. Lear's self-caricature speaks through the body, its inherent awkwardness, its vulnerability, its intemperate, insistent and often futile claim on others' attention. In this sense, he and the horse share the same predicament, though their wills are supposedly at odds.

Lear's pose when he is striding forward with long, thin legs stretched wide like a pair of compasses is repeated in several of his limerick illustrations. The unstoppable, cross-dressing 'Old Man on a hill, who seldom, if ever, stood still', the 'Old Man of Coblenz/The length of whose legs was

There was an Old Man on a hill, who seldom, if ever, stood still;
He ran up and down in his grandmother's gown,
Which adorned that Old Man on a hill.

Fig. 5.8 **The Old Man on a hill,** *Book of Nonsense*

immense' and the indecisive 'Old Man of Corfu, Who never knew what he should do' all have the same theatrical gait. Rather than walking, they are performing walking. They are going nowhere fast. This continuity demonstrates the close relationship between the theatre of Lear's self-caricature and his nonsense. The bendable, breakable and mendable bodies of the limerick protagonists are similar to Lear's own comic public vision of himself. All perform a dramatic version of physical excess, rushing, riding, jumping and getting tossed about. The reader laughs, knowing that the performance is absurd and unreal, but sensing also that the unreasonable behaviours depicted in the limericks have a real and truthful analogue in the common human experience of physical and emotional wishes too odd or extreme for polite expression. Lear would, in middle age, write a couple of limericks of which he is the explicit protagonist.

However, we should also be aware of discontinuities between Lear and the comic persona created in his nonsense. The limerick protagonists are predominantly 'old persons', and Lear represents the author of *A Book of Nonsense* as 'an old Derry down Derry/Who loved to see little folks merry'. In fact in 1846, when Lear published *A Book of Nonsense,* he was only thirty-four. He was not an *old* Derry down Derry at all. But as a carnivalesque figure who promised mirth to children, like Old King Cole, Old Mother Hubbard or Old Mother Goose, Lear was placing himself within a tradition that *was* extremely old. As Vivien Noakes points out, Derry down Derry was 'one of the fools of the traditional English mummers' plays'.[23] It is worth considering this figure in more detail. Mummers' plays were a practice dating from at least the eighteenth century and probably linked to much older festivals and masques; they were traditionally staged at Christmastime by itinerant groups of actors who were not professional players but were drawn from the local community and were often raising funds for food and drink to celebrate the season. In the Buckinghamshire mummers' plays, 'Hey Down Derry' or 'Don Derry' has a particular function. He is the announcer of the performance whose arrival signals its beginning. He calls on the assembly to make room for the entertainment, sometimes also pretending to sweep bystanders back with a broom that he carries for this purpose.[24] In some versions he is the Fool, but in others he is Father Christmas.

It is apt, then, that Lear invokes this figure on the title page of his *Book of Nonsense*, leaping and dancing with the audience of children. He is announcing his own entertainment at its commencement, like the mummer of old. And it is specifically a Christmas entertainment—Lear's books of nonsense were published in December to catch the gift market. James Williams has very persuasively analysed the figure of the Fool in Lear, arguing that 'Like a court fool, albeit less under the whip than King Lear's, Edward Lear enjoyed the intimacy of the powerful: he had their goodwill and their permission to behave eccentrically and he could be assured of their pardon'.[25] This analysis invokes the traditional art of fooling as a role licensed by the patron, who employs a clown to break social rules in limited circumstances. However, I think we can also see Derry down Derry as a kind of Father Christmas, a nonprofessional actor who brings physical gifts and a wider gift of harmony and goodwill to all, especially to children. If Carroll in his homilies linked himself with Christ (the 'unseen Friend, who once on earth blessed little children'), Lear is, here, more like Father Christmas or Yule, who *is* seen, and whose jollity is permissive. Christmas was in this period becoming increasingly commercially and symbolically important as a family festival; the tree and the gifts and merriment around it symbolised the radiant social circle of abundance that Victorians wished to conjure. Where Carroll resembles a theatrical impresario, directing the action crisply from behind the curtain, Lear represents his role as that of an itinerant player, participating at the centre of an impromptu entertainment.

Lear's grasp of the traditional aspects of what he was doing is extremely important to the way that *A Book of Nonsense* presents itself as a volume that encloses a long, popular history of oral rhyming and theatrical playing for children within the modern textual format of large pictures and print. The old and the new cohere. The entertainer visible in the cartoon on the title page, with his receding hairline and pointy elf's nose, looks nothing like the thirty-something Lear, except that he favours checked trousers. His shirt ruffle is reminiscent of that of the old person of Brill who wears a frill like a fish. The essential thing about him is that he is jigging in the air amongst the children, offering his book as a shared fulcrum of pleasure. The caption reads, 'So he made them a Book, And with laughter they shook, At the fun of that Derry down Derry!'. It is noteworthy that Lear refers to his authorial alter ego as 'making' children a book. This book is a handcrafted object. Lear has 'made' it in a sense that only an artist-author can claim to do who has both written the text and drawn the illustrations. It has the hall-marks of a personal gift, even when sold in a commercial bookshop. Lear's persona as the dancing Derry down Derry is part of that gift. Lear places his alter ego in the midst of his nonsense not principally as an author in the commercial sense but as a figure for the emotional transaction, beyond words, that the season invites. He is the maker of jokes that make children physically jump and shout. This is a dance involving both partners in phys-ical exuberance. The pleasure of their relationship will be key to the kind of performative friendship that Lear as author offers. As Derry down Derry he becomes a character from rhyme and song, an itinerant entertainer whose

Fig. 5.9 William Collins, *Happy as a King* (c. 1836). A print of this picture hung on Lear's wall in San Remo

advent means merriment. Lear inhabited this role very successfully for the rest of his life. He borrowed a mantle from literature, street theatre and folklore to become an embodiment of the kind of traditional figure of fun who is also a figure *for* fun, an acted metaphor that exists out of time and beyond meaningful criticism. When we ask ourselves as modern scholars why Lear for so long received so little critical attention from the academic community, one reason is surely that his persona deflected it.

This Child: Impotence as Power

Lear throughout his life constantly depicted himself as older or younger than he was; sometimes he acted the part of an old man, a spindleshanks with a stick, sometimes the role of child. This is a significant manoeuvre. It makes him unthreatening. He removes himself from the field of sexual competition, marshalling instead the instinctive sympathy and protection that belong by right to the very old and very young. Lear makes us care for him. One of the ways he does this is through self-formation as a character who signals that he needs or deserves to be cared for. Lear inhabits the role of wayward child even in his own diary, which he left to his dear friend and executor Franklin Lushington, knowing that he would read it and possibly pass it on (as he did) to others.

In his diary for 6 March 1864 (when he was forty-one), Lear writes, 'O bad day! O bad boy. O bad!' This was a day that began with an epileptic fit with two seizures, marked with crosses in the journal. I think we can infer from his self-admonition that Lear had been masturbating and that he thought doing so had brought on his 'demon'. Although it is rare for orgasm to cause seizures, it can do so and Lear believed in the linkage. The frequency of apparent physical retribution for desire must have made Lear's sexual life fraught, to say the least. A few months later, he notes, 'certainly we fall. . . . And the dreary penalty comes on'. On another occasion, Lear reports that he 'went to church, where I sate like a good boy til 4'.[26] By infantilising himself he creates a self-soothing acknowledgement that being dubbed 'good' or 'bad' is childish—adults do not need to submit to that kind of simplistic judgement and punishment. However, within the irony and playacting is a genuine need to recall being a child. Lear frequently refers to himself in his diary as 'this child'.[27] In the journals of his Indian journey from November 1873, he writes, 'Alas for the folly of this child!' and 'I look for 9 more days besides this, and well if this child's brain holds out'.[28] Later he notes, 'A passing elephant, & with other costumes, people etc—amazement prevailed over this child'. Seeing himself as a child enables Lear vividly to experience his own wonder, with a child's-eye view of the amazing elephants. It also puts him in touch with a sense of his own mental fragility: his vulnerable brain may not survive the excesses to which it is subjected. Like a child, Lear often records his age including fractions—64½—as if he is proud of small increments in his own growth towards a never-to-be-complete maturity.

To Chichester Fortescue, Lear also describes himself as 'this child': 'Lord Ebury and co. are coming to this child's studio'.[29] Fortescue can be a fellow infant: 'O my child! here is a gnat! Which, the window being open, is but gnatural. So I shuts up both vinder and letter, and goodbye'.[30] Lear creates physical linkages between the text and his environment as he is writing that reinforce its sense of intimacy and nearness; if the letter is a window through which the gnat enters, it flutters magically out of it again at Fortescue's end. One thinks of Keats's comparably intimate letters and his poem 'This living hand', in which writing conjures the body's physical and emotional ability to reach out and clasp the reader. Closing one letter, Lear cries with open mouth, conjuring his trademark 'O': 'O child! write! I can't any more'.[31] In another, from 1848, he wails to Fortescue: 'if real art is a *student,* I know no more than a child—an infant—a foetus:—how could I—I have had myself to thank for all education—& a vortex of society hath eaten my time. . . .'[32] Remaining a child is Lear's bitter complaint and his warm defence: at thirty-six, he claims that as an artist he hasn't yet been born.

In January 1850, Lear reported to Fortescue that (at the age of forty-seven) he had been admitted to Sass's School of Art, the training school for the Royal Academy. His feelings about his success in gaining entry were mixed. There was genuine delight: the acceptance represented acknowledgement of his talents as fit for the elite professional status of recognised artist in the British Establishment. Yet he also knew that he was far too old to stay the ten-year course, and that this training should have come earlier in his life, if at all. Lear characteristically handles these complex feelings by ventriloquising the child, with wobbly handwriting that mimics that of a child just learning to write:

> I tried with 51—little boys:—& 19 of us were admitted. And now I go with a large book and a piece of chalk to school every day like a good little boy.[33]

The two self-caricatures in the letter are telling. In one, Lear, alongside some babies, is in an anatomy lesson sketching a skeleton, which seems to be reaching forward to touch him like Death in the Dance of Death, beckoning him to the grave. In the other cartoon, Lear is being bullied by children. He is chain-weeping and has his knees awkwardly drawn up to his chin in a characteristically defensive posture while they pelt him with stones, prod him with a stick and leap tauntingly before his easel. The threat of being a child amongst children, with all its remembered torments, is vividly present. But the mortal threat of old age also looms. Lear is in-between. He is a child, yet not a child. It's an uncomfortable position. Yet it is also where he needs to be. These cartoons are about a specific event in Lear's life, yet they also speak a broader truth about how he positions his cartoon persona: inhabiting aspects of childhood vision and experience while simultaneously trying to escape or resolve its attendant miseries. The happy figure of Derry Down Derry on the title page of the 1846 *Book of Nonsense*, with eight loving and responsive children dancing round him, is almost the mirror image of the cartoon Lear here, surrounded by ten cruel or unresponsive children. 'What fun!' he begins this letter. *Fun* can be a pleasant diversion, but it can also mean something cruel: 'a cheat, a hoax, a practical joke'. The idea of Lear being a 'little boy' again and going back to school (where he had experienced real cruelty as a real child) rides a fine line between these two senses of the word. Lear's childlike persona gains poignancy and energy from a conflict inherent in its origins, which were both joyfully playful and unhappily defensive. A letter to Lady Reid from Corfu in 1857 confided, 'I have been learning Greek like a good little boy—& I really wrote a note to Sir James with only *one* mistake in it. I wish I were as advanced as your little boy'.[34] He does, and he doesn't.

He wrote to Emily Tennyson in October 1856 about a recent spat with his closest male companion, Franklin Lushington. Emily knew and loved Frank too, so she understood the underlying difference in their temperaments well:

> The impetuosity of my nature . . . cannot always be controlled & we have had one or two sad antagonisms—tho we are perhaps better friends afterwards: but our natures are so different, & he is so changed since I first knew him, while I have remained so absurdly the same—(I mean, he has become 70—& I have stuck at 20 or any boy-age all through my life—) that I feel convinced we are best when not with each other.[35]

Fig. 5.10 **Lear self-caricature at Sass's Academy (1850)**

Lear was forty-four when he wrote this letter; Franklin Lushington was thirty-three. Lear portrays himself as a child whose development is arrested while that of his friends moves on around him. Lushington has fast-forwarded into old age, while Lear remains on hold. Rather than accomplishing a 'voyage' into maturity, he has remained stuck at a 'boy-age'. This is Lear's explanation for the growing emotional gulf between them. It's not his fault. Their differences arise from natural relativity. Despite the word 'stuck', one senses Lear's pleasure at 'remaining so absurdly the same'. Like Rip Van Winkle, a fictional character introduced to the public by Washington Irving in 1819, or J. M. Barrie's Peter Pan, who would not appear on the stage until 1904, Lear gets to stay young and spongetaneous compared with his retiring (in imagination pensionable) melancholy younger friend. Absurdity has its advantages.

In another important friendship, with the Pre-Raphaelite artist William Holman Hunt, Lear also reversed his older status vis-à-vis the younger man. Hunt, the younger by some fifteen years, is always 'Daddy', while Lear plays at being his son: 'my dear little big boy' as Hunt calls him. Lear's imagined family of Pre-Raphaelite artists had other members too, with Bob Martineau (fourteen years younger than Lear) becoming 'brother Bob' and Thomas Woolner (thirteen years younger than Lear) 'uncle Tom'. Naughtily, Sir John Everett Millais (seventeen years younger) was sometimes 'my dear aunt'.[36] This role play, with its surface oddity, was initiated by Lear but clearly served an underlying psychological need for Hunt as well. Hunt, who was still deeply angry with his father—who had failed to educate Hunt as a painter, forcing him to work as a clerk for many years—plays at being the stern paterfamilias who counsels his son to work hard and behave morally. As Hunt mock-proselytises, 'I am always deeply interested in the successes of my son. And this the more that it proves the cultivating of industrious and sober habits, qualities, which—as I have always endeavoured to impress upon you, are of the utmost importance in a struggle with the difficulties of the world'.[37] Lear, responding with baby language, addresses Hunt as 'Bluffed Pa' (beloved father, but also, perhaps, deceived father).[38] This is an intimate form of nonsense—one that testifies to the deep psychological truths that can be told when we stop speaking in the language of adulthood and allow ourselves to use phonetic approaches to difficult words, which originate in the nursery. Lear doesn't usually employ nonsense words in his letters to Hunt, which makes his insistence on Hunt being 'Daddy' the more striking. In another letter, Hunt is 'o mi dear par'. Lear gains a kind of parity through this inverse parenting. When referring to parents, Lear normally uses his own coinage, 'parient', which he also uses in 'apariently' (his version of *apparently*). Nonsense here draws attention to a likeness between two words that do not have the same etymological root. In Lear's emotional vocabulary, people who are apparently your parents often don't behave in a fatherly and motherly fashion, whereas people who are not apparently your parents can and do. *Aperient* is also a word for a laxative, a kind of drug that Lear frequently used to remove 'stoppages' in his 'boles'. This verbal linkage might further suggest that parients are people who make you need to go.

Lear needed to stay a child, in some fashion, so that others would look after him. His most desperate diary entries are those he recorded when he had been left alone. When his servant Giorgio left for his annual visit to Corfu, Lear was stricken, abandoned, wretched. If there was any delay in receiving letters, he constantly feared that his closest friends were dead. Loss always threatened to be permanent and devastating. 'Abscence' (Lear's customary spelling again) was an abcess that needed to be lanced. It felt like someone absconding. Representing himself as an egg or a caterpillar, Lear kept the idea of developmental loss as something that was always immanent and imminent but not happening right now. To Fortescue, he wrote, 'I wish I was an egg and going to be hatched'.[39] And in another letter, when all his furniture had been packed up prior to a removal, 'I shall sit upon an eggcup and eat my breakfast with a pen. . . .'[40] Lear in this image is a miniature figure, literally feeding from his quill. In a self-caricature for Evelyn Baring in 1864, Lear (with a bad cold) is hanging from the bough of a tree in a bag, with a bird looking at him in a perplexed fashion. He might be an egg in an improvised nest, or a pupating caterpillar.[41] In 1855 he wrote to Henry Bruce, disparaging his own achievements beside those of the remarkable 'Landskipper' G. F. Watts and curling up as a 'a disastrous old caterpillar'.[42] Watts was one of the most respected artists of the period, a 'landscaper' in a painterly sense and a captain of artistic industry. But a 'skipper' is also a kind of butterfly, and Lear plays significantly on the pun. Lear, as artistic caterpillar, is undeveloped by comparison with Watts. Yet the comment contains a fascinating paradox, for caterpillars by definition cannot be old.

In a letter to Laura Campbell of 1873, Lear signs himself 'Bombyx Major'.[43] *Bombyx mori* is the Latin name for the silkworm. So again Lear is being a caterpillar, a larva that is unattractive but has great economic and social value (much more so as a caterpillar than it would as a moth), spinning its defensive cocoon in silk that is harvested by humans to make the finest cloth. This is a nice allegory for Lear's work. Lear's combined asser-

Fig. 5.11 **Lear self-caricatures in letter to Tennyson (1864)**

tion of smallness and 'major' status is revealing. As is so often the case with him, the apparently self-deprecating manoeuvre is also assertive. To Fortescue he confides the rather explicit image of 'gradually oozing out all my intellectual topographic bowels as a silkworm doth its caterpillary silk'.[44] He closes his letter to Laura Campbell with a cartoon of his tiny, rotund figure, bouncing along bareback on a huge elephant—a prospective vision of himself in India. Lear produced several versions of this cartoon in letters to friends. They can be compared with his cartoon antics on horseback in the 1840s, emphasising the comedy of tiny Lear, resplendent but ridiculous, not in control of his enormous vehicle. In fact when he reached India, he studiously avoided riding on elephants—such bumpy rides threatened to trigger his epilepsy—but it was vital that his comic persona should ride one. Like Humpty Dumpty on his wall, the egg-like 'Adopty Duncle' Lear needed the possibility of a fall to fully express the precariousness of his life and art. His integrity and his fragility were oddly linked.[45] In his dining room at San Remo, Lear displayed a print of a painting by William Collins, *Happy as a King*, which shows children swinging on a gate. One of them has fallen, but the central little boy is poised in a moment of joy, with both arms raised.[46] Lear had known Collins in Rome, so the picture doubtless had personal associations. Yet it also seems to express Lear's delight in ephemeral states that paradoxically can be kept forever in the air. In an awkward letter to Tennyson, requesting 'a nautograph' for a friend, Lear depicts himself either flinging his arms up like the boy in *Happy as a King* (if Tennyson says yes), or curling up like a caterpillar (if he says no).[47] It is interesting that Lear's never-completed illustrations to Tennyson, a project that occupied over thirty years of his life, are repeatedly referred to by him as 'eggs', 'larvae' and 'caterpillars'. These images of semi-development, which he so frequently applied to his own person, suggest how near the Tennyson illustrations came to his own identity and how vital it was that they, too, were guaranteed a kind of immortality by never being finished.

In order to draw attention to himself in a way that is also self-deprecating, Lear makes himself small in his self-caricatures—smaller and rounder as

Fig. 5.12 **Lear self-caricature on an elephant (1873)**

time goes on. Indeed one can often guess the date of Lear's undated manuscripts by the form that his self-caricatures take. In the 1830s and 1840s he is a hapless string bean. In the 1850s, his cartoon self-image is in transition, with a beard but with proportions more like those of an ordinary adult male. By 1860 his caricature self has settled into the plum-pudding form readers now know best: with a Falstaffian spherical belly, small head (dominated by beard and spectacles) and thin, often stick-like legs that protrude like those of a beetle from its carapace or of a bird from its feathered body. Sometimes the tail of his coat accentuates this likeness to a bird or insect. Mostly Lear appears in the guise of birds, insects and molluscs, which are relatively self-effacing and whose genitals are not at all prominent. His harmlessness makes him easy for the viewer to adopt as a pet. His impotence is paradoxically empowering.

Lear often draws himself with his arm confidentially placed around the shoulders of another creature or with their arms linked as they sit or walk and talk together. In a letter of 1865 to Lady Duncan and her daughter, he is accompanying two frogs in this way; in a letter to Gussie Bethell of 1883 he is walking with a slug and a snail; in another letter his companion is a parrot and in a fourth a 'henbird' with whom he is sharing a nest in a tree.[48] He doesn't mean the slug and snail well—he is leading them from their depredations on his garden to 'expiate their greedy sins' by being drowned in the cistern. In this blackly comic *passeggiata,* he acts rather like Carroll's Walrus and Carpenter. But in the other pictures his friendly conversation is genuine. The fact that in these drawings he is smaller than slugs and frogs is delightful. Little creatures are his fellows. This suggests his inconsequence, his eccentricity and his accessibility, all at once. He is a strange creature but also a familiar one whose geniality extends to the least among us, on the same privileged level in our affectionate regard as animals and children. The frogs who visit him unexpectedly prove to be potential patrons: '[they] were as good as to add that had I any oil paintings they would have been glad to purchase one—but the damp of their abode would quite efface watercolor art'.[49] Lear's story is humorously self-effacing, but the idea of an amphibious patron who makes excuses for not buying also hints at the difficulties under which the artist labours.

In one note of 1864 to Evelyn Baring, an important friend and patron, Lear is a bespectacled bee smoking a pipe, with the message spiralling out from his tiny figure like the smoke from his pipe or the circular passage of his flight. In another note from the same year, Lear is a snail with horns

Fig. 5.13 Lear walking with a slug and a snail (1883)

Fig. 5.14 Lear with frogs (1865)

that are suspiciously like ass's ears. The message is again written in spiral fashion on the layers of Lear's shell.[50] These are quotidian messages written in passing, of the kind that would now be sent by email. The cartoons add value to them, as witnessed by the fact that Baring preserved them. Lear deftly pokes fun at himself and secures the survival of his manuscripts simultaneously. In 1872 he wrote Baring a receipt for ten pounds that his friend had given him for a drawing of 'the seeders [Cedars] of Lebanon'.[51] The receipt is a cartoon Lear-goose, on whose plump and foolish body the receipt is written. Lear shows his writing as emerging from his cartoon self or written on it, as if he *is* his body of work and the pound of flesh in the artistic transaction comes from his own heart. Financial transactions between friends are always a little awkward. Lear regularly presents his cartoon body—as we saw earlier in his 'sukycide' drawing for George Scrivens—as a compensatory item. On the one hand it draws attention to the way in which Lear's art literally 'gives of himself', emerging from considerable physical and mental effort; on the other hand, it disarms and sublimates all transactions, lifting them into the realm of gift, of which Lear's persona is an ineluctable part.

Through such manoeuvres, Lear becomes a character, even in his own eyes. In his diary for April 1877, Lear reported that his child-friend Arnold Congreve 'took off his hat to the Willoby Wat'—meaning himself.[52] A wallaby is a small kangaroo; they roamed the grounds of Knowsley, so Lear would have been very familiar with them. In a typically nimble leap of imagination, his wallaby wit produces a willoby wat, a creature who features (as the 'Willeby-wat') in 'Calico Pie' (1869) and in 'The Quangle Wangle's Hat'(1872). The name 'willoby wat'—which phonetically suggests 'will obey what?'—recalls Lear's impetuosity, his assertion that 'I weary of restraint ever'.[53] Like the Scroobious Pip, whose obstinate refusal to be parsed as bird, fish or beast asserts the power of opacity, or the Akhond of Swat (whose heir Lear jokingly claims to be in another letter), the willoby wat is a creature whose qualities remain creatively mysterious. Its name doesn't give much away.

Lear had narrowly escaped being named after his father, Jeremiah,[54] a biblical name linked to previsions of doom; he liked to use a variety of self-invented comically 'long names' for himself, chiefly to astonish and amuse children to whom he was introduced. One of these was Adebika Kratoponoko Prizzikalo Kattefello Ablegorabalus Ableborinto phasyph. Another was Chakonoton the Cozovex Dossi Fossi Sini Tomentilla Coronilla Polentilla Battledore & Shuttlecock Derry down Derry Dumps. As Vivien Noakes has pointed out, the first of these names derives partly from a

Fig. 5.15 **Lear as a snail (1864)**

Fig. 5.16 **Lear as a goose (1872)**

memory game, originating in the 1820s, called *Aldiborontiphoskyphornios-tikos: A Round Game for Merry Parties*, by R. Stennett. The game proceeds through the alphabet, asking participants to recite aloud a paragraph of narrative that actually derives from a burlesque opera in a volume of *Shakesperiana*. It is absurdly complicated and difficult to recall. For example:

> ELEPHANT peeping in, as Dicky Snip the Tailor read the proclamation of Chronohotonthologos, offering a thousand sequins for taking Bombardinian, Bashaw of three tails, who killed Aldiborontiphoskyphorniostikos.[55]

There were various similar memory games of the period. In *The Gaping, Wide-Mouthed Waddling Frog,* players were warned that those who stumbled and forgot their lines were subject to forfeits. These included 'submitting to be tickled by the company for five minutes and repeating correctly five times, Villy Vite and his vife vent a voyage to Vindsor and Vest Vickham, vor Vitsun Vensday'.[56] One wonders if, by making his long name a ridiculous memory game of this kind, Lear was opening the door to tickling and other pleasant forfeits for those children who recited it incorrectly. Certainly he was announcing himself as a mythic figure of rank—Chakonoton the Cozovex sounds like a king or a pharaoh—who is also a figure of fun. 'Cozovex' hints at *convex,* like Lear's rotund belly in his late cartoons. Each of his long names contains contradictory elements. *Kratos* is Greek for power and *kalo* for good. *Poneó* is the Greek verb 'to toil'. 'Kattefello', however, phonetically suggests 'caterpillar', which is one of the organisms with which Lear habitually associates himself and is scarcely a powerful creature. In the second long name, Lear's cat, Foss, is present, and there are several feminine elements. *Potentilla tomentilla* is a herbaceous shrub with small yellow flowers, as is *Coronilla,* also known as 'scorpion-vetch'. Derry down Derry is an entertainer. But 'dumps' means a state of depression. 'Battledore and shuttlecock' was an early version of badminton, a game in which players must keep a feather-light object aloft. Lear's long names contain the contradictory qualities he projected as part of his self-image: male and female, powerful and impotent, old and young, playful and sad.

Names are usually given to us at birth. They proclaim our lineage. Lear's names suggest that his authority derives not from his family but from language, which is infinitely malleable; selfhood becomes a matter of choice and of play. We can glimpse the power dynamics involved in choosing one's mode of address in a letter Lear wrote to Evelyn Baring, in which he addressed Baring as Thrippsy Pillivinx and signed himself Slushypipp.[57] This may appear to be nonsense 'pure and simple', and doubtless Baring took it as such. But *pilliwinks* is a real word. It is an ancient instrument of torture. Lear likely absorbed it from the novels of Scott, or from Lecky's *History of Rationalism,* both of which he read avidly. *Thrips* are parasites, *tipsy* is drunk and *pilliwinks* is a thumbscrew. These are not things one can associate with one's patron outside of a nonsense letter. *Slushypipp,* meanwhile, is affectionately foolish, but it also suggests the pip of a fruit—something on its way to becoming something bigger. One thinks of the Scroobious Pip, Lear's nonsense creature who refuses to be categorised. These nonsense monikers subtly tip the balance of power in Lear's favour.

Even when Lear sent photographs of himself, which might seem the most concrete and inarguable material evidence of his visual identity, he managed to suggest the performativity of self. To Mrs Ford in 1865, he writes:

> I send you 2 photographs for your collection;—one, (the most professional,) was done this winter: the other (the head,) some time back: it is said by my friends to be a mixture of Socrates, Sir John Falstaff & Sancho Panza, & has an air prelusive of apoplexy.[58]

Lear in this analysis is a mixture of a classical philosopher of ethics; a roguish, fat old Shakespearean knight; and the illiterate but practical peasant sidekick to Don Quixote. Lear represents himself (through others' eyes) as a combination of real and fictional figures, aristocrat and peasant, tragic and comic, scholarly and foolish. One might say of Lear, as Hazlitt does of Falstaff, 'he is an actor in himself almost as much as upon the stage'.[59] The 'air prelusive of apoplexy' is a nice touch; Lear in his photograph looks furious, as if he is about to have a conniption. But appearances can be deceptive. Lear conveys his image in a way that simultaneously invites and preempts interpretation because he presents himself as a fictional character and an author simultaneously. In this instance, Lear's character comprises a mixture of other characters who themselves have representative qualities and combine eccentricity with universality. As Falstaff says of himself, 'Banish plump Jack, and banish all the world'.

Lear knew that his books, particularly his travel books, traded on the character 'Edward Lear' to amuse their audience. In 1885, he told fellow travel writer Amelia Edwards that he would give her a portion of his Egyptian diaries to read, with a view to possible publication:

> But I much fear your judgement—however it may approve of the illustrations—may not do so of the descriptive accompaniment. You see, there is & must be a great drawback in *My* writing which yours on a similar subject would not have:—& this is, that whatever *I* write would be Edward Lear—egotistical & unmitigated—fanciful—individual—

correct or what not—but nevertheless always *Edward Lear:*—
whereas what *you* write might be written by Mrs Tompkins, or
Queen Boadicea, or Lady Jane Grey, or Rizpah of Gileah, Joan
of Arc or anybody else—because 'A. B. Edwards' never appears
at all & don't claim—personally—a grain of sympathy.[60]

In this unusual and telling letter, Lear reveals that he is aware that his
writing is identified with his persona: it is *Edward Lear*. The character and
the writing may be 'fanciful' and 'egotistical', and even incorrect. But if his
words entertain, it is because *Edward Lear* is entertaining. By contrast, A. B.
Edwards does not appear as a character in her travelogues, to claim the reader's personal sympathy. Lear is rather rude in suggesting that Amelia Edwards's travel narratives (which he elsewhere admires) could be written by
any one of several historical women. Edwards was an intrepid and learned
explorer who had studied Egyptian hieroglyphs and history and whose cre-
dentials for writing her own Egyptian travelogue, *1000 Miles Up the Nile*,
included being part of a team who had made a major archaeological find at
Abu Simbel. Lear confessed in another letter to the patient Miss Edwards
that he persisted 'in believing that Queen Anne, Charles I—Edward 6—
Henry the 3rd & Egbert & Arthur, all lived in one simultaneous & sublime society & drank tea together in . . . Tumbridge Wells'.[61] He sometimes
proclaimed that he corresponded with 'every created human being capable
of writing since the invention of letters, except 'the prophet Ezekiel, Mary
Queen of Scots, and the Venerable Bede'.[62] To Lear, all history is basically
one long, ongoing, personal conversation.

His analysis of his relationship with living readers is shrewd. His journals are 'parts' of 'my ridiculous life', and 'numerous & minute as are the
hourly notices of my voyage—any cutting away or alteration would (to my
fancy) spoil all—& certainly destroy the Edward Learical nature of the
Diary'.[63] *Lyrical* is a word usually applied to poetry that directly expresses
the poet's own thoughts and sentiments. Here 'Learical' has a complex force.
It invokes the personal directness of lyricism, but also an inescapable self-
consciousness in which diarising and even living are inevitably forms of performance, to be retailed later for its ridiculous charm. The 'minuteness' of
Lear's writing is so essential to its character that to cut episodes would be
to destroy it; its failings and its attractions are indivisible. By 'minute', Lear
means 'detailed', but there is an accompanying sense of Lear's smallness that

Fig. 5.17 **Lear with a hive over his head (1885)**

makes his travel memoirs, as he explains to Edwards, perhaps not 'worth the 99th part of a grasshopper's eyelash,—but they might be so if considered as a part of this child's art life'.[64] The handwriting makes it hard to decipher whether Lear is saying 'art life' or 'ard life'. Perhaps its art lies in its vicissitudes. Lear tells Edwards that as a self-imposed penance for approaching her about publishing his Egyptian diaries, he will wear on his head 'a very large basket—formerly a beehive at dear old Mr Bell's at Selborne', and will sit on the terrace for an hour and a half: a comic self-effacement he illustrates. A modern reader can't help but be struck by the similarity of Edward Lear in this cartoon to the tubby, genial figure of Edward Bear (better known as Winnie-the-Pooh) in E. H. Shepard's drawing of him with a Hunnypot stuck on his head. In A. A. Milnes's children's books, it is Christopher Robin who occupies the role of the child within Hundred Acre Wood, just as Alice does in Wonderland. By contrast, Lear plays the role of child in his correspondence, using strategies to appear small and absurd that simultaneously win the reader over to a position of sympathetic identification where no portion of his writing can be cut without implicit injury to its author.

Call and Response: Correspondence and Role Play

As other commentators have observed, it is notable how often Lear's nonsense is contained within letters.[65] Like Keats's poems, many of Lear's best-known nonsense verses and stories are originally disseminated within epistles to particular recipients. They are gifts in circulation, which in their internal dialogue recall and celebrate the bandying involved in correspondence and the opportunities it offers for mutual role play.

Nonsense, indeed, is a game in which the reader is invited to take an active part. I was reminded of this when I was lucky enough in the course of my research to come across (in a suitcase in a Welsh garage) the lost half of a correspondence between Lear and the schoolmaster Edward Carus Selwyn, a friend Lear made late in life. Lear wrote nonsense for Selwyn. But Selwyn also wrote nonsense back, inventing illnesses— 'asthmotyphoidodyspnea'—and making a charming suggestion about Lear's home:

> How can you sell *a part of* Villa Tennyson? Will you begin at
> the roof and chimneys, or will you sell it for part of the year?
> Or will you sell the outside & retain the inside? I think the
> last is the best plan.[66]

These letters also discuss politics, literature and work and family concerns. They code-switch easily from nonsensical language and ideas to other literary registers. When Lear wrote nonsense in his letters to adult friends, he was inviting them to playact. To Henry Bruce, a Member of Parliament, he wrote with mock outrage, claiming to disbelieve that Bruce (absent on his last visit) had ever been in Corsica:

> I feel that therefore from this time a great Gulfscream stream
> steam dream—(I may say—bream)—rolls between us. One
> more chance remains for you. On the bustings (I would say
> Hustings) I shall examine you with the following parrotgraph,
> eggstracts from a work on Corsica I am writing: 'The sun,
> hidden by a cloud, lighted up the depths of the tops of the
> bottoms of the heights of the Corsican pinewoods. On their
> loftiest branches the sky blue moufflon was perched—pouring
> forth his plaintive but promethean warblings . . .' If you can
> describe the creatures eluded to in these words—well & good.[67]

Lear's evocation of the 'Gulfscream' of distance that separates him from Bruce is in fact a practical manifestation of its opposite: intimacy. Sheep don't fly, and Bruce is not really in the doghouse. But if he wishes to join in Lear's creative fantasy, the initial lines have been drawn for him to follow. Just as the rhymes of this nonsense letter roll forward, free associating from *stream* to *bream*, the ideas relating to birds (parrotgraph, eggstract, warbling) fly off at an angle, suggesting the way that written language can become oral, just as imaginary cerulean sheep can take to the air. Lear's nonsense is a form of blue-sky thinking that wants to go live.

Often Lear's games were live as well as epistolary. Lear liked to play at riddles and at 'epitaphs'. Helpfully, he gives us an example of one of these in his diary for 1887: 'Below these high cathedral stairs / Lie the remains of Agnes Pears. / Her name was Wiggs; it was not Pears, / But Pears was put to rhyme with tears'.[68] On this occasion it was Lord Northbrook and Lady Emma Baring who were participating in impromptu versification; 'fits of laughter' ensued. Death is supposed to be solemn, but the epitaph, which is not very different from a limerick, allows a person to be summarised in a way that explores the fiction of social identity.

Lear's poem 'The Akond of Swat', which revels in the opacity of identity, is a good example of the way in which his nonsense both emerges from social dialogue and generates it. Lear saw an item in the *Times of India* in July 1873 claiming that the akhoond (a high-ranking cleric and emir of an Indian province) had quarrelled with his son, who had left 'the parental presence . . . refusing to listen to the akhoond's orders to come back'. This oedipal rebellion inspired Lear to wonder who or 'why, or when, or which, or what' the Akond of Swat really was.

> Do his people like him extremely well?
> Or do they, whenever they can, rebel   or PLOT,
>   At the Akond of Swat?
>
> If he catches them then, either old or young,
> Does he have them chopped in pieces or hung   or SHOT,
>   The Akond of Swat?
>
> . . .
>
> Does he study the wants of his own dominion
> Or doesn't he care for public opinion   a JOT,
>   The Akond of Swat?[69]

Fig. 5.18 **Photograph of Lear (1862)**

Lear sent this 'call and response' poem in a letter to Chichester Fortescue.[70] When he finally published it in *Laughable Lyrics,* he did so with the explicit instruction that the monosyllabic rhymes 'ought to be shouted out by a chorus'. Lear had noted that little Janet Symonds liked to shout the last words of his nonsense songs.[71] Here he invites readers, old and young, to join in and act out—as if the left-hand passages are the riddle and the right-hand passages the rejoinder. Or one might think of the dialogue musically, as fast arpeggios for the left hand, which are answered on the right hand with a loud and violent chord.

Suggestively, the Akond, like so many of Lear's little kings and tyrants, has the imagined qualities of both a child and an adult. He may chop his subjects in pieces, or he may suddenly 'scream and wake' in the night and be brought a 'few small cakes'. Lear, as he does in 'The Scroobious Pip', uses the mystery of unfamiliar words to explore both the ultimate unreadability of the self and the coexistence of infantile and mature urges in adult psychology. In voicing and answering the queries—loudly, even rudely—an inner conflict that in private may be painful is temporarily resolved. Like the mysterious Akond, we contain the possibility of social and anti-social, ungovernable impulses. Precisely what we are escapes us. That is one of the reasons we need nonsense, which under its supposed blanket of absurdity offers us an opportunity to give ourselves away.

LEAR'S SELF-INVENTION IN VERSE

Lear's nonsense persona is also co-created through letters and the poems they contain. A good example of this is the 'Growling Eclogue' of December 1867, which Lear wrote for John Addison Symonds and his wife, Catherine. Lear had known Catherine since babyhood. The poem is in the form of an imagined dialogue between Edwardus (Lear) and Johannes (Symonds), who voice competing complaints. An eclogue in classical literature is a singing contest between shepherds. Often they vie to celebrate their love for a shepherdess and to extol the delights of Nature in the spring. Lear's eclogue is ironic on at least three counts: the competitors are not shepherds but writers; the season is winter; and they are griping rather than piping. This literary formation takes us right back to Lear's boyhood when he composed an eclogue in imitation of William Collins, a thinly-veiled complaint to his parents about leaving Bowman's Lodge for the miseries of town.

As he does in so many letters to friends, Lear makes a tour de force of moaning. The two singers growl in Augustan rhyming couplets that evoke unpleasant sounds and interruptions (German bands, mosquitoes, a draught from a cracked window). The pleasure of the piece lies in this teasing contrast between the harmony of classical poetry and the discordant prose of life. A duelling duet ensues.

E.— Why must I sneeze and snuffle, groan and cough,
    If my hat's on my head, or if it's off?
    Why must I sink all poetry in this prose,
    The everlasting blowing of my nose?

J.— When I walk out the mud my footsteps clogs,
    Besides, I suffer from attacks of dogs.

E.— Me a vast awful bulldog, black and brown,
    Completely terrified when near the town;
    As calves, perceiving butchers, trembling reel,
    So did my calves the approaching monster feel.

J.— Already from two rooms we're driven away,
    Because the beastly chimneys smoke all day:
    Is this a trifle, say? Is this a joke?
    That we, like hams, should be becooked in smoke?

. . .

E.— Alas! I needs must go and call on swells,
    That they may say, 'Pray draw me the Estrelles'.
    On one I went last week to leave a card,
    The swell was out—the servant eyed me hard:
    'This chap's a thief disguised', his face expressed:
    If I go there again, may I be blest![72]

As in so many of Lear's works, dialogue is at the heart of this poem's invitation to participate in its verbal game of battledore and shuttlecock. Lear includes thirty-two questions and alludes to twenty different voices or sources of noise, evoking the orchestral effects of musical theatre. Some might hesitate to call it a nonsense poem (there are no invented words, and it takes place within the 'real' world), but it shares with his other nonsenses a love of punning, of performance and of evoking sounds—'Last week I called aloud, O!O!O!O!'—that assert the emotional primacy of noise. The human voice as an instrument is not limited to language; it originates as a 'call' of displeasure and desire for attention, a cry, a growl. Lear builds the idea of call and response into the poem as well as the letter that encloses it, creating a double structure of sympathy and judgement as in the dramatic monologues so popular in the period. The poem involves both an internal audience (Catherine) and an external audience (the couple, their friends and family and eventually the wider circle of possible readers).

Lear establishes his comic persona through work of this kind, in which he is pictured as both a subjective speaker and an objectively viewed character. To the bulldog, Edwardus is merely an object, a set of edible 'calves', just as Johannes in the following stanza resembles a smoked 'ham'. In Lear's early epistolary poems he constantly compared himself with foodstuffs: a nervously warm curry, milk, a boiled pig. Here he returns to the idea of nervousness about being eaten, a comic victim of others' appetites. These appetites are aesthetic as well as literal. Lear often referred to himself as a 'damned dirty landscape-painter', a wounding comment made by two young Englishmen that he overheard in Calabria in 1847, whose power to upset him he overturned by making it a running joke. The 'Growling Eclogue' pokes fun at the thoughtless 'swells' (aristocrats) who nearly flatten Edwardus with their carriages while commanding his services as if the subjects depicted were more important than Lear's artistic treatment: 'Pray draw me the Estrelles'. This poem reinforces the class status of Edwardus as an artist who is not a servant, or a thief, or a bone for others' dogs to gnaw. But it does so in a self-deprecating manner, imagining Catherine Symonds judging Edwardus to be a 'bore', his complaints 'fudge' and condemning him to continue the existence he deplores:

> To make large drawings nobody will buy—
> To paint oil pictures which will never dry—
> To write new books which nobody will read—
> To drink weak tea, on tough old pigs to feed—

The poem combines lightness with learnedness. Lear is channelling memories of Alexander Pope, whose heroic couplets were standard educational fare for Regency schoolboys. Classical inversion and apostrophe combine with familiar, slangy lexis (chap, cove, swells). Catherine's judgement is similar to that of Clarissa in Pope's *The Rape of the Lock,* a gift poem that also circulated privately prior to its publication. Lear alludes to Augustan literary culture in this 'dispute poem' as well as to Augustan language and metrical structure.

Again he reinforces a double picture of himself to his friends, as someone who is highly capable, classically educated, witty—yet also needy, irritable, on occasion dull. His paintings and books are not successful in market terms. The natural rejoinder is to buy his pictures and read his books. When Lear circulates this kind of comic self-portrait he does so knowingly, binding himself to his audience with ties of mutual recognition and sympathy. The 'Growling Eclogue' found its way through private hands to Chichester Fortescue and his wife, Lady Waldegrave, whose social connections were wide and powerful. Lear's self-created persona was designed to be disseminated in this way in the gift economy, inspiring laughter and sympathy that might produce sales and commissions. Lear sends mixed signals. He needs 'tin', but if we regard our relationship with him as solely a financial transaction, we are part of the problem, behaving like the 'swells' who crush him beneath their chariot wheels. Our exchange needs instead to be framed, like the poem, within the context of conversation, of gift, of appreciative understanding. Edwardus solicits the reader's sympathetic friendship by emphasising his 'griefs' but also admits that his moaning may be judged, as Catherine in the poem judges it, to be groundless. His perceived competency and deficits are so intertwined as to be inseparable in a self-critical vision that presents his neediness as part of the gift.

Lear's most famous picture poem or song, 'The Owl and the Pussy-cat', was written around a week after the 'Growling Eclogue'. The 'Growling Eclogue' was not published until 1894, whereas 'The Owl and the Pussy-cat' became the leading work in *Nonsense Songs, Stories, Botany and Alphabets* (1871). But both were written in an identical context, evoking the ongoing spoken and written dialogue between Lear and John and Catherine Symonds. It should therefore, perhaps, not surprise us that the perfect happiness of the Owl and Pussy-cat conjured in the final lines of the poem should have been open—in Lear's mind at least—to a tragicomic sequel. In a letter of 1884 to Violet, the sister of Mrs James Cameron Grant, Lear explained that the Owl had long been a widower and that 'the Pussy I now have is the maternal Uncle of the original Pussy who went to the Bongtree Land'. He explains that the Pussy-cat died at New Guinea, after being troubled by savages and swallowing a document whose discovery would have led to 'acrostic results'. Whereat 'she fell off the tree and instantly perspired & became a Copse'. But he mentions that there are 'other accounts of the death of the Pussy-cat which are quite different from what I have belated above'.[73] She may alternatively have died from sucking a poisonous Broomhandle. Lear's imaginary endings to the Owl and Pussy-cat's tale smack of classical history combined with Jacobean tragedy in a comic cook-up of what he elsewhere calls 'authentic sauces',[74] worthy of *1066 and All That*. All history, being both belated and related, is inherently subject to revision. This letter demonstrates the way in which Lear conflates his own history (his actual cat) with that of his nonsense characters, but also the way that the field of his writing remains open to new and surprising developments. Wilkie Collins asked for a sequel to 'Mr and Mrs Discobbolos', and Lear similarly reversed the happy ending in part one of the poem. Because Lear's poems arise in the context of ongoing epistolary and actual conversation, they have a life in which readers continue to have a voice. Lear's poetry responds to others' questions and requests; it is like a live tree that can always form a new bud or branch.

Lear's persona was also created in dialogue. His two most famous poems that seem to be 'about' himself were produced in the context of playful repartee with friends. We must therefore be careful as critics in dealing with these pieces: they are less confessional and more performative than they might at first appear. The first was composed with Miss Bevan, the daughter of his friend William Bevan, who became British vice-consul at San Remo. Miss Bevan wrote poetry herself. She sent some to Lear in January 1879; he reported in his diary, 'very pretty copy of verses from Miss Bevan, very funny & nice'.[75] It was she who supplied the title line, 'How Pleasant to Know Mr Lear!', supposedly a comment she had overheard socially. The inverted commas within this poem are important. Lear is responding to an anonymous third person with a poem or song in the third person. The layers of irony are multiple.

Although Lear's comic style infuses the whole, we do not know how much Miss Bevan may have thrown into the mix. In his diary for 9 April 1879 Lear recorded, 'wrote out my and Miss Bevans verses of "How Pleasant to know Mr Lear"', which may imply that each of them worked on particular verses. It certainly suggests that Miss Bevan did more than supply the title.

Lear wrote to the Bevans that their ditty could be sung to the tune of Thomas Arne's 'How Cheerful along the Gay Mead'.[76] So the poem can also be read against Arne's 'Hymn of Eve' for the religious oratorio *Abel*, which concludes:

> Thee, Lord, who such wonders canst raise,
> And still canst destroy with a nod,
> My Lips shall incessantly praise,
> My Soul shall be wrapt in my God.[77] ♬

Knowing that Lear's words may be sung to this tune might alter how we view the rhyme between 'Lear' and 'queer' in Lear's first verse: it seems more provocative as a twist on the rhymes 'appear' and 'year' in Arne's religious paean by Eve in Eden. This is not a hymn of incessant praise, and its subject is far from God-like. It is a celebration of a character whose every quality is ambiguously delightful and repulsive. The movement of the verse allows for a setup followed by an undercutting riposte, as if the first couple of lines were spoken by Laurel and the second by Hardy. Dialogue and doubleness are part of the makeup of this self-consciously ironised tribute:

> 'How pleasant to know Mr Lear!'
>   Who has written such volumes of stuff!
> Some think him ill-tempered and queer,
>   But a few think him pleasant enough.
>
> His mind is concrete and fastidious;—
>   His nose is remarkably big;—
> His visage is more or less hideous;—
>   His beard it resembles a wig.
>
> He has ears, and two eyes, and ten fingers,—
>   (Leastways if you reckon two thumbs;)
> Long ago he was one of the singers,
>   But now he is one of the dumms.[78]

'"How Pleasant to Know Mr Lear!"' is full of words whose meaning is equivocal. *Pleasant* can mean 'pleasing' in a positive but weak sense—

♬ Listen to musical link #12 at edwardlearsmusic.com/audiotrail/#howpleasanttoknow 'moderately enjoyable'—but also 'ridiculous and peculiar'. A *pleasant* was once a name for a jester, somebody who amused others professionally by behaving absurdly. Lear is painting himself once more as a clown whose private life constitutes a public performance of absurdity. The ditty goes on to describe Lear's activities in terms that are equally on the edge. He has written 'such volumes of stuff'; again *stuff* can simply mean 'matter or substance of composition', but it also disparagingly means 'worthless ideas, rubbish', a sense of the word retained in the expression 'stuff and nonsense'. The line implies that all Lear's writing may be nonsense, whether he intends it as such or not. The fact that Arne's tune makes us sing 'stu-uff' and 'quee-er' over two beats gives more of a jeer to 'Lee-ar'. The author clearly isn't 'dumb', since he has composed this mocking encomium, yet he is also a character in a silent movie within it, miming with his ears, his eyes, his hands. His behaviour is simultaneously reticent and obtrusive. We teeter on the brink between laughing *with* Lear and laughing *at* him. In fact the doubleness of the verse, which conjures the first and third person perspective simultaneously, brilliantly requires that we do both.

The poem announces that 'His body is perfectly spherical;—/ he weareth a runcible hat'. G. K. Chesterton commented on this line that 'We accept him as a purely fabulous figure, on his own description of himself'.[79] The image conjures Lear's visual cartoons, in which his body is round and his legs stick out of it like needles out of a ball of yarn. It isn't accurate. Lear was not especially handsome by the standards of his period, but—as photographs reveal—he was not an ugly man either. In late middle age he put on some weight, but he remained tall for his era and remarkably fit. The tiny spherical Lear who wears 'a runcible hat' is a figment of nonsense. The persona is invested with many of the same attributes that Lear possessed in reality (a cat called Foss, the ability to read Spanish), but it is not identical with him. This makes it problematic when the poem tells us:

> He weeps by the side of the ocean,
>   He weeps on the top of the hill;
> He purchases pancakes and lotion,
>   And chocolate shrimps from the mill.

The final line of this verse seems fantastical. The third line is suspect. What then of the first and second? Should we believe in Mr Lear's tears? By placing the emotive portrait of 'Mr Lear weeping' within a frame of chocolate shrimps, Lear invites us to consider his grief as nonsensical (perhaps a weakness, perhaps a fiction). Yet it touches us for all that. Perhaps because grief itself *is* unreasonable and excessive, its conjunction with the ludicrous here intensifies its power. Normally one would expect 'walks' or 'sits' or 'waits' by the side of the ocean; the odd verb constitutes an emotional ambush. Lear's tragicomic persona repeatedly waylays the reader like this. Paradoxically he conjures the feeling of intimacy through the performance of a character who is separated by silence, loneliness, queerness and misinterpretation. However, his knowing, ironic self-portrait, with its jaunty tune, throws doubt on whether, and in what way, we can know Lear at all. As Lear commented in his diary after a friend's suicide, 'how little of the inner life is known'.[80] The invitation to know Lear provided by his comic writing and illustration is always equivocal.

'Some Incidents in the Life of My Uncle Arly' is a different kind of poem, more obviously nonsensical. Lear worked on it through various drafts and sent copies to friends. As Thomas Byrom was the first to note, 'Uncle Arly' is a pulled-apart version of the word 'Unclearly'; it also contains the name 'Lear'. So the poem is a little like Elgar's *Enigma Variations:* it contains clues that relate it to the author, yet it also announces its enigmatic status. It refuses to be clear.

> O my agèd Uncle Arly!—
> Sitting on a heap of Barley
>   All the silent hours of night,—
> Close beside a leafy thicket:—
> On his nose there was a Cricket,—
> In his hat a Railway Ticket;—
>   (But his shoes were far too tight.)

> Long ago, in youth, he squander'd
> All his goods away, and wander'd
>   To the Timskoop Hills afar.
> There, on golden sunsets blazing
> Every evening found him gazing,—
> Singing,—'Orb! You're quite amazing!
>   How I wonder what you are!'

> Like the ancient Medes and Persians,
> Always by his own exertions
>   He subsisted on those hills;—
> Whiles,—by teaching children spelling,—
> Or at times by merely yelling,—
> Or at intervals by selling
>   'Propter's Nicodemus Pills'.[81]

Lear's richly associative magpie mind took scraps from many different sources and wove them into the nest of nonsense. Procter's pills and ointments were ubiquitous in the mid-nineteenth century, advertised in national and regional newspapers. They were said to cure scurvy, itch, old wounds, bad legs, scald head, ringworms etc. Among them were Procter's Mild Aperient Family Pills, laxatives designed to relieve biliousness and indigestion.[82] Dr Nicodemus Pills is the name of a character whom Lear likely read about in the newspaper. He was reported in 1866 to be the 'bosom friend' of Doncaster town councillor and letting agent Cotnam Townsend, who was shockingly convicted at Leeds assizes of having let out a lady's house during the week of Doncaster horse races, supposedly to a respectable gentleman and his wife, but in fact as a brothel to serve racegoers during the holiday. Dr Nicodemus Pills bailed out Townsend financially.[83] One suspects that he was one of the shady beneficiaries of Townsend's racket. Like a dream, the nonsense poem allows us to see associations (Procter's pills / Dr Nicodemus Pills) that may be accidental, bits of similar-coloured fluff whirling in the mind's washtub, but may also be meaningful—depending on how we consider them.

'Some Incidents in the Life of My Uncle Arly', indeed, in its quiet way, seems to be a meditation on whether a little life has meaning. There is an indefinable pathos about a man whose struggles, like his tight shoes, are so parenthetical as to be practically invisible to others. Uncle Arly scrapes a living; he is joined by a cricket who becomes his companion; he sings; he yells; he dies. The 'little heap of Barley' on which he sits at the beginning and end of the poem recalls Lady Jingly's 'little heap of stones' in 'The Courtship of the Yonghy-Bonghy-Bò'. Uncle Arly's small and edible cairn is an apt marker of his unremarkable life. The lightness and transience of the three things he carries—a cricket, a hat and a railway ticket—also suggest the ephemerality of his passing. Yet, importantly, the cricket is also associated with immortality, through the Greek legend of Tithonus, who was transformed by the gods into a cricket when he asked to live forever. 'Tithonus' was one of Lear's favourites among Tennyson's poems. Emily Tennyson in a letter of 1858 urged Lear to 'be merry as a cricket henceforward & for ever'.[84] Dickens's popular novel *The Cricket on the Hearth* had also associated this creature in the Victorian mind with constancy and fidelity. Lear's poem explores the possibility of not mattering or meaning at all—and living forever—as realities that may be equally true. The relationship between being immortal and ephemeral, being remarkable and unremarkable, yelling and being silent, is at the heart of this odd little nonsense eulogy.

> Later, in his morning rambles
> He perceived the moving brambles
>   Something square and white disclose;—
> 'Twas a First-class Railway Ticket
> But in stopping down to pick it
> Off the ground,—a pea-green Cricket
>   Settled on my uncle's Nose
>
> Never—never more,—oh! never,
> Did that Cricket leave him ever,—
>   Dawn or evening, day or night;—
> Clinging as a constant treasure,—
> Chirping with a cheerious measure,—
> Wholly to my uncle's pleasure,—
>   (Though his shoes were far too tight.)
>
> So for three-and-forty winters,
> Till his shoes were worn to splinters,
>   All those hills he wander'd o'er,—
> Sometimes silent;—sometimes yelling;—
> Till he came to Borly-Melling,
> Near his old ancestral dwelling;—
>   —And he wander'd thence no more.

Vivien Noakes has described the poem as Lear's 'obituary', and certainly Lear identified with Arly in important respects,[85] but its relationship to the events of his life is not straightforward. Lear did not squander money as a young man—quite the reverse. His father's bankruptcy made him even in his twenties determined to save money and avoid debt. He did not as far as we know ever sell medications. The figure in Lear's cartoon of Uncle Arly is neither bearded nor bespectacled, as Lear's self-caricature at this period always is. Noakes takes the 'First-class Railway Ticket' that Arly finds in the brambles to mean Lear's patronage by the Earl of Derby, which was his ticket into high society. It may be so. However, at least one of the readers to whom Lear sent the poem, Edward Carus Selwyn, humorously suggested that the ticket was a warning against the temptations of travelling first class: 'Uncle Arly: who by the way strikes me as a prophecy in himself of what we shall come to, if we live to such an age. The excessive love of first-class railway tickets is what I am always preaching against, in vain'.[86]

So many of the references in this poem relate to more than one source that we shouldn't be too single-minded in our interpretation of the clues it furnishes. For example, as others have noticed, Borly-Melling is a near-anagram of 'merely boring'. But Melling is also a real place near Liverpool. These associations coexist. Similarly, the line 'Never—never more,—oh! never' recalls both Edgar Allan Poe's famous poem 'The Raven', which Lear quotes in his diary for 1871,[87] and Shelley's 'A Lament':

> O World! O life! O time!
> On whose last steps I climb,
>   Trembling at that where I had stood before;
> When will return the glory of your prime?
>   No more—Oh, never more!
>
> Out of the day and night
> A joy has taken flight;
>   Fresh spring, and summer, and winter hoar,
> Move my faint heart with grief, but with delight
>   No more—Oh, never more![88]

Lear set Shelley's poem to music, and he quotes it repeatedly in his diary. Its phrases were among his habitual expressions when reacting to feelings of loss. 'No more' and 'never more' resound through Lear's nonsense poems, from 'The New Vestments' to 'The Two Old Bachelors', embodying a self-contradictory loop where echoing repetition announces the inevitability of ending. Yet 'Uncle Arly' is not merely sad. In mentioning the Medes and Persians, Lear may well have been thinking of Cyrus, the ruler who united these peoples, and whose epitaph according to Xenophon and Plutarch ran, 'know that I am Cyrus the son of Cambyses who settled the Persian Empire, and ruled over Asia, therefore envy me not this little heap of earth. . . .'[89] Little heaps can be the monuments of great kings.

Lear worked on this poem occasionally between 1873, when he intended it as a gift for Lady Emma Baring, and 1886, when he revised it and issued it as 'the last Nonsense poem I shall ever write', sending fair copies to twelve friends, almost as if he were distributing locks of his hair to those who would mourn his passing.[90] It is thus personal and has pathos by association. One thinks of Christ breaking bread for the twelve disciples, saying 'this is my body; which is broken for you: this do in remembrance of me'. Yet one must also remember that the poem did not begin as 'last words' and that, even in 1886, Lear entertained different possible ideas for it, considering an ending in which Uncle Arly is borne aloft by the birds which he has fed through times of scarcity. That image of a man flying with birds is similar to Lear's comic self-portraits of 1842 and 1860, where he is swept away in a high wind to join the jackdaws.

Just as Uncle Arly is both a distinct personage and an adverb for what is indistinct—*unclearly*—the poem allows us the feeling of having been told something important and told nothing much at all. This is the secret of many of Lear's communications. Their very lightness, their apparent refusal to carry content, suggests its opposite. Unspoken emotion gathers in the space his 'nonsense' creates for thinking about what we might discover (like Uncle Arly) when we allow ourselves 'rambles' that don't apparently have any significance. Arly's forty-three years of wandering, 'sometimes silent;—sometimes yelling', recall Thoreau's dictum that 'the mass of men lead lives of quiet desperation'; but the cricket's 'cheerious measure', echoed in that of the poem, is altogether less bleak. Here, the theme of the poem— is a small, fugitive and frustrating life meaningful?—becomes also the question its nonsense method poses. The answer is yes, and no. In associating himself with Arly, Lear simultaneously proclaims his own insignificance and how much he means to others, creating an ephemeral token of affection with enduring power.

LEAR IN THE GIFT ECONOMY

Like the 'Growling Eclogue', neither of these poems was published in Lear's lifetime.[91] They are gift poems. For almost a decade they circulated only within a private circle as tokens of shared friendship. Although they are now available to the public at large, the intimacy of this original gift exchange lingers. The anthropologist Marcel Mauss, in his seminal study *The Gift* (1924), says that a defining quality of the gift is that 'even when it has been abandoned by the giver, [it] still possesses something of him'.[92] This is especially true of Lear's poems, cartoons and alphabets, which so often convey a verbal and/or visual picture of Lear as an explicit part of the gift. In making repeated presents of this kind, Lear performed a certain kind of ritual *abaissement* that was simultaneously an *élévation:* he insisted on his continuing presence in the recipients' lives, and developed a way of growling, yelling and being hideous that was also charming, funny and moving.

As a teenager, Lear compiled a gift album of verse and illustration; he also tried to contribute verses to Alaric Watts's *Literary Souvenir: A Christmas and New Year's Present,* a literary annual that gingerly occupied the territory between commodified object and personal gift. The 1820s and 1830s saw a proliferation of such annuals, often bound in watered silk, which combined sentimental poems, stories and pictures in a manner designed to recall the private album and to clothe the purchased text in personal raiment, linking *souvenir* as a meme to the giver's and recipient's personal memories. Lear grew up at a time when poetry was being repackaged by the publishing industry as a gift that could transcend the circumstances of commercial sale. At a moment of industrialisation and rapid expansion in publishing, poetry was particularly important for what it could signify as a form of expression that originated in feeling; gift status was one apparent hallmark of authenticity and of personal value independent of the ruthless economy of financial transaction. Lear's illustrated letters and gift poems were produced in this climate of intense interest in letters and poetry as forms of intimate gift exchange that also have the potential to be published.[93] Fascinated by the circle that had included Byron and Shelley, and connected to surviving members of that generation—such as Keats's friend the artist Joseph Severn, whom Lear knew in Rome and who gifted Lear a copy of Thomas Campbell's *Poetical Works*—Lear was well placed to learn from earlier Romantic practices of creative correspondence, shared composition and gift poetry.[94] His works are cognizant of the different and intrinsically higher value of the gift as something that ideally commemorates a shared moment of reciprocal affection. They have one eye on the private individual to whom the piece is immediately addressed and one on a wider assembly of readers that includes posterity.

Lear was prolific and adept at gift-giving. He recognised from a very early age that offering presents could both create and cement a relationship and alter its terms. His album for Miss Fraser is a case in point. She was a pupil, a paying client; Lear's 'prize' or gift, however, reverses this dynamic. Likewise in a letter to the Earl of Derby from 1833, Lear writes:

> I have taken the liberty of sending the accompanying drawing—of which I beg your Lordship's acceptance. It is a coloured lithograph of Emys Ornata (young)—a species which your Lordship wished me to figure from a specimen then living at the Gardens:—since, however, the animal died before I was able to sketch it, I thought it might please your Lordship to have a drawing of it—though only in Lithography, & I have accordingly procured the accompanying plate from Mr Bell's work.——It was drawn for Mrs B—by J. D. C. Sowerby—and from a living specimen. Hoping that your Lordship's health is better than (I am sorry to hear,) it has been of late, I remain My Lord, with the greatest respect Your Lordship's most grateful servant, Edward Lear[95]

Lear had been working with Sowerby on lithographs for Thomas Bell's *Monograph on the Testudinata* (published by subscription from 1832 to 1836), which would include the ornamented terrapin that Lear refers to here. He had been commissioned by the earl to make a drawing of the terrapin. Unable to complete the assignment, Lear gave him a lithograph. In doing so and in enquiring after the earl's health, Lear subtly shifts the ground of their relationship from one of financial transaction to friendship. By the 1840s, he was no longer signing himself 'your servant'.

Lear's long and vital correspondence with Emily Tennyson began with his wedding gift of paintings to the couple. His paintings hanging on their walls ensured Lear's foot in the door. He became a domestic presence in the Tennysons' daily lives. Lear's writings and drawings were talismans that represented him in his absence as a small, humorous, benign and mildly absurd presence in the family home. As these early letters reveal, Lear desperately wanted to illustrate Tennyson's poetry, paying an homage that had the potential to be both a money-spinner and a form of creative jousting. He found, through Emily, a way to be critically close to Tennyson without being (openly) closely critical. The gift offered safe passage to intimacy. In

a very different situation in the 1870s, Lear used gifts to emphasise his close-
ness to Hubert Congreve, the teenage son of his neighbour in San Remo,
for whom he had developed a passionate affection. Hubert was leaving to
study at Cambridge, and Lear was distraught at the prospect of his absence.
Lear gave Hubert copies of his nonsense books as a going-away present.
Hubert's father snorted that this was a pointless gift, as Hubert 'had them
by heart' anyway.[96] But this was precisely the point. Lear was ensuring that
Hubert remembered that he remembered him. Lear wanted fiercely to remain in Hubert Congreve's life. His gifts made sure of his physical presence there.

In a powerful cultural study of gift-giving, Lewis Hyde remarks that:

> . . . gifts do not bring us attachment unless they move us. . . .
> It is when someone's gifts stir us that we are brought close, and
> what moves us, beyond the gift itself, is the promise (or the
> fact) of transformation, friendship, and love. . . . Gifts bespeak
> relationship. As long as the emotional tie is recognized as
> the point of the gift, both the donor and the recipient will be
> careful to structure the exchange so that it does not jeopardize
> their mutual affection.[97]

The real power of the gift lies in the relationships it engenders and
strengthens. As Hyde persuasively argues, gifts are best understood not as
one-on-one exchanges (though they are often conceived as such in Western
society) but as acts of generosity that spread out to a network that comes to
include persons remote from the originating gift. Lear's gifts vividly show
this wider process in operation. He gave his books and paintings as calling
cards, gifts of sympathy in bereavement, wedding gifts, birthday presents
and parting gifts. However, in Italy he commonly also gave presents from
his garden of fruit (usually oranges), flowers and seed whenever they were
plentiful. These botanical gifts nicely illustrate the cyclic nature of gift-
giving as a form of free circulation that has natural rhythms of fertility at
its heart. From the earliest times, communities have understood that they
must sow in order to reap, and that circulating seed and harvest is the best
way of ensuring food security in lean times. Lear crowdsourced his garden,
with seeds donated by his sister in New Zealand, Sir Joseph Hooker at Kew,
the Bells at Selborne and friends in India, Italy and England. Many of his
plants embodied personal attachments; when he writes punningly of 'the

pease of my own garding', he conjures a web of goodwill whose roots derive from the many friends who cared for him.[98] When he sent seed, flowers or fruit from his garden to others, he was thus passing on the fruits of affection created in one quadrant of his social circle to those who occupied another. Indeed one might envision a model of Lear's gift-giving where at different points on the circumference lie his nonsense books, his travel books, his sketches and paintings, songs, botanical gifts, toys for others' children, financial sums (to his godsons and those in straitened circumstances) and letters, with their inclusions of cartoons and occasional poems. In many of Lear's relationships he gave from at least four of these points on the circumference but received increase from at least three other sources: artistic commissions, orders of books, letters of introduction, financial assistance and other forms of personal support as a result of the web of friendships he nurtured. I do not say this to suggest that Lear's gift-giving was disingenuous, rather that, like his gardening, it was highly effective. Lear's 'neediness' made demands on his friends that could be uncomfortable, but it was part of a relationship structure with gift-giving at its heart, in which Lear was as frequently a donor as a recipient, though the material value of his gifts was often less than that of those he received. He often expressed wonder that he had attracted such a wide and powerful circle of friends. But in truth he had tended this circle from his teenage years and knew that his professional viability and his private reputation for likability were inseparable. Lear's gifts and his work are so closely intertwined as to be only differentiable at certain moments in their production and distribution; often they move seamlessly from being one to being the other.

Lear's nonsense books gather together poems, songs, stories and pictures that were connected with a variety of friends and were given or performed privately as gifts—and re-present them to the public at large. Several famous children's books were first produced as gifts for individual children; best known are Carroll's *Alice in Wonderland* and Beatrix Potter's *Peter Rabbit*. It is no accident that the idea of gift origin is particularly potent in children's literature. Children are themselves gifts, and the idea that their arrival should be accompanied by gifts is culturally ubiquitous. The economic innocence of the gift mirrors that of the child; children represent a good more fundamental than monetary systems can realise. However, the works of Potter, Carroll and A. A. Milne are dedicated to individual children, who then stand in the position of muses for the particular character they inspired. Lear's four nonsense books are different because they were made for a *crowd* of diverse children and adults that continues to be the visual analogue for the mode of transmission Lear images for his songs and stories: a kind of social concert, like the one that takes place on the Quangle Wangle's hat. As with the Quangle Wangle's hat, which becomes a free space where all can find a home, the distinction between the book's existence as private and public object is blurred. The majority of the nonsenses and alphabets in his volumes were hand drawn by Lear the author-artist directly or indirectly as gifts; they were only afterwards reformed into books, which rapidly became gifts once more. Lear relied on Bush to send out copies of his nonsense works to friends; these gifts were exchanged for love and support of an intangible and literally invaluable nature.[99]

Lear has sometimes been criticised for being inept in his dealings with publishers, to the detriment of his profits. He cannot be blamed for the fact that Robert Bush, the publisher of *Nonsense Songs, Stories, Botany and Alphabets; More Nonsense;* and *Laughable Lyrics,* went bankrupt. However, Lear was hampered from the start by the fact that he didn't expect to make much money *directly* from his books. His first experience of publishing was by subscription, a funding model that was becoming dated in the Victorian period but has, arguably, revived in modern times in the form of crowd-funding. Lear wrote letters individually to his friends and acquaintances soliciting their willingness to subscribe for a copy of *Illustrations of the Family of Psittacidae or Parrots* in fourteen folios or, much later in his life, *Views in the Seven Ionian Islands* or *Journal of a Landscape Painter in Corsica.* Once he had a sufficient number of names, a publisher would print the volume. The system had the advantage of minimising risk for the publisher, but because authors were not paid until the work was complete and subscribers had received their copy, it didn't defray upfront the cost-intensive process of creating high-quality illustrated volumes. Lear's *Psittacidae* was never completed because the money ran out. However, he recognised that the primary return for the project was not cash but commissions; the extraordinarily high quality of the work served as a successful vehicle to promote the author's talents. Lear's travel books similarly gleaned very impressive lists of powerful subscribers, whose names were traditionally printed in the front of the volume as a form of thanks that was also an advertisement of the author's social standing. The book published by subscription is not a gift, but neither is the transaction it effects wholly financial. It privately asks the authors' friends and patrons to give their names and the promise of purchase as contributions to a joint enterprise. As commodities, such books are different from those offered for casual sale. The social circle they embody is intrinsic to their content and value. Most of the books Lear produced or contributed to in his lifetime were published by subscription or otherwise at his own initial expense. Lear was conditioned by his early experiences to think of his books as conduits first and products second.

Lear also needed to get things out for his own sake. His drawing of both landscape sketches and limericks had a compulsive quality of repeated action; both were sometimes produced in quantities of one hundred. He needed to be active to combat depression, and he needed to give to others in order to be given to at an emotional level. These needs were paramount. When Bush went bankrupt, the '3 succeeding absurd volumes' of nonsense, as Lear himself remarked in 1886, became, like the *Psittacidae*, 'very rare books'.[100] This wasn't an outcome Lear had produced directly, but it did reflect, I think, a gentlemanly ambivalence about submitting his art to solely economic transaction. He wished for popularity but sought a more personal relationship with those who valued his work that could stand above purely material considerations. This side of Lear caused him as a young artist to say he preferred to draw friends' animals because of their personal associations, rather than merely those specimens that happened to be available, and sometimes to avoid or snub potential customers for whom he had no personal sympathy. On one level, the market failure of 'the horrid man Bush' involved Lear's; financially speaking, his succeeding absurd volumes weren't absurdly successful to their author. However, as Lear recognised, their absence from the market increased their rarity value and worth as gifts. He offered them to John Ruskin as a token of appreciation after Ruskin's tribute to Lear's *Book of Nonsense* in the *Pall Mall Gazette:* a gift for a gift.

Lear's commercial value in his lifetime was not as high as it might have been; this is true of both his art and his writing. But appreciation of him in the gift economy was very high. These two facts are related, and their effect has been remarkably persistent. Lear's poetry, first created and circulated in the gift economy, has a value that is not primarily commodity value. It derives meaning partly from its, originally private, circulation from hand to hand and home to home. The figured absurdities of 'The Owl and the Pussy-cat' or the 'Growling Eclogue' are intimately linked to their emotional resonance as expressions of affection that solicit affection in return. Their 'nonsense' explores the redemptive possibility of being fully understood and appreciated despite being odd, opaque or confusing: the deep joy of communication between those who love one another. It matters that his 'nonsenses'

continue to feel like gifts, because this has helped to condition public response to Lear, which has tended toward affection, sympathy and personal
interest in his life—the kind of response gifts naturally elicit—rather than
critical evaluation. Lear offers himself, his books, his persona as a gift—
something we can't objectively criticise, because they are always connected to the emotion and the offer of relationship embodied in the gift
transaction.

Will the Real Edward Lear Please Stand Up?

The fact that Edward Lear's work circulated so successfully in the gift
economy, beloved by a large but select group of families and friends belonging to a particular social network, affected his reputation with the
public at large. He was for a long time not well known. The fact that from
his twenties he spent most of the year abroad made things worse. Many
people did not make the connection between the artist Edward Lear and
the author of the nonsense books, the first two of which were published
anonymously. Lear was quite a common name in the period; he might after
all have been Edward Lear, tallow chandler of Plymouth, or the Reverend
Edward Lear, vicar of Blackmoor.[101]

Mistakes were made in the press. A writer in the *Illustrated News* in 1862
thought that Lear's nonsense imitated that of John Parry, whose *Ridiculous
Things* had actually appeared in 1854, eight years after Lear's *Book of Nonsense.*[102] A *Times* reviewer of *Laughable Lyrics* in December 1876 referred to
him as Mr Edwin Lear.[103] James T Fields of Boston, who, as the publisher
of 'The Owl and the Pussy-cat' in the magazine *Young Folks*, should have
known better, printed in *Underbrush* (1877), his collection of sketches of eminent contemporaries, an account of 'Lear—Nonsense-Poet' that contained
several errors while claiming that Fields knew Lear intimately. Lear copied
it into his diary:

> He is a great, broad-shouldered, healthy Englishman, who
> spends a large portion of his valuable time in making children,
> especially, happy. He is the classmate & much-loved friend of
> Alfred Tennyson, (whose beautiful poem to E. L. means
> Edward Lear); & if you chanced, a few years back, to go to
> Farringford about Christmas-time you would have been likely
> to find a tall, elderly man, in enormous googles, down on

all-fours on the carpet, and reciting in the character of a lively
and classical Hippopotamus new nonsense-verses to a dozen
children, amid roars of laughter,—a very undignified position,
certainly, for one of the best Greek scholars in Europe, for a
Landscape painter unrivalled anywhere, & the Author of half
a dozen learned quartos of travels in Albania, Illyria, Calabria,
& other interesting countries! . . . A few years ago he was
obliged to build a cottage in Ravenna, in Italy, & live there a
portion of the year, in order to get time for painting & study;
for when he is in London the little people, whom he passionately loves and cannot live without, run after him, as they did
after the Pied Piper of Hamelin, to that extent he has no
leisure for his profession. . . .[104]

Lear certainly was not a classmate of Tennyson's, nor one of the best Greek
scholars in Europe (though he made valiant efforts to learn Greek in middle
age). He didn't build a cottage at Ravenna, and his chief reason for leaving
London was not that he was mobbed by children. But the anecdote of him
acting the Hippopotamus at Farringford is plausible, and the other asser-
tions are broadly true, though Lear would have disputed 'healthy'. The
mistakes are telling. Lear must have struck the purveyor of this gossip as
somebody who *could have been* an eminent classicist and a classmate of Tennyson but who was also a figure of Christmas revelry to whom children
were so hypnotically drawn that he had to flee them. 'Derry down Derry'
as a persona had done its work too well.

Lear the performer, rather than ignoring mistakes regarding his identity, chose to include them in his act. He opened his third nonsense book,
More Nonsense, with an extraordinary tale. Lear notes that regarding his
original *Book of Nonsense*, 'many absurd reports have crept into circulation',
such as 'that it was the composition of the late Lord Brougham, the late Earl
of Derby, &c.; that the rhymes and pictures are by different persons; or that
the whole have symbolical meaning. . . .' Lear assures us this is not the case.
He is the only sole begetter of his nonsense. Then he tells of an encounter
on a train between London and Guilford where he gained insight into the
rumours regarding the book's authorship. Two little boys have just been
given a *Book of Nonsense* and are 'loud in their delight'. An old gentleman in
the carriage explains that the writer is Edward, Earl of Derby, and that
LEAR is a teasing anagram of EARL. When ladies in the carriage express

their doubts, the old gentleman angrily insists, 'I am well aware of what I am saying: I can inform you, no such person as "Edward Lear" exists!' Lear then confronts him:

> Hitherto I had kept silence, but as my hat was, as well as my handkerchief and stick, largely marked inside with my name, and, as I happened to have in my pocket several letters addressed to me, the temptation was too great to resist, so, flashing all these articles at once on my would-be-extinguisher's attention, I speedily reduced him to silence.[105]

This incident has a wonderfully postmodern flavour. Lear is forced to argue for the objective existence of 'Edward Lear'. The audience threatens to 'extinguish' him, so he has to 'sit on' his audience. He chose to illustrate the incident, most unusually, both on the frontispiece and on the cover of the book, where 'EDWARD LEAR' appears in bright red letters in a font bigger than the title. The picture has Lear, drawn in a fairly realistic manner, facing off the startled 'old gentleman', who is rendered in the style of a cartoon figure, one of the old persons from Lear's nonsense volumes. In one way this cartoon is the ultimate revenge on the man in the train who doubted Lear's reality. Lear has turned him into an 'unreal' two-dimensional figure, discombobulated and absurd. But the double portrait is double edged. It is a mirror-pose of two people staring at one another in amazement with their hands up: a defensive posture. Lear presenting his hat looks a little like a stage magician, somebody who conjures illusions for a living. We can't see the writing on the hat or handkerchief or letter that is supposed to authenticate Lear's ownership and authorship. Lear would have been well aware that another anagram of his name was *real*. Here, who is REAL and who is LEAR is a matter of debate. In the end, he and the old man are equally just lines on the page. The strange meeting where two characters argue over which one is a figment of the other's imagination anticipates Pirandello.

One of Lear's favourite books was *Tristram Shandy,* and we can see in the preface to *More Nonsense* Lear's enjoyment of the paradoxes involved in the seeming authenticity of writing and drawing, whose representational nature undermines their own truth claims. Lear often writes jokingly beneath his self-caricatures, 'very like' or 'from a phoatograph'. Long before Magritte painted 'Ceci n'est pas une pipe' (1929), Lear was experimenting with the treachery of images. Presumably he didn't notice the mistake in

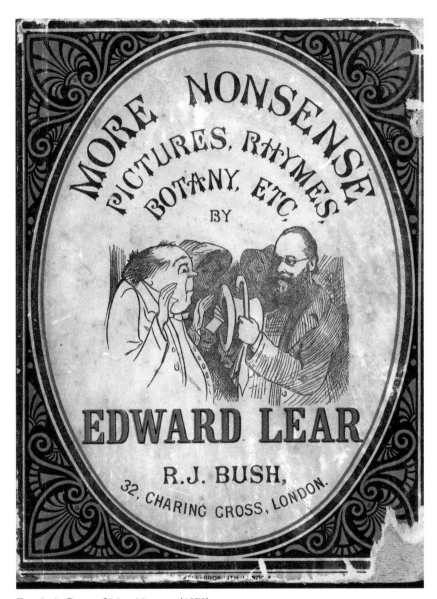

Fig. 5.19 Cover of *More Nonsense* (1872)

his introduction to *More Nonsense*, which said he had disposed of the copyright of his expanded *Book of Nonsense* to Routledge and Warne in 1843 rather than 1863. The claim to have reissued something in advance of its birth is certainly Shandyesque. In his *Illustrated Excursions in Italy* (1846), Lear had described an incident that occurred in the Abruzzi in the autumn of 1844. A drunken policeman asked to view his passport and, seeing the words 'Viscount Palmerston' written on it in large letters, insisted that Lear was the foreign secretary, who was at the time highly unpopular in Italy, and took him into custody. Lear's protestations were in vain. 'In spite of all expostulations, Viscount Palmerston it was settled I should be. There was nothing to be done'.[106] Lear had to wait placidly until someone who recognised him arrived and settled matters. It is interesting that in both these comic anecdotes, Lear is mistaken for a lord: the first Liberal prime minister and a reformist Liberal chancellor who did much to abolish the slave trade. As is so true of Lear's letters, self-assertion and self-mockery go hand in hand. Lear's farcical failure to gain proper recognition as an artist—which often saddened him in reality—is transformed into an amusing story that serves his comic persona.

In 1942, the *Yorkshire Post* reported, 'It is said that in his last years, when disinclined for callers, he would open his studio door dressed as his man-servant and bark out, "Mr Lear is ill"'.[107] This is perhaps a version of Henry Strachey's account of holidaying with Lear in San Remo, in which he mentions that Lear answered the door to repulse unwelcome visitors, announcing (untruthfully) that due to ill health he never showed his pictures now.[108] Certainly Giorgio was authorised to appear at the door—pretending to be his master—to dismiss beggars (Lear gave generously to charitable causes, but not to 'chance applicants').[109] And Giorgio got upset that Lear sometimes answered the door himself, ignoring the usual ceremony that dictated servants should do so. Lear's final revenge on those who didn't know him but thought that they would like to view him was to appear in disguise. In giving his callers the brush-off, he was also giving them the truth. 'Mr Lear' was always a performance. In appearing as his own servant, Lear was doing what his caricature-self had done for many years: opening a door to his inner world but letting the audience see only what he chose them to see.

AFTERLIFE: PITY AND PATRONAGE

Lear began to vanish socially before he died in reality. It is notable that roundups of children's literature in the late nineteenth century often don't mention him at all. In the absence of accurate knowledge about his output, myths arose. The *Ottawa Free Trader* of 25 May 1889 announced that 'a man has lately died in England who has done much to amuse children as well as grown folk'. As well as making a mistake about where

Lear had died, the article claimed he was 'the originator of *Mother Goose's Melodies*' and quoted a limerick supposed to be from the *Book of Nonsense:*

> There was an old fellow of Crewd,
> Who lived upon sawdust as food.
> It's cheap by the ton,
> And it nourishes one,
> And that's the chief virtue of food.[110]

This is indeed crude, and is certainly not by Lear. *Mother Goose's Melody* was in fact a much older collection of traditional rhymes and lullabies for children printed by John Newbery in 1760. It contained rhymes including 'High Diddle Diddle / The Cat and the Fiddle' and sonnets from Shakespeare. Collections of traditional nursery rhymes called *Mother Goose's Melodies* would continue to appear throughout the nineteenth and early twentieth centuries. It is intriguing that only a year after Lear's death, the Canadian author of this faulty eulogy believed him to be responsible for an older oral and musical tradition of nursery rhymes. Lear had already, it seems, become a figure like Mother Goose, whose authorship is largely symbolic.

As early as 1894, the *Globe* commented, 'So little is known of the late Edward Lear, the nonsense laureate, that Sir Edward Strachey's reminiscences of him in the "Atlantic Monthly" have peculiar interest'.[111] The art critic Paul Konody in the *Morning Post* of 16 March 1912, reviewing a charity exhibition of Lear's paintings in London, declared:

> Who is, or was, Edward Lear? may be the question asked by
> many artists and some art critics. . . . Edward Lear was an
> amateur in so far as he was not trained for the artistic profes-
> sion and never exhibited or sold his pictures. He sketched for
> his own amusement on his journeys through Italy, Corsica,
> Palestine and India, and he liberally distributed these records
> among his friends. Over a hundred of these water-colour
> landscapes have now been brought together in Piccadilly, with
> the result that this 'amateur' will henceforth have to be
> counted among the very masters of the English water-colour
> school. His development must have been very rapid. The
> drawings of Lake Thun, dated 1855, has the careful, hard
> precision and anxious concern with topographic facts that

mark the amateur and the beginner. The 'Corfu' of only three years later is the work of an experienced artist who has not only mastered his craft but has arrived at a personal style—who has found his own symbols for every fact in nature. Lear's 'symbols', his pictorial shorthand writing, are wonderfully expressive. They often recall the masters of the Far East, although they were found by him long before the appreciation of Chinese and Japanese art had taken root in Europe. The two sketches of 'Cephalonia' and the 'Lebanon' might almost be the works of a Japanese.[112]

It seems extraordinary that Lear, who exhibited and sold his paintings continually until the mid-1880s, should here confidently be described as an amateur who never did. It took a letter by the artist Arthur Cadogan Blunt to the *Times* to posit Lear's amateur status as 'surely inaccurate' on the basis of Lear's *Letters to Chichester Fortescue,* edited by Lady Waldegrave's niece, Lady Strachey, which referred to 'the sale of his sketches and paintings to his aristocratic patrons'. In fact, Lear's diaries show that he did enjoy access to Japanese artefacts, which he admired, in friends' homes. His landscapes were compared with Japanese art by a knowledgeable contemporary, Ernest Satow, who wrote on 1 January 1876 that Lear 'is an extremely clever artist, and some of his studies are almost Japanese'.[113] By 1912, cultural memory of Lear as an artist was shaky: it relied on Lady Strachey's edition of his letters.

The Stracheys, through various publications from 1888 to 1911, were deeply influential in shaping memory of Lear as a character. Edward Strachey, recalling Lear in a tribute of 1894, quoted Wordsworth's 'A Poet's Epitaph': 'And you must love him, ere to you / He will seem worthy of your love'.[114] Strachey painted a picture of an ageing Lear dwelling in the setting of 'his own pathetic nonsense of the Yonghy Bonghy Bo' that proved decisive in shaping how the poet would be seen by future writers—as a figure of pathos contiguous with his nonsense characters, always melancholy and infirm, yet warm-hearted and genial. It is old Lear rather than young Lear who has thus come down to posterity as the abiding image of the nonsense poet. The idea that one had to love Lear to understand why he was lovable was circular in its invitation to a form of appreciation based on subjective affection rather than objective analysis.

Evelyn Baring, Lord Cromer, supplied a preface to Lady Strachey's *Queery Leary Nonsense* (1911) in which he argued:

> It is to that chill penury against which Lear's life was one
> continuous and arduous struggle, that we probably owe
> productions which have been the delight of so many nurseries.
> He perhaps occasionally felt some slight disappointment that
> his fame rested not so much on his merits as an artist, as on
> the fact that he was known throughout the child-world as the
> author of 'Dumbledownderry'. But neither his impecuniosity
> nor his disappointment could sour his essentially lovable nature,
> or tinge with the least shade of cynicism a humour, which was
> above all things kindly and genial. He was too warm-hearted to
> be satirical. His laughter was, indeed, akin to tears.[115]

Baring, like Marianne North, was rightly struck by the fact that Lear could sing 'Tears, Idle Tears' at the piano and sob, and then hours afterwards spoof the same material, sending Baring a comic drawing of himself at the piano along with a nonsense version of 'Vivien's Song' from *Idylls of the King*. However, Baring's portrait of Lear forced by 'chill penury' to produce nonsense is simply untrue. And his assertion that Lear's 'laughter was . . . akin to tears' tends to suggest that Lear's comedy was just a way of weeping in public with a brave face. (In fact, based on the anecdote Baring relates, one might equally argue that Lear's tears were akin to laughter—since that is the actual order of events.) Rather than an emotionally labile artist who enjoyed flipping genre like a pancake in mid-air, Lear appears here as a tragic figure forced by poverty to clown: lovable, harmless, pitiable. To Lear's patrons, his neediness had always been uppermost; to them he had always seemed poor. They now drove the narrative of reminiscence. A memorialisation of Lear based on pity had begun. Lear's work would enjoy a rich and varied afterlife, but critical responses to it would henceforth be coloured by personal feeling for the pathos of Lear's own history.

His nonsense continued to be immensely popular with children. And it would be creatively influential on a panoply of modern poets and artists, from James Joyce, T. S. Eliot, and W. H. Auden to Elizabeth Bishop, Stevie Smith, and John Ashbery.[116] It is fascinating that Beatrix Potter directly related her own stories for children to Lear's nonsense characters. Potter's

Pig Robinson is the same pig, she tells us, who appeared with a ring at the end of his nose in Lear's 'song about the Owl and the Pussy Cat' (for which Potter had designed her own illustrations in 1897). Her *Tale of Little Pig Robinson* (1930) is a prequel that explains 'why the pig went to live in the land of the Bong tree'. In 1968, the same year that Edward Gorey illustrated 'The Jumblies' and Ogden Nash published his completion of 'The Scroobious Pip', the writers of Disney's animated film *Winnie the Pooh and the Blustery Day* made Milnes's Owl the nephew of Lear's Owl: he tells Pooh 'my uncle Clyde went to sea in a boat. He didn't give a hoot for tradition'. The *familial* relationship claimed for these creatures is deeply telling. Just as Lear himself had, in letters, made the Owl and the Pussy-cat characters with ongoing histories who were related to animals in his own life, new generations of writers for children expressed their sense of intimate, personal connection to Lear through constructing an imaginary genealogy that linked his characters to theirs.

But it is noticeable that by the 1920s a feeling that the whole Victorian period was not as 'great' as it wished to appear and that it had been a time of smug moral hegemony and sexual repression was affecting critical appraisals of Lear, whose nonsense, to some, now appeared to be a 'distorted representation' of the sentiment prevalent in the era. William Kerr in 1926 observed:

> A younger critic, looking through a series of Victorian poets
> and prophets, is impressed chiefly by their hairiness, and has
> suggested that, behind their whiskers, they were not as great
> as they wished to look: that, in the phrase of their own day,
> they were 'lions', and, like lions in the Zoo, have a self-
> conscious air that verges sometimes on charlatanism. Perhaps
> this is not how the Victorians really were, but how they look to
> us: each generation, looking back, seems to have its own blind
> spot, and Victorianism is ours. But from 1840 to 1890
> England was very moral and very self satisfied: the 'communal
> pressure' each epoch exercises on its children was powerful
> and constant: perhaps no period of fifty years shows En-
> glishmen so standardized, so incapable of serious difference
> from the moral attitude of their day. . . . This 'communal
> pressure' is as real and efficient as direct religious or political
> persecution: like persecution it drives differences and the spirit
> of revolt underground. The new psychology tells us what to

expect when natural impulses are inhibited and repressed—
they find indirect expression in dreams or in casual phrases
and irrelevant habits. Thus it is that Victorians, pressed into
that mould of their day, took refuge in 'Nonsense'. Lewis
Carroll gives a dream escape travesty of Victorian philosophy:
a lot of Victorian poetry and sentiment finds its distorted
representation in the work of Edward Lear.[117]

Kerr's thesis makes Lear more of a conduit than an agent. He is the night
mind of Victorian male self-satisfaction. According to Kerr, Lear's famous
question to Queen Victoria—'Oh, how did you get these beautiful
things?'—'bubbled up from his subconscious feeling like that of the child
who didn't see the Emperor's new clothes'. Lear's virtue, here, lies in a kind
of innocence, a failure to repress. Kerr avows that 'Lear was not a great artist,
or a great man, but he was a very lovable man'. Greatness and lovableness
are, in this article, inimical qualities. The guarantee of Lear's truthfulness
in this new age preoccupied with 'the new psychology' lies precisely in the
fact that he is minor. Like that of a child, his tongue is candid. There is no
room here for consideration of Lear's conscious artistry or power.

Angus Davidson's 1938 publication of a sensitive new biography of Lear,
which remarked that Lear 'remained always, himself, something of a
child',[118] stimulated fresh interest[119] in Lear's life and particularly in the
vexed question of his sexuality. Davidson hinted strongly that Lear had no
'romantic feeling' toward women and that 'the deepest feelings of his heart
were reserved for his friends . . . it is doubtful whether it was in Lushington's nature to have given Lear the close, unquestioning intimacy he de-
sired'.[120] George Orwell, responding in 1945 to R Mégroz's new collection
of the nonsense (the 1939 edition was notably called *A Book of Lear*),
commented that Lear 'never married, and it is easy to guess that there was
something seriously wrong in his sex life'.[121] This feeling of 'wrongness'
surrounding Lear's sexuality communicates itself also in Orwell's analysis
of Lear's poetry, which he likes when it is funny, but dislikes when it is
frail. Lear's poetry expresses 'a kind of amiable lunacy, a natural sympathy
with whatever is weak and absurd'. It is, Orwell decides, hard to believe
that Lear's considerable influence has been altogether good: 'The silly
whimsiness of present-day children's books could perhaps be partly traced
back to him'. The modern reader feels slightly as if Lear were a pupil in a
boys' school who had infected his classmates with a horror of field sports.

The question mark over Lear's masculinity, his poetry's sympathy with weakness and his possible responsibility for whimsiness in children's literature all point in one limp-wristed direction.

Perhaps not coincidentally, Lear's power in the art market remained very weak until the last quarter of the twentieth century, when his reappraisal as a visual artist led to a successful Royal Academy exhibition and prices for his pieces began to climb to their present high levels. In 1929, when many works that had been in Lord Northbrook's collection and the Lushington family collection were auctioned, a Lear watercolour could be bought for three to ten guineas. The American collectors Philip Hofer and William B. Osgood Field together amassed more than three thousand of Lear's watercolours during this doldrums, some of which cost them no more than five shillings.[122] Lear's paintings were simultaneously too numerous and insufficiently visible to the general public. A reviewer in 1942 commented, 'His pictures are rarely on the market now. Probably they still grace the houses of descendants of his many friends and patrons'.[123] Another retailed the commonplace 'that the delightful and nonsensical Edward Lear was a serious landscape painter is little suspected by the multitude of people who know by heart his limericks'.[124] Lear is ambiguously 'nonsensical' here; he is a producer of nonsense, but the placement of the adjective also implies that he is nonsensical as a person. No wonder, then, that the paired expression 'serious' (with its allied senses of 'substantial, considerable or impressive') seems inappropriate. Knowing Lear's work 'by heart' is a very potent tribute, but it can also lead to a refusal to consider the role of the intellect in creating or responding to it.

Samuel A. Nock in his 1941 essay 'Lacrimae Nugarum', one of the first academic papers to comment on Lear's verse, responded to Davidson's biography by asserting, 'Among the many writers of nonsense, Edward Lear seems to have been unique in writing in nonsense his emotional biography'.[125] Davidson has, Nock informs us, given a 'gratifying number of hints' that enable us to understand Lear's poems in autobiographical terms. 'Lear found in nonsense the vehicle of expression which other writers of nonsense neither found nor needed; and in that form he wrote about himself'. Nock continues:

> He was certainly not a great artist; he was at very best a good artist—and to call a man a good artist is about as complimentary as to call a girl a nice girl.[126]

Nock's comparison here is telling. Lear is the equivalent of a 'nice girl'. Again we are faced with the link between Lear's relative cultural impotence and his lovability. Great artists are by implication masculine: they transcend their emotions. Lear is feminine, and he writes his 'emotional biography' in nonsense. I was reminded on reading Nock of Lord David Cecil's 1934 account of Charlotte Brontë: 'Fundamentally, her principal characters are all the same person; and that is Charlotte Brontë. . . . The world she creates is the world of her own inner life; she is her own subject'.[127] Critics of this era, including Virginia Woolf, were wrongly inclined to believe that Charlotte Brontë 'owed nothing to the reading of many books'.[128] Like Charlotte Brontë, Lear was in fact a voracious and varied reader. He faced, however, a similar determination on the part of early critics to believe that his work stemmed chiefly from his own emotional life and body rather than responding to larger events or to others' work that he had read or seen or heard. This charge is often levelled at the feminine. *Lacrimae nugarum* means 'tears from nonsense' or 'tears from trifles'; Nock's choice of the feminine Latin word *nuga* tends to imply that, however delightful they may be, Lear's verses are sweet nothings, the peardrops of his teardrops.

LOVING LEAR: READING AND INTIMACY

The tradition of reading Lear's life story through his verse, and his verse principally or exclusively through his life story, has been remarkably resilient. Ina Rae Hark in 1982 noted, 'Commentators agree that the Bò is Lear himself, Lady Jingly Jones is Gussie Bethell, and the poem is a fictionalization of their abortive romance'.[129] Jackie Wullschläger (1995) confidently claimed that Lear's strange fantastical poems

> chart his life like an emotional barometer. The early limericks
> reflect his rage and frustration when he first entered upper-
> class nineteenth-century society. The poems of his middle
> years—'Calico Pie', 'The Duck and the Kangaroo'—celebrate
> his escape from Victorian constraint and narrow-mindedness,
> but tell also of a sense of alienation, his inability to fit in. The
> later poems . . . are about the sort of lonely wanderer that Lear
> became in his last years.[130]

Robert Douglas-Fairhurst, in a recent, excellent book on Lewis Carroll (2013), similarly asserts that Edward Lear's characters are 'to some extent . . . all disguised versions of himself'.[131] This is never said of Carroll or of Tennyson.

There have been, over the years, some wonderfully perceptive critical works on Lear, and, particularly since his bicentenary in 2012, Lear scholarship has been enjoying a renaissance. However, critical writing on Lear was for many years sparse compared with that accorded to other nineteenth-century writers and artists of comparable fame. Ann Colley's survey *Edward Lear and the Critics* (1993) doesn't quite fill 120 pages. Writers have preferred to come at Lear through biography, entering by the door of sympathy—the door he leaves invitingly open in all his letters and journals and travel books. And indeed the work that led research on Lear into a new era of meticulous scholarship was Vivien Noakes's sympathetic and moving *Edward Lear: The Life of a Wanderer* (1968), which remained for almost half a century the standard biography. Part of the success of Noakes's method lies in her use of free indirect discourse to give us imaginative access to Lear's thoughts and feelings, pairing her analysis of his inner state with direct speech from Lear's letters and diaries. We become familiar with Lear by overhearing him and absorbing the patterns of his prose, his play, his persiflage. Sometimes the outcome is so subtle that one is uncertain whether the reflection is Lear's or the author's:

> If he had been a free man, able to marry, then Gussie [Bethell] would have been an ideal wife. But he was not. As he saw it, the barrier of his epilepsy was total. Had he proposed and been accepted, it would have been a secret he would have had to have shared with her and possibly even with her family. This was unthinkable.[132]

The rhythm of Noakes's sentences here mimics that of a man who is weighing up the issues; it is a psychologically convincing account of Lear's marriage dilemma. But in fact, we have no concrete evidence that Lear's epilepsy, in his view, formed a barrier to his marriage to Gussie Bethell or even that she was ignorant of it. This is emotional guesswork. Lear may simply have decided that his temperament and Gussie's were not suited to being yoked together permanently; he may have recognised ambivalence on his part and on hers. Over many years he certainly allowed a wide variety of possible motives, some of them financial, and a wide variety of other people, to put him off. Lear was, all his life, very good at considering projects—from land purchases to trips abroad—and then backing out of them. His reverse gear was as formidably strong as his desire for company was tidal. The 'unthinkability' is Noakes's thought about what Lear may have thought was unthinkable.

Subsequent biographers have also used Lear's poems to set the scene for his life story and to illustrate the viewpoint they take on Lear's sexuality, which has been a source of critical controversy.[133] Thus Michael Montgomery, whose biography *The Owl and the Pussycats: Lear in Love, the Untold Story* (2012) is dedicated to refuting what he regards as the calumny of Lear's homosexuality, both uses Lear's illustration of the Yonghy-Bonghy-Bò proposing to Lady Jingly as his cover image and leads his introduction with the verse beginning:

> 'Lady Jingly! Lady Jingly!
> Sitting where the pumpkins blow,
> Will you come and be my wife?'
> Said the Yonghy-Bonghy-Bò.

Montgomery's contention is that Lear was exclusively heterosexual and wanted a wife; only illness, financial uncertainty and bad luck prevented him from becoming a family man.[134] In this reading, the kneeling Yonghy-Bonghy-Bò, suing for the affections of a woman surrounded by three hens, is Lear's avatar. He becomes the evidence for Lear's real position: as a slave to the charms of womankind. In a critical climate dominated by biography it has been tempting to read Lear's poems 'straight'—as concrete responses to concrete events in Lear's life. For critics like Montgomery, who would prefer a straight Lear, a straight reading of Lear as the Dong or the Yonghy-Bonghy-Bò can be one way of supporting their contention.

By contrast, those who prefer to see Lear as homosexual have also used his image in tandem with his writing to support their viewpoint. Nicholas Bentley in 1968, in an illustration for the *Sunday Telegraph*, presented Lear in a row of framed portraits next to Wilde and Swinburne.[135] In this line-up, Lear is unequivocally a gay icon. Auden's beautiful yet sad sonnet to Lear of 1939, '. . . affection was miles away:/But guided by tears he successfully reached his Regret', depicts Lear as a character whose surreally comic verse is a compensatory dream where he escapes from his 'Terrible Demon',

'Germans and boats' and hating his nose.[136] This implicitly frames Lear's unfulfilled sexuality with his other sadnesses as a sort of persecution from which Lear flees as Auden himself fled to America during World War II.

It is no wonder that readers feel for Lear. It is a reaction he carefully solicits. If they come to love Lear's writing, they usually come to love Lear too and to identify with him, to enter into his wishes and his wistfulness and to regret that he could not be paired in life, whether to a female or a male partner. If Lear's constant writing and painting was, at one psychological level, a plea not to be abandoned—to be cared for in perpetuity—sympathetic readers have ensured that it remains heard and honoured. Rightly so. Yet one must also recognise that singularity was vital to the character that Lear developed for himself. As Lear emphasised with bold pencil in his copy of Addison's essays from the *Spectator*, 'as for the word singular, I was always of opinion every man must be so, to be what one would desire him'.[137]

Lear liked to write comically about being mated and sometimes in loneliness wished he had a life companion, but he also knew that his singularity would be compromised by any such union. One must, I think, recognise the role of self-determination (rather than merely anxiety or bad luck) in Lear's persistent decision to live alone: he based his communicative persona upon a relationship with his readers that dramatised his peculiarity as a tragicomic state of being in play with them alone. If he had enjoyed the literal succession of having real children, the success of this character would not have been assured.

Lear is not the Pobble or the Dong or the Yonghy-Bonghy-Bò any more than Charlotte Brontë is Jane Eyre or Charles Dickens is David Copperfield. These characters do reflect aspects of the inner life of their creators, but they are by no means identical to them. The interesting question then becomes, Why has the critical tradition evolved in such a way as to favour biographical readings over any other kind of response to Lear's art? And here, I think, the intimacy that Lear solicits through his playful, rueful, physically demonstrative behaviour on the page and the visual and verbal persona he creates as a bridge—even a siege engine—into the reader's affections, is at the heart of the matter. Lear encourages a certain relationship with his audience where, as we have seen, self-mockery and self-promotion are codependent. He uses his small body, his speaking silence, his comic physical ineptitude or liability to be tossed and blown about, to signal accessibility, familiarity, friendliness. He broadcasts loneliness and thereby attracts sympathy. He flies, leaps, dances and stamps. He gains our trust through confiding his impetuosity, frustration, incompetence and vulnerability. He performs dependence and in certain ways solicits the status of a minor: a child, a caterpillar, an odd bird blown away by strong winds. He makes his lack of public recognition into part of the joke; Edward Lear is constantly mistaken for others, often for aristocrats in high public office. That comedy of error paradoxically makes the persona of Edward Lear—Socrates, Falstaff and Sancho Panza in one—powerful for its unknowability. His eccentricity becomes a kind of universality, his figure one that can contain and represent multitudes.

Most authors are known from vignettes painted by others. Jane Austen, sketched unsatisfactorily by her sister Cassandra, has come down to posterity as a tight-lipped lady with piercing eyes and arms defensively crossed. Charles Dickens is always at work, expansively velvet-draped in his study: either the young genius by Daniel Maclise or the bearded doyen by William Frith. Charlotte Brontë is a slight, wary figure by George Richmond, with a centre-parting and a serious mien like that of a schoolmistress. Almost uniquely amongst authors, however, Lear draws himself. He represents his face and body as comic artefacts, over and over and over again. He develops self-caricature into a fine art, producing some of the very first cartoon storyboards of the nineteenth century. He is animated. He advertises that he is part of his nonsense world; his comic body becomes integral to the pleasure that his work constitutes. This is increasingly the case once private self-caricatures of Lear—both verbal and visual—begin to be part of the public experience of reading his nonsense. Like that of Charlie Chaplin or Harold Lloyd, Lear's self-invented cartoon image becomes much better known than any realistic portrait of him by others. On the side of the Edward Lear pub on Holloway Road in London—in the neighbourhood of Lear's birthplace—there is a large stencil of the cartoon Lear in old age, with his spherical belly, his long stick legs, his spectacles. This is not Lear's body, but it is his sign, and it is a sign under which, appropriately, people gather to drink and make merry. Lear's work invokes sociability as its subject, its métier and its raison d'être. It brings together verbal, visual and musical forms of expression, just as it brings together the throng of improbable figures who leap and fly and sail in its pages. It offers itself as a gift. It is no wonder that reading it analytically has seemed, for many people, to be a form of misreading or overreading, a response to Lear that refuses the convivial invitation his work makes to us, countering a proffered wine glass with a magnifying glass.[138]

But to take entirely at face value the comic, small and ungainly figure of Lear that he promulgates in cartoons—the Lear who hangs on the horns of a mouflon or like a pupating caterpillar in a bag from a tree—runs the risk of re-creating in different form the patronage on which he depended during his lifetime. Lear performed dependency, just as he performed hanging from his inside-out umbrella when the wind sweeps him away, or as he memorably performed the hapless protagonist of the comic song 'Tea in the Arbour', who is menaced by flies and caterpillars, finds a frog in his tea, gets tar on his trousers, gets birdshot in his bottom and is finally caught in a mantrap. When Lear sang 'The Courtship of the Yonghy-Bonghy-Bò' or 'The Owl and the Pussy-cat' or 'The Quangle Wangle's Hat', he was, similarly, performing. Lear was a consummate actor. He made choices about how he came across on different occasions. As he recorded in his diary in July 1877, he attended a dinner party and 'being obliged to *act* one way or t'other' chose between 'Archepiscopal gravity—or very lively fun'.[139] The character he opted for that evening was a comic one: he 'rattled' the night away. If we assume that Lear's poetry is always chiefly and directly about his feelings at the moment of composition, we are reading cabaret as soliloquy.

As we have seen, Lear developed his cartoon vision of self over time, metamorphosing from string bean to plum pudding. But certain aspects of his performance remain consistent. He liked to portray himself as a bumbling character whose spectacles, absurdly large and hovering in advance of his face, figure a relationship to the world in which Lear is always a little behind, seeing things a beat later than others do. This is the precise opposite of the reality of his authorship of the cartoon, since he is in fact always several beats ahead of the audience. But it is vital to Lear's comic acting that there should seem to be a delay in his apprehensions that allows the reader to see before him. Lear's performance of unwariness is a blind that has been too effective in conditioning a response to his art as felt rather than considered.

Lear was, until heart trouble in his seventies forced him to slow down, a remarkably active person all his life. Aged fifty-three, he reported that he walked eight miles in two hours and two minutes, a brisk pace; in his sixties he climbed the foothills of the Himalayas. He possessed strong reserves of discipline and determination that drove him forward—despite the chains

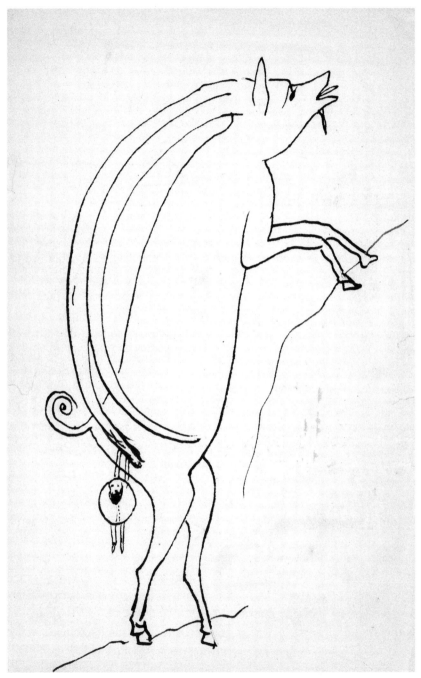

Fig. 5.20 'The landscape painter is enabled to ascend some of the highest tops of the Mountains of Crete by sticking on to a Moufflon's Horns' (1864)

Fig. 5.21 **Lear with Foss (1880s)**

of epilepsy and depression—to prodigious artistic output, including a prolific correspondence and considerable feats of travel and exploration, some
of it in wild terrain and under dangerous circumstances. He was an intellectual who liked the company of other intellectuals. His closest friends included some of the foremost Cambridge scholars of their generation; the
women whose company he preferred were authors, musicians, artists, travel
writers, linguists and translators. He read widely and thoughtfully all his
life, taking in periodicals and books in several languages that included philosophy and religion, poetry, essays, biography and letters, natural history,
travel, novels and parliamentary reports. He viewed art with the critical eye
of a practitioner; he listened to music with the quick ear of a singer and pianist. He was actively politically engaged by the issues of his day—particularly
in foreign policy. Lear was a dissenter, more involved with religious debate,
angrier and shrewder than his bumbling, unworldly, childlike persona
would suggest. He was also taller, slimmer, fitter, more capable, more at-
tractive to others, less isolated and less immune to sexual desire. In many
cases, we can read Lear only through the lens of his self-mockery: he is not
fully separable from it, as it is such an essential part of his letters, journals
and cartoons. But it is vital at least to recognise how Lear created and ma-
nipulated his persona and the effect that this has had on critical responses to
his work. Lear's dialogue is rooted in play with the adult reader as much as
with the child reader—play that draws attention to the persistence of the
child-self in adult psychology. Only by recognising Lear's self-fashioning as
a character and responding to his ideas, rather than merely to the pathos of
his biography, can critics fully appreciate his art. For 'Edward Lear' has
proved, in many ways, to be Lear's greatest and most enduring invention.

LIST OF ILLUSTRATIONS

Every effort has been made to identify copyright holders and obtain their permission for the use of copyright material. Notification of any additions or corrections that should be incorporated in future reprints or editions of this book would be greatly appreciated.

Figure Marginalia 'There was an Old Man of the Isles'
Edward Lear, *The Book of Nonsense* (London: Warne, 1888), 28. Reproduced from the
author's collection. This limerick first appears in *A Book of Nonsense* (1846).

INTRODUCTION

Figure I.1 **Lear and Foss**
Letter to Hallam Tennyson, 5 January 1876. Tennyson Research Centre, TRC/
LETTERS/5530-2. Courtesy of Lincolnshire County Council.

Figure I.2 **Lear's cartoon depiction of his ancestors**
Edward Lear: Holloway 1812–Sanremo 1888, ed. Rodolfo Falchi and Valerie
Wadsworth (Poggibonsi: Lalli Editore, 1997), 56.

Figure I.3 **'A Dream' storyboard**
Edward Lear, *Sleeping and Dreaming*. The Morgan Library and Museum, 2007.88k. Gift of
Mrs. Paul Pennoyer, 1963. Photo courtesy of the Pierpont Morgan Library, New York.

Figure I.4 **Lear leaping: self-caricature from his diary**
Edward Lear diaries, 1858–1888. *D* 29 February 1872. Houghton Library, MS Eng
797.3 (15), Harvard University.

CHAPTER I

Figure 1.1 **Lear's comically handwritten lyric from 'The Last Rose of Summer',
illustrating how it sounds when badly sung**
Edward Lear diaries, 1858–1888. *D* 23 October 1869. Houghton Library, MS Eng
797.3 (15), Harvard University.

Figure 1.2 **'S Singing', George Cruikshank**
George Cruikshank, *Comic Alphabet* (London: Tilt, 1836). © The Trustees of the
British Museum. All rights reserved.

CHAPTER 2

Figure 2.2a 'Old Woman of Leeds'
From *The History of Sixteen Wonderful Old Women* (London: Harris, 1821) (colour litho),
    English School (19th century) / British Library, London, UK / © British Library
    Board. All Rights Reserved / Bridgeman Images.

Figure 2.2b 'There was an Old Person of Leeds'
Edward Lear, *The Book of Nonsense* (London: Warne, 1888), 25. Reproduced from the
    author's collection. This limerick first appears in *A Book of Nonsense* (1861).

Figure 2.3a Lear's illustration for 'The Polly and the Pusseybite' (1866)
Edward Lear Miscellaneous Drawings, 1849–1866. Houghton Library, MS Typ 55.14,
    Harvard University.

Figure 2.3b Lear's illustration for 'The Polly and the Pusseybite' (1866)
Edward Lear Miscellaneous Drawings, 1849–1866. Houghton Library, MS Typ 55.14,
    Harvard University.

Figure 2.4 'A Polly-puss', Thomas Hood
Memorials of Thomas Hood, collected, arranged and edited by his daughter, with a
    preface and notes by his son (London: Moxon, 1860), 241. Reproduced from the
    author's collection.

Figure 2.5 'The Scroobious Pip'
Illustration for poem of the same name. Houghton Library, pga_typ_dr_805_l513_88c,
    Harvard University.

Figure 2.6 Lear as archbishop
Letter to Chichester Fortescue, 30 April 1885. Somerset Archives, South West
    Heritage Trust, DD / SH 337 C2 / 571. Courtesy of Somerset Archives and Local
    Studies, Somerset Heritage Centre.

Figure 2.7 Lear feeding unfortunate birds
Letter to Emily Tennyson, 14 January 1861. Tennyson Research Centre,
    TRC / LETTERS/5477-3. Courtesy of Lincolnshire County Council.

Chapter 3

Figure 3.1 'B was a Bat, Beautiful Bat!' from alphabet beginning 'A were some
    Ants'
Edward Lear, 'Alphabet', 1857. Yale Center for British Art, Paul Mellon Collection.

Figure 3.2 Blue and yellow macaw
The Gardens and Menagerie of the Zoological Society Delineated, ed. E. T. Bennett
    (London: Sharpe, 1831). Reproduced from the author's collection.

Chapter 4

Figure 4.1 'There was an old soldier of Bicester', Robert Cruikshank
Robert Cruikshank, *Anecdotes and Adventures of Fifteen Gentlemen* (London: Marshall, 1821). English School (19th century)/British Library, London, UK/© British Library Board. All Rights Reserved/Bridgeman Images.

Figure 4.2a 'There was an old soldier of Bicester'
Edward Lear, *Lear in the Original* (New York: Kraus, 1975), 34–35.

Figure 4.2b 'There was an old soldier of Bicester'
Edward Lear, *Lear in the Original* (New York: Kraus, 1975), 34–35.

Figure 4.3a 'L contemplates a ferocious horse with feelings of distrust'
Lear's cartoons of himself on horseback (1842). © The Trustees of the British Museum. All rights reserved.

Figure 4.3b 'L declares that he considers his horse far from tame'
Lear's cartoons of himself on horseback (1842). © The Trustees of the British Museum. All rights reserved.

Figure 4.3c 'K affectionately induces L to perceive that a thornbush has attached itself to his repugnant horse'
Lear's cartoons of himself on horseback (1842). © The Trustees of the British Museum. All rights reserved.

Figure 4.3d 'L is besought by K to sit back on his saddle'
Lear's cartoons of himself on horseback (1842). © The Trustees of the British Museum. All rights reserved.

Figure 4.4 'An Astronomer!!', George Moutard Woodward
'An Astronomer!!", drawn by George Moutard Woodward, etched by Thomas Rowlandson, from *Horse Accomplishments* (1799). Collection of Christchurch Art Gallery Te Puna o Waiwhetu, Sir Joseph Kinsey Bequest.

Figure 4.5 Lear's cartoon storyboard of scenes from 'Miss Maniac', plate 14
Illustrations of Miss Maniac. Houghton Library, MS Typ 55.6, Harvard University.

Figure 4.6a 'There was a young person of Janina'
Edward Lear, *More Nonsense* (London: Bush, 1872). Reproduced from the author's collection.

Figure 4.6b 'There was a young lady of Firle'
Lear, *More Nonsense*. Reproduced from the author's collection.

Color Insert

LIST OF ABBREVIATIONS

CV   Vivien Noakes, ed., *Edward Lear: The Complete Verse and Other Nonsense* (Oxford: Oxford University Press, 2001).

D   Edward Lear's Diary 1858–1888, 30 vols., MS Eng 797.3, Houghton Library.

LF   Lady Strachey, ed., *Letters of Edward Lear to Chichester Fortescue* (London: Unwin, 1907).

LL   Lady Strachey, ed., *Later Letters of Edward Lear* (London: Unwin, 1911).

LW   Vivien Noakes, *Edward Lear: The Life of a Wanderer,* rev. ed. (Stroud, UK: Sutton, 2004).

SL   Vivien Noakes, ed., *Selected Letters of Edward Lear* (Oxford: Oxford University Press, 1988).

Libraries and Other Manuscript Sources

Beinecke   Beinecke Library, Yale University, New Haven, CT

BL   British Library, London

Bod   Bodleian Library, University of Oxford, Oxford, UK

Houghton   Houghton Library, Harvard University, Cambridge, MA

NAL   National Art Library, Victoria and Albert Museum, London

NGS   National Gallery of Scotland, Edinburgh

NLS   National Library of Scotland, Edinburgh

NMS   National Museum of Scotland, Edinburgh

Pierpont   Pierpont Morgan Library, New York

Somerville   Somerville College, University of Oxford, Oxford, UK

Taunton   Somerset Archives, South West Heritage Trust, Taunton, UK

Lincoln   Tennyson Research Centre, Lincolnshire County Council, Lincoln, UK

Warne   Warne Collection, now managed by Penguin Random House and curated by the Victoria and Albert Museum, London

Unless otherwise noted, biblical quotations are taken from the King James Version of the Bible and dictionary definitions from the *Oxford English Dictionary* (OED). For reasons of space, a bibliography is not provided here; an excellent and constantly updated bibliography of works on Lear, curated by Marco Graziosi, can be found at https://nonsenselit.wordpress.com.

NOTES

Introduction

GENERAL NOTE: Lear's prose in his diaries and letters is, like his other work, delightfully idiosyncratic. It includes many unusual spellings (often reflecting inner wordplay, but sometimes merely a personal preference) and also portmanteau words, spoonerisms and neologisms. Readers should therefore assume that apparent oddities in quotations from his work are Lear's own. I have done my best, in transcribing over 10,000 manuscript pages of letters and diaries, to record what Lear wrote, but there may well be occasional misreadings; I apologise. For financial reasons, two illustrations that originally appeared the first edition of Lear's *A Book of Nonsense* (London: Maclean, 1846) and four that appeared in the third edition (London: Routledge and Warne, 1861) are reproduced here from the twenty-fifth edition, *The Book of Nonsense* (London: Warne, 1888), in my own collection. There are some small differences in the punctuation and capitalisation of these limericks at the various dates when they appear. For example, the limericks in the 1846 edition (but not in subsequent editions) are set in small caps; the Man of Whitehaven in 1861 dances with a 'Raven' rather than a 'raven'; and the Man of the Isles 'sung high dum diddle, and played on the fiddle', whereas in 1888 he 'sung "High dum diddle," and played on the fiddle'. I have otherwise followed *CV* in my presentation of limerick texts, though I note that Noakes capitalises Old Person, Young Lady etc in her reproduction of limericks from *More Nonsense* (London: Bush, 1872)— that is, she follows the conventions for limerick capitalisation established in 1861—whereas in my first edition of *More Nonsense* these epithets are not capitalised.

1. Queen Victoria, journal entry 15 July 1846, vols. 22 and 28, at www .queenvictoriasjournals.org.

2. *D* 2 August 1882, and *LL* 300, where Lear comments to Chichester Fortescue in 1884, 'I don't know if it is proper to call a sovereign a duck, but I cannot help thinking H. M. a dear and absolute duck'.

3. For discussion of Lear's beliefs, see Sara Lodge, 'Lear and Dissent', in *Lear and the Play of Poetry*, ed. James Williams and Matthew Bevis (Oxford: Oxford University Press, 2016), 70–88, and Jenny Uglow, *Mr Lear: A Life of Art and Nonsense* (London: Faber, 2017), esp. 306–310.

4. 'The Science of Nonsense', *Spectator*, 17 December 1870, 10.

5. This is changing, with strong signs of a revival of critical interest in Lear since his 2012 bicentenary. Among the important works on Lear published in the last few years are *Lear and the Play of Poetry*, ed. James Williams and Matthew Bevis

(Oxford: Oxford University Press, 2016), Robert McCracken Peck, *The Natural History of Edward Lear* (Woodbridge: ACC Art, 2016) and Jenny Uglow, *Mr Lear: A Life of Art and Nonsense* (London: Faber, 2017). I am aware of at least two other academic studies on Lear currently in preparation.

6. S. A. Nock, 'Edward Lear of the Nonsense Verses', *Sewanee Review* 49, no. 1 (1941), 68.

7. Ina Rae Hark, *Edward Lear* (Boston: Twayne, 1982), 78–79.

8. Lear to Henry Grenfell, 25 November 1884. 'I was born in 1812, the day Mr Perceval was shot'. Private collection.

9. For the Lear family's friendship with the Ayscoughs, Wilkinsons and Meacocks, see *D* 15 January 1880. William Wilkinson (1763–1833) married Jane Ayscough (1773–1838) and had twelve children. The Wilkinson and Ayscough families became well-known nineteenth-century cabinetmakers, upholders and furniture dealers. See www.airgale.com.au/histories/HISTORY OF THE WILKINSONS.

10. The Nevill family manufactured patent fleecy hosiery, lambs' wool and cotton goods at Langham Mill, Godalming, in the 1850s; they had previously been based in Stoke Newington. Both William and his son, the architect Ralph Nevill (1845–1917), who visited Lear in San Remo, were keen archaeologists. William's nephews Hugh and Geoffrey Nevill became eminent scholars: the first of Sri Lanka, its language, culture and zoology, and the latter of molluscs.

11. *D* 26 August 1873 recalls '"my uncle Col Leake" at the Queens Square select dinner parties'. Robert Martin Leake the elder's will (PROB-11-1816-437), in the National Archives at Kew, shows that Lucy Gale (wife of Thomas Augustus Gale and mother of Lear's friend Robert Gale) was his daughter.

12. *D* 31 October 1874.

13. *D* 5 August 1865.

14. *D* 6–7 November 1874.

15. Daniel Fowler in Frances K. Smith, *Daniel Fowler of Amherst Island 1810–1894* (Kingston: Agnes Etherington Art Centre, 1979), 106.

16. This cartoon appeared in the catalogue of the 1997 San Remo exhibition on Lear curated by Valerie Wadsworth (by whose permission I reproduce it) and Rodolfo Falchi. *Edward Lear: Holloway 1812–Sanremo 1888* (Poggibonsi: Lalli Editore, 1997), 56. The current whereabouts of the cartoon are unknown.

17. Samuel Warren, 'The Spectre-Smitten', in 'Passages from the Diary of a Late Physician', *Blackwood's Edinburgh Magazine*, February 1831, 363.

18. *D* 7 and 8 August 1872.

19. *D* 12 May 1886.

20. I am indebted to conversations with Professor Arjune Sen, head of the Oxford Epilepsy Research Group, for information on this topic. See also Andres M. Kanner, 'Depression in Epilepsy: Prevalence, Clinical Semiology, Pathogenic Mechanisms, and Treatment', *Biological Psychiatry* 54 (2003), 388–398.

21. *D* 19 June 1871.

22. *D* 8 April 1886.

23. *LW*, 11. For accounts of the boys who died at King's College School and a school in Darlington, see *Newcastle Courant*, 15 May 1885, 6.

24. For a fuller account of Lear's sexuality, see Peter Swaab, 'Some Think Him . . . Queer: Loners and Love in Edward Lear', in *Lear and the Play of Poetry*, 89–114. Lear mentions (*D* 6 July 1864) kissing a nursemaid in the back of a carriage as a young man, and an affair with a younger woman who had 'not much mind' in the Abruzzi in 1843; occasional casual sex is suggested by references to being attracted to follow prostitutes and a local waitress. An enigmatic reference (*D* 27 March 1873) to a 'most remarkable interlude'—'How *"the"* P.P. loved, died, and was buried'—also suggests sex as it conjures a line from *Much Ado about Nothing:* 'I will live in thy heart, die in thy lap, and be buried in thine eyes'. Various poetical allusions, as well as emotional outbursts and passionate reactions to their slights, presence and absence, reveal Lear's attraction to Franklin Lushington and Hubert Congreve.

25. *D* 28 June 1879. Lear mentions that the lines were taken from an American paper in 1871. This poem appeared in the *Charleston Daily News* on 25 May 1871, 4, and may also have been printed in other newspapers. It was anthologised in G. Westley, ed., *For Love's Sweet Sake* (Boston: Lee and Shepard, 1899).

26. *D* 8 January 1867.

27. *D* 15 December 1880. For the Giles sisters' school, see A. P. Baggs, Diane K. Bolton and Patricia E. C. Croot, 'Stoke Newington: Education', in *A History of the County of Middlesex: Volume 8, Islington and Stoke Newington Parishes*, ed. T. F. T. Baker and C. R. Elrington (London: Victoria County History, 1985), 217–223.

28. *D* 9 February 1867.

29. *D* 23 January 1882. This memory is stimulated by Rupert Ingleby's death in Adelaide on 6 December 1881, aged sixty-one. Ingleby became a distinguished Q.C. and Australian public figure.

30. *D* 14 September 1869.

31. *A List of the Governors and Officers of the Asylum for the Support of the Deaf and Dumb Children of the Poor* (Bermondsey: Printed at the Manufactory for the Employment of the Deaf and Dumb, Fort Place, 1817). Jeremiah is still listed as 'of Bowman's Lodge, Upper Holloway', although this period follows his financial crash. His involvement with the asylum was of long standing. The *Public Ledger*, 20 April 1807, 1, advertised the annual dinner for the President, Governors and Friends of the Asylum at the London Tavern, Bishopsgate Street, where some of the deaf children would recite verse. Jeremiah's name is prominent among the 'stewards' for this fundraiser.

32. *D* 9 September 1867. As is often the case, Lear underlines these words twice; italics fail to do justice to his multiple emphases.

33. *Times,* 8 August 1860, 5.

34. *D* 21 June 1880.

35. See also, of the Goldsmids' house, 'home-like & intellectual', *D* 31 October 1863.

36. *D* 7 July 1877.

37. *D* 17 October 1863.

38. *D* 15 March 1884. He recalls Evelyn Baring saying this in 1861.

39. *D* 10 June 1872.

40. *D* 15 August 1880.

41. See *D* 22 July 1877, where Lear conflates Gloucester's speech from *Henry VI* and Tennyson's 'Oenone'. Lear is writing to Hubert Congreve at the time, and his unconscious medley suggestively combines the voice of an old man and of a young woman in love with a beautiful youth.

42. See *D* 6 and 11 September 1871, where he is reading *The Antiquary* and *St Ronan's Well* 'with as much delight as 40 years ago'.

43. *D* 18 September 1861.

44. See for example his visit to Boscombe Priory, *D* 30 September 1869 and *D* 10–11 September 1883, where Lear is affected by drawing the 'Shelley memorial view' at La Spezia and thinking about Shelley's body being washed ashore.

45. *D* 9 August 1880.

46. *D* 5 June 1873. Thomas Moore ascribed these previously unpublished lines to Byron in *Letters and Journals of Lord Byron,* vol. 1 (New York: Harper, 1830), 56.

47. *Dublin University Magazine,* February 1833, 145. This magazine was founded in January 1833, so Lear was an early reader; it was unionist in tendency. Marco Graziosi and I both independently discovered this source; I am grateful to him for discussions of it.

48. Pierpont MS 2007.88k.

49. *D* 25 December 1867.

50. *D* 5 October 1880.

51. Among them were John Blencowe, Thomson Hankey and Henry Grenfell.

52. *D* 2 November 1868.

53. *LL,* 271.

54. *CV,* 435. I have assumed 'trunk' for Noakes's 'truck'.

55. 'Nonsense Lyrics', *Examiner* 18 November 1876, 1302–1303.

56. For Hengler's Circus see *Liverpool Daily Post,* 24 February 1866, 5. For Paulton's performances see the *London & Provincial Entr'acte,* 24 September 1870, 3, and the *Berkshire Chronicle,* 31 December 1870, 2.

57. *John Ruskin's Correspondence with Joan Severn: Sense and Nonsense Letters,* ed. Rachel Dickinson (London: MHRA, 2009), 177.

58. John Ruskin, *Pall Mall Gazette,* 15 February 1886, 2.

59. Letter to Henry Bruce, 24 November 1865. BL: R.P. 1470.

60. For example, Jean-Jacques Lecercle, in *The Philosophy of Nonsense* (London: Routledge, 1994), 35, argues that 'Nonsense does not seek to express the writer's emotions. Its main interest is in language, in the exploration and preservation of what Husserl calls the *formal* aspect of language'. Wim Tigges, in *An Anatomy of Literary Nonsense* (Amsterdam: Rodopi, 1988), 88, similarly asserts that 'an "ideal" nonsense . . . must fulfill the essential conditions of unresolved tension, absence of emotional involvement and an upgrading of its verbal and / or formal nature'. Elizabeth Sewell, in her otherwise excellent early study *The Field of Nonsense* (London: Chatto and Windus, 1952), 149, was inclined to regard Lear's nonsense songs 'technically as failures because in them the separation between player and material is beginning to fail, and the term "player" here will include both Nonsense writer and Nonsense reader'. It is, for me, precisely in this 'failure'—the complex emotional transference that the text enables—that the success of Lear's greatest work lies.

1. Returning to Lear: Music and Memory

1. *D* 28 August 1869. Elsewhere this work is a 'picture poem'. Word, image and music are all interconnected in Lear's mind.

2. Lear to Chichester Fortescue, 15 February 1859, Taunton DD / SH / 337 / C2 / 68.

3. *D* 22 April 1865.

4. *D* 8 February 1868.

5. For nonsense verses produced by thunder at Nárkunda, see Lear's Indian Journal 28 April 1874, Houghton MS Eng 797.4. Another of Lear's nonsense verses inspired by a place-name is 'Finale Marina! If ever you'd seen her', in which the Italian town is imagined as a captivating female. Lear in 1837 visited the Italian towns of Colico and Dongo, which may relate to his later verses 'Calico Pie' and 'The Dong with a Luminous Nose'.

6. *D* 10 November 1873.

7. *D* 1 May 1866.

8. *D* 6 February 1867.

9. *D* 17 March 1870.

10. *D* 6 May 1866.

11. See *D* 23 September 1865, where Gussie plays this piece and 'for a moment one's heart returned'. In *D* 21 June 1870, Lear reports hearing it in Nice and is distressed.

12. 'Land of the Stranger', arr. James Roe (Charleston: Siegling, 1830–1850?), University of South Carolina Library 785.42 T63n (17). Lear (*D* 21 May 1887 and 5 June 1887) recalls the song broadly as it appears in this version, but

typically recasts some of the lines, concluding, 'For Memory like the needle that guides the wandering Mariner home, tho the wind may be high & the skies may be dark, the needle still points to the pole'.

13. Edward Strachey, intro. to Lear, *Nonsense Songs and Stories* (London: Warne: 1894), x.

14. His sister Sarah was an accomplished pianist; it was probably she who taught him to play this instrument. In old age, Lear still treasured his sister Ann's guitar; it seems likely that she was his first guitar teacher. Music-making in this period was affected by gender conventions. Men often learned instruments like the violin, the flute and the clarinet that required accompaniment at musical soirees; women typically learned self-contained instruments such as the piano and the guitar so they could accompany themselves and others. See Derek Scott, *The Singing Bourgeois* (Milton Keynes, UK: Open University Press, 1989), 50. Lear's flexibility in playing different instruments is typical of his socially valuable ability to play a variety of different roles.

15. See the reproduction of this image in the colour insert.

16. Strachey, intro. to *Nonsense Songs and Stories*, x.

17. Emily Tennyson, *Lady Tennyson's Journal*, ed. James O. Hoge (Charlottesville: University of Virginia Press, 1981), 54, 17 October 1855: 'Mr Lear . . . sang for two or three hours. The whole of "Mariana," the whole of "The Lotos Eaters," "Ellen Adair," "Tears, idle tears," "Let the solid ground" . . . all his own settings'.

18. *D* 8 January 1866.

19. *D* 17 July 1876.

20. Lear to Mr and Mrs Henry Bruce, 25 September 1884, BL R.P. 1470. Lear mentions that he is negotiating with the publisher Hogg of Charing Cross for republication of 'all the Nonsense Songs & stories (not the "old persons") in one vol. with additions'; those additions were to include 'Mr and Mrs Discobbolos Part II'.

21. See *D* 21 December 1869, where Lear reports writing to Bush, his publisher, with this title.

22. Mrs Winthrop Chanler (nee Daisy Terry), *Roman Spring: Memoirs* (Boston: Little Brown, 1934), 29.

23. *D* 26 May 1872.

24. 'Fooly song' and 'nonsense ballads' *D* 11 December and 24 December 1871. 'The Akond of Swat' is 'an absurd fantasia'(*D* 27 July 1873), a word usually deployed in a musical context, which was only beginning in the nineteenth century to be used for poetry.

25. *D* 17 March 1877. F. C. Chattock, *The Two Old Bachelors* (Solihull, UK: self-published, 1879).

26. *D* 10 March 1885. Emily Josephine Troup, *The Daddylonglegs and the Fly* (London: Lucas and Weber, 1885).

27. John Ruskin, *Pall Mall Gazette*, 15 February 1886, 2.

28. Mostyn Pryce, *Musical Nonsense Rhymes* (London: Weekes, 1876).

29. For the latter, see *D* 20 December 1882, when he played this for General Ogle and his wife, to their delight.

30. Chichester Fortescue, '. . . *And Mr Fortescue': A Selection from the Diaries from 1851 to 1862 of Chichester Fortescue, Lord Carlingford,* ed. Osbert Wyndham Hewett (London: Murray, 1958), 54,137.

31. *D* 15 December 1878. He sings this and 'The Lady of Shalott' to William Bevan.

32. When he heard that Percy Bysshe Shelley's sisters were still alive, he excitedly made plans to send them paintings of Italy, which he had painted near the scene of their brother's death. See *D* 7 May 1880. This is one of many occasions when Lear reached out to Shelley and Byron via extant members of their circle.

33. The most substantial general discussion is Anne Ehrenpreis, 'Edward Lear Sings Tennyson's Songs', *Harvard Library Bulletin* 27 (1979), 65–85. See also Edmund Miller, 'Two Approaches to Edward Lear's Nonsense Songs', *Victorian Newsletter* (Fall 1973), 5–8, and I. A. Copley, 'Edward Lear—Composer', *Musical Opinion* (October 1980), 8–12.

34. Lear met Wordsworth in 1834 at Colonel Bolton's house in the Lake District (see *D* 22 October 1862). It is noticeable that this encounter, unlike Lear's visits to Byron's and Shelley's former abodes, inspired no exclamation marks. Lear quotes 'The Fountain' (*D* 4 March 1865), but a letter to Gussie Bethell of 18 June 1887 (*SL*, 282) shows that much of Wordsworth's verse was previously unknown to him. *LL*, 242, also suggests antagonism between Lear's cherished friend A. P. Stanley and Wordsworth, 'who opposed him always'.

35. As a dissenter, Lear was also exposed to congregational hymn singing in a way that would not become commonplace in Anglican churches until after 1820. Among the hymns that came back to him from time to time were Joseph Hart's 'Come Ye Sinners, Poor and Wretched' (1759) with its chorus 'If you tarry till you're better/You will never come at all', and Isaac Watts's 'There Is a Land of Pure Delight'.

36. Lear mentions having written, around 1828 or 1830, embarrassing letters to Sir George and Lady Smart (*D* 2 February 1866). Since Smart was one of the most prominent musicians, conductors and musical organisers of his day, the letters may well have been begging for admission to concerts or similar favours.

37. See *D* 17 January 1883, where he is 'greatly pleased' by Henry Strachey playing portions of *The Magic Flute* and 'other bits of Mozart'.

38. *D* 22 August 1884.

39. *D* 22 June 1879.

40. *D* 12 October 1873.

41. Lear to Fanny Coombe, 1 December 1838, Warne 10001.14.

42. *D* 29 December 1864.

43. *D* 21 June 1864.

44. E.g., *D* 10 November 1863, where Willy Nevill's wife plays Beethoven and Mendelssohn well; *D* 15 March 1876, where Hubert Congreve plays Beethoven's 'Adieu to the Piano'; *D* 9 January 1877, where Mrs Hanbury plays 'Chopin & a wonderful Hungarian chant divinely'; *D* 24 June 1877, where George Hall plays Mendelssohn beautifully.

45. Edward Rimbault, *Rimbault's Christy Minstrel Melodies* (London: Chappell, 1858).

46. For a discussion of Beuler, whose 'works were regularly featured at Vauxhall Gardens and The Royal Coburg', see David Worrall, 'Blake in Theatreland', in *Blake, Modernity and Popular Culture,* ed. Steve Clark and Jason Whittaker (Basingstoke, UK: Palgrave, 2007), 34.

47. For another example of old and new music programmed together, see *D* 11 October 1866, where Marianne North sang 'the Wanderer' (likely an old broadside ballad) and 'The Three Fishers' (a song by Charles Kingsley).

48. *D* 23 October 1869.

49. The Oxford Dictionary of National Biography notes that in 1818 Braham was described in the *Quarterly Musical Magazine and Review* as possessing 'the most extraordinary genius and aptitude for the exercise of his profession that was ever implanted in a human being'.

50. *D* 11 October 1868. Ward Braham was, in fact, not a professional singer. But early training made him quite capable of such impressive performances.

51. Marianne North, *Recollections of a Happy Life,* ed. Susan Morgan (Charlottesville: University Press of Virginia, 1993), 19.

52. *D* 11 March 1868.

53. *D* 8 June 1877.

54. *CV,* 5.

55. *CV,* 10.

56. Compare for example Biddy Fudge's versified journal description of Paris: 'Where *shall* I begin with the endless delights / Of this Eden of milliners, monkies, and sights— / This dear busy place, where there's nothing transacting / But dressing and dinnering, dancing and acting?' William Thackeray, *The Fudge Family in Paris* (London: Longman, 1818), 39.

57. A manuscript of this poem in a private collection owned by descendants of the Lear family is dated 23 August 1825.

58. *CV,* 3–4.

59. *D* 28 December 1865.

60. *D* 31 March 1878. Lear recalls getting someone else to go to Alaric Watts, editor of the *Literary Souvenir,* with his lines about Pisgah. He evidently also read the annuals the *Gem* and the *Bijou,* which he mentions elsewhere.

61. Derek Scott, *Singing Bourgeois,* 147.

62. Thomas Haynes Bayly, 'Isle of Beauty, Fare Thee Well!', melody by Charles Shapland Whitmore (London: Goulding and D'Almaine, 1834?).

63. *CV,* 14.

64. 'Mrs Jayfer's Advice' and 'Some Incidents in the Life of My Uncle Arly', in which the protagonist spends time in 'merely yelling'.

65. Thomas Haynes Bayly, "Oh! No, We Never Mention Her" (London: Goulding and D'Almaine, 1823–1824).

66. *CV,* 43.

67. Of course, contrafactum need not be parodic. Many composers set new words to established tunes without a sidelong glance at the tone of the original words and melody.

68. Lear, 'Sung by J—C—G . . . Esqr', 7 October 1826. Manuscript, private collection.

69. Compare hymn 12 from *The National Chartist Hymn Book* (Rochdale, UK: National Chartist Association, 1845), 11, which runs, 'Hoary age and sturdy youth,/All imbibe the sacred truth—/That your Maker made you free,/And demand EQUALITY!'

70. See Michael Henry Scrivener, *Radical Shelley: The Philosophical Anarchism and Utopian Thought of Percy Bysshe Shelley* (Princeton, NJ: Princeton University Press, 1982), 47.

71. Alfred Tennyson, 'You ask me why, though ill at ease', in *The Poems of Tennyson,* ed. Christopher Ricks (London: Longman, 1969), 490. The image may, alternatively, be of a river broadening out towards its estuary.

72. *LL,* 336. Lear reports that in old days he often used to hear Irving preach at the Caledonian Chapel. Irving was convicted of heresy in 1832.

73. *D* 17 April 1872.

74. *CV,* 428

75. Thomas Arne, *The Hymn of Eve from the Oratorio of Abel* (Liverpool: Hime, c. 1815), 3.

76. Olivia Clarke, *Parodies on Popular Songs,* with music by Sir J. N. Stevenson (London: Willis, 1826), preface. An Irish 'cronon' or 'cronane' is a monotonous chant or drone, a song without words.

77. North, *Recollections,* 29.

78. Miss Fraser's album (c. 1829–1830) is in a private collection. Lear's own album of sketches, bird pictures, poems and song is at NLS MS.3321, H.S.954.

79. Lear album, NLS MS.3321, H.S.954. This is the fair copy, dated 23 October 1829; the album also contains a draft.

80. Gerald Finley, *Angel in the Sun: Turner's Vision of History* (Montreal: McGill-Queen's University Press, 1999), 26.

81. Lear album, NLS MS.3321, H.S.954. See James Bird, *Dunwich: A Tale of the Splendid City* (London: Baldwin and Cradock, 1828), 24. Set in the Plantagenet

era, *Dunwich* tells of the forbidden romance between Bertha de Valeins and her lover, Mowbray. He signals his approach by '*three beacon-lights*', rather like Lear's Dong with a Luminous Nose.

82. Felicia Hemans, 'The Bride's Farewell', *The Poetical Works of Mrs Felicia Hemans*, vol. 2 (New York: Evert Duycinck, 1828), 161–162. The poem was set to music more than once: see also John Barnett, *The Bride's Farewell from the Queen's Boudoir* [a musical annual] (London: Jefferys, 1841).

83. M. L. Beevor and T. Williams, 'The Bride's Farewell', in *The Sylph; or Annual Pocket Melodist*, ed. T. Williams, vol. 1 (London: Williams, 1830), 74–75.

84. *CV*, 244.

85. Lear to George Coombe, 20 July 1835, Warne 10001.9.

86. Lear to George Coombe, 6 September 1836, Warne 10001.27. The Braddylls lived at Conishead Priory near Ulverston. A later diary entry makes it clear that Lear played the flute on this occasion, doubtless allowing the ladies to shine.

87. Jacob Beuler, 'The Nervous Family', 2nd ed. (London: Shepherd, 1864).

88. *CV*, 54.

89. *D* 24 September 1875.

90. J. Beuler, 'Tea in the Arbour', arr. A. C. Whitcombe (London: Paine and Hopkins, c. 1830).

91. J. Beuler, 'Wery Pekooliar, or the Lisping Lover', arr. J. Blewitt (London: Clementi, Collard, 1826), 2.

92. *CV*, 219.

93. Hubert Congreve, *LL*, preface, 20.

94. T. Hudson, 'The Cork Leg!', arr. J. Blewitt (London: Hudson and Collard, 1832?). The refrain varies from version to version.

95. For Lear's cartoons of popular songs from the Knowsley period, see Herman W. Liebert, ed., *Lear in the Original* (New York: Kraus, 1975). I reproduce them by kind permission of the firm of H. P. Kraus.

96. Lear, *By That Lake, Whose Gloomy Shore*, ed. Donald Gallup (North Haven, CT: John Henry, 1973).The picture story can be seen at www.nonsenselit.org/Lear/pstories/kiven.

97. Rowland E. Prothero, ed., *The Life and Correspondence of Arthur Penrhyn Stanley*, vol. 1 (London: Murray, 1894), 146–147.

98. *Lear in the Original*, 152.

99. *CV*, 37. The Houghton Library has made 'Miss Maniac' digitally available on its website, so the pictures can be studied in greater detail than *CV* permits. https://iiif.lib.harvard.edu/manifests/view/drs:48895553$1i.

100. Henry Rowley Bishop, *The Music in The Maniac or the Swiss Banditti: A Serio-Comic Opera*, words by S. J. Arnold (London: Goulding, D'Almaine, Potter, 1810), 129.

101. *Lear in the Original,* 148.

102. *Funny Books for Boys and Girls* (London: Bogue, 1856), 35–36. There is also a pool of tears in Gussie Bethell's 'The Ugly Princess and the Ogre's Son', in *Echoes of an Old Bell; and Other Tales of Fairy Lore* (London: Griffith and Farran, 1865), 72.

103. *D* 19 July 1873. They met at Moore's publisher, Longman's. Lear reports that he has just read through eight volumes of Moore's diaries. He also recalls meeting Samuel Rogers in 1850.

104. *D* 23 July 1865. Moore remains part of Lear's repertoire to the end; see *D* 7 August 1882, where he quotes 'How dear to me the hour when daylight dies', and 15 September 1882, where he plays *Irish Melodies* to the Drummonds and Mundellas.

105. Thomas Moore, *The Poetical Works of Thomas Moore* (Philadelphia: Crissy, 1835), 319.

106. Ibid., 339.

107. Thomas Moore, *The Works of Thomas Moore* (Leipzig: Fleischer, 1833), 226.

108. Lear to Fortescue, 12 September 1873, *LL,* 161.

109. *Works of Thomas Moore,* 213.

110. Thomas Hood, *Whims and Oddities, Series 1* (London: Lupton Relfe, 1826), facing p. 13.

111. *The Universal Songster or Museum of Mirth* (London: Jones, 1834), 207.

112. *Lear in the Original,* 170.

113. Lewis Carroll, *Alice's Adventures in Wonderland,* ed. Hugh Haughton (London: Penguin, 1998), 105–106.

114. *Lear in the Original,* 144.

115. William Thackeray, 'Sorrows of Werther', reprinted in *A Victorian Anthology,* ed. Edmund Clarence Stedman (Boston: Houghton Mifflin, 1896), 305.

116. Lear to George and Fanny Coombe, n.d. August 1837?, Warne 10001.24.

117. Lear to Fanny Coombe, 8 July 1837, *CV,* 508.

118. Muzio Clementi, *Introduction to the Art of Playing the Pianoforte* (Leipzig: Peters, 1801), 20.

119. Edmund Law Lushington, a Cambridge friend of Tennyson's, married his younger sister Cecilia Tennyson, so the two families were related.

120. Lear to Emily Tennyson, 5 October 1852, Lincoln 5399.

121. Ibid.

122. See Hubert Congreve's preface to *LL,* 20, for a discussion of Lear's fondness for spread chords and his 'once fine tenor voice'. Later commentators often note that Lear's voice deteriorated with age, and he was obliged to 'vamp' his songs.

123. Emily Tennyson to Lear, 16 April 1859, Lincoln 5459.

124. *D* 8 July 1877.

125. *D* 3 March 1858.

126. *D* 13 November 1868. In the conversation Lear reports, Tennyson turns from discussion of the death of Franklin Lushington's son to lament his own history: 'I nearly died of teeth: I was given over, & lay for dead a long time'. It is as if Tennyson's nearly abandoned inner child can't bear to be usurped by other children, even dead ones.

127. *D* 29 January 1862. Lear's medleys at the piano made this point just as effectively as his better-known nonsense versions of lines from Tennyson, e.g., in his letter to Fortescue of 12 September 1873, where 'to watch the crisping ripples on the beach' (from 'The Lotos-Eaters') becomes 'to watch the tipsy cripples on the beach'. *LL,* 161.

128. *D* 16 June 1867.

129. Charles Tennyson, *Alfred Tennyson* (London: Macmillan, 1949), 441.

130. *D* 13 May 1861.

131. *LL,* 232.

132. E.g., '. . . *and Mr Fortescue': A Selection from the Diaries from 1851 to 1862 of Chichester Fortescue, Lord Carlingford,* ed. Osbert Wyndham Hewett (London: Murray, 1958), 54, 137.

133. Evelyn Baring in *Queery Leary Nonsense,* ed. Lady Strachey (London: Mills and Boon, 1911), 7. See also Lear's parody of the same line at *D* 20 September 1870, 'In gnats, if gnats be gnats'. Conrad Noel, a child during Lear's San Remo years, recalled that after dispensing presents of oranges from the pockets of an ancient greatcoat, 'He would . . . go to the piano and play melodious airs, some serious and some comic, and would sing to us one or other of the nonsense rhymes'. Conrad Noel, *An Autobiography,* ed. Sidney Dark (London: Dent, 1946), 7.

134. *D* 11 May 1877.

135. *CV,* 241–242.

136. *Mother Goose's Melody* (London: Power, 1791), 64.

137. Hugh Haughton, 'Edward Lear and "The Fiddlediddlety of Representation"', in *The Oxford Handbook of Victorian Poetry,* ed. Matthew Bevis (Oxford: Oxford University Press, 2013), 352–369.

138. *CV,* 247.

139. L. M. Budgen, *Episodes of Insect Life* (London: Reeve Benham and Reeve, 1850), 223.

140. *CV,* 238.

141. Thomas Wright, ed., *Early English Poetry, Ballads, and Popular Literature of the Middle Ages,* vol. 4 (London: Richards, 1841), 85.

142. *CV,* 255.

143. James Bird, *The Emigrant's Tale* (London: Baldwin and Cradock, 1833), 3.

144. *CV,* 422. The Dong also recalls the many abandoned or bereaved characters in Tennyson's verse.

145. See *The British Minstrel: A Collection of All the Ancient and Modern Songs* (London: Vernor and Hood, 1820), 404–405.

146. Lucretius, *De Rerum Natura*, trans. Martin Ferguson Smith (Indianapolis and Cambridge: Hackett, 2001), 116.

147. *D* 29 January 1866.

148. See also Beuler's 'Wery Pekooliar', or Thomas Hood's 'Faithless Sally Brown'.

149. 'Dash My Vig!' in *The Universal Songster or Museum of Mirth*, vol. 1 (London: Jones, 1827–1832), 31.

150. See OED and also Charles Darwin, letter to Emma Darwin, 5 April 1840: 'Be Sure you give Mr Hoddy Doddy a kiss from me!' (meaning the baby). *The Correspondence of Charles Darwin*, ed. Frederick Burkhardt and James A. Secord, vol. 2 (Cambridge: Cambridge University Press, 1986), 263.

151. *D* 10 November 1880.

152. *CV,* 325.

153. *D* 7 May 1863, 'nil save the white barrel earthen broken-handled jug'.

154. The protagonist resembles a statue of Bacchus on a turtle that Lear would have known from the Giardini di Boboli in Florence. Lear's title also recalls that of Longfellow's popular poem *The Courtship of Miles Standish* (1858), which features a different kind of love triangle, but an equally no-nonsense heroine.

155. Byron, *Childe Harold's Pilgrimage* (London: Murray, 1837), 247, canto IV, verse 178.

156. *D* 26 January 1874.

157. Philip Hofer, 'The Yonghy-Bonghy-Bò', *Harvard Library Bulletin* 15, no. 3 (July 1967), 237.

158. *D* 8 December 1875. Eleanor Frances Poynter was the author of *My Little Lady* and *Ersilia*, novels that Lear appreciated.

159. 'Nonsense Lyrics', *Examiner,* 18 November 1876, 1302–1303. This critic was willing to see Lear's best songs as 'important' and asserted that 'we recognise . . . the voice of the first great Nonsense Poet of the age'.

160. 'Christmas Books', *Times,* 21 December 1876, 6.

161. James and Horace Smith, 'Drury's Dirge', in *Rejected Addresses or the New Theatrum Poetarum* (London: Miller, 1812), 42.

162. Benjamin Humphrey Smart, *An Outline of Sematology or an Essay towards Establishing a New Theory of Grammar, Logic and Rhetoric* (London: Richardson, 1831), 217.

163. William Dobson, *Poetical Ingenuities and Eccentricities* (London: Chatto and Windus, 1882), 220.

164. C. M. Bowra, *The Romantic Imagination* (Oxford: Oxford University Press, 1950), 279.

165. Emile Cammaerts, *The Poetry of Nonsense* (London: Routledge, 1925), 85.

166. Michael O'Neill, 'Edward Lear and Romanticism', in *Lear and the Play of Poetry*, ed. James Williams and Matthew Bevis (Oxford: Oxford University Press, 2016), 51.

167. *D* 11 February 1867. A cartoon from the 1830s belonging to the Hornby family, reproduced in Vivien Noakes, *Edward Lear: The Life of a Wanderer* (London: BBC, 1985), 47, shows Lear standing amazed before an orchestra who are breaking out of a parcel, playing their instruments, rather like the blackbirds who break out of a pie in the nursery rhyme. The eight instrumentalists include a flautist, two string players, an accordionist and four brass players, including somebody who is playing the serpent. This illustration does not appear in subsequent editions of the book from other publishers.

168. Lear to Fanny Coombe, 1 December 1838, Warne 10001.14.

169. Lear, *Illustrated Excursions in Italy*, vol. 1 (London: McLean, 1846), 17.

170. Lear to Emily Tennyson, 30 December 1860, Lincoln 5477.

171. Lear himself wondered about how music worked on the mind. Having been moved by the lovely music of the Philharmonic Society in Corfu on 20 April 1866, he reflected in his diary that he knew not 'if the perception that music acts on the mind as any other noise does—by affecting the nerves—is well to have been cherished: one respects music less as technical result rather than spiritual spontaneity. . . . Anyhow, just now I am affected as of old'.

172. Louisa Alcott, 'Eight Cousins', *Good Things for the Young of All Ages*, 6 March 1875, 214.

2. Nonsense and Nonconformity

1. *D* 11 May 1866.

2. Emily Tennyson, *Lady Tennyson's Journal*, ed. James O. Hoge (Charlottesville: University of Virginia Press, 1981), 267.

3. Lear's explosions, which he understood to be physiological as well as psychological, were usually provoked by being 'controlled' or feeling abandoned. Religious intolerance could detonate both these triggers simultaneously.

4. *LL*, 187.

5. Lear to Emma Parkyns, 18 December 1871, private collection.

6. *D* 1 October 1865.

7. *D* 12 October 1868.

8. *D* 30 June 1865.

9. *D* 4 April 1869.

10. *D* 23 January 1870.

11. *D* 1 October 1865.

12. *D* 17 September 1862.

13. *D* 24 August 1862.

14. *D* 7 July 1861.

15. Lear to Emily Tennyson, 28–29 October 1855, Lincoln 5340–1.

16. John Morison, *The Fathers and Founders of the London Missionary Society: A Jubilee Memorial* (London: Fisher, 1844), 496–498.

17. *D* 29 December 1873.

18. The Lear family home, Bowman's Lodge, was close to two chapels, Holloway Chapel and Union Chapel, that supported an Independent dissenting community, and it is possible that they worshipped here.

19. *LL*, 250.

20. According to the Test Act of 1672, holders of public office had to take the oaths of allegiance and supremacy and receive communion, duly certified by Minister and Churchwarden, according to the usage of the Church of England. Some Protestant dissenters were willing to swallow these conditions in order to become MPs, while privately rejecting Anglicanism.

21. Richard D. Floyd, *Church, Chapel and Party: Religious Dissent and Political Modernization in Nineteenth-Century England* (Basingstoke, UK: Palgrave, 2008), 9.

22. *LL*, 250.

23. See also, for example, *D* 11 December 1863: 'Mr Hawkins—a tory-loud-speaking & a bore'; or 24 December 1867, of Lord Percy: 'he is full of swell vulgar curiosity & narrow Toryism'.

24. *D* 25 November 1861.

25. Lear to Emily Tennyson, 10 May 1865, *SL*, 205.

26. *LF*, 252.

27. *D* 24 September 1863.

28. *D* 8 December 1863.

29. See Lear to Lady Waldegrave, 15 March 1863, where he notes the twenty-third sermon he has heard on Lot's wife 'and other unpleasant legends', *LF*, 276.

30. *D* 22 March 1868. See also on 18 October 1868 at the Clives' house: 'a long funxion of prayers—indescribably queer'.

31. See also *D* 8 January 1860: 'Mr Thomas preached an absurd sermon about responses, kneeling & c'.

32. Lear to Emily Tennyson, 10 May 1865, *SL*, 205.

33. *LF*, 150.

34. Mary Anne Schimmelpenninck, *The Life of Mary Anne Schimmelpenninck*, ed. Christiana C. Hankin (London: Longman, 1860), 5.

35. *LW*, 270.

36. Ibid., 4, 22.

37. Lear bought a copy of Arnaud Berquin's *The Looking-Glass for the Mind* in 1885 and signed his name in it. Since he signed it, he evidently didn't mean to give it as a gift. The book was a reprint of the 1792 edition, and the most likely explanation of its presence in Lear's library is that he bought it out of nostalgia for a text he had enjoyed in childhood.

38. *D* 22 September 1861. The last words of this entry are hard to read. I previously thought that they were 'lying conveniently lowly', but a better computer screen and zoom function on the digitised text suggests 'conventionality'.

39. *D* 18 January 1858 and 14 May 1858.

40. *LF*, 150.

41. Ann to Fanny Lear, 12 February 1859, Houghton HOU GEN*2003 M-27. Emphases original.

42. Mary Boswell to Frederick Lear, undated, Houghton HOU GEN*2003 M-27. Emphases original.

43. Lear to Fortescue, 22 August 1877 and 20 July 1879, *LL*, 208, 221.

44. *LL*, 49.

45. *LL*, 330.

46. Edward Lear to Frederick Lear, 24 January 1873, Houghton HOU GEN*2003 M-27.

47. *D* 31 December 1867.

48. *D* 26 March 1861.

49. *The Philokalia*, ed. G. E. H. Palmer, Philip Sherrard and Kallistos Ware, vol. 3 (London: Faber, 2010), 237.

50. *LF*, 150.

51. *LF*, 285.

52. *D* 28 April 1866.

53. *CV*, 54. Compare Jacob Beuler, 'The Nervous Family', 2nd ed. (London: Shepherd, 1864).

54. *D* 21 August 1859.

55. *CV*, 139, 145.

56. Ina Rae Hark, 'The Jew as Victorian Cultural Signifier: Illustrated by Edward Lear', *Bucknell Review: Journal of Letters, Arts and Sciences* 34 (1990), 83. Hark argues that Lear compartmentalizes his views of Jews by context. There is some truth in this. However, I feel she underestimates the progress Lear made in thinking about Judaism once he had been exposed to intellectual debate and close friendship in Jewish circles. His views were progressive compared with those of many contemporaries.

57. *D* 6 January 1861.

58. Reference to these friendships emerges continuously in Lear's letter and diaries. But see *D* 21 February 1881: 'I took leave of that truly *Xtian* woman, the *Jewess*

Lady G.: by which I mean she has all the Christian qualities Christ recommended, & which Christians too generally have *not*'. Also *D* 23 October 1873: 'discussion of Jewish matters with the intelligent & unorthodox little Hungarian jew Bela Steiner', and *LL*, 98: '. . . if Judaizing all England would do us any good—why not?'

59. *LF*, 105.

60. Lear to Amelia Edwards, 18 October 1885, Somerville SC/LY/SP/ABE 102.

61. *D* 29 August 1863.

62. *D* 18 October 1859.

63. *LF*, 19.

64. Andrew W Tuer, *Pages and Pictures from Forgotten Children's Books* (London: Simpkin, Marshall, Kent, 1898–1899), 134.

65. *SL*, 139.

66. *D* 14 October 1868.

67. *D* 9 July 1859.

68. The image of the two bachelors being bashed with a book appears in gold and black on the red cover of Bush's first edition of *Laughable Lyrics* (1877). It emphasizes the difference between the humorous, accessible book that lies within the cover and the 'awful book' *on* the cover.

69. Lear's poem, written in the 1870s, predates publication of Tennyson's 'The Ancient Sage' (1885), though it is possible that Lear heard an early version of this material in the Tennyson home. Hermit sages crop up in many eighteenth- and early nineteenth-century poems, e.g., William Hodgson's 'The Hermit and His Dog' (1800) and Pleydell Wilton's 'Clifton' (1816).

70. James Orchard Halliwell, *Popular Rhymes and Nursery Tales* (London: Russell Smith, 1849), vii.

71. Lady Eastlake, 'Children's Books', *Quarterly Review* 75, no. 147 (1844), 2.

72. William Lisle Bowles, *The Little Villager's Verse Book; Consisting of Short Verses for Children to Learn by Heart* (London: Whittingham, 1837), 5.

73. Sara Coleridge, *Pretty Lessons in Verse, for Good Children; with Some Lessons in Latin in Easy Rhyme*, 4th ed. (London: Parker, 1845), 63.

74. In fact the last limerick in one volume of *A Book of Nonsense* (London: Maclean, 1846) about the 'Old Man of Kildare' is arranged over five lines; the others are printed over three lines. Lear would experiment with different layouts, from the two-line limericks of his earliest Knowsley efforts to three-, four- and five-line limericks, but they always have structural symmetry, like a crystal. Indeed one might compare limericks to snowflakes in their pleasing combination of identity and difference.

75. Aldous Huxley, *On the Margin* (London: Chatto and Windus, 1923), 170.

76. George Orwell, 'Nonsense Poetry', *Tribune*, 21 December 1945, 13.

77. Thomas Dilworth, 'Society and the Self in the Limericks of Edward Lear', *Review of English Studies* 45, no. 177 (January 1994), 43, talks very well about the 'dual identification' that the limericks produce. I disagree, however, with his view that the 'overall experience of moving from one picture-limerick to another is of interior disorientation and unease'.

78. 'Lear's Nonsense Books', *Spectator,* 17 September 1887, 1252.

79. *The History of Sixteen Wonderful Old Women* (London: Harris, 1821), 4. It is noticeable that John Parry in his 'Stray Leaves from A Book of Nonsense', in *Ridiculous Things* (London: McLean, 1854), plate 11, is also much *meaner* to his exclusively female eccentrics than Lear is. For example: 'There was a sly spinster of Swansea,/Who never would let her "dear John" see, / What she had in her pockets/But it proved to be "rockets"!/So, *up* went Miss Skylark of Swansea!' This 'sly' lady is blown up, losing her legs and hand, in a manner that casts implicit aspersions on spinsters.

80. Ibid., 6.

81. Ibid., 16.

82. *CV,* 114.

83. *D* 6 August 1862.

84. *CV,* 171.

85. *LL,* 269.

86. Lear to Chichester Fortescue, 3 October 1857, Taunton DD/SH337/C2/24.

87. Lear to William Holman Hunt, 7 January 1865, *SL,* 202.

88. Lear, when reading Charles Grover's *Folk Songs of Southern India* (1871), called them 'hymns' because of their 'antipolytheistic and anticaste tendencies', *D* 24 September 1874.

89. Lear to Emily Tennyson, 10 May 1865, *SL,* 205.

90. Lear to Lady Ashburton, 25 June 1876, NLS Acc 11388 84.

91. *The Child's Alphabet Emblematically Described and Embellished by Twenty-Four Pictures Brought into Easy Verse for the Tender Capacities of Young Readers* (London: Evans, c. 1820), 13.

92. Alphabet made for Gertrude Lushington, 1867, repr. *CV,* 133.

93. *D* 16 March 1862.

94. *D* 9 March 1862.

95. *D* 28 February 1864.

96. *D* 1 April 1860.

97. *D* 17 January 1858.

98. *D* 14 March 1881.

99. *LF,* 41.

100. Ibid.

101. *LL,* 99.

102. *D* 19 April 1859.

103. *D* 22 February 1863 notes that he talked with the Reverend Clark, whose sermon 'on the old ridiculous Lot's wife story' irritated him: 'Why must he say that non-communicants have some crimes or what not which prevent their joining their fellow Xtians? I am conscious of none—& only always refrain because I will join no church intimately whose dogmas are so loathsomely blasphemous as ours in the Athanasian Creed'. This is not wholly true. Lear did not believe in transubstantiation. His need for control—his desire to be accepted but to retain his ability to walk out and to refuse communion—is typical both of a physical irritability and an intellectual resistance that are vital to his artistic character.

104. In this context, the Catholic Faith is principally identified as belief in the Trinity.

105. Lear to Holman Hunt 15 October 1856, Harry Ransom Center, University of Austin, Texas MS-2415, box 1, folder 4.

106. *D* 13 February 1873.

107. Indeed, he regarded 'reason' as 'God's attribute', contrasting it with 'the Priest's art—"religion"'. Lear to Emily Tennyson, 6 March 1861, Lincoln 5481. Lear goes on to argue that 'if a man comes to believe that bread & wine made yesterday is the flesh & blood of a person dead 2000 years ago—how can he laugh at Timbuctoo and MumboJumbo'.

108. William Hartpole Lecky, *History of the Rise and Influence of the Spirit of Rationalism in Europe*, vol. 1 (London: Longman, 1865), xviii.

109. Lecky, *A History of European Morals from Augustus to Charlemagne*, vol. 1 (New York: Appleton, 1869), 99.

110. *SL*, 216. Lear had been close to A. P. Stanley from the 1830s; he knew Benjamin Jowett through Tennyson.

111. *D* 18 February 1870.

112. Ieuan Ellis, *Seven against Christ: A Study of 'Essays and Reviews'* (Leiden, Brill: 1980), ix.

113. For a full discussion of the controversy, see *Essays and Reviews: The 1860 Text and Its Reading,* ed. Victor Shea and William Whitla (Charlottesville: University of Virginia Press, 2000).

114. Frederick Temple, 'The Education of the World' in *Essays and Reviews* (London: Longman, Green, Roberts, 1861), 43.

115. Lear to Holman Hunt, n.d. 1869, BL RP 3731.

116. See Hood, *Complete Poetical Works* (London: Frowde, 1911), 561–562.

117. *LF,* 225.

118. John William Colenso, *The Pentateuch and Book of Joshua Critically Examined* (London: Longman, 1865), 27.

119. *LL,* 49.

120. Lear to Lady Waldegrave, 15 March 1863, *LF,* 276–277.

121. *LL,* 49.

122. *CV,* 214–218.

123. Lear to Emily Tennyson, 9 October 1856, *SL,* 139.

124. Exodus 33:2.

125. Deuteronomy 7:1–3.

126. In Italy in 1867, Lear encountered a dining place with 'very queer old pictures' including 'a dance of ducks, geese and all sorts of creatures dressed as men & women, & an orchestra of similar brutes above'. *D* 9 May 1867.

127. The 'Jerusalem artichokes' may refer to the '39 Articles'; there may also be an embedded private joke about a Mr Ballantine, whom Lear nicknamed the Jerusalem Artichoke. See *D* 9 February 1864.

128. *CV,* 409–410.

129. *D* 14 October 1880.

130. *CV,* 391–392.

131. *D* 13 July 1866. The soothy-beautiful letter was from Gussie.

132. *CV,* 388.

133. 'The Science of Nonsense', *Spectator,* 17 December 1870, 10.

134. Daniel Karlin, '"The Owl and the Pussy-Cat", and Other Poems of Love and Marriage', in *Lear and the Play of Poetry,* ed. James Williams and Matthew Bevis (Oxford: Oxford University Press, 2016), 222.

135. *CV,* 239.

136. See *D* 3 September 1872 for one of many instances.

137. OED, first entry is 1387.

138. 'The Owl and the Pussy-cat' was written as a gift 'picture poem' or song for Janet Symonds. Many of Lear's other works were first created as gifts for particular individuals, then incorporated into published volumes that became Christmas gifts. I discuss this phenomenon more fully in Chapter 5.

139. G. K. Chesterton, 'A Defence of Nonsense', in *The Defendant* (London: Brimley Johnson, 1901), 48.

140. Carroll was a deacon in the Church of England, who, despite having Pusey for a godfather, had broad views that included the possibility of universal salvation. However, Lear's religious ideas were far more heterodox. Carroll's nonsense is 'high church' where Lear's is 'low church', in the sense that Carroll directs his dialogic narratives from the top while Lear's medleys have a more open participative structure.

141. Holbrook Jackson, 'Masters of Nonsense' in *All Manner of Folk: Interpretations and Studies* (London: Grant Richards, 1912), 36.

142. Ibid., 37.

143. *D* 8 March 1868.

144. *D* 7 December 1879.

145. *LL*, 190.

146. Thomas Hardy, 'The Oxen' (1915), in *Thomas Hardy: The Complete Poems,* ed. James Gibson (Basingstoke, UK: Palgrave, 2001), 468.

147. Lear to Gussie Parker, 1 March 1880, private collection.

148. *D* 17 January 1866.

149. *D* 12 May 1862.

150. *D* 8 June 1877.

151. *D* 14 April 1878.

152. *D* 23 March 1871. 'Hope' is underlined three times, as is 'know', which is also in blacker ink to indicate greater emphasis.

153. Lear to Amelia Edwards, 26 October 1885, Somerville SC/LY/SP/ABE 103.

154. *LL*, 106, 271.

155. *D* 9 March 1868.

156. *D* 11 December 1870.

157. *D* 31 May 1875.

158. *Thames Star,* 3 August 1875, vol. 7, 2.

159. *CV,* 432. This poem may also relate to the discussion of religion and Positivism in Lear's letter to Gussie of 1 March 1880, referenced above.

160. *D* 24 April 1870.

161. *D* 25 September 1881.

162. *LL*, 270–271.

163. Ibid., 273.

164. Edward Adolphus Seymour, *Christian Theology and Modern Scepticism* (London: Bain, 1872), 173–174.

165. Lear's marginalia to Joseph Addison, *Spectator,* vol. 1 (London: Routledge, 1886), 14, private collection.

166. *LL*, 239.

167. Lear to Mrs Stuart Wortley, *CV,* 437.

168. Lear to Fortescue, 30 April 1885, Taunton DD/SH 337 C2/571. In an early letter to Fanny Coombe (3 March 1837), he had asserted that he was neither going to 'turn cannibal, nor become Bishop of Salisbury'. This highly unorthodox pairing is typical of his letters from first to last. Warne 10001.7 36.

169. James T. Fields, *Underbrush* (Boston: Osgood, 1877), 56.

170. Draft of 'Some Incidents in the Life of My Uncle Arly' written on the endpapers of the *Spectator,* vol. 4, and of C. F. Gordon Cumming, *At Home in Fiji* (Edinburgh and London: Blackwood, 1885), the latter verse dated 5 July 1886. Private collection. In piecing together these two different drafts of verses for 'Uncle Arly', I am speculating. But the imagery of flying with birds is so pervasive in Lear's cartoons that I think the inference is warranted that this version was meant to end with Arly flying. Further words and phrases in the

'Fiji' notes—'in the road', 'in the lane', 'parks', 'field', 'beyond' and 'pond'—
suggest the progress of the flight.

171. In *D* 19 September 1880, Lear records his friend Edward Carus Selwyn telling
him that, when he was a curate at Jarrow, 'the natives used to call out "Protestant Quack Quack Quack!"'

172. Lear to Holman Hunt 15 October 1856, Harry Ransom Center, University of
Austin, Texas MS-2415, box 1, folder 4.

173. *CV,* 546.

174. Lear to Norah Bruce, 24 December 1870, BL R.P. 1470.

175. Job 27:3

3. Queer Beasts

1. Lear to Lady Digby Wyatt, 31 July 1872, private collection.

2. *D* 26 April 1862.

3. *D* 24 March 1862.

4. *D* 3 May and 11 October 1861.

5. *D* 7 February 1861.

6. Tyndall's Bakerian Lecture 'On the Absorption and Radiation of Heat by
Gases and Vapours, and on the Physical Connexion of Radiation, Absorption,
and Conduction' can be found here: https://archive.org/details
/philtrans01149074. Mike Hulme argues in *Exploring Climate Change through
Science and in Society* (Abingdon, UK: Routledge, 2013), p. 62, that 'Tyndall
demonstrated that a group of polyatomic gases—a group later collectively
named "greenhouse gases"—possessed distinct and differential radiative
properties with regard to infra-red radiation. . . . His work suggested the possibility that by altering concentrations of these gases in the atmosphere human
activities could alter the temperature regulation of the planet'.

7. Jonathan Smith, *Charles Darwin and Victorian Visual Culture* (Cambridge:
Cambridge University Press, 2006), 95.

8. Lear to Ellen Newsom, 4 June 1874, NAL 86.RR.25.

9. Robert McCracken Peck in his recent, engaging book *The Natural History of
Edward Lear* (Woodbridge: ACC Art, 2016), pp. 107–108, discusses the
proposal made by Lord Derby in 1835 that Lear should accompany Audubon to
America on a joint natural-history and painting expedition. Audubon, probably
wisely, scotched the suggestion, but the two artists admired each other's work.

10. Drewitt family archive, West Sussex Record Office, Add. M. 31. 611, 3.

11. Lear to Fanny Coombe, 17 March 1835, Warne 10001.31. (For evidence of
Lear buying fossils for George, see also his letter to Fanny Coombe of 1
February 1837, Warne 10001.12.)

12. Ibid.

13. Lear to William Jardine, 5 September 1834, NMS [25] Box 3, file 64.

14. Lear to William Jardine, 14 October 1835, NMS [25] Box 3, file 64.

15. Daniel Brown, *The Poetry of Victorian Scientists: Style, Science and Nonsense* (Cambridge: Cambridge University Press, 2013), 11.

16. Royal Society Library Lending Register MS/403. Of course, library borrowing is not conclusive evidence of reading. But Darwin's keen professional interest in John Gould's work suggests that he would have borrowed Lear's *Gleanings* with a view to attentive perusal.

17. Charles Darwin, *The Zoology of the Voyage of HMS Beagle 1834–1836,* vol. 3 (London: Smith Elder, 1842), 15.

18. John Gould to William Jardine, 17 April 1832, NMS [19] box 2, file 35.

19. *Proceedings of the Fifth Meeting of the British Association for the Advancement of Science,* Dublin, 10–15 August 1835 (Dublin: Dixon Hardy, 1835), 110.

20. *D* 10 January 1869.

21. See *D* 23 July 1872, where Miss Darwin and her uncle Erasmus come to see pictures, returning on the 25th.

22. He announces in *D* 13 December 1866 that he is reading Darwin, 'the usual', implying that this has been going on for a time.

23. *D* 3 February 1867.

24. *D* 24 April 1870.

25. Lear, *Journal of a Landscape Painter in Corsica* (London: Bush, 1870), 71.

26. Thomas Bell, *A History of British Quadrupeds* (London: Van Voorst, 1874), 11. There are now eighteen recognised species of British bat.

27. Ibid.

28. Another good example of how Lear's early work in natural history directly informed his nonsense is his transposition of information about the robust parrot from *The Naturalist's Library,* in which the birds pursue 'their favourite fruit, a kind of cherry', to his story 'The Seven Families of the Lake Pipple-Popple', in which the seven parrots fight over a cherry. *The Naturalist's Library* sought to make the scientific claim that the parrots were properly regarded as a family—a taxonomic group ranking above 'genus' and below 'order'. In Lear's nonsense story, the word *family* hovers suggestively between this scientific sense and a more conventionally domestic one. When the naughty offspring of each of the seven families die as a result of failing to follow parental guidance, and their parents jump into pickling bottles, there is an expressive tension between our sense that this conclusion is perfectly natural—in the wild, 'families' often become extinct—and our sense that the mass suicide constitutes a social outrage.

29. Lear to William Jardine, 17 April 1834, NMS [25] box 3, file 64.

30. *D* 26 June 1869.

31. Lear to William Jardine, 19 February 1834, NMS [25] box 3, file 64.

32. This technique, which Lear deploys in several of his Knowsley watercolours of birds and animals, was doubtless learned from the artists who hand-coloured his Psittacidae lithographs.

33. See Lear to William Lizars, 5 November 1834, NMS [25] box 3, file 64. Lear notes that 'the few who draw animals with accuracy sufficient for a zoologist are in smaller proportion than you would imagine'. He mentions W. Harvey and T. Landseer.

34. McCracken Peck posits that this may be because Lear lacked expertise in foreign landscapes and flora to conjure such detailed habitats. But in *The Naturalist's Library,* as in Lear's earliest album sketches, the detail of landscape is there; it is simply not coloured; this makes the brilliantly coloured parrots stand out.

35. Lear, drawing of a night monkey, 1830s, Houghton MS Typ 55.12.

36. Lear to William Jardine, 17 April 1834, NMS [25] box 3, file 64.

37. Prideaux Selby, *The Naturalist's Library,* vol. 10, *Ornithology: Parrots* (London: Chatto and Windus, 1845), 129–130.

38. 'Reviews', *The Naturalist* 1 (1837), 231.

39. Isobel Charman, *The Zoo: The Wild and Wonderful Tale of the Founding of London Zoo* (London: Penguin, 2016), 208–216.

40. Ibid., 278.

41. Brown, *Poetry of Victorian Scientists,* 18.

42. Lear to Fanny Coombe, June 1835, Warne 10001.21.

43. *D* 26 November 1865.

44. 'Hippopotamouse Rabbitte', by descent from the Coombe family, private collection.

45. Pierpont MS 2007.88i.

46. James Bischoff, *Sketch of the History of Van Diemen's Land* (London: Richardson, 1832), 52.

47. This drawing was auctioned by Bonhams in 2016. It can be viewed at www .bonhams.com/auctions/23577/lot/48/.

48. Rev W. Bingley, *Animal Biography; or Anecdotes of the Lives, Manners and Economy of the Animal Creation,* vol. 2 (London: Phillips, 1803), 224. Bingley was a fellow of the Linnean Society. He notes of owls that 'the head is round, and formed somewhat like that of a Cat' and that owls are 'as useful in clearing the fields of Mice, as the Cat is in ridding the house of these destructive little animals'.

49. Compare the feathers sticking out of the hat of the Judicious Jubilant Jay (who is certainly female) in Lear's *More Nonsense* (London: Bush, 1872).

50. Lear to George Coombe, 6 September 1836, Warne 10001.27.

51. Lear to Chichester Fortescue, 16 October 1847, Taunton DD / SH 337 C2 / 2.

52. Charles Kingsley, *Glaucus or the Wonders of the Shore,* orig. pub. 1855 (London: Macmillan, 1890), 93.

53. Charles Darwin, *On the Origin of Species: A Facsimile of the First Edition* (Cambridge, MA: Harvard University Press, 1964), 455.

54. OED gives 1450 as the first usage for *bluebottle* meaning a cornflower; 1600 for the first usage meaning a beadle; and 1703 for the first usage meaning a fly.

55. *D* 24 September 1864.

56. Lear to Mrs Digby Wyatt, 31 July 1872, private collection. In the original the lines are run on. I have given a fresh line to each speaker to make the theatrical dialogue easier to read; Lear elsewhere follows this convention.

57. In *Journals of a Landscape Painter in Southern Calabria* (London: Bentley, 1852), 85, Count Garrolo is like 'a caged armadillo'. In *Journals of a Landscape Painter in Albania* (London: Bentley, 1851), 45, a solitary elder in blue and yellow robes is 'very like an encaged macaw'.

58. On sales figures for *On the Origin of Species* see www.theguardian.com/science /2008/feb/09/darwin.bestseller. For zoo visiting figures in the 1850s, see Charman, *The Zoo*, 307.

59. *The Surrey Zoological Gardens* (London: Tilt, 1835?), 128–131.

60. Thomas Peckett Prest, ed., *The London Singer's Magazine* (London: Duncombe, 1835), 25.

61. 'The Zoological Gardens', *Durham County Advertiser*, 15 July 1831, 11, reprinted from the *Atlas*.

62. Takashi Ito, in *London Zoo and the Victorians* (Woodbridge, UK: Boydell, 2014), describes how tickets were forged and sold on the bus and in the pub, while the brass-necked also crammed in, attaching themselves to ticketed parties.

63. John Parry, *Ridiculous Things* (London: McLean, 1854), 10.

64. 'The Lounger at the Clubs', *Illustrated Times*, 8 February 1862, 91. Since the first edition of Lear's 1846 *Book of Nonsense* had been small, and Lear's reputation as a humourist was not consolidated until its reissue in the 1860s, it mistakenly seemed to this reviewer that Parry was the originator and Lear the copyist.

65. *CV*, 172. As discussed in my general headnote, Noakes follows the 1861 edition of *A Book of Nonsense* in capitalising 'Raven'. The illustration of this limerick from 1888 (reproduced in this book) chooses a different layout and does not capitalise 'raven'. It is interesting to consider the marginally different symmetry / asymmetry between man and bird that this implies.

66. The old person of Bree appears in *More Nonsense* (1872). The man of Ems appears in *A Book of Nonsense* (1846). People mirroring animals, birds and fishes becomes a more prominent theme in Lear's limericks in the 1861 edition of *A Book of Nonsense,* and the question of whether humans can teach or learn from other animals is explored most explicitly in the limericks in *More Nonsense*.

67. Freud, *Civilisation and Its Discontents*, in *The Future of an Illusion and Other Works,* ed. James Strachey (London: Hogarth, 1961), 123.

68. *CV*, 354.

69. See also 'The Story of the Four Little Children Who Went Round the World', in which Violet makes herself a parrot-feather headdress, but also knits a 'small woollen frock' for various fishes. These children are awkwardly poised between becoming animals, exploiting them and 'saving' them.

70. *The History of Sixteen Wonderful Old Women* (London, Harris, 1821), 2.

71. In Lear, *More Nonsense*.

72. It is common, for example, to find an ass, a cow, a quail and a whale.

73. *The Alphabet of Animals Intended to Impress Children with Affection for the Brute Creation* (London: Society for Promoting Religious Knowledge among the Poor, undated), 7.

74. Lear's owl in 'The Owl and the Pussy-cat' is described as an 'elegant fowl', an unusual pairing of noun and adjective that directly echoes Dorset's rhyme on 'owls / inelegant fowls'. The tetrameter complaint of 'The Nutcrackers and the Sugar Tongs' also closely resembles this verse.

75. Catherine Dorset, *The Peacock 'At Home'* (London: Murray, Harris, 1809), 5.

76. *CV*, 276.

77. Matthew Bevis, 'Edward Lear's Lines of Flight', *Journal of the British Academy* 1 (2013), 50.

78. *D* 22 February 1865.

79. Augusta Bethell, 'The Discontented Sparrow', in *Echoes of an Old Bell; and Other Tales of Fairy Lore* (London: Griffith and Farran, 1865), 9.

80. Ibid., 12.

81. *D* 18 March 1872. On 19 March Hubert took away his drawing of the 'Discobolos head' and Arny his drawing of the ball.

82. *CV*, 321–322.

83. 'The Science of Nonsense', *Spectator*, 17 December 1870, 1506.

84. *CV*, 207–208.

85. *The Surrey Zoological Gardens*, 64–67.

86. D. H. Lawrence, 'Kangaroo', in *Birds, Beasts and Flowers!* (London: Seltzer, 1923), 146.

87. Leigh Hunt, 'A Visit to the Zoological Gardens', *New Monthly Magazine*, August 1836, 483.

88. *The Gardens and Menagerie of the Zoological Society Delineated* (London: Sharpe, 1831), 55.

89. A very early cartoon shows a huge female ostrich with a bonnet and bloomers being accompanied by a male kangaroo who is half her size, bearing an umbrella. See Herman W. Liebert, ed., *Lear in the Original* (New York: Kraus, 1975), 215.

90. Pierpont, McCrindle MA 7461. In the original manuscript the 'quadruped' becomes '1st Q', but I have retained 'quadruped' here for ease of reading.

91. *D* 8 July 1883.

92. See '... *and Mr Fortescue': A Selection from the Diaries from 1851 to 1862 of Chichester Fortescue, Lord Carlingford,* ed. Osbert Wyndham Hewett (London: Murray, 1958), 86.

93. *SL*, 204.

94. *D* 12 April 1862.

95. Lear to Emily Tennyson, n.d. 1859?, Lincoln 5460.

96. As Jonathan Smith remarks in *Darwin and Victorian Visual Culture,* p. 60, Darwin's description of this process in barnacles in his *Monograph of the Sub-Class Cirripedia* (1854) used language that was neither clinical nor detached: 'barnacle sexuality is insistently rendered in human terms . . . his references to "husbands" kept in female "pockets" and to short-lived males with enormous penises whose sole purpose was reproduction also betray broad anxieties about female polyandry and males simultaneously potent and parasitic'. Recent findings in marine biology were widely popularised in the slew of books about the seashore that appeared in the 1850s, from David Landsborough's *Popular History of British Zoophytes and Corallines* (1852) to Charles Kingsley's *Glaucus* (1855) and Philip Gosse's *Tenby: A Sea-Side Holiday* (1856). Thousands of middle-class Britons took to collecting marine specimens and examining them under the microscope, as Lear's unpleasant brother-in-law Richard Boswell did. Dr Hassall, Lear's friend in San Remo, specialised in the study of zoophytes.

97. Kingsley, *Glaucus,* 44.

98. *CV,* 397.

99. Ibid., 524.

100. *LW,* 9.

101. *D* 17 May 1859.

102. *CV,* 395–396.

103. Daniel Karlin, 'Poems of Love and Marriage', in *Lear and the Play of Poetry,* ed. James Williams and Matthew Bevis (Oxford: Oxford University Press, 2016), 215.

104. 'Swimming in the Channel', *Dover Express,* 30 August 1872, 3.

105. The broadside by Tom Haines, 'I Wish that I Could Swim like J. B. Johnson!' (Bod, Roud Number V7340) begins, 'Oh! would I were a little fish'.

106. *CV,* 452–453.

107. Sally Shuttleworth, *The Mind of the Child: Child Development in Literature, Science, and Medicine, 1840–1900* (Oxford: Oxford University Press, 2010), 40.

108. Ibid., 278.

109. Ibid., 256.

110. *D* 29 December 1863.

111. Charles Darwin, *On the Origin of Species* (London: Ward, Lock, 1901), 154.

112. Charles Kingsley, *The Water-Babies* (New York: Dover, 2006), 55.

113. Jean-Jacques Lecercle, *Philosophy of Nonsense: The Intuitions of Victorian Nonsense Literature* (London: Routledge, 1994), 4.

114. D'Arcy W. Thompson, *Nursery Nonsense or Rhymes without Reason* (London: Griffith and Farran, 1864), 53.

115. Charles Leland, *Johnnykin and the Goblins* (London: Macmillan, 1877), 21.

116. Charles Lamb to Samuel Taylor Coleridge, 23 October 1802, repr. *The Life, Letters and Writings of Charles Lamb*, ed. Percy Fitzgerald, vol. 1 (London: Gibbings, 1892), 420.

117. Priscilla Wakefield, *An Introduction to the Natural History and Classification of Insects* (London: Darton, 1816), preface.

118. Lear, *Nonsense, Songs, Stories, Botany and Alphabets* (London; Bush, 1871).

119. *D* 4 November 1872.

120. *D* 8 March 1872.

121. Anthony Mundella, *'Secular and Religious Education': An Address as President of the Sunday School Union at Exeter Hall May 8th 1884*, 4.

122. *D* 14 January 1863.

123. *LF,* 148.

124. Lear to Mary Mundella (draft), c. 1885, Houghton MS Eng 797.

125. Lear, *Views in the Seven Ionian Islands* (London: Lear, 1863), XVII, View from the village of Galáro, Zante. This nursery rhyme, which Lear quotes in his travel notes on Zante, dates back at least as far as the mid-seventeenth century.

126. *Examiner,* 18 November 1876, 1303.

127. Anna Henchman, 'Homology and the Logic of Nonsense in Edward Lear', in *Play of Poetry,* 196–197.

128. 'Science of Nonsense', 1506.

129. See *CV,* 511.

130. *D* 28 March 1872.

131. Kingsley, *Glaucus,* 86.

132. E. W. Cooke, *Grotesque Animals: Invented, Drawn and Described by E W Cooke FRS, FGS, FZS etc* (London: Longmans, Green, 1872), vi. The legend Cooke has appended to the plate reproduced here, 'Les Femmes Sont Extremes', identifies one of his 'composite creatures' as female. This kind of interspecies play often gives rise to questions about what might be identified as creating male and female 'characters', where the parts are neither one thing nor another.

133. Walter Savage Landor, 'Imaginary Conversations', in *The Works of Walter Savage Landor,* vol. 1 (London: Moxon, 1846), 506.

134. *SL,* 208.

4. Dreamwork: Lear's Visual Language

1. Lear, *Nonsense Songs, Stories, Botany and Alphabets* (London: Bush, 1871). We lack evidence about precisely when Lear composed this alphabet and whether it was conceived, like so many of his other alphabets, for a particular child before it was prepared for book publication. The manuscript can be seen at Lear, Alphabet, 'A was once an apple-pie' (undated), Houghton, Edward Lear Miscellaneous Drawings, 1849–1866, MS Typ 55.14.

2. *D* 24 August 1864. See also 26 June 1871, where he says that he has a dream 'once in 10 years or so' and it is more of a memory of a voice or face than a dream.

3. Sigmund Freud, *Jokes and Their Relation to the Unconscious,* trans. James Strachey (London: Penguin, 1991), 219.

4. Lear, *More Nonsense* (London: Bush, 1872).

5. Lear to Mrs Scrivens 8 April 1868, Houghton MS Typ 782. There follows an Aladdin's lamp, with the initials Emma Elizabeth Muro Ferguson in the border; then a staircase, in which the initials have become the railing; a champagne flute for Anne Glass; a moonlight on the Nile for Cecilia Susan Scott; and an egg for Anne Scrivens.

6. *D* 3 March 1871 alludes to the monograms he is making for Louisa Isaak and Agnes Mary Clark.

7. Lear to George Coombe 24 July 1835, Warne 10001.11.

8. *D* 25 September 1866.

9. See Lear's drawings in Herman W. Liebert, ed., *Lear in the Original* (New York: Kraus, 1975), 34–35.

10. Anon. (perhaps Richard Scrafton Sharpe, illus. Robert Cruikshank), *Anecdotes and Adventures of Fifteen Gentlemen* (London: Marshall, 1822), 4.

11. See *D* 5 October 1864. The magic lantern slides of Switzerland delighted him.

12. *SL,* 205.

13. T. Hudson, 'The Cork Leg!', arranged by J. Blewitt (London: Hudson and Collard, 1832?). This particular song sheet features an illustrated cartoon sequence by Joe Lisle.

14. Twenty-one drawings, British Museum, catalogue number 1970, 0411, numbered 24 onwards.

15. Illustrations of Miss Maniac, Houghton, MS Typ 55.6.

16. James Stuart, *Poems on Various Subjects* (Baltimore, MD: Dobbin and Murphy, 1812), 46.

17. Liebert, ed., *Lear in the Original,* 206–207.

18. Ibid., 208–209.

19. Ibid., 210.

20. Tobias Smollett, *The Adventures of Sir Launcelot Greaves,* in *The Miscellaneous Works of Tobias Smollett,* vol. 5 (Edinburgh: Doig, 1811), 197.

21. Lear's biographers have found no evidence of Jeremiah Lear's incarceration. It is intriguing, however, that Lear, in writing of the discomfitingly accurate recollections of a Holloway neighbour from his childhood, Mrs Hansard (*D* 27 March 1881), describes this shameful episode in his father's life as if it were true: 'no doubt she equally well remembered that he was imprisoned for fraud & debt, & that 2 of my brothers suffered for deserting the Army & for forgery'. This seems too particular a memory to be altogether false, and it throws light on Lear's family embarrassments as not only financial but also moral. Perhaps Mr Lear was briefly arrested by bailiffs and confined while surety was sought for his debts.

22. *CV,* 111.

23. Robert Southey, 'The Cataract of Lodore', in *Poems, Chiefly Manuscript, and from Living Authors,* ed. Joanna Baillie (London: Longman, 1823), 282–283.

24. Liebert, ed., *Lear in the Original,* 152.

25. Thomas Byrom, *Nonsense and Wonder* (New York: Dutton, 1977), 120.

26. Ibid., 138.

27. Freud, *Jokes,* 215.

28. Liebert, ed., *Lear in the Original,* 47–48. Lear would redesign this limerick in his *Book of Nonsense,* where the element of pleasure is less pronounced and the result is less effective.

29. See Hassett, '"Does It Buzz?": Image and Text in Lear's Limericks', *Victorian Literature and Culture* 45, no. 4 (December 2017), 685–707.

30. Lear, *More Nonsense.*

31. *CV,* 107.

32. Compare Lear's comic illustration for *The tragical life and death of Caius Marius Esqre,* where Caius Marius 'sits among the ruins' of Carthage in what is ambiguously a baby's high chair or a throne. *The tragical life and death of Caius Marius Esqre late her Majesty's Consul-general in the Roman state: illustrated from authentic sauces by Edward Lear* (1841), repr. Justin G. Schiller (New York City: Schiller, 1983).

33. Lear, *More Nonsense.*

34. Daniel Fowler in Frances K. Smith, *Daniel Fowler of Amherst Island 1810–1894* (Kingston: Agnes Etherington Art Centre, 1979), 103.

35. See for example the *Manchester Courier,* 11 January 1862, suppl., 3, which argued of *A Book of Nonsense* that 'this happy reproduction of true child-pictures' would bring back to the adult's recollection 'those primitive struggles of yours with the graphic art'.

36. 'Christmas Books', *Graphic,* 30 December 1871, 635.

37. 'Evening Amusements', *Western Flying Post, Yeovil,* 18 February 1862, 7.

38. 'Children's Books—III', *Examiner,* 24 December 1870, 826.

39. See *D* 27 May 1859, where he is making a 'library of letters' for the Blencowes' little boy.

40. Lear, *A Nonsense Alphabet* (London: Victoria and Albert Museum, 1977). This alphabet was made in 1880 for Charles Geffrard Pirouet.

41. Gertrude Lushington's alphabet (c. 1865), Houghton Ms Typ 55.3.

42. H. A. Page, 'Child-World', *Contemporary Review,* May 1879, 7–26, 9.

43. Lear to Fortescue, 16 September 1863, *LF,* 295: 'What's the difference between the Czar and the "Times" paper? One is the type of Despotism: the other the despotism of Type'.

44. Anon., *The Pretty ABC, Being a Complete Alphabet to Entice Children to Learn Their Letters* (London: Evans, 1810). It includes 'The Life and Death of a Apple Pye' and also 'A Curious Discourse That Passed between the Twenty Five Letters at Dinner-Time'.

45. Anon., *The Invited Alphabet, or, Address of A to B; Containing His Friendly Proposal for the Amusement and Instruction of Good Children* (London: Darton, 1818), 5.

46. Patricia Crain, *The Story of A: The Alphabetization of America* (Stanford, CA: Stanford University Press, 2000), 45, see also 56.

47. Lear, Alphabet, 'A was once an apple-pie' (undated), Houghton, Edward Lear Miscellaneous Drawings, 1849–1866, MS Typ 55.14, repr. Lear, *Nonsense Songs, Stories, Botany and Alphabets.*

48. Most commonly, Lear's letters are animals and birds. This echoes many early alphabets, but Lear's drawings, reflecting his mastery of natural-history painting, are more vivacious and accurate, his rhymes more inventive and amusing.

49. Lear, *A Nonsense Alphabet.*

50. This is the opening of *The New England Primer,* of which six million copies were printed between 1690 and the mid-nineteenth century. It was still current as *The Child's Alphabet Emblematically Described and Embellished by Twenty-Four Pictures Brought into Easy Verse for the Tender Capacities of Young Readers* (London: Evans, 1820).

51. Edward Hindman, *The Amusing Alphabet for Young Children Beginning to Read* (London: Taylor, 1812).

52. Mrs Winthrop Chanler (nee Daisy Terry), *Roman Spring: Memoirs* (Boston: Little Brown, 1934), 29.

53. Anon., *The Children's Moral Alphabet by an Octogenarian* (Kettering, UK: Waddington, 1879), preface. 'A was an Archer who Shot at a Frog' was published as *Tom Thumb's Play-Thing* (London: Evans, 1809) and as *A was an Archer* (London: Dean 1859), and even later as *A was an Archer* (London: Harrap, 1920).

54. 'A was an Archer who Shot at a Frog' was published as *The Child's New Play-thing* (London: Cooper, 1742) and was constantly reissued: as *Tom Thumb's Play-Thing* (London: Evans, 1809), as *A was an Archer* (London: Dean 1859) and (still later) as *A was an Archer* (London: Harrap, 1920).

55. Lear's 'J was a small jackdaw' is in *A Nonsense Alphabet*. For the origins of 'There was an old woman' (Roud Folk Song 797) see James Orchard Halliwell, *Popular Rhymes and Nursery Tales* (London: Russell Smith, 1849), 14.

56. For example, *The Victoria Alphabet* (London: Routledge, 1856).

57. Crain, *The Story of A*, 50.

58. The first of Lear's Xerxes rhymes given here is from Gertrude Lushington's alphabet (see above); the second is *Alphabet, 1857,* in the Yale Center for British Art; the third is from 'A was once an apple-pie', Houghton MS Typ 55.14.

59. Anon., *Invited Alphabet*, 2–3.

60. Compare *The Alphabet Ladder* (1822) in which 'Y was a Youth that had great Discerning' (see Crain, *The Story of A*, 75) or *The Child's Scripture Alphabet* (London: Darton and Clark, 1845) in which 'Y, is the Youth who, though killed by a fall,/was raised up to life at the word of St Paul'.

61. Lear, 'Alphabet, No.6', *Laughable Lyrics* (London: Bush, 1877).

62. Lear, 'Once I had a Mucous Membrane', Houghton MS Typ 55.14, item 93. The poem deals with a mucous membrane, a layer of tissue located in the nose, mouth, urethra and anus that protects the body from pathogens and keeps sensitive areas moist. In Lear's story, the blue-green membrane escapes from its multiply padlocked box and is cooked and eaten by a married couple who at first seem happy, but then, being hungry, quarrel. It is hard not to see this as a story of sexual anxiety. Protective physical borders are vulnerable to attack and absorption by others. But they are also hard to defend because of their own desire to escape control.

63. Lear, *Nonsense Songs, Stories, Botany and Alphabets*.

64. *Lady Tennyson's Journal*, ed. James O. Hoge (Charlottesville: University of Virginia Press, 1981), 6 June 1859, 136.

65. *D* 3 September 1867. The British Library has recently acquired a manuscript, uncatalogued at the time of writing, that includes Lear's monogram for Ida Waldegrave Money, Lady Waldegrave's niece. It cleverly 'finds' the I, W and M in the umbrella and coattails of two figures, seen from the rear.

66. *SL*, 250. Thomas Rowlandson had experimented with such comic use of pictograms in his 'Yorkshire Hieroglyphics!!' (1809), and their existence as a form of playful puzzle is documented from the late eighteenth century. See *High Spirits: The Comic Art of Thomas Rowlandson* (London: Royal Collection Trust, 2013), 208–209.

67. Lear to Mrs Scrivens, 8 April 1868, Houghton MS Typ 782.

68. *D* 11 March 1860.

69. *D* 24 December 1859, 'woke exhilarious'; 15 March 1880, 'dismy dreamal'.

70. *D* 9 April 1883.

71. *D* 26 June 1869.

72. *D* 25 February 1868.

73. *D* 19 April 1862.

74. Ann Colley, 'Limericks and the Reversals of Nonsense', *Victorian Poetry* 26, no. 3 (Autumn 1988), 285. There are brilliant accounts of Lear's landscapes, such as Charles Nugent's *Edward Lear: The Landscape Artist* (Grasmere, UK: Wordsworth Trust, 2009), but, excepting biographers, the people who write about Lear's poetry and those who write about his landscapes are rarely the same people. I was struck at the 2012 Oxford bicentenary Lear conference both by the excellence of the papers and by the fact that Lear's landscapes received little notice.

75. *D* 12 June 1875.

76. *D* 1 June 1870.

77. *D* 10 May 1862.

78. Christopher Bollas, *Being a Character: Psychoanalysis and Self Experience* (London: Routledge, 1997), 21, 34–35.

79. Ibid., 20.

80. *D* 23 June 1877.

81. Lear, *Langdale,* private collection.

82. Alfred Tennyson, 'To E. L., on His Travels in Greece', in *The Poems of Tennyson,* ed. Christopher Ricks (London: Longman, 1969), 993.

83. This version of *Kasr-es-Saad* is in a private collection, but can be viewed in Vivien Noakes, *The Painter Edward Lear* (Newton Abbot and London: David & Charles, 1991), 94. An earlier version (1856) is in the Fine Arts Museum of San Francisco.

84. Kirby Olsen, 'Edward Lear: Deleuzian Landscape Painter', *Victorian Poetry* 31, no. 4 (1993), 347–362, considers Lear within the 'comic picturesque' tradition and according to theories of the sublime in art but ultimately concludes that he 'deterritorializes the boundaries' created by earlier aesthetic theorists.

85. *D* 2 July 1885.

86. He complains in his diary for 19 July 1869 that Holman Hunt's portraits are 'hard & not good in some respects'.

87. Of course, neither the V-shaped composition nor the use of a flight of birds to link land and sky is unique to Lear. He was grounded in the artistic tradition of Claude and Poussin, who both use V-shaped symmetries in their harmonious landscapes, and was highly aware of both older Italian art and modern work by artists he admired, such as Albert Bierstadt, who favoured this format.

88. Noakes, *Painter Edward Lear,* 11.

89. See Lear's painting of Arta 1848–1849, NGS D 5551.8.

90. Lear's painting of Corfu 17 February 1864, five p.m., and 8 March 1864, five p.m., NGS D.5551.24.

91. Noakes, *Painter Edward Lear,* 12.

92. *Kithira,* NGS D. 5551.30.

93. *Suli*, 6 May 1849, NGS D.5551.4. See colour plate.

94. *Karyes, Mount Athos*, Courtauld Gallery D.2007.DS.24. See colour plate.

95. William Holman Hunt, *Pre-Raphaelitism and the Pre-Raphaelite Brotherhood*, vol. 1 (London: Macmillan, 1905), 332.

96. *D* 13 November 1859.

97. In a letter to Holman Hunt of 7 February 1857, Lear notes, 'When I say "I wish I had gone to the Academy when you did"—you may suppose I don't say that out of love for the Academy for itself. Tout au contraire, I believe that had J. Millais foregone the ambition of place and position, & had he steadily worked with all those who, as he once did, set their faces against conventionalities and still do so,—art in England & who knows where else besides—would have gained life & respectability'. It seems here that he is saying he would have liked to have been, like Millais, an RA in order to join the original PRB rebellion from within. Houghton MS Eng 797.

98. Lear to William Holman Hunt, April 15 1882, BL RP 3731.

99. Lear to Holman Hunt, 2 May 1857, private collection.

100. Elizabeth Prettejohn, introduction to *The Cambridge Companion to the Pre-Raphaelites* (Cambridge: Cambridge University Press, 2012), 7.

101. *D* 27 August 1869.

102. *Lady Tennyson's Journal*, 104.

103. Anon., 'Local News: School of Design', *Worcestershire Chronicle*, 14 September 1853, 4.

104. Anon., 'Exhibition of the Society of Arts', *Worcestershire Chronicle*, 25 October 1854, 6.

105. Lear to Emily Tennyson, n.d., Lincoln 5411.

106. *D* 12 February 1873.

107. It is also true, as Richard Cronin suggests, that 'Lear's Tennyson illustrations often seem designed not so much to illustrate the poems as to point attention to the difficulty of deciding whether the poems create their own world or refer to the world outside them'. Richard Cronin, 'Edward Lear and Tennyson's Nonsense' in *Tennyson among the Poets*, ed. Robert Douglas-Fairhurst (Oxford: Oxford University Press, 2009), 268.

108. Lear to Holman Hunt, 9 February 1853 *SL*, 120.

109. Lear to Holman Hunt, 21 September 1870, John Rylands Library Manchester MS 42.

110. Lear to Holman Hunt, 7 July 1854, BL microfilm RP800(1–4). Sir Edwin Landseer's contribution to the 1854 Exhibition, *Royal Sports on Hill and Loch*, featured members of the royal family with two dead deer, a dead salmon and three dogs. It is easy to see why Lear disdained this torpid canvas, and why he found Daniel Maclise's vast and improbable history painting, *The Marriage of Strongbow and Eva*, unnatural.

111. Lear to Lord Derby, n.d. 1854, Liverpool Central Library 920 DER (14)/ 152/12/7.

112. Allen Staley, 'The Painter of Topographical Poetry', in *Impossible Picturesquenesss: Edward Lear's Indian Watercolours*, ed. Vidya Dehejia (Middletown NJ: Grantha, 1989), 108.

113. Peter Levi, *Edward Lear: A Biography* (London: Macmillan, 1995), 136.

114. See *D* 31 December 1872, where Lear looks over Turner's sea engravings and then works on the sea in his own *Akrokeraunian Walls*. Lear felt that Turner's 'almightiness' raised him above biographical criticism: 'like Shakespeare, his works proclaim the man', *D* 2 February 1872.

115. *D* 16 November 1871. Noakes, *Painter Edward Lear,* 13.

116. *D* 3 November 1874.

117. *D* 24 August 1872.

118. Lear to Henry Grenfell, 23 October 1862, private collection.

119. Vivien Noakes, *Edward Lear 1812–88 at the Royal Academy of Arts,* exhibition catalogue (New York: Abrams, 1986), 156.

120. Alfred Tennyson, 'You ask me why, though ill at ease', in *The Poems of Tennyson,* ed. Christopher Ricks (London: Longman, 1969), 490.

121. Noakes, *Painter Edward Lear,* 69.

122. Noakes, *Edward Lear 1812–88,* 20.

123. John K. Howat, in *American Paradise: The World of the Hudson River School* (New York: Metropolitan Museum, 1987), 287, confirms that this picture was exhibited at Maclean's Gallery in 1866.

124. Eleanor Jones Harvey, *The Voyage of the Icebergs: Frederic Church's Arctic Masterpiece* (New Haven, CT: Yale University Press, 2002), 66.

125. *D* 28 November and 7 December 1869.

126. Lear to Henry Grenfell, 23 October 1862, private collection.

127. *D* 2 July 1875.

128. 'A Batch of Exhibitions', *Illustrated Times,* 30 March 1867, 206.

129. *D* 9 May 1863.

130. *D* 27 December 1859.

131. Lear to Sir Digby and Lady Wyatt, 13 August 1871, private collection.

132. *D* 10 January 1867.

133. *D* 1 February 1867.

134. *D* 5 January 1867.

135. *D* 23 April 1863.

136. Lear, *Views in the Seven Ionian Islands* (London: Lear, 1863), XVII View from the Village of Galáro, Zante.

137. *CV,* 412–413.

138. Lindley Murray, *Murray's English Reader* (London: Burrill, 1818), 132. This speech was also widely reprinted in *Elegant Extracts* and other texts designed to give younger readers models from which to learn eloquence.

139. *D* 28 January 1871.

5. Inventing Edward Lear

1. Lear to Amelia Edwards, 26 October 1885, Somerville SC/LY/SP/ABE 103.

2. Lear to Lee Warner, 13 October 1876, Athenaeum Club Library, London.

3. *D* 3 July and 8 August 1884.

4. Lear to George Scrivens, 7 August 1866, repr. *CV,* 211.

5. Lear to Marianne North, 8 June 1871, Somerville SC/LY/SP/ABE 96.

6. Robert Douglas-Fairhurst, *The Story of Alice* (London: Harvill Secker, 2015), 216.

7. Ibid., 237.

8. 'Journal 1829', *CV,* 10–11.

9. 'Scrawl', *CV,* 48–49.

10. Lear to Mr and Mrs George Coombe, 18 March 1840, Warne 10001.1.

11. Lear to Fanny Coombe, 19 May 1837, Warne 10001.25.

12. *D* 6 May 1881. For another version of Mariana's lament see *CV,* 458. Also, of himself, 'I was "half sick of shadows"—said this Lady of Shalott', *D* 29 November 1867.

13. *D* 14 June 1860. See also *LL,* 98, where Lear tells Fortescue in a letter of 24 'Febbirowerry' 1868 that he shall 'go on in a meandering mashpotato manner, male and female after his kind, like an obese gander as I am. . . .' The mash-up of food, gender and goosiness here is suggestive.

14. The word appears frequently in his early letters from 1830–1840, e.g. to the Coombes, 3 March 1837, Warne 10001.7.

15. Lear to George Coombe, 20 July 1835, Warne 10001.9.

16. Ibid.

17. This cartoon sequence is reproduced in *Lear in the Original* (New York: Kraus, 1975), 177–184.

18. Lear, 'Illustrated Story in Eight Scenes', drawn for Lady Susan Percy, 28 February 1842, Beinecke Koch Collection GEN MS 601, box 25, folder 549.

19. *OED.*

20. Lear, *A Walk on a Windy Day* (ten drawings), 24 December 1860, Beinecke Koch Collection, GEN MS 601, box 78, folder 1420.

21. See Lear to the Coombes, 3 January 1837, Warne 10001.29, which describes travelling in deep snow: 'I cannot describe,—were I Munchhausen himself, half the hideous adventures that befell us!'

22. *CV,* 190.

23. *CV,* 481.

24. Alfred Heneage Cocks, 'The Wooburn Version of the Mummers' Play' and 'The Penn Version of the Mummers' Play', *Records of Bucks* 9, no. 3, 222–226, and 10, no. 3, 172–175. See also Alison Uttley, *Buckinghamshire* (London: Hale, 1950), and H. Harman, *Sketches of the Bucks Countryside* (London: Blandford, 1934).

25. James Williams, 'Lear and the Fool', *Lear and the Play of Poetry,* ed. James Williams and Matthew Bevis (Oxford: Oxford University Press, 2016), 19.

26. *D* 25 February 1872.

27. For example, *D* 25 February 1877. As Charles Lewsen has noticed, this habit seems to have begun, or to have become entrenched, after the death of his sister and surrogate mother, Ann, in 1865.

28. Lear, Indian Journal, 13 and 27 November 1873, Houghton MS Eng 797.4.

29. *LL,* 114.

30. *LL,* 188.

31. *LF,* 269.

32. *LW,* 76.

33. *SL,* 108–109.

34. Lear to Lady Reid, 27 February 1857, NLS Ac.10089.

35. Lear to Emily Tennyson, 9 October 1856, Lincoln 5443.

36. Henry Strachey saw a letter by Lear addressed to Millais: 'My dear aunt, I send you a drawing of my cat to show you how I am getting on'. See E. Strachey, ed., *Nonsense Songs and Stories* (London: Warne, 1894), ix.

37. Holman Hunt to Lear, n.d., John Rylands Library, Manchester Eng MS 1214/12.

38. Lear to Holman Hunt, 12 August 1857 and 21 April 1861, BL, microfilm RP800 (1.4).

39. *LF,* 139.

40. Ibid., 308.

41. *CV,* 186.

42. *SL,* 130. See also a letter of 29 September 1882 to Lady Strachey, in which Lear paradoxically describes himself as 'this old blind child'. Taunton DD/SH C/2480 71/4.

43. Lear to Laura Campbell, 21 October 1873, Beinecke GEN MSS 601, box 25, folder 540.

44. Lear to Fortescue, 24 February 1868, Taunton DD/SH/337/C22/288. In Lear to Edward Carus Selwyn, 7 August 1886, he confided that he was planning 'to perform Chrysalis vocations previous to entering another state'—a slightly more conventional, Christian image of himself as caterpillar preparing for the metamorphosis and flight of the soul as a 'butterfly' to heaven. Private collection.

45. *SL,* 18.

46. *D* 4 May 1878.

47. Lear to Alfred Tennyson, 27 June 1864, Lincoln 5504–2.

48. The illustrations not reproduced here can be seen at *CV,* 191, and *LL,* 142.

49. *CV,* 192.

50. Ibid., 187.

51. Ibid., 393.

52. *D* 14 April 1877.

53. *D* 4 August 1860.

54. See *D* 27 September 1862.

55. R. Stennett, *Aldiborontiphoskyphorniostikos: A Round Game for Merry Parties* (London: Newman, 1823), 11.

56. *The Gaping, Wide-Mouthed Waddling Frog: A New and Entertaining Game of Questions and Commands* (London: Newman, 1823).

57. Lear to Evelyn Baring, n.d., in Lady Strachey, ed., *Queery Leary Nonsense* (London: Mills and Boon, 1911), 6.

58. Lear to Mrs Ford, 30 June 1865, John Wilson Manuscripts Ltd. catalogue archive, https://www.manuscripts.co.uk/stock/21111.HTM.

59. William Hazlitt, *Characters of Shakespeare's Plays* (1817) repr. (London: Dent, 1921), 147.

60. Lear to Amelia Edwards, 26 October 1885, Somerville SC/LY/SP/ABE 103.

61. Lear to Amelia Edwards, 9 October 1885, Somerville SC/LY/SP/ABE 101. Lear claimed to Fortescue in 1877 that in the hubbub of London he nearly lost 'all ideas about my own identity, & if anybody should ask me suddenly if I am Lady Jane Grey, the Apostle Paul, Julius Caesar or Theodore Hook, I should say yes to every question', *LL,* 204. Historical mash-ups appealed to him.

62. *SL,* xi.

63. Lear to Amelia Edwards, 17 December 1885, Somerville SC/LY/SP/ABE 104.

64. Lear to Amelia Edwards, 18 October 1885, Somerville SC/LY/SP/ABE 102.

65. On Lear's letters see Hugh Haughton, 'Playing with Letters: Lear's Episthilarity', *Play of Poetry,* 223–243.

66. Edward Carus Selwyn to Lear, 11 July 1886, private collection.

67. Lear to Henry Bruce, 3 July 1866, BL R.P. 1470.

68. *D* 20 April 1887. He calls these 'Welsh epitaphs', but alludes to the game elsewhere simply as 'epitaphs'.

69. *CV,* 399.

70. Lear to Fortescue, 12 September 1873, *LL,* 162. The spelling is 'Akhond' in the manuscript, but became 'Akond' in *Laughable Lyrics.*

71. *D* 29 January 1868. Jane Symonds 'shouts out all the ends of the songs'. This dialogue poem recalls Lear's earliest birthday verses for Ann, which similarly play with the outrageous return of a single rhyme.

72. *CV*, 234–235.

73. Ibid., 450–451.

74. *The tragical life and death of Caius Marius Esqre late her Majesty's Consul-general in the Roman state: illustrated from authentic sauces by Edward Lear* (1841), repr. Justin G. Schiller (New York City: Schiller, 1983).

75. *D* 29 January 1879.

76. Lear to William Bevan, 14 January 1879, BL 61891 f.110.

77. Thomas Arne, *The Hymn of Eve from the Oratorio of Abel* (Liverpool: Hime, c. 1815), 3.

78. *CV*, 428–429.

79. Chesterton, 'A Defence of Nonsense', in *The Defendant* (London: Brimley Johnson, 1901), 45.

80. *D* 27 July 1872.

81. *CV*, 456–457.

82. See for example an advertisement in the *Teesdale Mercury*, 1 February 1860, 1.

83. 'Leeds Assizes', *Sheffield Independent*, 14 April 1866, 12.

84. Emily Tennyson to Lear, 26 August 1858, Lincoln 5457.

85. For example, he refers to breathing difficulties in old age as his 'boots being far too tight' and connects this to the line in 'Uncle Arly'. *D* 14 June 1886.

86. Edward Carus Selwyn to Lear, 30 May 1886, private collection.

87. *D* 23 August 1871.

88. Percy Bysshe Shelley, *The Poetical Works of Percy Bysshe Shelley* (London: Moxon, 1861), 596.

89. Plutarch's account of Cyrus's epitaph was variously translated. This is from Nathaniel Wanley, *The Wonders of the Little World; or a General History of Man*, vol. 2 (London: Longman, 1806), 119.

90. *CV*, 546.

91. The 'Growling Eclogue' was published in the *Atlantic Monthly* in May 1894; 'How Pleasant to Know Mr Lear' was published in *Nonsense Books* (Boston: Roberts, 1888) but is best known from *Nonsense Songs and Stories*; 'Some Incidents in the Life of My Uncle Arly' was also published in *Nonsense Songs and Stories*.

92. Marcel Mauss, *Essai sur le don*, trans. *The Gift* (London: Routledge, 2009), 15.

93. A great deal of good work has been done in the last thirty years on the importance of the gift economy for Romantic literary and social culture. See for example Sarah Haggarty, *Blake's Gifts* (Cambridge: Cambridge University Press, 2008); Simon Jarvis, 'Wordsworth's Gifts of Feeling', *Romanticism* 4

(1998), 90–103; Angela Keane, 'The Market, the Public, and the Female Author: Anna Barbauld's Gift Economy', *Studies in Romanticism* 18, no. 2 (January 2008), 161–178; and Matthew Reynolds, *Real Money and Romanticism* (Cambridge: Cambridge University Press, 2010). Lear's practices make him a good candidate for study within a more detailed consideration of the Victorian gift economy than my book allows.

94. An auction catalogue of 21 February 1929 lists as item 541: Campbell, (T.), 'Poetical Works inscribed to Edward Lear by Joseph Severn, Paris 1822'. It seems likely that the auctioneer misread 1842 as 1822. Private collection.

95. Lear to the Earl of Derby, 27 November 1833, Knowsley Collection, Knowsley Hall. Repr. courtesy of the Earl of Derby.

96. *D* 19 November 1877.

97. Lewis Hyde, *The Gift* (Edinburgh: Canongate, 2007), 71.

98. *D* 17 April 1872.

99. See for example *D* 27 August 1876, in which he writes that fifty-five copies are to be sent to friends.

100. *SL,* 278.

101. For Mr Edward Lear tallow chandler and melter, see *Western Daily Mercury,* 20 July 1864, 1; for the Reverend Edward Denison Lear, see *Derby Mercury,* 2 July 1884, 6.

102. 'The Lounger at the Clubs', *Illustrated Times,* 8 February 1862, 91.

103. 'Christmas Books', *Times,* 21 December 1876, 6.

104. James T. Fields, 'My Friend's Library', in *Underbrush* (Cambridge, MA: Welch, Bigelow & Co., 1877), 54–55. Lear transcribes this in *D* 1877, before the first entry for January. He repunctuates it, but otherwise makes only slight changes.

105. Lear, *More Nonsense* (London: Bush, 1872), vii.

106. Lear, *Illustrated excursions in Italy,* 2 vols. (London: McLean, 1846), vol. 1, 126–127. This describes events of 28 September 1844.

107. *Yorkshire Post,* 18 March 1942, 2.

108. Strachey, introduction to *Nonsense Songs and Stories,* x.

109. *D* 17 April 1879.

110. *Ottawa Free Trader,* 25 May 1889, 3.

111. 'Literary Gossip', *Globe,* 12 May 1894, 6.

112. Paul Konody, *Morning Post,* 16 March 1912.

113. Ernest Satow, *A Diplomat in Japan: The Diaries of Ernest Satow 1870–1883* (Raleigh, NC: Lulu Press, 2009), 146.

114. Edward Strachey, 'Talk at a Country House', *Atlantic Monthly* (May 1894), 632.

115. *Queery Leary Nonsense,* 7.

116. These influences are explored in detail in *Play of Poetry*. As I hope is clear, my intention in the final movement of this chapter is not to attempt a comprehensive review of Lear's critical afterlife, but to explore certain instances where reaction to Lear's 'child-like' character and/or the pathos of his life story have shaped critical reaction to his work.

117. William Kerr, 'Edward Lear', *Gloucester Journal*, 27 November 1926, 13.

118. Angus Davidson, *Edward Lear, Landscape Painter and Nonsense Poet* (London: Murray, 1940), 10.

119. R. L. Mégroz, *A Book of Lear* (London: Penguin, 1939), 8, noted, 'there are many signs of a revival of popular interest in Edward Lear'.

120. Davidson, *Edward Lear*, 67.

121. George Orwell, 'Nonsense Poetry', *Tribune*, 21 December 1945, 13.

122. Vivien Noakes, *The Painter Edward Lear* (Newton Abbot and London: David & Charles, 1991), 28–29.

123. *Yorkshire Post*, 18 March 1942, 2.

124. *Scotsman*, 5 November 1931, 11.

125. S. A. Nock, 'Edward Lear of the Nonsense Verses', *Sewanee Review* 49, no. 1 (1941), 68.

126. Ibid., 70.

127. David Cecil, *Early Victorian Novelists: A Revaluation* (London: Constable,1934), 121–122.

128. Virginia Woolf, *The Common Reader* (London: Hogarth Press, 1925), 200.

129. Ina Rae Hark, *Edward Lear* (Boston: Twayne, 1982), 78–79.

130. Jackie Wullschläger, *Inventing Wonderland: The Lives and Fantasies of Lewis Carroll, Edward Lear, J M Barrie, Kenneth Grahame, and A A Milne* (London: Methuen, 1995), 68.

131. Douglas-Fairhurst, *The Story of Alice*, 168.

132. *LW*, 186.

133. Susan Chitty, au contraire, in *That Singular Person Called Lear* (London: Weidenfeld and Nicolson, 1988) argues for Lear's homosexuality and chooses to focus on the period of his life spent with Franklin Lushington. She contends that Lear only writes about wanting to find a wife in moments of stress.

134. Michael Montgomery, *The Owl and the Pussycats: Lear in Love, the Untold Story* (Brighton: Pen Press, 2012).

135. See National Portrait Gallery, online Later Victorian Portraits Catalogue. 'Pen and ink caricature drawing by Nicholas Bentley . . . with Oscar Wilde and Algernon Charles Swinburne stamped on verso for publication in *Sunday Telegraph* c. 1968.'

136. W. H. Auden, 'Edward Lear', in *Another Time* (New York: Random House, 1940), 12.

137. Addison, *Spectator*, no. 424, 4 (Lear's annotated copy), private collection.

138. For a recent example of the annoyance that academic criticism of Lear can inspire, see Anthony Madrid, 'Some "Ozbervatims" on Edward Lear', *Paris Review*, 19 January 2017, 5.

139. *D* 13 July 1877.

ACKNOWLEDGEMENTS

This book was written at a time of great sadness and personal difficulty. I am deeply grateful to all those who have helped me through it, both personally and practically, in ways too numerous and too subtle to record fully here.

Firstly, I would like to acknowledge three people who died during the years when I was researching Lear and writing about him. My baby daughter (born and died 2013), whose death cracked and blackened me as lightning splits a tree, but from whose loss I gained understanding of the depths of love and the need for forgiveness. My clever and creative mother (1947–2016), who introduced me as a baby to poetry and to Edward Lear, and who died a sudden and terrible death, far too young. And Yiannis Hayiannis (1972–2017), a dear friend and the kindest of men, who remained encouraging and enthusiastic about this project until he succumbed to a cruel disease. They are all in this book, somewhere.

Secondly, I am grateful to a legion of wonderful people, fellow researchers and readers and private owners of Learobilia who have helped me to understand and to think about Lear, and to access Lear's writings and artwork and personal effects. It is a huge privilege to see Lear's paintings, letters and other materials firsthand, particularly those in private homes; nothing has given me greater pleasure in my research or a deeper sense of connection to Lear's circle and his gift for friendship. I cannot name everyone here, but particular thanks are due to David Attenborough, Quentin Blake, Hugh Bredin, David Bretherton, Charlotte Brudenell, Ann Colley, Richard Cronin, the Earl of Derby, Basil and Clare Dewing, Stephen Duckworth, Clemency Fisher, Rowena Fowler, Peter Gillies and his family, Marco Graciosi, Derek Johns, the Lygon family, Harry and Mary Martineau, David Michell, Michael O'Neill, Adam Phillips, Elizabeth Prettejohn, Margot Selwyn and her family, Justin Schiller, Derek Scott, Arjune Sen, Ralph Steadman, David and Richard Stileman, Peter Swaab, Jenny Uglow, Judith Van Damm and Valerie Wadsworth. Matthew Bevis and James Williams organised a bicentenary conference on Lear and a subsequent essay collection, both of which helpfully sharpened my ideas. Several valuable new works on Lear have emerged since 2012 and are still emerging. When new books appeared during the course of my own writing, I have responded in endnotes, if not in the text. Jenny Uglow's wonderful new biography appeared just as my own book departed for the publisher. I had not read it when I submitted my book in draft, but I have greatly enjoyed discussing Lear with her, and her generous, insightful and supportive comments on my manuscript have been extraordinarily valuable.

The Noakes family generously made available to me some of the material in Vivien Noakes's extensive archive before it went to its permanent home at Somerville College. I am deeply grateful to them for this important service, and would like also to bow before the work of Vivien Noakes, whose meticulously researched and beautifully written work on Lear forms the foundation on which modern study of Lear is built. David Owen Norris, musician, composer and musicologist par excellence, helped me greatly to understand Lear's music. Thanks to him and to singers Amanda Pitt and Mark Wilde, and to Chawton House, for enabling me to record the songs Lear wrote, collected and sang, so that they are now publicly available for all to hear. We only had financial resources for one day of recording; the results are inevitably rougher in their sound quality than they would be if we had been granted the luxury of multiple takes. But the songs give a very lively sense of what a nineteenth-century concert on a nineteenth-century piano in a private home might have been like.

Charles Lewsen is the deserving dedicatee of this volume, a belated eightieth birthday present, not only for the particular help and encouragement he has given me, but for his dedication of over fifty years of private, unpaid and largely unsung devotion to Lear research and to helping those who study Lear. At Harvard University Press, I have had the very best of care from everyone—from my anonymous reader to the art department—but especially from my editor Ian Malcolm. Thank you so much for your patient guidance and your enthusiasm. The Bugatti of publishers has spoiled me forever; I now believe that speed, beauty and perfectly gentle stops come as standard.

I owe a great debt to libraries, librarians and curators in many places, but especially to Stephen Lloyd at Knowsley, Peter Hughes at Madresfield Court, Hope Mayo at the Houghton, Adrienne Sharpe at the Beinecke, Katherine McConnell at Somerville College, Anita O'Brien of London's Cartoon Museum, Nicholas Doyle at the University of South Carolina

Library, and Sheila O'Connell, formerly of the British Museum. I am also especially grateful to the people and institutions who allowed me freely to reproduce images of their Lear artefacts, including the Berger Collection, Denver Art Gallery; the Rt. Hon. Lord Derby; the Houghton Library; H. P. Kraus, Lincolnshire County Council; the Lygon family; Melissa Minty of Penguin Random House for permission to reproduce material in the Warne Collection; the Principal and Fellows of Somerville College; South West Heritage Trust; and several owners of private collections. For permission to quote from Lear manuscript material in their collections, thanks are also due to the Athenaeum Club, London; the Beinecke Library; the Bodleian Library; the British Library; the John Rylands Library Manchester; Liverpool Central Library; the National Library of Scotland; the National Museum of Scotland; the Pierpont Morgan Library; and the Harry Ransom Center at the University of Texas. A Leverhulme Fellowship made the work on this book possible by granting me time away from teaching; no gift has ever made more difference to me. I am grateful also for support from the Carnegie Trust for travel to the Houghton Library; to the Russell Trust, which supported my project to record Lear's music; and to the Royal Society of Edinburgh, which has generously funded the provision of illustrations for this volume.

Finally, I would like to thank my friends and family for their unflagging support. Contrary to dinner-party myth, writers are quite boring. At least they often seem to have the quality of Tennyson's brook: 'for men may come and men may go, but I go on for ever'. For six years I have been going on about Lear, and moaning about my inability to do his work justice in a single monograph, or at all, and it has sometimes seemed to me (and doubtless to others) as if the work would never be done. Well, here it is. For getting it there, special thanks are due to my first readers, Guy Ducker and Susan Manly. You both have sharper eyes and wits than I do, and a restorative sense of humour. Guy Lesser took time out to visit American libraries for me when I was incapacitated by pregnancy; he deserves many martinis when I am next in Manhattan. Helen Maslen, meanwhile, did me the most extraordinary kindness of acting as my research assistant pro bono. This work included transcribing a large file of letters and sourcing permissions for many of the images that illuminate the text. Thank you, Helen, for giving so much of your time in retirement to working for free. For friendship, help and encouragement along the road, I am grateful to Michael Alexander, Henrik Bindslev (who patiently explained John Tyndall's 1861 lecture on thermodynamics), Gavin Boyter, Elizabeth Burke (whose Radio 4 Playlist series inspired me to research Lear's music), Robert Crawford, Guy Cuthbertson, Laura Dishington, Rachel Garlick, Kim Gilchrist, Linda Goddard, Juliet John, David Lemon, Virginia Mallin, Elena and Neil McGugan, Gerald and Fiona Montagu, Kate Ó Súilleabháin, Mario Relich, Maeve Rutten, Jyoti Sigouin, Angus Stewart and Lynnette and Richard Wood.

The last words must go to those closest to me. Thanks to my ever-kind, patient father, who bore with the fact that I could not always be with him during six gruelling months of chemotherapy. Thanks to my lovely in-laws, John and Judy Ducker, for sustaining meals and supportive child care. And thanks beyond words to my dearest Guy (research assistant; photographer; tamer of paperwork; bringer of tea; assuager of despair) and Rosamund: the lights of my life and companions of my darkness.

INDEX